Working-Class Life

Peter R. Shergold

Working-Class Life
The "American Standard"
in Comparative Perspective
1899–1913

University of Pittsburgh Press

This volume was published with the cooperation of the Pennsylvania Historical and Museum Commission in its continuing attempt to preserve the history of the people of the Commonwealth.

Published by the University of Pittsburgh Press, Pittsburgh, Pa. 15260
Copyright © 1982, University of Pittsburgh Press
All rights reserved
Feffer and Simons, Inc., London
Manufactured in the United States of America

Library of Congress Cataloging in Publication Data

Shergold, Peter, R., 1946–
  Working-class life.

  Includes bibliographical references.
  1. Cost and standard of living—United States—History. 2. Cost and standard of living—Great Britain—History. I. Title.
HD6983.S45   339.4'7'0973   81-50921
ISBN 0-8229-3802-2   AACR2

To my mother and father,
K. D. and A. A. Shergold,
for their support and encouragement.

This much is certain: the American worker lives in comfortable circumstances. . . . He is well fed. . . . He dresses like a gentleman and she like a lady, and so he does not even outwardly become aware of the gap that separates him from the ruling class. We ought never to forget the continuous progress that "economic prosperity" in the United States has made . . . the economic situation of the average labourer improved and . . . the increasing affluence in his standard of living gave him the opportunity to experience the temptation of material depravity. All Socialist utopias came to nothing on roast beef and apple pie.

Werner Sombart, *Why Is There No Socialism in America?*

Contents

Tables

Charts and Graphs

xv

Acknowledgments

This work began as a set of vague and ill-formed ideas, was written as a doctoral dissertation, and emerged—after a long and difficult metamorphosis—as a book. Professor Charlotte Erickson, of the London School of Economics, persuaded me to complete the Ph.D. Without her constant encouragement, assistance and advice it would never have been finished. Professor Dirk Hoerder organized a stimulating conference (at the University of Bremen in November 1978), which brought together European scholars working on American labor history. At that meeting I benefited enormously from the criticisms made by Professors Alan Dawley, David Brody, and Herb Gutman, as from the detailed comments made earlier by Professor William Ashworth. And throughout the 1970s the slow path to publication was eased by my friends and colleagues in Sydney, Australia, who read, typed and/ or lived with this manuscript: to Srinivasa Ambirajan, Braham Dabscheck, Ian Inkster, Fay Johns, David Meredith, Charleen Nicolle, Steve Nicholas, Bill Purcell, and Christine Mikula Shergold, I offer my thanks. None can be blamed for the analytical weaknesses and the errors of interpretation that remain.

Working-Class Life

1
Introduction

Preparing to celebrate the nation's Bicentennial in 1976, and desirous of providing background information on a sector of American life that "visitors are invariably interested in observing," the United States Information Service decided to send a reporter to interview Thomas C. Cochran, emeritus professor at the University of Pennsylvania and doyen of American business history. It was not long before the questions turned to the condition of the manual workers in the era in which American business developed its modern characteristics.

> *Q:* We have spoken about the new industries and the new technologies, but what about the new people—the immigrants who came to the United States in waves in the late 1800's and early 1900's, the "huddled masses" which the Statue of Liberty at the entrance of New York's Harbor welcomed?
> *A:* The United States had, of course, a scarcity of labor. Consequently, workers were paid better in the United States than elsewhere.[1]

The reasons for the question, and implications of the answer are clear. Analysis of industrial productivity, capital investment, technological prowess, and entrepreneurial ability is well enough; but to many the success of American capitalism, and the degree to which economic growth has created a greater society, may best be assessed in terms of the material benefits that they have provided for the working population: the extent to which growth has increased per capita income and resulted in a more equitable distribution of that income throughout society.

Assessment of the benefits and costs to labor from the industrial revolution and/or the maturation of capitalism has most frequently depended upon temporal comparison. In contrast, this study employs a spatial yardstick in order, it is hoped, to "add a new dimension to the flat perspective which the purely national view of living standard reveals."[2] The central question posed here is whether Cochran's claim that American labor enjoyed unparalleled affluence and preeminent

3

material conditions—an untested assertion that has by now attained the stature of historiographical truism—survives empirical investigation. More specifically, it is asked, did early twentieth-century Americans have a standard of living superior to their British counterparts?

There is more than intrinsic value in measuring the wages gained and standard of life experienced by American workers. Comparative investigation has far wider implications. The Rothbarth-Habakkuk thesis, for example, relates American technological change to relative factor prices. Noting the comments of contemporary European visitors to the United States, Rothbarth and Habakkuk suggest that the United States was a high-wage economy in the nineteenth century: while land was abundant, labor remained scarce, inelastic, and dear, and as a result the cost of labor relative to capital was higher than in Britain. This increased the capital-intensity of manufacturing production, stimulated technological inventiveness, and hastened the introduction of more—and perhaps superior—labor-saving machines.[3] The thesis has received a great deal of critical attention from economic historians in recent years, but unfortunately the fervor of the theoretical debate has not been matched by historical investigation.[4] Indeed, as Paul David observes, there appears to exist a "tacit agreement to decide the issue without the benefit of further empirical research."[5] To hypothesize that real wages were significantly greater in the United States than in Britain, and that rates were higher vis-à-vis the rental price of capital equipment, requires more than theoretical elaboration. Assessment of comparative wages at different times would, at the least, provide a valuable basis for further historical analysis.

The implications of research on comparative living standards reach far beyond the confines of technological history. Frequently texts on labor history incorporate explicit comments as to the condition of manual workers in the United States in relation to their counterparts in Europe, to explain the peculiar characteristics of the labor movement which developed within it. The essentially conservative nature of many American unions, their "pure-and-simple" pragmatism, their emphasis upon "bread-and-butter" issues and "business" objectives and concomitant rejection of utopian ends—all these are often related to the allegedly superior material welfare of the individuals who composed them.

It is true that a wide variety of explanations have been presented for the failure of radical philosophies to gain a stronger foothold among American workers. Some historians believe that the reasons for failure lie within the radical ranks. Early twentieth-century fights between revolutionary and gradualist elements, between socialists and anarcho-syndicalists, between "borers-from-within" and "dual unionists" dissipated energy that might otherwise have been directed against the capitalist class. Such factionalism, it has been suggested, reflected an attempt—albeit an unsuccessful one—to resolve the "basic dilemma of ethics and politics," namely, how to work within capitalist structures while seeking their ultimate overthrow.[6] More commonly, historians have sought explanation for the comparative failure of American socialism in the nature of the surrounding socioeconomic environment. Lacking a feudal tradition, the United States had, by the early nineteenth century, become a formal democracy in which most male citizens were enfranchised; in consequence, opposition to the political process was mitigated, and demands for an independent labor party reduced. Moreover, the ethnic heterogeneity of the work force and high degree of social mobility among wage earners prevented the emergence of class consciousness. Other more specific reasons have also been postulated. The strong antisocialist stand taken by the Catholic Church and the conservative leadership that Samuel Gompers gave to the emerging American Federation of Labor (A. F. of L.) both weakened radical alternatives.[7]

Yet underlying many analyses, and featured prominently in some, is a belief that American capitalism offered the manual worker a standard of life superior to that experienced by his counterpart in Europe, and that this advantage lessened employee discontent and reduced revolutionary sentiment. Philip Taft, for example, attributes the absence of a strong radical tradition in the United States to the fact that American soil was "not as fertile for the diffusion of Socialist influence as other parts of the world." According to Taft, a major reason for the relatively barren conditions was the greater material satisfaction experienced by American workers. In similar vein, Taft explains the lack of philosophy in American unions in terms of the special economic conditions within which they developed. "In many instances compelled to bid for a small pool of labor, entrepreneurs were forced to offer high returns. . . . Thus workers in the United States found that the possibility to improve their standard of living was no idle dream."[8]

Taft's views are echoed, with varying degrees of forcefulness, by other prominent historians of American labor. An early exponent of this thesis, Warren B. Catlin, believed that the abundance of natural resources in the United States and the safety valve to labor offered by the immense areas of fertile, free land had put American wage earners at a premium. Wages were raised so high that despite the vast transatlantic migration of labor, American workers continued to earn far more than English colleagues. By the late nineteenth century, American wages were "higher then they had ever been anywhere in the course of history."[9]

Similarly, Henry Pelling indicates that a major element of continuity in American labor history has been the high wages paid, as a result of which "the average standard of living is higher in the United States than elsewhere." Pelling admits that by the early twentieth century there were many who expressed skepticism as to the economic superiority of the American worker, but he remains unconvinced by such contemporary pessimism. The stream of immigrants was unabated, he notes, and "even Edwardian England, for all its [social welfare] legislation, continued to send a proportion of its working class to the United States."[10] Furthermore, most British labor agitators still believed that American workers were better off, even though it "was somewhat embarrassing for British union leaders to have to admit that in spite of the weakness of the American unions, rates of wages were much higher in American industry than in British. The difference in the cost of living was not sufficient to account for this."[11]

Other historians also share Taft's belief that the manual workers' superior standard of life in the United States explains, in large measure, the generally moderate program of American unions. "The effect of increasing economic affluence in undermining support for revolutionary behavior must be emphasized," John Laslett claims. While the economic downturn of the late nineteenth century aggravated European labor discontent and channeled workers into more radical organizations, no such far-reaching consequences occurred in the United States "because wage levels in [that country], although also subject to fluctuations, remained—even during a depression—in relative terms considerably higher than those in Europe."[12]

Howard H. Quint, analyzing the origins of American socialism in the late nineteenth and early twentieth centuries, suggests that one of the most formidable obstacles to gathering worker support was that "living standards were generally higher than those of any other country in the world." Marc Karson presents a similar hypothesis, in which the inability of socialism to attract American workers is deemed to indicate the resiliency of an economy based upon the private ownership of production. An "expanding American capitalism has been financially capable of meeting the unions' continual economic demands," Karson says. "It is the economic facts of the worker's own experiences that nurture his loyalty to the existing economic system."[13]

Occasionally the causal link between economic conditions and union formation has been reversed. Thus a study commissioned by the International Labour Office states that American trade unions, wealthy, powerful, and influential, had through long years of struggle "succeeded in helping to bring about a continuous rise in the living standards of the workers which no country in the world has exceeded."[14]

Yet while the historical mainstream has emphasized the superior standard of life enjoyed by American manual workers, both as a general condition, and particularly in the years in which the A. F. of L. rose to dominance, agreement has not been universal. Philip Foner, for instance, offers a very different picture of American labor conditions from that indicated in most texts. The "Promise of American Life," before which so many historians have genuflected, is criticized as illusory. "From the turn of the century until 1914 a living wage was the exception not the rule for one-half to two-thirds of American wage-earners," Foner contends in a typical passage. "There was little more to life than an endless routine of work, eat, sleep, and work."[15]

Melvyn Dubofsky also suggests that in spite of an improvement in the standard of living of American workers between 1877 and 1917, "poverty remained a fact of life for most working-class families and a condition of existence for many." Indeed, Dubofsky hypothesizes that the failure of the Industrial Workers of the World (IWW) derived not from American affluence, as is usually contended, but rather from the fact that too many workers were "locked in the subculture of poverty."[16] The United States, in short, possessed a sizable *lumpenproletariat* who were unable to respond to the syndicalist utopia presented by the Wobblies.

What is disturbing in all these explicit analyses, and even more so in those numerous labor histories that simply imply the material superiority of American workers, is the paucity of evidence. The collection, refinement, and presentation of quantitative and qualitative data is not, of course, an easy task. I am painfully conscious of the weaknesses and ambiguities of the present study. The attempt to assess comparative living standards was fraught with difficulties, and many remain inadequately resolved. It was with some relief, therefore, that I fortuitously discovered an epigram which provides the combination of justification and apology sought as a preface to this initial effort at employing a statistical framework to assess one aspect of working-class life:

> Our doubts are traitors,
> And make us lose the good we oft might win,
> By fearing to attempt.

The author? Clearly, William Shakespeare. And the play? *Measure for Measure*. Doubts remain, qualifications abound—but let measurement begin.

2
Methodological Considerations

A Grain of Salt

Labor historians today generally share a common perspective that emphasizes the comparative affluence of American workers. This view is supported by little statistical evidence. By contrast, writers of the late nineteenth and early twentieth centuries tackled the question of comparative living standards with almost obsessive ardor, and presented voluminous evidence. Yet no contemporary consensus emerged. The evenly balanced debate remained open-ended.

To a large extent the abundance of contemporary literature reflects a fierce debate within radical ranks as to the nature of American capitalism. Some observers argued that even by the 1880s the conditions of labor in the United States had deteriorated to a level at which they were no better than those experienced on the other side of the Atlantic. In 1886 Edward Aveling and his wife Eleanor Marx toured America under the auspices of the Socialist Labor Party. They found that the "average condition of the working-class in America [was] as bad as it [was] in England," and claimed that American socialists, unfettered by the vestiges of feudal society, would soon act as a vanguard of world revolution.[1]

Similarly, Eugene Debs, writing at the turn of the century, contended that the United States had already "become Europeanized in respect of the suppression of exploited and discontented workingmen." And fellow American socialist Charles Russell, explaining the home-grown nature of his political convictions, argued that poverty in his native country was virtually as prevalent as in England: the "East Side of New York [was] only in degree less terrible than the East End of London; the essential character of its conditions [was] the same."[2]

Other radicals remined unconvinced. Although they agreed that American laborers were worked brutally, and that ever-greater amounts of surplus value were extracted from them, yet economic conditions allowed the capitalist to pay the wage earner more than in Europe. In essence, the American worker was exploited, but still had material advantages not experienced abroad: the American proletariat was far less degraded.[3] Thus the German Werner Sombart claimed in

1906 that the superior economic condition of American workers was largely responsible for the failure of socialism to blossom. "On the reefs of roast beef and apple pie socialist Utopias of every sort are sent to their doom."[4]

The *International Socialist Review* refused to publish Sombart's analysis, claiming that he wrote "nonsense on the conditions of American workers," but other Americans were not so sure. Morris Hillquit, certainly, believed that the preeminent cause for the retardation of American socialism was that manual workers in the United States still enjoyed some actual advantages over their brethren in Europe. The favorable labor market meant that even during industrial depressions, "the wages of American workingmen were, on the whole, better, and the standard of living higher, than those of European wage-workers." Similarly the Communist William Z. Foster, looking back on the development of American syndicalism, stressed the importance of the comparatively favorable economic situation in the United States, which deterred the emergence of strong class identity. The "traditionally higher wage and living standards," he argued, created "bourgeois property illusions" and predisposed workers to syndicalist tendencies, thereby stifling socialist consciousness.[5]

Debate on the comparative well-being of American labor was not confined to radicals, nor was the dogmatic assurance with which so many arguments were presented. Governments on both sides of the Atlantic were just as concerned to assess the standard of life offered to manual workers and equally aware of the political implications of their findings. At the governmental level, however, there was a far more strenuous attempt to employ "objective" measurement techniques and a far greater willingness—it might be cynically contended—to quantify inherent convictions.

The Parliament of the United Kingdom debated the subject with vehemence. "On the average," claimed Basil Peto in the House of Commons in 1912, "every man [in the United States] can save as much every week as every man can earn in this country."[6] It was a view that, although widely held, was challenged from diverse quarters. J. M. Robertson, parliamentary secretary to the Board of Trade, refuted Peto's statement as simplistic and, noting that American wage figures varied tremendously, accused the Conservative spokesman of looking at only the highest-paid occupations. The Labour member of Parliament for Norwich, George Roberts, added his own qualifications, remarking that wage rates cited outside the context of prices were of little relevance in estimating a comparative standard of life. "On the other hand," continued Roberts, reminiscing on his recent visit to

America, "I found where trades were less well organized or completely disorganized, that the conditions of the workers was quite as bad as anything with which we are acquainted in this country."[7]

A week later the honourable members crossed swords again. Donald Macmaster and Harold Smith stated that the American worker was "infinitely better off" in real terms, and that the British artisan, appreciating this fact, was leaving to work in the United States. Joseph Pointer, in contrast, reiterated the views of his Labour party comrades that the United Kingdom had "not many conditions so bad as those that are to be found in America." "The conditions for employees in the United States are very bad indeed," said Pointer, sketching a picture of industrial depravity. "The social conditions are bad, the housing conditions, the number of hours of labour, and so on, are all bad from top to bottom and from start to finish."[8]

To anyone ignorant of the context of the tariff reform agitation within which the debates took place, it might seem surprising that all sides were to a large extent basing their arguments upon the statistical ·evidence recently published in the British *Enquiry into Working Class Rents, Housing . . . Retail Prices . . . [and] Rates of Wages.*[9] Moreover, this investigation of twenty-eight towns in the United States, made in February 1909, was no mean document. In a prefatory analysis, G. R. Askwith of the Labour Department clarified the methodological difficulties of the survey and cautioned against abuse of the data. Unfortunately, few M.P.s appear to have read Askwith: the *Enquiry* was treated as an encyclopedic source in which to look for affirmation of one's beliefs and, if one chose material selectively, the necessary "evidence" did not prove difficult to find. To tariff reformers, protected Americans had to be shown as economically superior to the inhabitants of free-trade Britain; consequently, they stressed those comparative wage rates that illustrated most convincingly that earnings across the Atlantic were far greater than those at home. At least fifteen times prior to publication of the report, the presidents of the Board of Trade, at first Churchill and later Buxton, were questioned as to the reasons for delay, and it was openly suggested that the *Enquiry* was being held back by the Liberals because it would provide Conservative tariff reformers with too deadly an ammunition. "Why was not that report published prior to the recent General Election?" Robert Houston asked heatedly in April 1911. "If the report was not ready, why was not the election postponed, seeing that in many constituencies throughout the country the main issue was Free Trade versus Tariff Reform?"[10]

The free traders, for their part, denounced the reformers' interpretations as biased. They claimed that more careful scrutiny of the *Enquiry,* and especially of those sections which explored the cost of living in the United States, would not allow "protectionists" to "adduce much of advantage to [their] Tariff Reform propaganda." Furthermore, it was noted, the largest differences in wage rates occurred in American industries that gained little from protection—the building trades, for example—while some of the worst American labor conditions prevailed in the highly protected steel industry. In fact, suggested the Labour member, William Brace, recently returned from a tour of the United States, the country was "a democracy in revolt against the enormous cost of living," a fact that had "compelled the American politician to make overtures to reduce the tariff walls so that it might be possible for the American democracy to live cheaper than it did at the present time." This view was in turn condemned as propagandistic: Brace's speech, complained A. D. Steel-Maitland, "savoured rather of the breezy air of the hustings than of the arguments sometimes adduced in this House."[11]

Such contradictory interpretations of the 1909 *Enquiry* in the House of Commons illustrate the attempts made in the opening years of the twentieth century to compare the well-being of British and American workers. Statistics as to comparative wages and prices were important not for their intrinsic value but rather as numerical cudgels with which to bludgeon one's opponents. Whether the argument concerned tariff reform, the role of trade unions within society, or the advantages of introducing government welfare measures, the politicians' strategy was to outstatistic the enemy, to defeat him in a numerical war of attrition. The source of the evidence was relatively unimportant. Although the 1909 *Enquiry* was most frequently cited in the fiscal reform debates, testimony as to the American standard of life was also garnered from the U.S. Bureau of Labor Statistics, the "Pittsburgh Survey,"[12] the Commission of the Federal Council of Churches, the Massachusetts Bureau of Labor Statistics, consular reports, Ralph Chapin's study of New York, "a Year Book published by one of the Agencies in America," and even a personal letter from the secretary of the U.S. Department of Agriculture.[13]

Another source of information to which parliamentarians frequently referred was the Mosely Industrial Commission.[14] In 1902 Alfred Mosely, a South African diamond millionaire, financed and led a delegation of twenty of the United Kingdom's most important unionists on a three-month visit to the States. Unfortunately, they found themselves imprisoned within the tour's arrangements. Shepherded about in the nicest possible way, wined and dined and taken on tours of model factories and housing settlements, they were rarely able to make their own private investigations. It says much for the unionists' integrity that many of them noted the limitations placed upon them by such constricting hospitality. The "rapid tour through the principal cities, visiting places of interest under the auspices of the 'Civic Federation' was extremely interesting," wrote James Fox of the Association of Iron and Steel Workers, yet he also noted that his observations were in consequence "of a somewhat superficial character." Similar criticisms were made by Alex Wilkie, T. Jones, and G. J. Lapping. "My experience with several employers," claimed the representative of the Amalgamated Society of Leather Workers, "was that although I was very courteously received, I was only allowed to look around the establishment as a special favour in a very superficial manner."[15]

It is not surprising, therefore, that statistical evidence was almost entirely absent from the commission's *Report of the Delegates,* nor that on many important questions the unionists' essays contradicted one another. Lapping's belief that the British skilled worker was "equally as well off as the American employe [*sic*]" was not shared, for instance, by George D. Kelly of the Lithographic Printers, who expressly denied that the American artisans' higher wages were "swallowed up" by the higher cost of living.[16] The Mosely Commission, useful as it was in many other ways, had but little to offer in terms of quantitative data and contained few unambiguous conclusions.

British interest in the American workers' conditions was reciprocated. The British *Enquiry* of 1909 was matched in the United States by the Senate investigation of 1910 chaired by Cabot Lodge. The four-part *Wages and Prices Abroad* published information on the previous decade collected from American consuls throughout the world. But the statistics thus received from abroad were barely used in the Select Committee's investigation entitled *Wages and Prices of Commodities.*[17] The final document consisted of a *Majority Report* and a *Minority Report,* a division reflecting ideological tensions similar to those manifested in the British parliamentary debates over the 1909 *Enquiry.* The *Majority Report* concluded that the American worker's "standard of living had steadily advanced" and that workers in the States were the most affluent in the world, whereas the *Minority Report* asserted that wages had not kept pace with prices since 1900 and disputed the assumption that the American laborer was better off than his counterpart in Britain. The *Majority Report* laid the blame for rising prices, where blame was attached, upon consumer extravagance, the introduction of trading stamps, the rise of large-scale advertising, an increase in the amount of packaged goods, and upon the new expectations of American laborers. The *Minority Report,* in contrast, argued that the roots of the supposed decline in the American standard of living were much more basic, attributing blame to the survival of tariff barriers and to the growth of manufacturing and retailing "trusts."

Thus American interpretations of the available quantitative material suffered, as they did in the United Kingdom, from a need to defend preconceived notions, a politicization of data that was well appreciated by contemporaries. "It is necessary to take current statistics, and even official statistics, with a grain of salt," noted the Frenchman Levasseur in 1900. "Partizans of protection are particularly open to suspicion in this matter because they like to make it appear that labor is more highly paid in America than in other countries."[18] Thus the marked interest that Britons and Americans exhibited in comparative studies of the respective conditions of the manual labor force in their two countries was not matched by a commitment to objectivity. Contemporary investigations provide valuable data upon which statistical analysis may be based, but they supply no incontrovertible conclusions.

A Point of Departure

The reciprocal interest that Americans and Europeans have recurrently shown in each others' living standards has borne little fruit in historical scholarship. The notable exception to this sweeping generalization, and the starting point of the present study, is E. H. Phelps Brown's statistical interpretation of comparative wage rates, earnings, and prices. There can be no doubt that these data, which he and his associates painstakingly constructed and which were analyzed with meticulous scholarship, remain a sound basis for future work. The investigations present an informative guide to extant sources, clearly delineate the pitfalls awaiting the unwary researcher, and tackle the difficult methodological obstacles with tremendous skill.[19]

Nevertheless, the conclusions must be treated with caution. The aggregated nature of the statistical evidence presented may not be the best manner by which to gauge the comparative standard of life enjoyed by British and American workers. Phelps Brown judges that relative annual wage earnings, expressed in composite units of consumables, were 18–23 percent greater in the United States than in the United Kingdom in 1909.[20] The accuracy of this conclusion will be assessed in due course. At this stage it is more crucial to question the validity of the measurement technique. Two major criticisms must be lodged.

First, wage differentials based upon skill may be just as relevant to understanding the condition of labor as the aggregated mean. It is imperative that the relative rewards paid to skilled and unskilled employees be known. And even then, as statisticians have long been aware, the emerging picture may hide more than it reveals. Indeed, at the beginning of this century the United States Bureau of Labor, assigned to collect data on the standard payments received by American workers, noted that "an average rate of wages is almost meaningless unless limited to an occupation."[21]

Second, regional variations in wage rates need to be distinguished. The observant contemporary Arthur Shadwell, an early exponent of comparative analysis, contemptuously dismissed nationwide aggregation. Terms such as "American workman," "American wages," and "American prices" were, he contended, absurd.[22] Shadwell was correct. Investigation of national living standards must clearly identify the geographical bases of the compared data sets lest conclusions be attributed to biased sampling procedure.

Thus the present study began from the premise that analysis of the standard of life of manual workers should be conducted at a detailed level of disaggregation. I believed that only then could statements as to the comparative well-being of American and English employees be made with assurance. At the outset I decided that evidence, quantitative and qualitative, should be collected from regions possessing similar demographic and economic characteristics and a comparable economic climate; and that wage rates should refer to a work force categorized by occupation and skill level. As the study progressed, however, I found that this emphasis upon disaggregation of data required extension into other areas of investigation. Not only was it necessary to estimate prices for specific items, but also the type of retail outlet and time of purchase had to be considered. It was also necessary to distinguish household expenditure by ethnicity as well as by family income. Quantification, it soon became apparent, compelled incessant qualification.

Equally crucial was the decision as to which income measure to use as the basis of analysis. A number of alternatives existed: wage rates, which represent payment for a given input of work—per hour, per piece—for a standard week; earnings, which may include payments gained through overtime awards or productivity bonuses; and family income, which incorporates the contributions made by wage earners other than the breadwinner and/or payments derived from nonwage sources. Data could be presented for hourly, weekly, or annual time periods and could be derived from established rates—union or customary—or from payroll statistics. Which was most appropriate?

The methodological questions posed were complex. Eventually I decided that in terms of judging comparative living standards, the adult male wage rate paid per hour of labor for a standard work week provided the least ambiguous measure. Such hourly rates are less valuable than annual payroll earnings in constructing time series, for they are less sensitive to economic fluctuations: rates, for example, have a characteristic downward rigidity in times of depression.[23] However, in terms of spatial comparison at a set point in time, hourly rates are preferable. They allow one to estimate the standard of living in terms of a composite "basket of goods" that could be acquired from a clearly defined measure of timed labor input.

It is true that the definitional measure is as narrow as it is clear. Any estimate of the comparative standard of living experienced by workers in the 1900s requires adjustment for transatlantic variations in the number of hours worked in a standard week, differential hourly rates according to the amount of labor performed, the prevalence of seasonal or cyclical unemployment, and the contribution made by working wives and children to family income. Many of these areas warrant and receive detailed attention in this study. The difficulty remains of how to interpret such findings. To select but two examples: is it possible to view differences in weekly hours of labor as a tradeoff between income and leisure; or to see variations in the participation of married women in the paid workforce as a choice between household income and household services? Whatever the answer, it is imperative that the historian distinguish between those variations in the American and British standard of living resulting from differences in the number of family hours devoted to income-earning activities and those derived from differences in the standard wage rate received per hour of employed adult male labor. It is this latter measure, the payment per timed unit of labor, that provides the clearest indicator of how wage earners' work was exchanged for consumed goods and services in the marketplace.

A Choice of Location

The desire for disaggregated analysis and geographical specificity determined that this study would be a tale of two cities. However, the choice of location was difficult. It was necessary to select two regions, one in the United States and the other in England, that might be accepted both as typical of early twentieth-century urban-industrial society and as comparable with each other.

Pittsburgh, "the greatest hive of human industry on the face of the earth," presented itself as an obvious choice on the American side.[24]

Seventh-largest city in the United States by 1900, and fourth in respect to the value of its manufactured products, Pittsburgh represented to many contemporaries the acme of American industry. It was a city that few serious European travelers excluded from their itineraries and one that fascinated—and sometimes horrified—Americans. But to which English city would it be most justifiably compared? Therein lay the crux of the problem.

One obvious answer was suggested by contemporary accounts that claimed, with tedious repetitiveness, that Pittsburgh was "the Birmingham of America." As early as 1814, the *Niles Register* had referred to the young American city in such terms, and visitor David Thomas echoed the phrase two years later. By the twentieth century the comparison had lost none of its earlier appeal. Lincoln Steffens, for example, seeking a quick description of Pittsburgh in 1903, still considered the time-honored tag appropriate.[25]

Yet the alert historian, imbued with the inquiring spirit of Hercule Poirot, might be forgiven for seeing the clues laid too thick, for thinking the answer too obvious. Pittsburgh's prosperity was founded, it might be argued, upon a single industry, the production of iron and steel, whereas Birmingham possessed a more diversified economic structure, based upon a crowded proliferation of small workshops. If it was an English steel town that was sought, might Sheffield have been a more suitable choice? Investigation suggested not. The disaggregated nature of the data presentation removed the necessity for the economic structures of the two compared communities to duplicate each other.[26] I did not deem it of vital significance that Pittsburgh had relatively more steel mill laborers or bricklayers than Birmingham, or relatively fewer morning newspaper compositors or cabinetmakers, so long as the wage paid to each occupation could be accurately determined for both cities.

Within this detailed analytic framework, the major factor in determining comparability was not economic structure but population size. A study of local wage variations conducted in Britain in 1899 revealed a distinct correlation between the rates paid to various occupations and the size of the town in which the worker resided. "The variations in wages in the same trade from town to town [were] considerable," it was noted. The "large towns [showed] the highest wages, and if we may neglect the smallest towns we may say of the rest with an approach to accuracy, 'The larger the town the higher the wage.' " An investigation carried out in the United States in 1937 presented similar conclusions. Although the correlation was imperfect, statistical data "very definitely" substantiated the "generally held belief that wages in large cities [were] higher than in small communities." More recent examination supports this claim.[27]

Most studies reveal a positive relationship between money wages and city size. Evidence on the cost of living is less clear. To the extent that larger cities have greater population density, one might expect land values, and therefore rents, to be higher. However, there is little evidence of other prices being correlated with city size. A study of Britain indicates that regional price differences were minor relative to wage variations.[28] Investigation of the United States suggests, by contrast, that there existed substantial regional cost-of-living variations in the late nineteenth century, but that these bore little relationship to city size. Nevertheless, since price differences were not as great as relative differences in money wages, it is probable that American real wages still positively correlated with city size.[29]

As occupational wage rates were to be compared, and as such rates varied within each country in relation to city size, then it seemed sensible, *ceteris paribus,* that two communities of relatively equal population should be chosen. Since the base years for investigation were 1906–1907, Birmingham appeared a more valid choice than Sheffield. Interpolation from decennial census data indicated that by 1906 Birmingham had a population of 524,000. Pittsburgh had a population of 501,000, approximately 4 percent less than that of the Midlands city but 12 percent greater than Sheffield's 418,000.[30]

Population size was not the only reason for the selection of Birmingham. Even if urban economic structure had been the major factor determining comparability, Sheffield would not have been the automatic choice to compare with Pittsburgh. The fascinating story of Pittsburgh's economic development has yet to be told with analytic rigor: suffice it here to note that the stereotyped image of a one-industry town is misplaced.[31] While Pittsburgh's prosperity did depend upon the output of its blast furnaces, steel works, and rolling mills, the city's economic structure was broadly based by the early twentieth century. Manufacturing activity was far more diversified, and the manufacturing sector much less significant, than most accounts suggest.[32]

In 1908 Pittsburgh held its sesquicentennial celebration, the climax of which was a spectacular pageant of floats designed to illustrate the city's history and to acclaim its industrial might: "A huge Bessemer steel converter, belching forth its flames and sparks, was the donation of the Jones and Laughlin Steel Company. The H. J. Heinz float representing Ceres, Goddess of Plenty, surrounded by brightly gowned young women and luscious fruits and vegetables, was a 'climax of gorgeousness.' . . . Beauty in the industries was demonstrated by the

Pittsburgh Plate Glass Company. . . . The Electric Renovator Company had Cinderella in a corner, while a vacuum cleaner run by a motor was shown in contrast."[33]

American Vice-President Charles W. Fairbanks, reviewing the parade, was impressed: it was, he said, "the greatest demonstration" he had ever witnessed.[34] Certainly it was informative, for it sketched the outline of Pittsburgh's economic structure. The manufacture of steel products, processed foods, glassware, and electrical goods, together with liquor, "stogie" cigars, railway cars, and the output of machine shop and printing press, provided a wide range of employment opportunities for Pittsburgh's wage earners.

It is true that the production of Crucible, Bessemer, and open-hearth steel dominated Pittsburgh manufacturing enterprise. By 1909 the output of ferrous metal accounted for 32.7 percent of the city's total value-added production, and the steel mills and furnaces employed about one-third of the manufacturing work force. Nevertheless, it would be simplistic to view Pittsburgh as a one-industry city. Of the $94.9 million value added by manufacturing enterprise, 12.4 percent derived from foundries and machine shops, 6.7 percent from printing and publishing, 4.4 percent from liquor production, 4.4 percent from bakery and confectionery articles, 4.0 percent from canning and preserving, and 2.6 percent from the manufacture of tobacco products, predominantly cigars. An additional 29.0 percent derived from a wide variety of manufacturing activities, most notably slaughtering and meat-packing, and the production of electrical machinery, glass, clothing, brass and bronze, tin and copper, ice, soap, bricks and pottery, paint, coke, cork, and locomotives.[35]

If one shifts attention from value-added production to the distribution of the work force, it becomes apparent that Pittsburgh had a more diversified economic base than is generally suggested. Indeed, Table 1 indicates that if total metal production, rather than ferrous metal production, is taken as the measure, Pittsburgh's manufacturing sector bore closer resemblance to that of Birmingham than to that of Sheffield. The American city was less dependent upon the processing of metals than either of the British cities, and—reflecting an early twentieth-century building boom—far more dependent upon construction activity. Machine shops and engineering establishments, although of vital importance as employers of labor in all three cities, were of less significance in Pittsburgh and Birmingham than in Sheffield. Similarly, metal production, the output of foundries and machine shops, and construction were, taken together, the most substantial employers of manufacturing labor in each of the cities; but Birmingham and Pittsburgh had a lower percentage of workers engaged in these fields than did Sheffield: 60.3 percent and 66.8 percent as compared to 76.8 percent.

Moreover, Birmingham and Pittsburgh had relatively more wage earners employed in printing and food processing and in the manufacture of clothing, bricks, tiles, pottery and electrical apparatus than did Sheffield, while the American city had a larger percentage of its workforce engaged in tobacco workshops. It would seem fair to argue that if Pittsburgh's manufacturing sector was less diversified than that in Birmingham, it was more diversified than that in Sheffield.

Table 2 extends analysis to the total male labor force, revealing that a far smaller proportion of Pittsburghers were employed in manufacturing than in either British city, and a greater proportion employed in domestic and personal service, building and construction and professional fields. The percentage of male workers engaged in transportation was similar in all three cities. Birmingham and Sheffield had a

Table 1

Distribution of Workers in the Manufacturing and Construction Industries: Pittsburgh, Birmingham, and Sheffield, 1910–1911

Manufacturing Sector	% of Total Manufacturing Work-Force Engaged in Industrial Sector		
	Pgh	Bhm	Shfd
Iron and steel production	33.0	18.1	39.6
Nonferrous metal production	1.4	11.8	8.6
Unspecified metal production	—	11.2	2.6
[Total metal production]	[34.4]	[41.1]	[50.8]
Machine shops/Engineering	11.6	11.3	16.3
Building/Construction	20.8	7.9	9.7
Food processing	3.7	2.2	2.0
Clothing manufacture	6.7	8.5	5.2
Brick/Pottery/Glass production	2.6	1.0	0.7
Woodworking/Furniture production	2.2	4.6	3.1
Tobacco manufacture	2.2	a	0.1
Electrical apparatus	1.9	1.6	0.9
Publishing/Printing	1.8	2.8	1.3
Leather goods	0.9	2.9	1.4
Electricity/Gas production	0.4	1.1	1.2
Jewelery trades	0.3	7.9	1.2
Cardboard boxes/Paper bags	a	1.5	0.3
Other manufacturing industry	10.5	5.6	5.8
Total	100.0	100.0	100.0

Sources: Great Britain, *Census,* 1911, Vol. 10, pt. 2, Table 13; U.S., *Census,* 1910, Vol. 4, Table 3.

a. Less than 0.1 percent.

similar share of their male workers engaged in manufacturing (58.5 percent and 56.1 percent, respectively), a segment considerably larger than in Pittsburgh (41.0 percent). Perhaps the most unexpected contrast between the American and British cities was that the former had a much more substantial percentage of its workforce involved in trade and commercial pursuits. In the two decades before 1900, there had been "a steady drift of important enterprises from [Pittsburgh] proper to the surrounding boroughs and townships."[36] At the same time, the city had confirmed its position as the nodal point of its economic hinterland. British investigators found in 1909 that Pittsburgh was "fast becoming the administrative and commercial headquarters of the local iron, steel, coal, coke and glass industries, and the general distributing centre for commodities required in the surrounding manufacturing area."[37]

In short, Pittsburgh, although it still proudly boasted the appellation "Iron City," possessed a far more diversified economic structure than its eponym suggested. In the bases of its manufacturing activities, as in its population, it had by 1910 more affinity with Birmingham than Sheffield. The American city's nonmanufacturing enterprises were of greater importance than in either British city, but again it was Birmingham's intersectoral distribution of male workers which most closely matched that in Pittsburgh. In light of such facts, it seemed most appropriate to concentrate attention upon Birmingham and Pittsburgh; and it was from those two cities that most of the circumstantial, qualitative evidence was collected. Nevertheless, at times when the statistical conclusions demanded validation, or in circumstances in which

Table 2
Male Work Force: Pittsburgh, Birmingham, and Sheffield, 1910–1911

Industrial Sector	Number of Male Workers			% of Male Workers		
	Pgh	Bhm	Shfd	Pgh	Bhm	Shfd
Professional, government	11,272	7,153	6,920	6.1	4.3	4.6
Domestic, personal	11,766	5,708	4,718	6.5	3.4	3.1
Transportation	15,706	15,449	11,495	8.6	9.3	7.6
Trade, commerce	46,013	26,933	24,580	25.3	16.2	16.3
Manufacturing	74,522	97,558	84,459	41.0	58.5	56.1
Building, construction	20,905	12,406	10,944	11.5	7.5	7.3
Agriculture, mining	1,775	1,469	7,412	1.0	0.9	5.0
Total	181,959	166,455	150,528	100.0	100.1[a]	100.0

Sources: Great Britain, *Census,* 1911, Vol. 10, pt. 2, Table 13; U.S., *Census,* 1910, Vol. 4, Table 3. See Appendix Table 6 for the occupations in each industrial sector.
a. Error due to rounding.

quantitative analysis appeared to be biased by the selection of Birmingham, I have introduced data from Sheffield. The impact of such substitution the reader may shortly judge.

A Matter of Time

"It was the best of times, it was the worst of times." So Charles Dickens began his tale of Paris and London, and so, too might one introduce the 1900s in Pittsburgh and Birmingham. The hardships both cities had suffered in the depression of the early 1890s has become a distant if haunting memory. At either end of the first decade of the twentieth century were conditions of prosperity, characterized by relatively high levels of production and low levels of unemployment: between, separated by an all-too-brief boom, recession and depression.

It is difficult to quantify these trends with greater precision. A range of reliable economic indicators is not available for either city, and even the relevant national aggregate figures are scanty and inadequate. Table 3 presents data that can be accepted with some degree of confidence. Where city and national indices can be compared—for unemployment/pauperism in Britain and Birmingham, for production in the United States and Pittsburgh—local conditions appear to have mirrored those of the nation as a whole. More importantly, the movement of the economy appears to have been similar in both cities/countries, although there are indications that the scale of cyclical variation was greater in America. On both sides of the Atlantic, the years from 1899 to 1913 can be divided into four major periods, as suggested in Chart 1: the economic climate of the late 1890s, improving since 1896, stabilized in the opening years of the twentieth century and fell into recession in 1903–1904; from 1905 conditions advanced once more, with output and employment accelerating from mid–1906; the panic of late 1907 swiftly ended the boom and heralded two years of depression. Early signs of recovery in 1909 proved short-lived; there were some indications of improvement in 1910, but only from 1911 did production and employment levels rise substantially.

Within this general economic environment, both cities still faced individual problems. It has already been noted that by 1900 Pittsburgh's glass factories and coke plants, iron foundries and steel mills, which had molded the city in their own satanic image, sought to leave the overcrowded riverbanks and smoke-draped hills to relocate in areas where land was cheaper, raw materials more readily accessible, and transportation less constricted by topographical constraints. But this transition from a manufacturing to a commercial city was eased by

Table 3

Economic Conditions: the U.S. and the U.K., 1899–1913
(Index numbers: 1907 = 100.0)

Year	United Kingdom Production[a]	United Kingdom Unemployment[b]	Birmingham Pauperism[c]	United States Production[d]	United States Unemployment[e]	Pittsburgh Production[f]
1899		54.1	80.1	64.1	232.1	61.7
1900	87.6	67.6	85.4	64.1	178.6	57.3
1901	87.2	89.2	88.5	71.2	142.9	71.3
1902	89.8	108.1	92.4	81.4	131.1	80.0
1903	90.1	127.0	94.9	80.8	139.3	78.4
1904	90.3	162.2	100.0	77.6	192.9	74.4
1905	94.7	135.1	98.1	89.7	153.6	95.0
1906	97.5	97.3	93.6	97.4	60.7	102.8
1907	100.0	100.0	100.0	100.0	100.0	100.0
1908	97.0	210.8	110.8	81.4	285.7	62.7
1909	97.5	208.1	113.4	106.4	182.1	96.4
1910	100.1	127.0	112.1	110.3	210.7	101.0
1911	104.6	81.1	106.4	103.8	239.3	89.4
1912	106.4	86.5	103.2	124.4	164.3	110.7
1913	114.0	56.8	97.5	130.1	153.6	109.5

Sources: Col. 1: K. S. Lomax, "Production and Productivity Movements in the United Kingdom Since 1900," *Journal of the Royal Statistical Society*, 122 (1959), 196; Col. 2: B. R. Mitchell and Phyllis Deane, *Abstract of British Historical Statistics* (Cambridge, 1962), p. 65; Col. 3: Parish of Birmingham, *Statistics as to the Number of Indoor and Outdoor Poor* (Birmingham, 1906), p. 6; Col. 4: Edwin Frickey, *Production in the United States, 1860–1914* (Cambridge, Mass., 1947), p. 54; Col. 5: Stanley Lebergott, *Manpower in Economic Growth: The American Record Since 1860* (New York, 1964), Table A3, p. 512; Col. 6: University of Pittsburgh, *Industrial Databook for the Pittsburgh District* (Pittsburgh, 1936), pp. 29–35.

a. Industrial production in the U.K., excluding building.   b. Percentage of unemployment in all British trade unions presenting returns.   c. Percentage of indoor and outdoor poor in Birmingham district in December.   d. Manufacturing production in the U.S.   e. Percentage of civilian labor force unemployed.   f. Production of iron and steel in Allegheny County.

Chart 1
Economic Activity: Pittsburgh and Birmingham, 1896–1913

Years	Pittsburgh/U.S.	Birmingham/U.K.
1896–1904 (Boom, 1896–1898) (Recession, 1903–1904)	The trend since 1896 of substantially reduced unemployment and increased production peaked in 1902; a significant reversal of the trend occurred in 1903–1904.	After some years of much improved economic conditions 1899 began a period of worsening unemployment with the sharpest rise in 1903–1904; industrial production rose slightly in 1901–1902, but fell again in 1903–1904.
1904–1907 (Boom, 1906)	Production rose steeply in 1904–1905 and unemployment fell in 1905–1906; production in 1906 was not reached again until 1912, and the level of employment in 1906 was not equaled prior to the outbreak of the First World War.	There was a substantial improvement in employment and output, especially in 1906.
1907–1909 (Depression, late 1907–1909)	Between late 1907 and 1908, production fell precipitously and unemployment soared.	There was a heavy increase in unemployment from the winter of 1907, peaking in 1909; production fell sharply in 1908, not attaining the 1907 level again until 1911.
1909–1913 (Boom, 1912–1913)	Early signs of recovery in 1909 proved short-lived: only from 1911 did production and employment levels rise substantially.	A sharp increase in production occurred along with a concomitant reduction in unemployment: in both areas the major improvement occurred in 1912–1913.

a boom in construction stimulated both by increased demand for dwellings to house Pittsburgh's swelling immigrant population and by the desire of commercial enterprises to secure headquarters in a downtown location.

Birmingham's early twentieth-century problems were more painful. The city's leather and gun trades had been adversely affected by the lull in demand which followed the conclusion of the Boer War, while the gun, flint glass, and jewelery industries faced unparalleled competition from cheap goods imported from the United States and Germany—a fact to which the growth of tariff reform agitation in Birmingham bears convincing testimony.[38] "The Yankees' [gun] exports have been coming over for some time in such a manner as to cause unfair competition with our goods," bemoaned the *Birmingham Magazine of Arts and Industries* in 1902. "What the country wants, is . . . not . . . ugly machine-made articles of utility, but . . . artistic hand-made goods."[39] When the gun trade did recover from the prolonged depression, it was the superior class of weaponry that primarily benefited. This is apparent from the reports of the American consul in Birmingham, Albert Halstead. "Domestic business in sporting guns . . . is distinctly improved over recent seasons," he wrote in the winter of 1911; "almost every manufacturer of *good . . . guns* is said to be overwhelmed with work." Six months later he reiterated that the "1911 demand for *the best grade of guns* was the best of any year in the century" (my italics).[40]

The city's imitation jewelery also found its position in the domestic market seriously challenged by competition from imported German goods. Although the industry fought hard to retain its share of home consumption by integrating plants and reducing production costs, the post–1910 trade revival was due to increased activity in articles of superior quality. In the 1890s cheap jewelery had formed the greater share of the Birmingham industry. In contrast, the "position in 1913 was reversed, and the output of high-class jewellers exceeded in value at least that of cheap jewellers."[41]

The city's leather trade likewise faced a decline in demand, especially for military items. George Power of the Midland Leather Trades Federation testified before a parliamentary committee in 1908 that it was "patent to everyone" that since the end of the Boer War, the region's saddle trade had been in a "very bad state." The representative of the Birmingham branch of the Union of Saddlers and Harness Makers agreed, claiming that things had gone "pretty smoothly down to 1902," and that wages had been "fair," but that after that date remuneration had declined substantially. He was convinced that the decrease in wages had resulted from the slackness of trade.[42]

However, even when economic conditions declined into a recession in 1903–1904, and the localized distress spread to other sectors of Birmingham industry, not all the city's trades were adversely affected. While the cycle industry "was not of an encouraging nature," and "business in the glass and pottery industries was most disappointing," the engineering trade "did not . . . fare so badly," and the iron and steel works "were generally speaking, fairly well employed."[43]

The downturn had a wider impact in Pittsburgh. In 1903–1904 iron and steel production, building activity, railway earnings, and bank deposits all fell, unemployment rose, and many Pittsburgh workers saw their wages reduced.[44] Yet the recession was, as in Britain, short-lived. By 1905 in Pittsburgh and by 1906 in Birmingham, most industries operated at near full capacity. A mood of guarded optimism prevailed. The Birmingham Chamber of Commerce reported that trade in 1906 was "a great improvement on that in 1905," and conditions continued to better during the first half of 1907.[45] So too in Pittsburgh, where the output of iron and steel had risen 38.2 percent and railway earnings 25.5 percent in the two years since 1904. Yet the substantial improvement in economic conditions experienced in 1906–1907 represented a reprieve, not a recovery.

In October 1907 a financial crisis occurred in the United States. It was written into American history as the "rich man's panic," but the poor bore the major burden of the ensuing depression. And nowhere more so than in Pittsburgh. According to John R. Commons, "Hardly another city in the [United States] was hit as hard or stunned as long by the panic as Pittsburgh."[46] Tonnage production in all branches of Allegheny County's iron and steel industry fell substantially (by 39.1 percent between 1906 and 1908). The number of building permits issued by the city declined precipitously, and the gross earnings of railways operating out of Pittsburgh were much reduced. Those on the Pennsylvania Railroad line (west), for example, fell by 17.3 percent between 1907 and 1908, although mileage operated increased slightly.[47] Even in less obvious areas, the statistical impact of the depression was readily apparent. Consumption patterns, both industrial and private, were clearly affected. After years of considerable development, the sale of natural gas declined by 17.1 percent in the two years ending March 31, 1909, whereas in 1904, in spite of the "depression in manufacturing operations in the Pittsburgh district," consumption fell by only 6.0 percent. In the two years ending June 30, 1909, the number of street railway passengers per mile was reduced by 14.1 percent. Between 1903 and 1905, in contrast, the number dropped by only 7.5 percent. Even Pittsburgh's saloonkeepers must have viewed pessimistically the groups of dejected workingmen who crowded their premises, for consumption of beer fell by 21.9 percent in the two years ending the last week of October 1909.[48]

Pittsburghers would have been well aware of the human hardship hidden behind the statistical data—the blast furnaces shut down, the magnificent machinery silent, the river valleys free of the grimy haze that signified prosperity. The Pittsburgh plants of United States Steel reduced their work force substantially, and by the end of 1907 one-half of the big pig iron concerns controlled by the corporation lay inactive. The Zug Iron and Steel plant was idle, and the Oliver and Snyder Steel Company ran at two-thirds capacity. The Crucible Steel Company saw its volume of business drop 55 percent. It operated at a loss from November 1, 1907, to June 30, 1908, and was obliged to suspend dividends.[49]

Conditions were similar outside the steel industry. Activity ceased on many construction sites, and new building projects lay dead upon the draftman's board. A few miles downstream at Aliquippa, for instance, all work was halted on the new Jones and Laughlin plant, and 800 building workers were laid off. The Westinghouse plants, forced into a receivership that closed down the Pittsburgh Stock Exchange for fourteen weeks, made redundant many "hundreds of men." In February 1908 all the switches and side tracks in the vicinity of Pittsburgh were blocked by idle railway cars. Such "teddy bears" (as the empty cars were contemptuously nicknamed) meant unemployment or under-employment for hundreds more of the city's workers. The Pennsylvania Railroad alone had more than four hundred locomotives and 77,000 freight cars standing unused; one, as the *Commercial and Financial Chronicle* noted, for each shareholder. Even college graduates were unable to find employment commensurate with their academic qualifications, and a number eventually had to accept work collecting fares for the Pittsburgh Railways Company. Deep, indeed, hung the depression over Pittsburgh when the president of one of the city's leading firms, Harbison-Walker Refractories, could claim that the company had "been fortunate in operating its plants at 57% of their normal capacity." "Smokestacks ceased to belch forth their black currents," claimed Representative Garrett of Tennessee in congressional debate with Pittsburgher James F. Burke "and over the land arose the pale steam of the charity soup house."[50]

Pittsburgh's business and political leaders boomed their confidence that the city's prosperity would be rapidly restored. George Westinghouse, in the midst of legal wrangles over the control of the manufacturing enterprises he had created, told a *New York Times* reporter from his Pittsburgh office that there would not be "any serious industrial depression . . . if people [would] only keep their heads." George T. Oliver, commenting in December 1907, believed that after a short period of "rest and comparative inaction," conditions would improve: by summer 1908, he adjudged, business would be "moving on its wonted grooves." The committee that organized Pittsburgh's sesqui-centennial celebrations, facing criticism for indulging in unnecessary extravagance at a time of financial stringency, published with relief a letter of support from Andrew Carnegie written in November 1908 congratulating the city's residents "upon the evidence of returning pros-perity which everywhere abounded."[51] But such optimism rang hollow. Prosperity was not speedily restored in Pittsburgh. The amount of steel manufactured in Allegheny County in 1906 was not exceeded for six years; gross earnings of the Pennsylvania Railroad remained below the 1906 level; and the building boom of the early years of the century was not equaled again before the First World War. Recovery was slow and erratic. Only from 1912—when masses of the city's Turks, Bulgarians, and Greeks left to fight each other in the Balkan Wars—did the city bask once more in the peace of sulfurous prosperity.

The period from late 1907 to 1910 was one of depression in Birming-ham also, although the severity of the economic nadir was tempered by the fact that the upturn of 1906–1907 had been less pronounced there than in the American city. Nevertheless, by 1908 the Birmingham Board of Guardians pleaded that industrial conditions had "become chronic," a view shared by E. V. Birchall, who characterized the twelve months previous to April 1909 as a period of "exceptional distress." Mr. J. S. Taylor was indubitably correct when he declared that "there were few businessmen who were not glad to see the back of 1908, which . . . for all round depression, was undoubtedly one of the worst years experienced in Birmingham during the [previous] quarter of a century."[52]

It is scarcely surprising, therefore, that the visit of Victor Grayson to the city in 1908 as a guest of the Birmingham Labour Church aroused "great public interest . . . in consequence of his vigorous and uncon-ventional agitation on behalf of the Unemployed." The Hippodrome was filled to capacity and thousands had to be turned away. But the most sustained pressure for greater aid to the city's unemployed came from an independent organization, the Right-to-Work Committee, composed of delegates from the Independent Labour party and the Social Democratic Federation as well as from the Labour Church. Although created in 1904, the committee reached its zenith of activity in the winter of 1908, successfully battling the Watch Committee and chief constable for the right to use Chamberlain Square as a meeting place, attempting to persuade the Education Department to provide more free school breakfasts, and loudly castigating the Distress Committee for alleged ineptitude. Yet their 1908–1909 report proved to be their last, for as the decade drew to a close, the long-awaited improvement finally occurred. After that report, explained the committee's secretary, Annie G. Evans, in a letter to Birmingham's chief librarian, "there was a boom in trade and very little unemployment. The Right-to-Work Committee therefore thought it was wise to cease operations and wait till the time came when it would again do useful work."[53]

Halstead, the American consul, concurred. Business conditions, he reported, "were far better during the first half of 1910 than in the corresponding period of 1909, unemployment has been steadily decreasing, exports of goods that are Birmingham's speciality have increased . . . and there is a greater confidence." The Birmingham Chamber of Commerce and the district's Grocers' Protection and Benevolent Association were more circumspect in their conclusions. Although 1910 was "fairly satisfactory as [regarded] the amount of employment and wages," the year was deemed "by no means so satisfactory from the trade point of view." However, by the following year expressions of optimism were less guarded, and by 1912 the general upturn in business conditions was apparent to all. "The trade revival, which set in in 1909 and continued throughout 1910 and 1911, not only endured but increased in 1912," exclaimed the editor of the chamber of commerce *Journal* with relief. "It would be no exaggeration to say that taken as a whole, the industries of Birmingham and district have rarely, if ever, been better supplied with orders than they are now."[54] The coal strike and industrial unrest stole newspaper headlines, but it was military rather than economic events that clouded the horizon.

In short, statistical data and circumstantial evidence both suggest that the business cycles in Pittsburgh and Birmingham were similar in the early twentieth century. It was a period characterized by relative prosperity through to about 1902, recession in 1903–1904, a brief upturn followed by years of bitter depression from 1908 to 1910, and an accelerating improvement thereafter. This would appear to be true of Sheffield also, for in that city, "after some years of prosperity associated with the Boer War and the building boom, unemployment became again widespread in most trades in 1903. . . . The years 1908–10 were again years of depression. . . . Fuller employment returned in 1910 and lasted until the boom of 1913."[55] Variations in economic activity were not identical in the British and American cities, but the cyclical movements did exhibit a high degree of correlation. Certainly the parallel experience of the cities justifies the presentation of data from the same year and an analytical framework comparing the same time span.

3

Wage Rates

Wage Movements, Wage Margins

Records of the wage rates paid to workers in Pittsburgh and Birmingham in the early twentieth century have survived in a wide range of documents, presented with varying levels of detail and accuracy. The investigations carried out by governmental organizations and private institutions, the records of city council meetings, union organizers, and arbitration tribunals, and the reports of consular officials and interested travelers—all provided a firm statistical foundation upon which analysis could, with caution, be built.[1] From these sources it proved possible to construct a time series of adult male hourly rates for the 1899–1913 period, covering thirty-one occupations in the British city and ninety in the American, each tabulation incorporating evidence of the wages paid to workers employed in a variety of industrial sectors and possessing different levels of manual skill. The rates were subsequently converted to index numbers. 1907 was selected as the base year because the greatest number of individual observations were recorded for that year and because it transpired that 1904–1908 was a period of stability, a plateau in the upward movement of money wages.[2]

Tables 4A and 4B present these series categorized by industrial sector. In virtually all industries in both cities, the major increases in hourly rates occurred prior to 1902 and after 1911, with the upward advance far more pronounced in Pittsburgh. In Birmingham wage movements were similar in all industries, although rates paid to municipal employees (including police) and to workers in brass foundries rose somewhat faster, and rates paid to metal tradesmen somewhat slower, than the average. In the American city interindustry variations were more marked, with rates paid to bakers, building tradesmen, and railway workers rising substantially more, and rates paid to printing employees considerably less, than the norm.

The major statistical difficulty was to place a more precise value on the citywide average or norm. In some cases the occupational wage rates from which time series were constructed were available only for a few years, in others, only for one city, and in yet others, the years for

Table 4
Hourly Wage Rates by Industry: Pittsburgh and Birmingham, 1899–1913
(Index numbers: 1907 = 100.0)

A. Pittsburgh

Sector	1899	1900	1901	1902	1903	1904	1905	1906	1907	1908	1909	1910	1911	1912	1913
Building[a]	64.1	68.1	79.7	93.4	95.8	96.5	98.2	97.7	100.0	102.4	104.5	104.5	107.4	110.5	119.0
Bakeries[b]	64.5	95.3	100.0	100.0	100.0	100.0	100.0	100.0	100.0	100.0	100.0	100.0	100.0	136.1	136.1
Metal trades[c]	74.2	77.9	83.4	86.4	93.1	91.1	90.8	96.6	100.0	102.0	100.6	105.4	106.3	112.6	118.5
Printing[d]	89.2	90.1	90.7	91.7	99.0	98.8	97.8	97.3	100.0	100.8	106.6	106.6	106.6	107.3	108.4
Railways[e]	70.3	70.3	70.3	83.5	83.5	83.5	83.5	100.0	100.0	100.0	100.0	118.7	118.7	119.9	119.9
Street railways[f]	77.1	77.1	81.8	85.8	89.8	91.8	94.5	97.1	100.0	98.1	98.1	102.8	100.7	102.6	102.6
Breweries[g]									100.0	100.0	100.0	100.0	105.0	105.0	105.0
Municipal employment[h]	75.2	87.6	87.6	87.6	87.6	87.6	87.6	87.6	100.0	100.0	100.0	100.0	105.0	105.0	105.0
Steel mills[i]			90.5	98.5	98.5	89.0	93.6	93.6	100.0	100.0	100.0	100.0	100.0	100.0	112.4
Police[j]	84.1	84.1	84.1	100.0	100.0	100.0	100.0	100.0	100.0	100.0	100.0	106.4	106.4	106.4	119.0

Source: See Appendix Table 1.
a. Based upon bricklayer, carpenter, plumber, painter, inside wireman, and structural iron worker.
b. Based upon first hand, second hand, third hand.
c. Based upon blacksmith, machinist, patternmaker, iron molder, boilermaker.
d. Based upon compositor, linotyper, stereotyper, proofreader.
e. Based upon engineer, fireman, conductor, brakeman.
f. Based upon median wage of motorman.
g. Based upon washhouse man, brewhouse man, bottlehouse man, route driver.
h. Based upon public laborer, garbage man.
i. Based upon steel mill laborer.
j. Based upon patrolman, lieutenant.

B. Birmingham

Sector	1899	1900	1901	1902	1903	1904	1905	1906	1907	1908	1909	1910	1911	1912	1913
Building[a]	96.4	97.3	100.0	100.0	100.0	100.0	100.0	100.0	100.0	100.0	100.0	100.0	100.0	100.9	104.4
Bakeries[b]				100.0	100.0	100.0	100.0	100.0	100.0	100.0	100.0	103.9	103.9	103.9	108.8
Police[c]	96.2	96.2	96.2	96.2	100.0	100.0	100.0	100.0	100.0	100.0	100.0	100.0	100.0	100.0	108.1
Metal trades[d]	98.2	98.6	98.6	98.6	98.6	98.6	98.6	98.6	100.0	100.0	100.6	100.6	100.6	102.2	102.2
Printing[e]	94.5	94.5	94.5	99.0	99.0	99.0	99.0	99.0	100.0	100.0	100.0	100.0	100.0	101.4	101.4
Woodworking[f]	93.6	100.0	100.0	100.0	100.0	100.0	100.0	100.0	100.0	100.0	100.0	100.0	100.0	100.0	106.1
Electrical trades[g]									100.0	100.0	100.0	102.2	102.2	102.2	104.6
Municipal employment[h]	91.8	95.9	95.9	95.9	95.9	95.9	95.9	100.0	100.0	100.0	100.0	111.6	111.6	113.0	113.0
Brass trades[i]	98.6	100.0	100.0	100.0	100.0	100.0	100.0	100.0	100.0	100.0	100.0	111.6	111.6	113.0	113.0

Source: See Appendix Table 1.

a. Based upon bricklayer, carpenter, plumber, painter, plasterer, stonemason.
b. Based upon first hand, second hand, third hand.
c. Based upon minimum rates for constable, sergeant.
d. Based upon machinist, patternmaker, blacksmith, iron founder, borer/slotter, heavy plater, riveter, farrier's fireman, farrier's doorman.
e. Based upon compositor (morning newspaper/weekly newspaper), lithographer, bookbinder.
f. Based upon cabinetmaker, upholsterer.
g. Based upon instrument/switchmaker, armature winder, electrical fitter.
h. Based upon gas stoker, gas laborer.
i. Based upon brass finisher, brass laborer.

which statistical information existed were different in the two cities. This complicated the calculation of mean index numbers of wage rates. Three methods of estimation were therefore employed: in the first the annual mean was based upon all the occupational rates for which data were available; in the second the mean was calculated only from those occupations for which data were collected for each year between 1899 and 1913; and in the third the mean was derived only from those occupations for which statistics existed for both Pittsburgh and Birmingham. The initial method was superior in terms of extending the sample base; the second produced a far more satisfactory foundation for a time series; but the third possessed greater validity for purposes of comparison. In fact, as Table 5 shows, the difference between the three calculations was surprisingly small. Discrepancies were further narrowed when the indices were converted to three-year moving averages, a conversion undertaken in order to reduce those statistical errors that might have resulted from changes in the sample base and/or differences in the methods of collecting and recording rates, and to express with more clarity the long-term secular movement of wages.

It should be noted that the means calculated were in no instance weighted to make allowance for the number of workers employed in each occupation. Unfortunately, the detailed information necessary to construct such an index accurately did not appear to exist. It was possible, however, to make an estimate for Pittsburgh. The results suggested that the twenty-three occupations in Table 5 (estimate ii) comprised 13.3 percent of the Pittsburgh adult male manual work force at the end of the first decade of the twentieth century, and that the ninety occupations used to construct the index for base year 1907 (estimate i) accounted for 41.2 percent. When I excluded from the reckoning clerical workers, domestic servants, and retail store workers—employees in sectors for which no reliable wage data could be found—the twenty-three occupations comprised 38.8 percent of the remaining (blue-collar) manual labor force, and the 90 occupations 62.5 percent.[3]

In order to test the variation between a weighted and an unweighted mean, I selected twenty-five occupations in which an estimated 45,823 workers—or 59.4 percent of Pittsburgh's blue-collar work force—were engaged in 1910. Data were compiled for the years 1901–1913.[4] Mean indices were then estimated employing different calculating procedures. There existed, for instance, 19,686 steel mill laborers but only 22 stereotypers: in the calculation of the unweighted mean, each occupation contributed 4.00 percent ($\frac{1}{25}$), whereas in the calculation of the weighted mean, steel mill laborers accounted for 42.96 percent of the final index ($^{19,686}/_{45,823}$) and stereotypers but 0.05 percent ($^{22}/_{45,823}$). Nevertheless, Table 6 indicates that the difference between the weighted and unweighted mean index was small. The weighted wage index advanced somewhat more slowly between 1901 and 1913 (38.1 percent compared to 41.6 percent) and revealed greater fluctuations in movement, but the general similarity is remarkable. Indeed, the apparent similitude between mean indices regardless of method of construction or size of sample base suggests that the movement of the majority of occupational wage rates conformed relatively closely to the overall trend.

Graph 1 expresses these tabulations diagramatically. It is readily visible that the movement of wages was similar in Pittsburgh and Birmingham although the upward progress of rates was much faster in the former: in the American city hourly rates advanced by 54.5 percent between 1899 and 1913, compared to 7.5 percent in Birmingham.[5] In both cities the pattern of wage development may be summarized as a period of relative stability from 1903 to 1908 with more impressive rates of growth at each end of the decade, particularly at the turn of the century and in the years following 1910. In general, movements in money wage rates and cyclical variations in economic activity appear to

Graph 1
Hourly Wage Rates, 1899–1913 (1907 = 100.0)

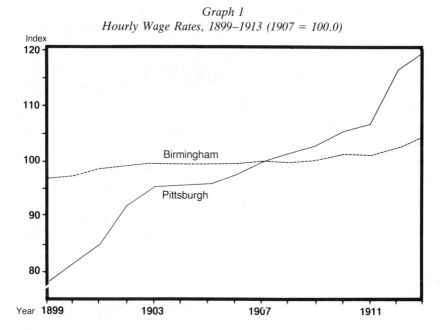

Table 5

Movement of Hourly Wage Rates: Pitsburgh and Birmingham, 1899–1913

A. Index Numbers, Base Year 1907

	Pittsburgh						Birmingham					
	Estimate i[a]		Estimate ii[b]		Estimate iii[c]		Estimate i[a]		Estimate ii[b]		Estimate iii[c]	
Year	n[d]	Index	n[d]	Index	n[d]	Index	n[d]	Index	n[d]	Index	n[d]	Index
1899	28	74.3	23	72.3	11	77.3	28	96.8	26	96.8	11	97.2
1900	33	81.9	23	78.9	12	81.2	33	97.8	26	97.4	12	97.4
1901	34	85.2	23	83.2	12	85.3	33	98.3	26	98.0	12	98.4
1902	39	91.0	23	89.9	15	92.5	36	98.9	26	98.7	15	99.0
1903	43	93.0	23	93.2	17	95.3	36	99.1	26	99.0	17	99.5
1904	47	94.9	23	92.9	19	95.9	36	99.1	26	99.0	19	99.4
1905	49	94.5	23	93.1	19	95.9	36	99.1	26	99.0	19	99.4
1906	50	97.6	23	97.0	19	97.2	37	99.3	26	99.0	19	99.4
1907	90	100.0	23	100.0	20	100.0	40	100.0	26	100.0	20	100.0
1908	82	101.7	23	101.2	16	101.4	39	100.0	26	100.0	16	100.0
1909	79	102.8	23	102.4	16	102.8	39	100.3	26	100.2	16	100.4
1910	75	107.6	23	106.7	16	105.6	38	101.4	26	100.7	16	101.1
1911	74	109.1	23	107.7	16	106.7	37	101.5	26	100.8	16	101.1
1912	74	113.3	23	114.9	16	116.5	37	102.4	26	102.0	16	102.1
1913	75	117.1	23	119.1	16	119.4	36	104.7	26	103.7	16	104.5

B. *Mean 3-Year Moving Average Index Numbers, Base Year 1907*

	Pittsburgh						Birmingham					
	Estimate i[a]		Estimate ii[b]		Estimate iii[c]		Estimate i[a]		Estimate ii[b]		Estimate iii[c]	
Year[e]	n[f]	Index	n[d]	Index	n[f]	Index	n[f]	Index	n[d]	Index	n[f]	Index
1900	v	80.7	23	78.6	v	81.7	v	97.8	26	97.7	v	97.9
1901	v	86.2	23	84.5	v	86.7	v	98.5	26	98.3	v	98.5
1902	v	89.9	23	89.3	v	91.5	v	99.0	26	98.9	v	99.2
1903	v	93.2	23	92.6	v	95.1	v	99.2	26	99.2	v	99.5
1904	v	94.3	23	93.7	v	96.2	v	99.3	26	99.3	v	99.6
1905	v	95.9	23	94.9	v	96.8	v	99.4	26	99.3	v	99.6
1906	v	97.6	23	97.3	v	98.2	v	99.7	26	99.6	v	99.8
1907	v	100.0	23	100.0	v	100.0	v	100.0	26	100.0	v	100.0
1908	v	101.7	23	101.8	v	101.9	v	100.3	26	100.4	v	100.3
1909	v	104.2	23	104.0	v	103.8	v	100.8	26	100.6	v	100.7
1910	v	106.7	23	106.2	v	105.5	v	101.3	26	100.9	v	101.1
1911	v	110.2	23	110.5	v	110.2	v	102.0	26	101.5	v	101.6
1912	v	113.4	24	114.6	v	114.8	v	103.1	26	102.5	v	102.8

Source: See Appendix Table 1.

a. Estimate based on all occupations for which data were available for any given year, i.e., varying sample frame, maximum occupational coverage.

b. Estimate based upon only those occupations for which data were available for every year, 1899–1913, i.e., constant sample frame, reduced occupational coverage.

c. Estimate based upon only those occupations for which data were available for both Pittsburgh and Birmingham in any year, i.e., varying sample frame, but occupational base in both cities is identical for any given year.

d. n indicates number of occupations in sample base.

e. Central year of 3-year moving average.

f. Number of occupations in sample base varies, i.e., the moving average has been calculated from the indices of three consecutive years, although the number of occupations from which these indices were deduced fluctuated.

have been positively correlated. However, this broad statement demands qualification. Hourly rates rose fastest during the more prosperous years of the late 1890s and the boom preceding the First World War. Yet while upturns in the economy were accompanied by advances in money wages, hourly rates exhibited downward rigidity during years of depression. This was particularly noticeable in Pittsburgh, where fluctuations in economic activity and changes in wage rates were both substantially greater than in Birmingham.

Part of the explanation for this apparent stability of hourly wages during the years of low output and high unemployment relates to the criterion of comparative analysis employed. As previously noted, wage

Table 6

Weighted and Unweighted Mean Indices of Hourly Wage Rates: Pittsburgh, 1901–1913
(Base Year 1907)

Year	n	Single Year		3-Year Moving Average	
		Unweighted Mean Index[a]	Weighted Mean Index[b]	Unweighted Mean Index[a]	Weighted Mean Index[b]
1901	25	84.1	85.3		
1902	25	89.8	92.3	89.5	92.0
1903	25	93.0	94.2	92.4	93.6
1904	25	92.5	90.2	93.4	93.6
1905	25	92.9	92.2	94.7	93.8
1906	25	96.9	94.9	97.2	97.2
1907	25	100.0	100.0	100.0	100.0
1908	25	101.4	100.6	101.8	101.9
1909	25	102.3	100.5	104.2	104.3
1910	25	107.2	107.1	106.4	106.7
1911	25	108.0	107.8	110.7	109.8
1912	25	114.7	109.8	114.6	113.5
1913	25	119.1	117.8		

Sources: See Appendix Tables 1 and 3.

Note: n = number of occupations in sample base. The occupations and the number of Pittsburghers engaged in each category in 1910 comprised: bricklayers (1,250); carpenters (3,999); plumbers (635); painters (1,845); structural ironworkers (189); plasterers (459); tile layers (69); first-hand bakers (305); second-hand bakers (305); third-hand bakers (305); blacksmiths (1,310); machinists (5,345); patternmakers (485); iron molders (1,790); boilermakers (526); compositors (458); linotypers (457); stereotypers (22); railway engineers (853); railway firemen (632); railway conductors (690); railway brakemen (1,246); street railway motormen (1,759); public laborers (1,200); and steel mill laborers (19,686). The total was 45,823.

a. Mean calculated as if there were an equal number of workers in each occupational category.

b. Mean weighted according to number of workers in each occupational category.

rates have generally been more inflexible than earnings. As productivity falls, short time increases and underemployment rises, weekly earnings decrease, and—less noticeably—average hourly earnings are reduced. Thus although rates of pay held for those Birmingham workers who retained their jobs during the bleak years of 1904 and 1908, it is likely that earnings declined. In Sheffield real earnings "rose sharply after the depression of 1893 to a peak in 1899, to decline, in 1902–5 and again in 1908–9, to levels barely above those of previous depressions." It may well be true that in Birmingham, as in the Yorkshire city, the earnings "level of 1899 was not reached again until the height of the boom of 1913."[6] This pattern was similar to that for the United Kindgom as a whole.[7] While wage rates generally held firm, earnings fell.

The same phenomenon probably occurred in Pittsburgh. Estimates of average hourly earnings in American manufacturing suggest a decrease from 19.1¢ in 1907 to 18.4¢ in 1908, and only a slight advance to 18.6¢ in 1909.[8] But it would be foolhardy to attribute the stability of Pittsburgh rates in 1907–1909 to statistical deception. First, one is left to explain why rates declined in the 1904 recession and not in the far severer downturn of 1908. Second, the downward rigidity of wages during the latter depression evoked much comment in the contemporary press. Indeed, the reports of newspapers and journals not only referred to wage stability but also attempted to analyze it.

Explanations took two basic forms. The first might be termed "institutional." Contemporaries noted a conscious decision on the part of manufacturers, especially in the steel industry, to maintain both prices and wages at their predepression level and to reduce output in relation to demand. In 1905 the United States Steel Corporation declared that it was "the policy of manufacturers to keep the furnaces, mills and transportation works in operation to their full capacity whenever practicable. Obviously this is wise. It results in . . . lower prices generally to the domestic purchaser; and it secures continuous employment."[9] Two years later the corporation pursued a decidedly different approach, and it spent a great deal of effort in persuading other steel producers to alter their management philosophies accordingly. Thus it was the consensus of opinion at an informal conference of leading steel manufacturers, held at the Pittsburgh University Club in October 1907, that "any radical reduction in steel prices would not help the situation but would make it worse, and hence . . . that the only remedy for the market was to cut down output, which will be done"—an opinion rapidly made official. Within a fortnight Frederick Baackes, vice-president of the corporation's subsidiary, the American Steel and Wire

Company, circulated a well-publicized letter to departmental managers and salesmen. The message was unmistakable: "My instructions to you are: indulge in no cutting of any kind; maintain schedule prices absolutely. This is no time to think of anything else. No additional sales would result from a drop of any kind."[10]

Price stability was one side of the coin; wage stability was the other. Although substantial reductions in the wages of all classes of labor were contemplated, the corporation decided not to implement them because it wanted to maintain prices. "It was deemed advisable not to make any reductions in wages in view of the fact that there were to be no official reductions by the Steel Corporation on iron and steel products," commented a journalist from *Iron Age*. Some independent steel producers found it difficult to accept the corporation's position. In Pittsburgh, Jones and Laughlin certainly toyed with the idea of reopening idle plants at reduced wages. But the oligopolistic position of U.S. Steel eventually enabled it to persuade potential mavericks not to re-fire furnaces and thereby instigate a price war. By December 1907 it was apparent that the corporation's leadership had been reluctantly accepted. In that month consultations over the prospective wage basis for 1908 were concluded with an agreement to maintain existing scales. "The Steel Corporation," noted the *New York Times*, had "saved the day by refusing to accede to the demands of the independents for a wage reduction to take effect after the 1st of the year."[11]

Contemporary comment suggests that other Pittsburgh employers responded favorably to the arguments of U.S. Steel—arguments given a great deal of space in the local and national press. The attitude of the railway corporations toward the depression showed a remarkable similarity to that expressed by steel corporation executives: namely, that reduced freight and passenger rates (and reduced wage rates) would not materially increase the volume of traffic, and that it was best to leave stock idle, reduce the work force, and use the months of inactivity to carry out maintenance work. The public statements of the railway officials, it is true, may have been rationalizations of a position forced upon them by presidential pressure. In February 1908 Theodore Roosevelt wrote to the Interstate Commerce Commission demanding explanation of the fact that a number of railroad companies had "served notice of a proposed reduction of wages on their employees." Such a reduction, he asserted, would result in investigation both by the commission and by the Department of Labor to see if wage cuts were attributable to the past misconduct of the railroads. Not surprisingly, the *Commercial and Financial Chronicle*, whose columns had constantly inveighed against Roosevelt, attacked the president with fervor:

his action was "a lighted brand thrown into a powder magazine."[12] But the potential explosion never occurred, no wage reductions were made, and further presidential action was not required.

It is difficult to find in other industrial sectors evidence of a conscious decision by employers to uphold wage rates in the face of substantially decreased activity, but there can be little doubt that such a sentiment did prevail. Pittsburgh's construction leaders were almost certainly aware of the stand taken by the New York Building Trades Employers' Association, that while there were "more idle people [in November 1907] . . . than at any time within the previous four or five years, . . . reducing wages would not increase the volume of business";[13] certainly rates were not reduced in the Pittsburgh building trades.

Most contemporaries, however, devoted much greater attention to a second factor in explaining the stability of wage rates through the 1908–1909 depression. This explanation stressed the safety-valve nature of emigration. Nearly all the foremost journals of the day believed that wage maintenance resulted to some extent from the departure of many foreign workers for their homelands, and it was widely accepted that this efflux of migrant labor was economically advantageous. "How much worse," asked the *Commercial and Financial Chronicle,* "would be the situation but for this safety-valve of emigration?" The question was rhetorical, for the journal had no doubt that it had been "a decidedly favorable development that so considerable a portion of the alien element has been so well circumstanced as to be able to make a temporary sojourn abroad."[14] At the same time, the number of foreigners entering the United States declined markedly.

Circumstantial evidence suggests that the *Chronicle* was correct in its assertion that never in American history had the movement of aliens been so strongly away from the country as in 1908, and that for the first time ever the net annual movement of migrants was outward.[15] The ratio of departing male steerage passengers to recorded male immigration stood at 0.746 for the year ending June 30, 1908, compared with only 0.231 during the previous year. More significantly, the outflow:inflow ratio was substantially greater than in the recession of 1904 when, for a corresponding twelve-month period, the figure stood at 0.381.[16]

Although it is impossible to estimate the proportion of departing migrants who came from Pittsburgh, it is probable that Allegheny County contributed a greater number of such workers than any other similarly sized area in America. Trainloads of anxious aliens converged on New York City from throughout America, but the traffic was "noticeably heavy from the Pittsburgh district and territory adjacent." In the single month following the financial panic, 15,000 foreigners departed the city, two-thirds on the Pennsylvania railroad and one-third on the Baltimore and Ohio, and by August 1908 "many thousands" of foreigners had returned to Europe from the Iron City.[17]

That a large number of migrants left Pittsburgh is scarcely surprising. The shutdown of the city's manufacturing plant was extensive, and immigrant workers, notably Italians, Slavs, and Hungarians, were the first to be dismissed from employment. In part this was because they were engaged in unskilled occupations most susceptible to redundancy; and in part because employers deliberately laid off "new" immigrants rather than native-born Americans or "old" immigrants. "Dissatisfied with Latins Pittsburgh Manufacturers Discharging Them by the Hundreds," headlined the *New York Times,* suggesting a racial interpretation. "After having experimented with foreign labor for a number of years the big manufacturing concerns of the Pittsburgh districe [*sic*] have decided that they will not do. According to the manufacturers, one intelligent American, Englishman, German or Irishman can do the work of two 'foreigners.' "[18] Whether or not this report accurately reflected the ethnic biases of employers, there can be no doubt that in Pittsburgh's steel industry American workers who faced unemployment were downgraded in skill and found jobs at a lower level, replacing immigrants who had previously been employed at such tasks.[19]

As immigrant workers were the first to be made redundant, so they were the last to receive relief aid. The floating loans and bond issues raised in Pittsburgh to create employment gave preference to American citizens, a provision heartily condoned by the city's labor papers. The system was abused, for there developed a flourishing black market in foreign naturalization papers, and aliens thereby secured work "for which actual bona fide citizens of Pittsburgh alleged that they applied in vain." Nevertheless, such discrimination in relief work must have persuaded many unemployed immigrants to depart.[20]

Whatever the reason for the departure of so many foreign workers, contemporaries were aware of the importance of such a movement in upholding wage rates. The large-scale emigration of late 1907, editorialized the *New York Times,* simplified the unionists' "tasks of maintaining wages without the use of 'entertainment' committees. Every wage-earner taken off [the] declining labor market strengthened it naturally." John R. Commons, present in Pittsburgh at the time of the depression, noted that "thousands of foreigners left precipitately for Europe. For such unskilled laborers as stayed and could find work, the rate of pay held." Local labor leaders agreed. "The immigrants are now turning emigrants," asserted the *National Labor Tribune.* "In this way the pressure on home labor of the permanent class . . . will be reduced."[21]

Such statements might well be criticized as simplistic. Rather than viewing the migrant nature of American society as a safety valve in times of depression, some economists would argue that dependence upon a work force recruited abroad actually accentuated cyclical trade movements. Possibly the depression of 1908–1909 was deepened by the large number of immigrants who had entered America in the boom before the crash, and wage levels were maintained only because rates had been held down by the presence of such alien labor in the prosperous year preceding the trough.[22] But a more fundamental question arises from this present account: namely, why were wage rates upheld in the "great economic convulsion" following the financial panic of 1907, "a panic of the first magnitude," when they had fallen in the "slight industrial disorganization" of 1903–1904?[23] A partial explanation appears to have been the revised managerial policy evident, at least in the steel industry and on the railroads. There is a second possible explanation, however, which requires that the relationship between wage levels and cyclical movements in economic activity in an immigrant society be analyzed more subtly than usual.

It has been seen that both statistical and qualitative evidence show that Pittsburgh wages were far more rigid in the 1908–1909 depression than in the less severe downturn of 1903–1904. These two characteristics suggest that there was a degree of unemployment/underemployment that immigrants were willing to "ride out" and another, harsher level that proved sufficiently distressing to persuade foreign-born workers that the difficulties and traumas of returning overseas were worthwhile. Thus the labor supply/demand ratio may have been higher, and the consequent downward pressure upon wage rates greater, the *milder* the industrial trough experienced.

Let us assume that hourly wage rates were determined by just two variables, the number of job-hours offered and the supply of workers available to occupy them. In a minor recession the number of job-hours offered may have been reduced, but insufficiently to have had an adverse impact upon net immigration; in a major depression the number of job-hours available may have been decreased far more substantially, and for a much longer period, but with the result that emigration was encouraged and immigration discouraged. If this occurred it is possible that the number of job applicants per job-hour offered might have been higher in a period of comparatively mild decline in industrial activity than in a period in which production fell precipitously. In short, the relative tightness of the labor market might have been directly related to the severity of the economic downturn. Therefore, paradoxical as it may first appear, downward pressure upon wages would have been greater in a minor recession (such as in 1904) than in a major depression (such as in 1908).

Between 1899 and 1913 most Pittsburgh and Birmingham occupations experienced an increase in money wage rates. However, evidence from both cities suggests that generally it was unskilled or semiskilled employees who gained the most substantial advance: that is, the margin between the hourly rates paid to skilled and unskilled workers decreased. In contrast, historical accounts have usually indicated that the long-term secular trend toward reduced wage differentials in the United States and Britain only occurred during the exigencies of the First World War.[24] Indeed, it has been suggested that in the two decades prior to the outbreak of hostilities, percentage margins actually widened.[25] Unfortunately, the quantitative data presented to substantiate such hypotheses have been too restricted to warrant sweeping assertions. No fewer than three major studies have based their conclusions upon wage rates paid in the building trades.[26] More extensive statistics, derived from a wider range of industrial and occupational categories at the local level, reveal a general reduction in skill differentials before 1914. While historians have presented imposing evidence that "the margins between the wages of skilled and unskilled labor narrowed considerably from 1914 to 1920," data from both Pittsburgh and Birmingham suggest that this phenomenon was merely an acceleration of a tendency already evident, and not, as generally supposed, a sudden departure from historical precedent.[27]

It is true that differentials widened in the Pittsburgh building trades, but that experience represented the exception rather than the rule. Tabulation of the wage data in Appendix 3 indicates that while the first decade of the twentieth century saw percentage wage margins related to skill increase in the city's construction and engineering industries and remain constant in the district's coal mines, differentials narrowed in the printing, woodworking, brewing, and baking industries, on the railways, and in municipal and police employment. So, too, in Pittsburgh's iron and steel industry, where statistical evidence supports the proud boasts of Charles M. Schwab, president of U.S. Steel, and Willis King, vice-chairman of Jones and Laughlin, that wage differentials had narrowed considerably since the Homestead Strike of 1892. By 1901 there was "no aristocracy of labor by which one man [received] $100 a day and another $1": wages were "more generally distributed among all the men in the mill than formerly."[28]

Thus the claim of a touring British delegation that there existed a "tendency in the American steel industry . . . to establish the general wage on the basis of common unskilled labor" could be legitimately extended to other sectors of Pittsburgh's economy.[29] Table 7 suggests that an index of hourly wage differentials (based upon the less skilled wage as a percentage of the more skilled wage) rose from 62 in 1899 to 73 in 1914, representing a significant reduction in skill margins. Data compiled in Appendix 4 and summarized in Table 7 indicate that this trend was apparent in Birmingham also. Wage data from the British city's industries reveal a perceptible, if less pronounced, narrowing of wage differences based upon skill: from 69 in 1900 to 73 in 1913.

Table 7
Hourly Wage Differentials: Pittsburgh and Birmingham, 1899–1914
(Less Skilled Wage as % of More Skilled Wage)

| Year | Pittsburgh | | | | Birmingham |
	Index[a]	Index[b]	Index[c]	Index[d]	Index[e]
1899	58.8			61.6	
1900	62.1			65.0	69.4
1901	61.7			64.6	69.4
1902	62.9			65.9	69.7
1903	63.2	60.8		66.2	69.9
1904	63.7	61.4		66.8	69.9
1905		60.1		65.4	69.9
1906		61.3		66.7	69.9
1907		63.2	68.8	68.8	69.8
1908			69.5	69.5	69.8
1909			69.1	69.1	69.8
1910			70.1	70.1	73.0
1911			70.7	70.7	73.0
1912			71.6	71.6	73.2
1913			71.7	71.7	72.9
1914			72.8	72.8	

Sources: See Appendix Table 4. For fuller details of calculations, see Peter R. Shergold, "Wage Differentials Based on Skill in the United States, 1899–1914: A Case Study," *Labor History*, 18 (1977), 163–88, esp. Table 3.

  a. Mean of engineering, mining, baking, printing, steam railway, municipal park service, police: Appendix Table 4A.

  b. Mean of engineering, mining, building, baking, printing, steam railway, police: Appendix Table 4A.

  c. Mean of engineering, mining, building, baking, printing, steam railway, brewing, steel manufacturing: Appendix Table 4B.

  d. Chain index calculated from previous three columns: e. g., 1906 = 68.8 (61.3/63.2) = 66.7.

  e. Mean of building, baking, metal trades, printing, police, brass trades: Appendix Table 4C.

Reasons for the decrease in skill differentials were not readily apparent. Detailed examination of the Pittsburgh data suggested that no single cause provided a persuasive explanation for the wage narrowing. To some extent trade union negotiating tactics were responsible. Craft unions, such as in the highly demarcated building trades, argued for wage increases that preserved traditional differentials, and industrial unions such as the United Brewery Workmen fought for flat-rate, across-the-board increases that effectively improved the wages of unskilled workers expressed as a percentage of the wages paid to more skilled colleagues. Managerial policies were also crucial. Facing a weak and defeated Amalgamated Association of Iron, Steel and Tin Workers, Pittsburgh's large steel mills and iron foundries handed down decisions that reduced wage margins and, more importantly, lowered the power and prestige of the industry's skilled employees. To some extent narrowed wage margins were attributable to technological advances which, through the introduction of more efficient machines and through the institution of more effective workplace organization, reduced the level of skill required of the craftsman and/or raised the productive capability of the unskilled worker. This could be witnessed, in the early twentieth century, in such diverse innovations as the car dumpers, skip hoists, and Wellman chargers of the city's steel mills; the new keyboards installed in newspaper printing offices; and the salimeters and hygrometers introduced at the H. J. Heinz pickle plant on Pittsburgh's North Side. However, while the pressure of industrial unions, managerial policy, and technological advance together narrowed wage differentials, the increasing immigration of unskilled workers to the city would have tended to exert a countervailing influence. This will be considered in more detail soon.[30]

Perhaps the single most potent force toward reduced wage differentials in Pittsburgh between 1899 and 1914 was the upward movement of prices. The scale and significance of this inflation will be considered in detail in chapter 5. Suffice it here to note that retail prices rose from the late 1890s, after three decades of deflation, and as they advanced pressures were exerted upon the supply of labor sufficient to distribute subsequent (and consequent) wage increases in a manner that narrowed percentage skill differentials. There was a close correlation between rising prices and reduced occupational wage differentials, suggesting that inflation may have significantly contributed to decreased margins.[31]

The mechanics of this process remain unclear, but four primary forces may be at play. First, as prices rise labor becomes increasingly concerned with wage levels and correspondingly less interested in wage structure. Second, there is a superficial fairness in the award of flat-rate wage increases in response to advances in the cost of living. Third, flat-rate increases are the speediest form of wage award to negotiate, and the easiest to administer. Fourth, and perhaps most significant, there is more urgent pressure upon unskilled workers to achieve wage increases, insofar as inflation makes it impossible to maintain their subsistence living standard, whereas the more skilled, better-paid employees can temporarily absorb price advances within the limits of existing budgetary surplus.[32]

In short, it may be that a subsistence theory of wage differentials is required, in which labor supplies of diverse skill (and income) are seen to react differently to real price rises. To the extent that unskilled workers lived closer to the subsistence line than their skilled colleagues, they would have reacted to price advances with greater vigor and would more stridently have demanded wage increases to match rises in the cost of living. Here the reader may well ask if it is meaningful to analyze American skill differentials in terms of subsistence, an absolute measure of poverty. By European standards, surely, even the least skilled, lowest wage earner was relatively affluent and possessed an ability to save. Yet contemporary commentators were far less convinced of this fact than have been most historians. Many observers believed that Pittsburgh's laborers lived a precarious existence, expending virtually all income upon necessities: they earned a "paltry wage which [made] the cost of maintaining the lowest standard of living compatible with decency and comfort a little more than [they could] provide."[33] The validity of such assertions must now be assessed.

A Place to Get Rich, a Place to Go Under

Whatever the conjunction of forces responsible for the narrowing range of wages in Pittsburgh and Birmingham in the first fifteen years of the twentieth century, Table 7 has shown that the trend was more pronounced in the American city. Nevertheless, wage data indicate that by 1906–1907 differentials remained far less substantial in Birmingham: that city's unskilled employees received a larger percentage of the wage of their skilled colleagues than was the case in Pittsburgh. Graph 2, based upon Tables 8 and 9, shows that in the building, engineering, and printing industries, in bakeries, and in public road work, the difference in the hourly wage rate paid to skilled and unskilled workers was less substantial in Birmingham than in Pittsburgh. Moreover, the overall wage spectrum was greater in America.

Thus while Birmingham's average hourly rate, expressed in money terms, was only 43.8 percent that in Pittsburgh (for twenty occupations) and that in Sheffield 45.5 percent (for seventeen occupations),

Table 8
Hourly Wage Rates for 20 Occupations: Pittsburgh, Birmingham, and Sheffield,
1905–1907

		Hourly Wage Rates		
Occupation	Year	Pgh	Bhm	Shfd
Engineering laborer	1905	15.8¢	9.2¢	9.6¢
Baker, third hand	1907	18.5	10.3[i]	?
Baker, second hand	1907	21.5	11.5[i]	?
Public laborer[a]	1906	21.9	12.2	11.7
Baker, first hand	1907	27.7	13.7[i]	?
Foundry blacksmith[b]	1906	29.0	16.5	18.2
Building laborer[c]	1906	29.9	13.7	11.7
Bookbinder	1906	30.6	15.0	16.5
Machinist[d]	1906	31.6	16.5	18.2
Compositor, b.&j.[e]	1906	32.7	16.2	16.7
Boilermaker[f]	1906	33.4	17.5	18.0
Patternmaker	1906	36.3	17.5	18.0
Machine woodworker[g]	1906	39.2	17.3	16.2
Painter	1906	42.6	17.3	15.2
Carpenter	1906	43.8	19.3	18.3
Plumber	1906	50.0	19.3	18.3
Stonemason	1906	55.0	20.3	19.3
Plasterer	1906	56.3	20.3	18.3
Compositor, m.n.[h]	1906	58.6	22.8	21.9
Bricklayer	1906	63.1	19.3	19.3

Source: See Appendix Table 1.

a. Sheffield rate for public sweepers and water department laborers; Birmingham rate for gas department laborers.

b. Birmingham and Sheffield rates for engineering smiths.

c. Pittsburgh rate for hod carriers; Birmingham and Sheffield rates for bricklayers' laborers.

d. Birmingham and Sheffield rates for fitters and turners.

e. Pittsburgh rate for book-and-job compositors; Birmingham and Sheffield rates for weekly newspaper compositors.

f. Birmingham and Sheffield rates for heavy platers; light platers received 16.5¢ in both cities.

g. Birmingham and Sheffield rates for cabinetmakers.

h. Morning newspaper compositors.

i. Birmingham bakers were paid a standard weekly rate whether they worked the 60-hour day shift or the 54-hour night shift. Hourly wage rates are based upon the midpoint, 57 hours.

Table 9

Hourly Wages of Various Occupations in the Building, Printing, Machine Shop, and Baking Trades, 1905–1907[a]

			Wage Indices		
Sector	Occupation	Year	Pgh	Bhm	Shfd
Building	Bricklayer	1906	211.0	140.9	165.0
	Plasterer	1906	188.3	148.2	156.4
	Stonemason	1906	183.9	148.2	165.0
	Plumber	1906	167.2	140.9	156.4
	Carpenter	1906	146.5	140.9	156.4
	Painter	1906	142.5	126.3	129.9
	Bricklayer's laborer	1906	100.0	100.0	100.0
Printing	Compositor, m.n.[b]	1906	191.5	152.0	132.7
	Compositor, b.&j.[c]	1906	106.9	108.0	101.2
	Bookbinder	1906	100.0	100.0	100.0
Machine-shop	Patternmaker	1906	229.7	190.2	187.5
	Boilermaker	1906	211.4	190.2	187.5
	Machinist	1906	200.0	179.3	189.6
	Foundry blacksmith	1906	183.5	179.3	189.6
	Engineering laborer	1905	100.0	100.0	100.0
Baking	First hand	1907	149.7	133.0	?
	Second hand	1907	116.2	111.7	?
	Third hand	1907	100.0	100.0	?

Sources: See Appendix Table 1.

a. Expressed as percentages of the wage paid to the least-skilled occupation in each sector.

b. Morning newspaper compositor.

c. Book-and-job compositor (Pittsburgh): weekly newspaper compositor (Birmingham and Sheffield).

there was considerable occupational deviation from the mean. This deviation was not random. In general, lower-paid employees in Birmingham and Sheffield were in a less disadvantaged position vis-à-vis their Pittsburgh counterparts than were higher-paid employees. Almost without exception those workers paid less than 35¢ per hour in Pittsburgh possessed an income advantage over their British counterparts less than the mean; those paid in excess of that sum possessed an income advantage greater than the mean.

This fact is presented forcibly in Graph 3, where the rates paid for Birmingham occupations are plotted as percentages of the rates paid for the same jobs in Pittsburgh. If the wage spectrum had been identical in the British and American cities, the derived percentages would have remained constant no matter whether the comparison was made between bricklayers or engineering laborers. Such was not the case. Nor was the statistical distribution about the mean random. There was a trend: the higher the Pittsburgh wage, the lower was the Birmingham wage expressed as a percentage of it. The Birmingham bricklayer, Table 10 shows, received only 30.6 percent of the rate of his Pittsburgh

Graph 2
Wage Differences Between Skilled and Unskilled Workers: Pittsburgh and Birmingham, 1905–1907

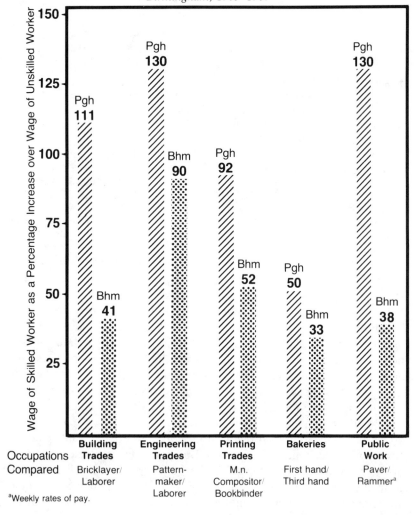

Occupations Compared	Building Trades	Engineering Trades	Printing Trades	Bakeries	Public Work
	Bricklayer/ Laborer	Pattern- maker/ Laborer	M.n. Compositor/ Bookbinder	First hand/ Third hand	Paver/ Rammer[a]

[a]Weekly rates of pay.

counterpart; in contrast, the engineering laborer obtained 58.2 percent of the hourly payment earned by a worker engaged in similar work in the Iron City. In between these two extremes, a fairly obvious pattern emerged, the Birmingham (or Sheffield) wage ratio (y/x) falling as the Pittsburgh wage (x) rose. Indeed, it proved possible to posit a linear relationship between the two variables, expressed mathematically by the formula: $y/x = 65.73 - 0.52x$. That is, for every one-unit increase in the number of cents paid per hour in Pittsburgh, there was a 0.52-unit decrease in the percentage of the Pittsburgh wage represented by the Birmingham wage. When the correlation regression line was superimposed upon the scattergram, the large majority of observations fell close to it. A statistical test of the significance of the relatively tight grouping of observed data around the line of correlation indicated that r = 0.958.[34] There was therefore an extremely high negative relationship between the two

Table 10
Hourly Wage Rates: Birmingham and Sheffield, 1906[a]

Occupation	Hourly Wage Stated As % of Pittsburgh Hourly Wage	
	Bhm	*Shfd*
Bricklayer	30.6	30.6
Carpenter	44.1	41.3
Plasterer	36.1	32.5
Plumber	38.6	36.6
Painter	40.6	35.7
Stonemason	36.9	35.1
Building laborer	45.8	39.1
Compositor, b.&j.	49.5	51.5
Compositor, m.n.	38.9	37.4
Bookbinder	49.0	53.9
Engineering laborer	58.2	60.8
Patternmaker	48.2	49.6
Machinist	52.2	57.6
Foundry blacksmith	56.9	62.8
Boilermaker	52.4	53.9
Baker, first hand	49.5	n.k.
Baker, second hand	53.5	n.k.
Baker, third hand	55.7	n.k.
Machine woodworker	44.1	41.3
Public laborer	55.7	53.4

Sources: See Appendix Table 1.
Note: n. k. = not known.
a. Except engineering laborer (1905) and bakers (1907).

variables, although it must be understood that the regression of *y/x* on *x* was obviously noncausal in nature. If the occupational sample base was representative, it suggests that Birmingham wages (as ratios) might be predicted with a high degree of probability from known Pittsburgh rates and vice versa.[35]

It has been shown that in the early twentieth century all Pittsburgh

Graph 3
Hourly Wage Rates: Pittsburgh and Birmingham, 1905–1907

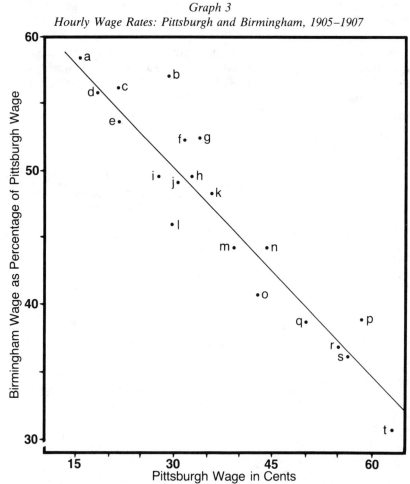

a. Engineering laborer, b. Foundry blacksmith, c. Public laborer, d. Third-hand baker, e. Second-hand baker, f. Machinist, g. Boilermaker, h. Book-and-job compositor, i. First-hand baker, j. Bookbinder, k. Patternmaker, l. Building laborer, m. Machine woodworker, n. Carpenter, o. Painter, p. Morning newspaper compositor, q. Plumber, r. Stonemason, s. Plasterer, t. Bricklayer.

workers received hourly wage rates substantially superior to those paid in Birmingham or Sheffield. However, the higher the financial status of the American manual worker (a status reflecting, at least to some extent, superior skill), the greater was his comparative wage advantage. Within the American city, wage differentials were, in all industries, wider than in Britain, and the overall range substantially more extended.[36]

The contrast between the hourly rates received by Pittsburgh's skilled artisans and common laborers did not go unnoticed by contemporaries. Many travelers, it is true, observed only the high wages being paid to skilled workers and believed that beneath the city's smoky, grimy exterior lay a workers' paradise. The city's name, suggested Casson, "should be spelled—Pitt$burgh." According to William Lucien Scaife, Pittsburgh's skilled artisans earned "more than most professional men."[37] But others lowered their gaze and noted the unskilled workers' difficulty in making ends meet. Data gathered in 1915 by canvassers of the Metropolitan Life Insurance Company revealed that average weekly income for fully employed laborers was only $9.90, or 16.5¢ an hour for a sixty-hour week. The Pittsburgh Christian Social Service Union asserted that this was inadequate to purchase family necessities, a view that was far from unique. The Pittsburgh Association for the Improvement of the Poor, analyzing the continuing demands made upon its relief services, concluded that unemployment, sickness, and immorality were but the final crushing blows on the path to poverty: "in many instances the wages were inadequate to meet the necessary expenses of the family, for the cost of living and high rents were not in proportion to their earnings." Similarly, John Commons concluded that "common labor in the district was . . . paid less than the standard of family subsistence."[38]

Thus while observers mentioned, in some astonishment, the high wages paid to skilled artisans, social investigators pointed out, in horror, the insufficient income received by day laborers. Pittsburgh was, wrote the British visitor Arthur Shadwell, a city of extemes. Appalled by a society in which steel mill rollers and heaters earned, as he believed, seven times more than laborers, he described the city as "a place to toil in and get rich—the best I daresay in the world; and . . . a place to toil in and go under—the worst in the world."[39]

Contemporary observers of Birmingham's work force were more troubled by labor immobility than by low wages. The prevailing wage rate for male laborers was deemed satisfactory, but it was attained at an early age, and there was little opportunity of promotion into skilled employment. "When children leave the elementary school it is comparatively easy to find them situations where they will earn a fair wage for three or four years," reported the Birmingham Ladies' Union of Workers in 1907, "but . . . there is no prospect of learning any trade, with the result that eventually they join the large army of unskilled workers."[40] In addition to the lack of opportunity for job advancement offered such workers, social investigators were concerned about the period of unemployment to which this section of the labor force was particularly susceptible. It is not perhaps surprising that Birmingham was the first local authority in Britain to take advantage of the Employment Act of 1910, establishing Juvenile Employment Exchanges controlled by the Education committee and the Board of Trade: nor that the city coined its own term for the disconsolate groups of youths who lounged on street corners, caps pulled down over their eyes, waiting for casual employment as laborers—the "peaky blinders."[41]

Statistical evidence and circumstantial comment both suggest that there was, in material terms, far more of an "aristocracy of labor" in the United States in the first decade of the twentieth century. Wage differentials were substantially wider than in Britain. It was Pittsburgh's skilled tradesmen, not laborers, who experienced the greatest money wage superiority over their Birmingham counterparts. In contrast, Victor Clark's encyclopedic study of American manufacturing estimated that wage differences between that country and Britain were much greater in unskilled occupations, and much of Habakkuk's analysis of nineteenth-century technology was postulated upon the premise that in the United States "an increased demand for labor raised the wages of skilled labor *less* than the wages of unskilled labor . . . [and] that the premium on artisan skills was generally lower in America than in England."[42] In short, the comparative wage/skill differentials appear to have reversed by the end of the century.[43] Why?

Habakkuk suggests that the comparatively greater supply of skilled labor in early nineteenth-century America derived largely from the superior popular educational facilities in that country, and the consequent wider diffusion of literacy. By the twentieth century, English educational institutions had probably experienced a relative improvement. More significantly, the large number of Slavic and Italian migrants entering the United States in the final decades of the century meant that an increasing percentage of the work force was functionally illiterate. Generally unable to speak English, frequently unacculturated to industrial life, they appeared to many Americans little short of brutish. "They don't seem like men to me hardly," John Griswold, a Scotch-Irish Pittsburgh furnace boss, commented in exasperation in 1907. "They can't talk United States. You tell them something and they just look and say 'Me no fustay, me no fustay', that's all you can get out of 'em." Indeed, Pittsburgh laborers able to communicate in English, in an environment in which thousands of workers were "as dumb as horses" in their ignorance of the language, were paid an extra 2¢ per hour.[44]

This undereducation of the new immigrants (at least in terms of the abilities required in industrial America) more than offset the improvement in educational facilities available to children brought up in the United States. As a result there was an increasingly low elasticity of substitution between the skilled and unskilled sections of the labor force: the mass of immigrant laborers were effectively barred from promotion to skilled employment and offered only their unskilled manual labor in competition with one another.

A second explanation relates to union organization. Throughout most of the nineteenth century, the upgrading of unskilled to skilled labor had been less impeded in the United States than in Britain by trade union restrictions and apprenticeship rules. The emergence of the A.F. of L. late in the century, and its unions' increased concentration upon job control, meant that the advantages American employers experienced in this respect were severely reduced. At the same time the practical problems involved in organizing the ethnically heterogeneous work force—difficulties compounded, no doubt, by the exclusive attitude of many American employees, who consciously sought to protect their jobs from immigrant usurpers—meant that unions were usually craft-based, and that far more upward pressure was exerted upon the wages of skilled artisans that upon the rates paid to common laborers. In contrast, the rise of "new unionism" in England meant that an increasing number of unskilled occupations were organized alongside more skilled ones.

A third explanation derives from the concept of the frontier West as a safety valve for urban eastern labor. Some historians argue that in the first half of the nineteenth century, the pulling power of American agricultural expansion had been felt most on unskilled labor, for it was the worker without special industrial skills who stood to make the largest relative gain from turning to farming. But although land became progressively cheaper as the century advanced, the effective costs of settlement rose, and the lure of land therefore exerted relatively greater influence upon skilled workers able to accumulate capital.

Probably the single most important factor, however, at least in Pittsburgh, was the increased scale and changing nature of immigration. The difference between old and new migrants has often been exaggerated, but there can be little doubt that the mass immigration of the post–Civil War period did contain relatively fewer skilled workers than did earlier waves. Certainly the overall supply of labor was increased proportionately faster than the supply of skilled labor. Thus the wider range of wages in Pittsburgh at the beginning of the twentieth century reflected the city's more elastic supply of unskilled (migrant) labor. Whereas foreigners accounted for only 0.4 percent of Birmingham's population (1901), in Pittsburgh foreign-born whites comprised 25.5 percent of the city's residents (1900). Employed males in Birmingham decreased by 0.9 percent between 1901 and 1911, while in Pittsburgh between 1900 and 1910 they increased by 19.8 percent and 48.0 percent of this increase resulted from an advance in the number of foreigners in the work force.

The importance of industrially unskilled immigrants in Pittsburgh's labor force was a result not only of the number of foreign-born entering the city but also of their demographic structure. The age of the migrants was highly favorable to production, with far fewer old- and young-age dependents than characterize a stable (immobile) society, and this affected the demographic framework of the society within which the immigrant community existed in diaspora. Consequently, Birmingham and Sheffield had far fewer males in the productive age group (from fifteen to forty-four years, inclusive) than did Pittsburgh. Of 273,589 males in the American city in 1911, 63.9 percent fell in the productive age category; in Birmingham the equivalent figure was only 49.7 percent, and in Sheffield, 48.9 percent.[45]

Pittsburgh epitomized migrant America. The massive inflow of foreign workers into the city created substantial pressures toward a long-term widening of wage differentials. The increasing percentage of foreign-born common labor was possibly paid less for its muscle-power than native common labor, although recent research has failed to validate the existence of widespread wage discrimination.[46] Large-scale immigration into the American city may nevertheless have widened differentials insofar as the supply curve of unskilled workers would have been far more affected by net immigration than that of skilled workers and, unless the supply curve of the unskilled was perfectly elastic, the inflow of labor would have depressed the wage rates paid to unskilled workers.[47] The large numbers of immigrants who arrived in Pittsburgh from the 1880s brought few industrial skills with them, and those skills they did possess could be given little expression until they mastered the English language. Most were absorbed into the ranks of the unskilled, the skilled laborer remaining comparatively unaffected by the competition of foreigners. Rates for skilled artisans were therefore maintained at a high level—the supply of such workers being relatively inelastic—but the comparative plentitude of unskilled labor tended to keep wage rates low.

Moreover the immigrants, as consumers, may have actually increased demand for the limited supply of skilled labor and thereby have contribued to widened differentials. "In some trades," noted a British inquiry, immigration tended "to increase [wage] rates, as in the case of some skilled branches of the building trades that were stimulated by the demand for house accommodation, created by the influx of a non-competing foreign element."[48]

The comparatively low level of wages among Pittsburgh's unskilled workers also reflected more competition between such employees than was true of the more homogeneous and stable structure of Birmingham. The psychology of immigrant laborers, already mobile in the spatial sense, seems to have been different from that of relatively settled British workers. Uprooted from their home environment and having come to America primarily for economic gain, Pittsburgh's southeast European workers were more willing to undertake whatever jobs were available, and more ready to change occupations in response to demand. As a result, the city's labor market was a ferment of mobility. In the prosperous year of 1906, one large machine works—presumably MacKintosh, Hemphill, and Company—had to hire no less than 12,000 employees in order to maintain a force of 10,000 and another major manufacturing enterprise estimated that 2,000 workers had to be employed annually in order to keep 1,000 permanent positions filled. It was with good reason, therefore, that John Commons characterized Pittsburgh's unskilled laborers as "a restless, movable, competitive rank-and-file."[49]

The contrast with the Birmingham labor force was great. Birmingham's trades did not experience entirely concurrent seasonal depression, and observers were convinced that "in a properly organized labor market it [was] probable that most of [the temporarily unemployed] would have worked for several employers each year, instead of working for only one master during his busiest season." The Birmingham worker seems to have been far more willing to "play" until employment in his particular field returned. Frank Tillyard, secretary of the Lord Mayor's Relief Fund in 1905, saw this as a sign of the moral decline of the city's laboring men who, he claimed, requested aid from the fund rather than take up partial, temporary employment.[50] On the other hand, those in charge of the Distress Committee shared similar qualms about giving out temporary work to which applicants were not accustomed: "There is a natural hesitation," noted the 1907 report, "about sending a skilled workman to do rough work in the open air."[51]

Birmingham's work force was immobile horizontally as well as vertically. "It seems that even the lowest grades of labor in Birmingham are more or less professional," claimed a bemused contemporary. The "filers and polishers in the metal trades remain filers and polishers; if there is no filing or polishing to be done they are unemployed, and they do not to any great extent take up other lines of work; every branch of every trade has its own stagnant reservoir."[52]

The Pittsburgh laborer, therefore, appears to have been a far less specialized factor of production than the laborer in Birmingham, and the greater competitive activity within the Pittsburgh work force may well have been partially responsible for the comparatively low wages earned by the city's unskilled employees. It is true that none of the socioeconomic pressures frequently attributed to mass immigration seem to have been sufficient to prevent the narrowing of wage differentials in the post-1900 period, and even in the preceding decades there was only a slight increase in differentials.[53] Nevertheless, in terms of spatial comparison—if not of temporal—the contribution that successive waves of immigrants made to Pittsburgh's economy must be afforded a significant role in explaining that city's far wider range of hourly wage rates vis-à-vis Birmingham.

Analysis of occupational wage dispersion about the mean thus indicates that the differential between skill levels in Pittsburgh was substantially greater than in Birmingham, and also that the overall wage spectrum was much wider in the American city. The common assertion or implicit assumption of historians that the American worker experienced a standard of living superior to his counterpart in England must therefore be considerably qualified. This is especially true in light of contemporary observation that the manual labor force of the United States contained "an abnormally large proportion of unskilled and semiskilled workers," a fact that "would affect appreciably any general 'weighted' comparison between the level of wages in the two countries."[54]

Unfortunately, there are few statistics by which to compare the percentages of skilled, semiskilled, and unskilled workers in British and American industry. Because the British censuses generally characterized the work force by industry rather than by skill, occupational comparison with the American censuses proved impossible. The British census of 1911 did, however, provide a rough indication of skill levels within the building and construction trades. In this industry, at least, unskilled occupations comprised a smaller proportion of the total manual labor force in Birmingham (and Sheffield) than was true of Pittsburgh. In the American city bricklayers, masons, carpenters, painters, and plumbers totaled 52 percent of building employees, and laborers

48 percent; in Birmingham a liberal estimate of laborers and navvies in the construction industry suggested that they comprised only 36 percent of the total force; in Sheffield the equivalent statistic was 42 percent.[55]

In the steel industry too, available data indicate that the United States was more dependent upon unskilled workers. Common labor comprised approximately 42 percent of the steel mill work force in Allegheny County in 1907, while another 7 percent earned wages no greater than those paid to unskilled laborers. Estimates for Yorkshire steel mills, including Sheffield, suggest that general laborers totaled just under 30 percent of manual employees.[56] It behooves the economic historian who compares average American and British wages to proceed with extreme caution: in some way the averages compared must be weighted in regard to the different skill structure in the two countries. Certainly here is an area that will require much more attention in the future.

A Time for Toil, A Time for Leisure

Attention thus far has been devoted to a comparison of hourly wage rates in the British and American cities. It is now necessary to consider the number of hours worked by employees in Pittsburgh and Birmingham, and the weekly earnings received for such labor.

Appendix 5 indicates that the number of hours worked in a full-time week remained relatively static for most Birmingham occupations in the first thirteen years of the twentieth century. Bricklayers and plasterers had their hours reduced from 54 to 51 in 1909, and nearly all building tradesmen secured a half-hour cut in the work week in 1913. In the printing industry, morning newspaper compositors had their weekly hours cut from 50 to 48 in 1902, and their colleagues were awarded a less substantial reduction in 1912. Metal trades employees also made a little progress toward a shorter working week, some workers gaining a 48-hour week in 1907. Many, however, continued to labor 53 hours, and by 1913 the minimum full-time week had risen to 50 hours. They were not the only group to see their working week lengthened once more. Farriers' doormen and firemen, whose full-time hours declined from 56.5 in 1899 to 55.5 in 1900, saw a return to their former work week in 1913. In other occupations the work week remained unchanged. Bakers, who worked a 54-hour week when employed at night and a 60-hour week when engaged during the day, experienced no reduction in their hours of labor; and woodworkers continued to work a 54-hour week.[57]

Pittsburghers, on the other hand, found that their full-time working week was substantially shortened. In the building trades most employees worked a 44-hour week in 1913, whereas in 1900 hours had varied from 48 (for plasterers) to 60 (for structural iron workers and inside wiremen). This significant decrease in hours was matched by other sections of the city's labor force. Metal tradesmen had worked a full-time week of between 57.5 and 60 hours in 1899, but 54 hours was general by 1907. By 1913 blacksmiths and their helpers had had their hours cut even further, working only 48 hours. Printing house employees, who worked approximately 54 hours in 1900, had their week reduced to about 48 hours by 1907. In that year a new agreement gained the strongly unionized brewery workers a shorter working week: engineers, firemen, and pipe fitters derived most benefit, finding their day cut from 10 to 8 hours, while other brewery and bottle house employees won the 48-hour week.

Appendix 5 suggests that the full-time working week had gravitated toward 48 hours by 1913. Yet there remained many jobs, for which data are more fragmentary, in which weekly hours were substantially in excess of that total. In the city's steel mills, the 72-hour week continued to be worked, and in blast furnaces the 84-hour week remained normal, in spite of increasing opposition from many quarters. In April 1911 Charles M. Cabot succeeded in introducing a critical resolution to the annual meeting of U.S. Steel stockholders. "Whether viewed from a physical, social or mental point of view, we believe the 7-day week is detrimental to those engaged in it," reported the investigating committee established in response to this resolution. A "12-hour day of labor followed continuously by any group of men for any considerable number of years means a decreasing of the efficiency and a lessening of the vigor and virility of such men."[58]

The steel corporation was unmoved. Elbert Gary, presenting the "official" viewpoint, argued that the 12-hour day was "not physically detrimental to the men, because the work [was] intermittent, and for the further reason that the introduction of machinery [had] eliminated most of the arduous physical labor." Long hours, in consequence, remained the norm in Pittsburgh's steel mills. In 1911 laborers worked an average of 75.6 hours in the district's blast furnaces, 74.3 hours in Bessemer converters, and 73.2 hours in open-hearth plants. Many of their colleagues toiled even longer: in the blast furnaces, for example, larry men, skip operators, blowers, stove tenders, keepers, pig machine men, and helpers all worked an 84-hour week.[59]

Other Pittsburgh workers shared their plight. Stokers for the gas companies also labored through an 84-hour week, while electricians and engineers employed by the electric light and power companies worked 65 hours. Shop workers too had long hours. At the start of the century, the Salespeople's Assembly No. 4097, a last stronghold of Knights of Labor influence in Allegheny County, negotiated successfully with the city's leading stores. As a result, the workday began at 8 A.M. and ended at 5:30 P.M., except on Saturdays, when late-night shoppers had to be served until 9 P.M. In other words, retail clerks worked 58.5 hours per week (including lunch breaks). By 1905, the agreement having expired, the assembly found itself too weak to renegotiate a similar contract, and weekday hours were extended until 6 P.M. increasing the full-time working week to 61 hours.

Hours were especially long in the transportation sector. Boat men, the "Mike Finks" of the Allegheny and Monongahela rivers, worked 12 hours a day, seven days a week. It is scarcely surprising that they possessed a reputation for toughness, earning a "stake" and then "knocking off" until their money had been spent in a cathartic bout of drunken revelry. The hours of railway workers were almost as exhausting. Men employed in the yards and sidings worked shifts of 12 hours' duration and were expected, in an emergency, to labor for up to 48 hours at a stretch. The motormen and conductors of the street railways generally worked shorter days of from 9 to 10 hours in length. But although 10.6 hours was the maximum "straight" run, "swing" shifts must have seemed considerably longer. Such shifts, necessary one week in four, required that the employee work from 5 A.M. until 10 A.M., rest until 4 P.M., and then work again until 9 P.M. The hours of teamsters were likewise severe. Up at 5 A.M. to feed, clean, and harness their horses, Pittsburgh's drivers usually began deliveries an hour later. Although a quitting time was rarely stipulated, it generally took about ten hours to finish the day's route.[60]

Weekly hours in the English cities rarely reached such heights. In Yorkshire iron and steel workers averaged only 54.7 hours for a full work week in 1906, and there is no reason to suppose that equivalent data from Sheffield alone would differ markedly.[61] In Birmingham workers in many occupations labored fewer hours in a full week than their colleagues in Pittsburgh. Tramway drivers and conductors, for instance, averaged 54 hours per week; gas stokers worked daily shifts of only 8 hours duration; and the Shop Act of 1911, which compelled shopkeepers to close not later than 1 P.M. on at least one weekday every week, resulted in a "weekly half-holiday for the majority of [Birmingham's] shop-assistants."[62]

In summary, the number of hours worked in a full-time week varied far more, between occupations, in Pittsburgh than in the British cities.

In Birmingham few employees enjoyed the 44-hour week that by 1913 was general in the construction trades of the American city. Indeed, the 48-hour week, worked by Pittsburgh's printing house, brewery, and municipal employees, was rare in Birmingham. On the other hand, few Birmingham workers labored more than 56 hours each week: virtually all occupations had a full-time week of between 50 and 54 hours. The range of hours worked, like the hourly income paid, was far wider in Pittsburgh. Members of the American labor aristocracy were not only richer than their British counterparts—they were also more leisured.

The long hours expected of many Pittsburgh workers meant that few of them possessed the necessary spare time to watch sporting contests. Undoubtedly many followed the exploits of Honus Wagner, the "Flying Dutchman," and his ability to hammer home runs made him a popular hero. Thanks to his tremendous batting power, the Pittsburgh Pirates gained the National League baseball championships in 1901, 1902, and 1903 and celebrated the opening of Forbes Field in 1909 by winning the World Series. Yet relatively few workers had the weekly half-holiday necessary to enjoy the spectacle. There existed, of course, aficionados of the game willing to forsake rest in order to urge the Pirates to victory from a 25¢ seat in the bleachers. "They have work to do—for the most part—and they should be sleeping or eating," reported a local journalist. "But they would rather do without sleep or without a square meal deliberately eaten, than miss a minute of a ball game . . . even if they go on their 'night turn' in mill or factory minus the rest that should be theirs." Generally, however, support for Pittsburgh's most popular sport came from the "middle and relatively leisured classes."[63]

In Birmingham, by contrast, tens of thousands of spectators, mostly working-class, spent bleak, wintry Saturday afternoons roaring allegiance to one of the city's great soccer teams. Aston Villa drew the largest crowds by the 1890s, but West Bromwich Albion and Birmingham City (Small Heath) also attracted enthusiastic supporters—workingmen able to find identity with "their" team's glory, and fortunate enough to escape briefly from the difficulties of everyday life. Some workers' representatives were clearly irritated by this infatuation with soccer, seeing it as a threat to more legitimate leisure pursuits. T. Jones of the Midland Counties' Trades Federation found the absence of such spectator enthusiasm in the United States one positive aspect of American life. "There is but little football played," he noted with relief, "and no time is lost in going to see it, a thing we should do well to copy." American commentators frequently agreed. Price Collier, for example, was shocked by the British workers' dedication to soccer. "The attendance at games on Saturday is very large," he observed. "Even in these days of distress in the shipbuilding and cotton industries, when the problem of the unemployed is a serious one, there is no lack of sixpences and shillings to gain entry to the football games."[64]

It is, of course, a matter of debate whether the time and money spent by soccer fans was wasted. There can be little question, however, that the half-day Saturday that enabled the tremendous development of such spectator sports in Birmingham would have been welcomed by a considerable number of Pittsburgh workers. Many employees in the city's ironworks and steelworks, as they sweated in the noise and glare of furnace and mill or doused tired limbs under the yard tap, must have daydreamed of carefree afternoons spent at Forbes Field. That, in essence, was the opinion of Terence Flynn, Jones' colleague on the Mosely Commission. The "Saturday half-holiday, so much favoured by English workers, [had] not yet obtained general recognition [in the United States]" he confirmed. But the "movement in its favour [was] becoming a popular one, mainly owing to a desire to attend Saturday afternoon sports."[65]

By multiplying the hours of work in a full-time week by hourly wages, we can calculate the standard weekly rates paid to various occupations.[66] Rates for twenty-four occupations in the British and American cities are compiled in Table 11. These weekly rates may then be compared as the hourly rates were; namely, by representing the wage for a Birmingham or Sheffield trade as a percentage of the wage paid to a similar trade in Pittsburgh (see Table 12).

The result of such tabulation does not require fundamental amendment to the premises posited earlier. It is true that the weekly wage spectrum in Pittsburgh was not as wide as the hourly range, for those jobs paying high hourly rates (such as trades in the construction and printing industries) generally required fewer hours than jobs paying relatively low hourly rates (such as the engineering, iron and steel, and bakery trades). Moreover, insofar as those in occupations with the highest hourly rates in Pittsburgh tended to work fewer hours than their counterparts in Birmingham or Sheffield, the transatlantic variation between weekly rates was somewhat less substantial than the difference between hourly rates. Conversely, those Pittsburgh jobs with relatively low hourly wage rates tended to require more hours in a full-time week than their equivalent occupations in the British cities, so that the difference in weekly rates was concomitantly greater.

Nevertheless, the principal conclusions derived from analysis of hourly data remain unaltered: the higher paid the Pittsburgh occupation, the lower was the wage of that occupation in Birmingham or Sheffield stated as a percentage of the American city's rate. It was the higher paid and, to some extent at least, the more skilled employees who experienced most income advantage from residence in Pittsburgh. Hourly wage rates, standard weekly wages, and hours of work were all

Table 11

Weekly Hours of Labor and Weekly Wage Rates of Occupations: Pittsburgh, Birmingham and Sheffield, 1905–1907

Occupation	Year	Hours in a Full Work Week			Weekly Wage		
		Pgh	Bhm	Shfd	Pgh	Bhm	Shfd
Engineering laborer	1905	57.5	53.0	54.0	$ 9.09	$ 4.87	$ 4.87
Baker, third hand	1907	65.0	57.0[a]	n.k.	12.03	5.85	n.k.
Baker, second hand	1907	65.0	57.0[a]	n.k.	13.98	6.58	n.k.
Public laborer	1906	48.0	n.k.	48.0	10.51	5.88	5.60
Baker, first hand	1907	65.0	57.0[a]	n.k.	18.01	7.80	n.k.
Foundry blacksmith	1906	61.0	53.0	51.0	17.69	8.75	9.26
Building laborer	1906	48.5	54.0	49.5	14.50	7.40	5.78
Bookbinder	1906	54.0	52.0	51.0	16.52	7.80	8.40
Machinist	1906	58.5	53.0	51.0[b]	18.49	8.75	9.26
Compositor, b.&j.	1906	54.0	52.0	51.0	17.66	8.42	8.53
Boilermaker	1906	58.0	53.0	54.0	19.37	9.28	9.73
Patternmaker	1906	56.0	53.0	54.0	20.33	9.28	9.73
Machine woodworker	1906	54.0	54.0	54.0	21.17	9.34	8.77
Painter	1906	48.0	56.5	49.5	20.45	9.77	7.54
Carpenter	1906	48.0	51.0	49.5	21.02	9.84	9.04
Plumber	1906	48.0	54.0	49.5	24.00	10.42	9.04
Stonemason	1906	48.0	51.0	49.5	26.40	10.35	9.55
Plasterer	1906	48.0	54.0	49.5	27.02	10.96	9.04
Compositor, m.n.	1906	48.0	48.0[c]	50.0	28.13	10.96	10.96
Bricklayer	1906	48.0	54.0	49.5	30.29	10.42	9.55
Public paver	1909	n.k.	n.k.	n.k.	30.38	8.75	n.k.
Public rammer	1905	n.k.	n.k.	n.k.	13.20	6.36	n.k.
Tram conductor	1907	n.k.	n.k.	n.k.	16.20	n.k.	6.80
Steel mill laborer	1906	72.0	n.k.	54.7[d]	12.00	n.k.	5.39

Sources: See Appendix Tables 1 and 5.

Note: n.k. = not known.

a. Bakers worked 54 hours (full-time) when working at night and 60 hours (full-time) when working during the day.

b. Some workers were employed for 48 hours in a full week: others were employed for 54 hours. The weekly wage was the same.

c. The *Annual Abstract of Labor Statistics* consistently stated that, after 1902, the daily newspaper compositor worked a 48-hour week, although the *Report on Standard Time Rates for Wages* (1906) indicated that the compositor was working a 52-hour week.

d. Mean hours worked in full-time week for 8,874 iron and steel workers.

far more variable than in the British cities. Some Pittsburgh workers gained far higher money wages and some labored fewer hours, but for many occupations the American experience was less advantageous. Whether or not all Pittsburghers enjoyed real material advantage vis-à-vis their British counterparts will shortly be calculated.

Table 12
Weekly Wage Rates: Birmingham and Sheffield, 1906[a]

Occupation	Weekly Wage Stated As a % of Pittsburgh Weekly Wage	
	Bhm	*Shfd*
Engineering laborer	53.6	53.6
Baker, third hand	48.6	n.k.
Baker, second hand	47.1	n.k.
Public laborer	55.9	53.3
Baker, first hand	43.3	n.k.
Foundry blacksmith	49.5	52.3
Building laborer	51.0	39.9
Bookbinder	47.2	50.8
Machinist	47.3	50.1
Compositor, b.&j.	47.7	48.3
Boilermaker	47.9	50.2
Patternmaker	45.6	47.9
Machine woodworker	44.1	41.4
Painter	47.8	36.9
Carpenter	46.8	43.0
Plumber	43.4	37.6
Stonemason	39.2	36.2
Plasterer	40.6	33.5
Compositor, m.n.	39.0	39.0
Bricklayer	34.4	31.5
Public paver	28.8	n.k.
Public rammer	48.2	n.k.
Tram conductor	n.k.	42.0
Steel mill laborer	n.k.	44.9

Sources: See Appendix Tables 1 and 5.
Note: n. k. = not known.
a. Rates not for 1906 are listed in Table 11.

4

Family Income

The wage received for a standard week's work represented only one measure of the material standard of life enjoyed by workers. Income received by male breadwinners fluctuated according to the extent of overtime worked or unemployment suffered. Equally significant, the take-home pay of male household heads was frequently increased by the income earned by wives and/or children. The father's wage was "almost invariably supplemented by the earnings of the members of the family," noted a Birmingham medical practitioner in 1914. Investigating the diet of the city's laboring classes, he was "often astonished to discover . . . how large [was] the income of a family where the man's wage [was] under 25/- per week."[1] Clearly these additional earnings would have had a major impact upon the scale and direction of family expenditure. It was therefore necessary to attempt to assess the various components of family income and to quantify the level of income additional to that earned by the husband.

Bent Backs, Sickly Children, Suffering Mothers

Female workers played a far greater role in the economic life of Birmingham than of Pittsburgh. Table 13 suggests that approximately one-third of the British city's workers were women and girls (33.1 percent in 1901, 34.7 percent in 1911), compared with about one-fifth of the American city's laboring population (18.5 percent in 1900, 22.1 percent in 1910). During the 1900s female employment increased faster in Pittsburgh. Nevertheless, by 1910–1911, 41.3 percent of Birmingham women aged ten years and over were engaged in paid employment, compared to only 24.9 percent in Pittsburgh. These figures included, in both cities, all women who regularly earned money from participation in the work force, even if they were not actually employed on the day of census enumeration; they also incorporated wives who materially assisted their husbands in earning income and women who received income for work performed at home.[2]

The latter fact was particularly relevant to the British city, for although the significance of "outworkers" in Birmingham's economy was declining, the number of women so employed was still high. The Women's Industrial Council reported rather despairingly in 1909 that factory inspection of homework would require "many more than 16 [inspectors] to each centre of industry of the approximate size of Birmingham . . . since these [workers were] to be numbered by thousands, scattered about in back streets and tenements."[3] But outwork was an extravagant system requiring that work be given out in small quantities, and necessitating a considerable waste of time in fetching and carrying. Increasingly, therefore, the homeworker became a superfluous factor in production, unable to survive the transition of industry to mechanized, capital-intensive, integrated factory units, while the increased standardization of manufactured goods disinclined employers to risk handing out work to unsupervised persons. Many former strongholds of Birmingham homework scarcely survived into the twentieth century—brushmaking, chair-caning, and shoe-repairing, for example—and the decade 1901–1911 witnessed the decline of other outwork trades. The census statistics for 1911 reveal that whereas the

Table 13
Labor Forces Classified by Sex: Pittsburgh and Birmingham, 1900–1901, 1910–1911

City	Year	No. of Workers Male	No. of Workers Female	Composition of Work Force Male	Composition of Work Force Female	Percentage of Sex Employed[a] Male	Percentage of Sex Employed[a] Female
Birmingham	1901	167,905	83,116	66.9%	33.1%	86.7%	39.5%
Birmingham	1901[b]	167,905	84,101	65.3	34.7	86.7	40.0
Pittsburgh	1900	151,933	34,563	81.5	18.5	83.3	20.3
Pittsburgh	1900[b]	151,933	36,259	77.9	22.1	83.3	21.3
Birmingham	1911	166,455	88,419	65.3	34.7	85.1	41.3
Pittsburgh	1910	181,959	51,678	77.9	22.1	82.9	24.9

Sources: Great Britain, *Census*, 1901, Vol. 8, Table 35; 1911, Vol. 10, Pt. 2, Table 13; U.S., *Census*, 1900, Special Report, "Occupations at the Twelfth Census," Table 42; 1910, Vol. 3, Table 13; Vol. 4, Tables 3, 8.

a. Percentage of sex of persons aged 10 years and over.

b. Data adjusted for underenumeration of female workers in 1900–1901 censuses. Formula for adjusted totals was:

$$n^{adjusted} = [n^i \times (s^i + h^i)] + [(s^{ii} - h^{ii})/(n^{ii} - n^i)]$$

where $n^{adjusted}$ is the adjusted number of employed females in 1900–1901;

$\quad n^i \quad$ is the stated number of employed females in 1900–1901;

$\quad n^{ii} \quad$ is the stated number of employed females in 1910–1911;

$\quad s^i \quad$ is the stated number of shopkeepers (female) in 1900–1901;

$\quad s^{ii} \quad$ is the stated number of shopkeepers (female) in 1910–1911;

$\quad h^i \quad$ is the stated number of housekeepers (female) in 1900–1901;

and $\quad h^{ii} \quad$ is the stated number of housekeepers (female) in 1910–1911.

number of employed women had increased in most listed occupations, there had been a substantial decline in the number engaged in laundry work compared to the previous decade: from 2,463 to 1,628. The preface to the 1911 census concluded that the "striking decline in the number of women workers and the displacement of female by male labor [were] associated with the reduction in the numbers working in small and hand laundries, in the houses of private employers, and in their own homes, which [had] resulted from improved organization of laundries and the extended use of machinery."[4]

Homeworking survived primarily in those industries in which mechanization had not superseded handcraft, or where production demand fluctuated widely and in which the outworker consequently provided a solution to temporarily increased labor requirements. The most important remaining home occupations, excluding extended domestic chores such as housecleaning, baby-sitting, and home laundry work, were paper-box making, leather-stitching (mostly by "old hands"), burnishing for the jewelery trades, gunstock-cleansing (a home trade unique to Birmingham), and of greatest significance, hook-and-eye carding. "There are streets," noted Cadbury, "where as one passes along on a summer's day one may see the carding done in nearly every house."[5]

Such homework does not appear to have been common in Pittsburgh, nor did women workers participate so fully in that city's factories. It might be argued that the more diversified industrial structure and small workshops of the British city offered far more opportunity for the employment of females than did the less diversified, heavy manufacturing environment of Pittsburgh; and that the contrast in the importance of women workers merely reflected the difference in the cities' economic structures. Yet such an analysis is too simplistic. The comparison between Birmingham and Pittsburgh reflected international differences: by 1910–1911, 32.5 percent of British women (aged ten years and over) worked, compared to only 23.4 percent of American women.[6]

Moreover, to view Pittsburgh as a heavy-industry steel town is only partially correct. The city possessed some of the world's largest blast furnaces and rolling mills but it also had the biggest pickle and cork factories in America, manufactured a substantial amount of clothing, turned out hundreds of thousands of cheap cigars each year, mass-produced cakes, biscuits, and confectionery, and possessed a number of large printing and publishing houses—all substantial employers of female labor. It is scarcely surprising that when Mrs. John van Vorst wished to experience life as a factory operative at first hand, she selected Pittsburgh as an easy city in which to gain employment, for it "[exceeded] all other cities of the country in the variety and extent of its manufacturing products."[7] In addition, the development of the city as a major commercial center brought increased opportunities for female employment as clerks, cashiers, telephonists, and stenographers.

Perhaps more important, the assumption that women were confined to light or semidomestic industrial occupations is based more in historical myth than in empirical reality. The "dippers" of the Birmingham bedstead trade were composed almost exclusively of women, whose task it was to lower bed frames elbow-deep into vats of black paint, while a "very rough class" undertook japanning and blacking. The steel pen industry employed 7,000 Birmingham women who dominated every stage of the production process beyond the actual furnace work and steel-rolling. Hundreds of Birmingham women exhibited "maimed and scarred fingers as the result of their service in its deafening press shops." And even the press girls and dippers had a social status higher than that which contemporaries accorded to the "lowest types of girl" engaged in the city's metal-polishing shops. These young women washed, it was noted with some horror, from the same yard tap as the men, and worked in an atmosphere "dirty from the metal dust and blackened lime which [flew] from the revolving polishing wheels."[8]

In Pittsburgh, too, women were engaged in dirty and heavy occupations. One-third of the Oliver Iron and Steel Company's nut-and-bolt workers at the start of the century were women, mostly Poles and Hungarians, employed at the nut-tapping machines and daily drenched in lubricating fluids. The plant's foreman remembered that they "were engaged in sloppy work, so greasy . . . [that] the clothing of some girls, as they worked, resembled greasy dishrags." It was a situation that was to provide valuable ammunition for critics of David B. Oliver when he became the director of the Pittsburgh Board of Education in the next decade. In a stinging attack, the *Pittsburgh Leader* informed its readers that the Oliver fortune had been swelled by the labor of women and children: by "bent backs, sickly children, suffering mothers and stones over the graves of women cut down when they should have been enjoying the glories of young womanhood."[9]

Oliver, however, was not the only Pittsburgh industrialist to employ female labor to perform such tasks. The city's lamp-manufacturing plants engaged women as riveters and press stampers, while in the mills Slavic women, "rough-skinned and stolid . . . with muscular strength and readiness to do disagreeable things . . . [opened] the sheets of tin still warm from the furnaces . . . and [carried] heavy trays in foundries where they had displaced men."[10]

Even jobs that were theoretically "light" were often unhealthy and exhausting in practice. Women employed in the Pittsburgh stogie industry worked in crowded rooms "gray-brown with the fine dust of heat-dried tobacco leaves." In winter no ventilation was allowed for fear that cold would numb the nimble fingers of the rollers and molders and hence retard their speed. Hugh O'Donnell, a Pennsylvania factory inspector, claimed that conditions rivaling "those commonly attributed to the black pit of Calcutta were to be found every day in these shops."[11] And work was equally tiring in the far more hygienic pickle factory presided over by the welfare-conscious H. J. Heinz. "I have stood ten hours," a woman worker recorded despondently in her diary. "I have fitted 1,300 corks; I have hauled and loaded 4,000 jars of pickle. My pay is seventy cents." Indeed, work conditions within the factory were often harsher for the women than for the men who labored under Heinz's benevolent despotism. On Saturday mornings, "scrubbing day," men were equipped with mops and hoses, while the women were expected to clean the floor on their hands and knees.[12]

Finally, it should be noted that in similar occupations in Pittsburgh and Birmingham, the percentage of females employed was almost always greater in the British city. Table 14 shows that even in Pittsburgh occupations that were undertaken primarily by women and engaged a larger percentage of the total female labor force in that city than they did in Birmingham, the jobs generally employed a greater proportion of male workers than was the case in the British Midlands. This was particularly notable in the tobacco industry, which employed 3.4 percent of Pittsburgh's female workers, more women than in any other manufacturing activity except dressmaking. Yet the much smaller Birmingham tobacco industry was far more dependent upon women workers than was the case in Pittsburgh. In fact, the only Pittsburgh occupations that employed significantly more females in the labor force than did the same occupations in Birmingham were teaching and housekeeping.

This difference between the role of women workers in Great Britain and the United States was noted by contemporaries. Robert Holmshaw of the Sheffield Cutlery Council, for instance, a visitor to America in 1902, observed that burnishing was there "done by men with tools used here by women." In Birmingham, in contrast, burnishing was so dominated by female workers that Cadbury could recommend the trade to women not only because it was a skilled occupation but also because of the edifyingly moral climate of a workshop empty of men![13]

The occupational distribution of women workers presented in Tables

14 and 15 suggests that the majority of the Pittsburgh female labor force was engaged in the tertiary sector of industry, while most of Birmingham's women workers contributed to the success of the city's secondary industry. In short, Pittsburgh women served; Birmingham women manufactured. In the manufacturing area of greatest relevance

Table 14

Leading Occupations of Female Labor: Pittsburgh and Birmingham, 1900–1901

Occupation	% of Total Female Labor Force Engaged in Each Occupation		% of Total Labor Force Engaged in Occupation Who Were Female	
	Pgh	Bhm	Pgh	Bhm
Servant/Waiter	31.1	16.8	83.1	89.3
Dressmaker/Milliner	10.4	5.3	99.1	99.8
Sales assistant[a]	7.3	7.4	37.5	35.7
Clerk/Copyist[b]	7.2	3.2	22.7	32.6
Teacher	5.2	2.2	86.3	77.1
Laundry worker	4.6	3.0	84.9	97.7
Tobacco/Cigar worker	3.4	0.1	61.5	78.0
Seamstress/Shirtmaker	2.9	1.7	98.3	97.7
Housekeeper[c]	2.6	0.7	91.3	76.9
Nurse/Midwife	2.5	1.1	93.0	99.3
Tailor	1.3	2.5	28.2	51.6
Woodworker	1.1	2.6	25.7	26.0
Metal trades worker	0.6	19.8[e]	1.0	24.3
Paper-box/bag worker	0.3	2.5	85.5	94.6
Leather worker	0.1	2.6	1.7	47.9
Toolmaker	[d]	4.2[f]	0.8	47.8
Brass worker	[d]	4.1[g]	0.5	20.6
Jewelery worker	[d]	3.4	[d]	34.8

Source: See Table 13.

a. Includes all retail dealers.

b. Includes stenographers and typists in Pittsburgh; there was no such category in Birmingham.

c. Includes boarding house and eating-house keepers.

d. Less than 0.1%.

e. Most importantly in the production of tinplate, which engaged 1.4% of the Birmingham female labor force (0.1% in Pittsburgh) and whose total work force was 41.6% female (3.7% in Pittsburgh); in electroplate manufacture, which employed 1.4% of the working women in Birmingham and whose total force was 41.2% female; and in bolt-and-nut production, which employed 1.3% of the city's female workers and whose total force was 63.4% women.

f. Most importantly in the production of steel pens, in which 3.5% of the entire Birmingham female labor force was occupied, and which provided 91.4% of the workers thus engaged.

g. Excluding brass founders and finishers, the brass trade provided jobs for 3.7% of the city's female workers, who occupied 32.4% of the labor force so employed.

Table 15

Male and Female Employees Classified by Occupational Grouping: Pittsburgh, 1900/1910, and Birmingham, 1901/1911[a]

A. 1900–1901

Industrial Sector	No. of Male Workers		No. of Female Workers		Composition of Labor Force				Industrial Distribution			
					Male		Female		Male		Female	
	Pgh	Bhm	Pgh	Bhm	Pgh	Bhm	Pgh	Bhm	Pgh	Bhm	Pgh	Bhm
Professional	8,050	5,949	2,502	2,937	76.3%	66.9%	23.7%	33.1%	5.3%	3.5%	7.2%	3.5%
Domestic/Personal	6,807	5,501	15,526	21,569	30.5	30.5	69.5	79.7	4.5	3.3	44.9	26.0
Transportation	11,996	14,590	62	79	99.5	99.5	0.5	0.5	7.9	8.7	0.2	0.1
Trade/Commerce	30,465	25,461	7,433	9,775	80.4	72.3	19.6	27.7	20.1	15.2	21.5	11.8
Manufacturing	93,569	113,218	9,030	46,054	91.2	71.1	8.8	28.9	61.6	67.4	26.1	55.4
Agriculture/Mining	1,046	1,016	10	50	98.7	95.3	1.3	4.7	0.7	0.7	—	0.1
Unclassified	—	2,170	—	2,652	—	45.0	—	55.0	—	1.3	—	3.2
Total	151,933	167,905	34,563	83,116	81.5	66.9	18.5	33.1	100.1	100.1	99.9	100.1

B. 1910–1911

Industrial Sector	No. of Male Workers		No. of Female Workers		Composition of Labor Force				Industrial Distribution			
					Male		Female		Male		Female	
	Pgh	Bhm	Pgh	Bhm	Pgh	Bhm	Pgh	Bhm	Pgh	Bhm	Pgh	Bhm
Professional	11,272	7,153	3,751	3,097	75.0%	69.8%	25.0%	30.2%	6.2%	4.3%	7.3%	3.5%
Domestic/Personal	11,766	5,708	22,209	20,330	34.6	21.9	65.4	78.1	6.5	3.4	43.0	23.0
Transportation	15,706	15,449	136	121	99.1	99.2	0.9	0.8	8.6	9.3	0.3	0.1
Trade/Commerce	46,013	26,933	14,322	13,510	76.3	66.6	23.7	33.4	25.3	16.2	27.7	15.3
Manufacturing	95,427	108,709	11,233	50,414	89.5	68.3	10.5	31.7	52.4	65.3	21.7	57.0
Agriculture/Mining	1,775	1,469	27	34	98.5	97.7	1.5	2.3	1.0	0.7	0.1	—
Unclassified	—	1,255	—	913	—	57.9	—	42.1	—	0.8	—	1.0
Total	181,959	166,455	51,678	88,419	77.9	65.0	22.1	34.7	100.0	100.0	100.1	99.9

Source: See Table 13.

a. For occupations in each sector, see Appendix Table 6.

to Birmingham and Pittsburgh—the metal trades—the contrast in the role of women was substantial. In the British city almost one-quarter of metal workers were female; across the Atlantic a mere one-hundredth were so employed. Throughout the decade the production industries of Birmingham employed approximately five times the number of women workers engaged in the Pittsburgh manufacturing work force.

But the greater importance of the manufacturing sector in Birmingham was not sufficient to account for the larger number of females employed. Analysis of the manufacturing work force alone reveals that the female proportion was almost three times larger in the British city: 31.7 percent of Birmingham's manufacturing workers were women in 1911, compared to 10.5 percent of Pittsburgh's in 1910. The contrast in the number of employed females in the two cities can be effectively understood as a contrast in the activity of women engaged in manufacturing industry. By 1910–1911 the number of women employed within the paid labor force was 36,741 greater in Birmingham than in Pittsburgh. The English city possessed 39,181 more women within manufacturing industry, but in all other sectors—domestic and personal, trade and commerce, transportation and professional—the number of Birmingham women workers was less than in Pittsburgh.

The concern of British social reformers for working women largely centered on their employment in manufacturing industry. Edward Cadbury was not alone in his belief that Birmingham's working women faced "grave moral danger" from the increasing sexual integration of the manufacturing labor force, nor alone in his indignation that a "considerable number" of girls were forced to leave employment because "someone in authority was forward." To minimize the likelihood of such incidents at his confectionery factory at Bournville, Cadbury inaugurated a system of "red badge men" of tested moral integrity, and it was these men alone who were admitted to those areas of the plant where women were employed.[14]

Similar expressions of concern were voiced in Pittsburgh. It was "well known," recorded S. P. Breckinridge in 1906, "that the unregulated mingling of men and women under conditions of darkness, fatigue, and the excitement due to the constant apprehension of danger may give rise to immoral intercourse." Pittsburghers affirmed this attitude. The city's surveyor of customs, Mahlan M. Garland, ex-president of the Amalgamated Association of Iron, Steel and Tin Workers, explained to the Industrial Commission in 1901 that "our people work very hard, and they are about half clad. Women being in the same neighborhood, it does not tend to elevate their morals to see men running around with their shirts off and all that sort of thing." Charles Reed Zahniser agreed, reporting in 1915 that the integration of the sexes in Pittsburgh's candy factories and laundries had resulted "in a great deal of immorality." One of the most common complaints against the city's stogie-manufacturing workshops was that male and female employees worked in close proximity. William Matthews visited one cellar in 1905 where "huddled at least fifteen people, men and young girls making stogies . . . . The laws of God and the laws of men [were] violated every day."[15]

Factories and workshops were seen as the first downward step on the path to sin. According to Pittsburgh's Columbian Council of Jewish Women, girls employed in factories became "immoral in their private conduct"; they were "girls who [frequented] Dance Halls of the lowest grade and . . . [became] an easy prey to unscrupulous dealers in human flesh." Tobie (stogie) factories, in which large numbers of Jewish women worked, were to a large extent responsible for "the Jewish people . . . furnishing . . . a great deal more . . . than the average rate of immorality in [the] community."[16]

Fears of factory-inspired licentiousness stalked Pittsburgh's social workers. Their speeches and writings bore eloquent testimony to an abiding concern with the threat to social standards posed by manufacturing employment. Given the comparative insignificance of female employment in the city's manufacturing sector, the emphasis appears obsessive; indeed, their fears probably contributed to the lack of opportunity for women to find work within Pittsburgh's mills and factories. Yet their vision of crowded, busy workshops as dens of vice was not borne out by their own inquiries. Not only did relatively few Pittsburgh women engage in manufacturing industry, but available evidence indicates that those who did were no looser in their sexual mores than other members of society. Believing that morality, like city government and packaged food, could be improved by Progressive legislation, the city established in 1913 a Morals Efficiency Commission. The detailed study of Pittsburgh's prostitutes that emerged found that of the 506 girls from whom data were collected, 231 had previously been engaged in domestic and personal service, 188 had come straight from home, and only 85 had fallen from the straight and narrow road of manufacturing life.[17]

It is difficult to typify the conditions under which women toiled. In both cities were concerned paternalistic employers such as Cadbury and Heinz. The latter, for example, was so determined that his women employees should retain their femininity that he provided them with separate lockers and dressing rooms, clothed them in dainty uniforms, organized cooking and sewing classes for their benefit, arranged a women-only social group—inevitably the "57 Club"—and even installed a manicurist department. At the other extreme were the many employers who made little special arrangement for women workers. "Girls who are in service are generally much more quiter [*sic*] and more ladylike than those which work in a factory," wrote one Birmingham woman. "In gentlemens houses there are proper lavertories [*sic*] and ventilators." Birmingham factories rarely provided such facilities, nor did those in Pittsburgh. The rudimentary toilets provided at the Oliver Iron and Steel Company were "a kind of industrial afterthought, a dingy place of thin tongue-and-grooved boards, and one side for men, the other side for women." Even the provision of this minimum privacy seems to have presented problems, for the women workers were "in the habit of congregating there as in a sanctuary. Of course no man could cross that threshold, so if [the forewoman] was not around to act as a sheperdess [*sic*], the old Irish foreman would slyly turn a valve that sent a cloud of steam into their retreat."[18]

We have seen that analysis of the labor force by industrial sector reveals that the larger number of female workers in Birmingham was primarily attributable to their greater employment in manufacturing. Table 16 indicates the comparative importance of working men and women by age, and suggests equally significant differences between the British and American city. The pattern of employment was similar in both cities. Peak male employment occurred in the 20 (21)–44 year age group, although for most men paid work was a lifelong activity: in contrast the zenith of female industrial activity was reached in the 16–19 (20) age group, and as women aged, so the likelihood of their working declined. However, as age increased, the importance of females in the work force diminished far more rapidly in Pittsburgh than in Birmingham: in the 14–15 year group the percentage of employees who were females was similar (39.3 percent in Pittsburgh, 47.7 percent in Birmingham); but by age forty-five and upward the female components were markedly different (12.9 percent in Pittsburgh, 24.4 percent in Birmingham). Whereas the percentage of males at work in Pittsburgh was only slightly less than in Birmingham, the percentage of Pittsburgh females occupied was roughly half that in Birmingham in all age categories from fourteen years upwards.

Although the legal age for full-time employment was fourteen years in both Pittsburgh and Birmingham, the number of children at work was much larger in the British city, as was their proportion of the labor force. Birmingham girls younger than sixteen accounted for 8.4 percent of the total females employed, more than twice the 3.9 percent in

Table 16

Labor Forces Classified by Age and Sex: Pittsburgh and Birmingham, 1910–1911

City	Age Grouping	Sex	Total Population	No. Employed	% Employed	Sex Composition of Workers (%)	Age Distribution of Workers (%)
Birmingham	10–13 years	Male	21,226	602	2.8	83.4 }100.0	0.4
		Female	21,294	120	0.6	16.6	0.1
Pittsburgh	10–13 years	Male	18,258	254	1.4	71.1 }100.0	0.1
		Female	18,562	103	0.6	28.9	0.2
Birmingham	14–15 years	Male	9,658	7,982	82.7	52.3 }100.0	4.8
		Female	10,033	7,291	72.7	47.7	8.3
Pittsburgh	14–15 years	Male	9,037	2,983	33.0	60.7 }100.0	1.6
		Female	9,335	1,929	20.7	39.3	3.7
Birmingham	16–19 years	Male	18,506	17,738	92.9	49.1 }100.0	10.7
		Female	20,848	18,357	89.0	50.9	20.8
Pittsburgh	16–20 years	Male	28,815	20,983	81.3	60.4 }100.0	11.5
		Female	27,713	13,769	49.7	39.6	26.6
Birmingham	20–44 years	Male	99,628	98,628	99.0	66.7 }100.0	59.3
		Female	109,210	49,282	45.1	33.3	55.7
Pittsburgh	21–44 years	Male	121,356	118,818	97.9	79.8 }100.0	65.3
		Female	108,280	30,099	27.8	20.2	58.2
Birmingham	45+ years	Male	46,381	41,505	89.5	75.6 }100.0	24.9
		Female	52,753	13,369	25.3	24.4	15.1
Pittsburgh	45+ years	Male	42,276	38,921	87.9	87.1 }100.0	21.4
		Female	43,969	5,778	13.1	12.9	11.2

Source: See Table 13.

Pittsburgh; and Birmingham boys of similar age comprised 5.2 percent of the total male labor force, almost three times as great as the 1.8 percent in Pittsburgh. Whereas in 1910–1911, 82.7 percent of Birmingham lads (aged fourteen and fifteen) were already out at work, only 33.0 percent of their Pittsburgh counterparts were; and the equivalent figures for girls were 72.7 percent and 20.7 percent.

It was not only age that distinguished female employees in the two cities. The difference between the conjugal condition of women workers in Pittsburgh and Birmingham was also substantial. The contrast in the participation of employed single and widowed females in the work force was, as Table 17 shows, notable; the difference in the contribution made by married women to the work force, astounding. In 1910–1911, 18.5 percent of Birmingham married women were engaged in paid labor compared to only 3.5 percent in Pittsburgh.[19]

This difference in the conjugal status of working women was reflected in contemporary comment upon women's labor. In Birmingham and Britain, major concern was expressed with regard to working wives and the detrimental effect such work could have upon the family. "It is a general opinion," noted Clementina Black, "especially among persons of the middle class, that the working for money of married women is to be deplored."[20] Such opinion, vocal in Birmingham, moved the city's health department to instigate a survey of the city's married female workers in 1908, with the aim of establishing the relationship (if any) between infant mortality and employed mothers. The investigation, carried out by Dr. John Robertson, rejected "middle-class" indictments. A study of the working-class families convinced him that the "home conditions of those industrially employed [did] not differ to any large extent from those not so employed," that infant mortality was higher in families in which the mother did not work, that the health of children in families in which the mother worked was as good as in those in which the mother stayed at home, and that the industrial work undertaken by women was "often much lighter and more wholesome than that done by many mothers." He argued that the "class of women" who sought employment had more drive and ambition than their housewife neighbors and were more "thrifty and energetic . . . determined not to get below the poverty line, nor yet to neglect their home duties." His controversial conclusion was that in Birmingham "the type of industrial employment in vogue [did] not appreciably influence the health of the mother or her infant when the standard of comparison [was] that of women in equally poor circumstances who [were] not employed industrially."[21]

Table 17

Conjugal Condition of Females Aged 16 and Over: Pittsburgh, 1900/1910, and Birmingham, 1901/1911

City/Year	No. of Females				No. of Females at Work				% of Females at Work			
	Total	Single	Widowed/ Divorced	Married	Total	Single	Widowed/ Divorced	Married	Total	Single	Widowed/ Divorced	Married
Pittsburgh (1900)	144,964	49,217	16,257	76,490	32,355	26,517	3,620	2,218	22.3	49.3	22.3	2.8
Birmingham (1901)	178,840	65,150	19,782	93,908	73,699	52,142	6,661	14,896	41.2	80.0	33.7	15.9
Pittsburgh (1910)	179,773	60,465	20,574	93,734	49,646	40,690	5,555	3,406	27.6	67.3	27.0	3.5
Birmingham (1911)	182,811	65,300	20,468	97,043	81,008	55,031	8,037	17,940	44.3	84.3	39.3	18.5

Sources: See Table 13; U.S. Census, 1900, Vol. 7, Table 32; 1910, Vol. 6, tables 38 and 49, and Vol. 8, Table 13; Bureau of the Census, Bulletin, No. 69 (1900), "Child Labor in the United States," Table 205. Some figures are estimates: see Ch. 4, n. 19.

In Pittsburgh, however, most attention was directed toward unmarried female employees. The superintendent of Pittsburgh's Methodist Episcopal Church Union, while acknowledging that wives were sometimes forced to seek jobs in order to aid their husbands, railed most eloquently against the "employment of girls and young women in rolling cigars or operating some automatic machine that [required] neither ability nor training of intellect or character [and] which [was] not fit preparation for wifehood and womanhood." Mrs. Perry Starkweather, a Pennsylvania factory inspector, shared his belief, informing a Pittsburgh audience in 1909 that the greatest evil of female labor was the predominance of unmarried women who were prevented by their occupation from training as competent housewives.[22]

The Earnings of Wives and Children

Before the contribution of wives and children to weekly family income could be estimated, two basic problems had to be tackled: the extent to which wives and children aided the family exchequer had to be established numerically, and the average income from such sources needed to be assessed.[23] Both, in turn, required that the number of family units be estimated. Census definitions of family included institutional groups (such as hotels and hospitals) and single persons, neither of which provided an adequate basis for calculating the extent of per family income derived from wives and children. Instead, the number of married women was taken as a proxy for the number of family units in Pittsburgh and Birmingham. I was then able to estimate total earnings for a standard work week in "normal" families made up of a husband, wife, and perhaps, children.

This presupposes that the same proportion of Pittsburgh and Birmingham adult males had the status of husband within normal families. Methodological objections might be raised insofar as the prevalence of such normal families differed between the two cities. It has been suggested, for example, that American males were more likely to be single than their British counterparts. If this were true in Pittsburgh, and if the conjugal status of its workers differed considerably from that in Birmingham, then comparison of estimated family earnings would represent a statistical illusion. Such does not appear to have been the case. The number of married men was similar in both cities. In 1900–1901, 51.2 percent of Pittsburgh males aged fifteen years and over were married, compared to 54.6 percent in Birmingham. In 1910–1911, 42.8 percent of Pittsburgh males remained single, compared to 38.4 percent in Birmingham. Thus while there was a greater likelihood of British males residing within a normal family unit, the difference was not sufficiently large to materially affect calculations.[24]

Moreover, it is generally contended that the greater incidence of single males in the United States was a result of immigration. It has been assumed that the unskilled labor force of early twentieth-century American cities was preponderantly composed of unmarried immigrants: while they saved a high proportion of earnings for remittance to extended families overseas, they were generally unable to enjoy the financial contribution made by wives and children in the United States. This theoretical profile does not reflect the Pittsburgh experience. In 1910, 62.6 percent of that city's immigrant white adult males were married, compared to only 46.7 percent for native-born whites, and 54.1 percent for blacks. In part this was because a greater share of foreign-born males were represented in those age categories in which rates of marriage were highest (twenty-five to sixty-four years), but in every age group (until age sixty-five and over) there existed a higher incidence of marriage among foreigners. However, such data probably overestimate differences within Pittsburgh, for it is likely that a larger percentage of immigrants lived apart from their wives. It should also be noted that there does not exist much evidence that rates of marriage were substantially lower among unskilled workers. Census investigation in 1900 revealed that 51.2 percent of Pittsburgh's male workers were married, compared to 49.0 percent for general laborers and 55.2 percent for steel mill laborers.[25] There is then little reason to suppose that the conjugal status of workers in ethnically heterogeneous Pittsburgh differed markedly from that in Birmingham, that the prevalence of normal families was significantly different, or that family size varied—in both cities families averaged 5.4 persons. Comparison of weekly earnings in normal families is not an artificial quantification divorced from historical reality.

It has been established that, in 1911, 18.5 percent of Birmingham wives worked, and that in 1910 the "range of probability" stretched from a minimum of 3.5 percent of Pittsburgh married women at work to a maximum of 5.8 percent.[26] Estimates of the number of family units in which the wife worked are presented in Table 18. Based upon the mean probability of 4.6 percent, the difference between Pittsburgh and Birmingham may be expressed as follows: for every Pittsburgh family in which the wife was employed, there were 4.0 such families in Birmingham.[27]

The major problem encountered in estimating the financial role of children was to calculate what proportion of working juveniles contributed to parental income. An obvious premise was that the earnings of

Table 18

Average Number of Wives and Children at Work per Family: Pittsburgh and Birmingham, 1910–1911

City	No. of Family Units[a]	No. of Married Women at Work	No. of Children at Work[b]		No. of Married Women at Work (per 100 Family Units)	No. of Children at Work (per 100 Family Units)	
			Male	Female		Male	Female
Birmingham	97,043	17,940	30,757	30,357	18.5	31.7	31.3
Pittsburgh	98,734	3,406[c]	24,220	15,801	3.5[c]	24.5	16.0
Pittsburgh	98,734	5,727[d]	24,220	15,801	5.8[d]	24.5	16.0
Pittsburgh	98,734	4,542[e]	24,220	15,801	4.6[e]	24.5	16.0

Source: See Table 17.

a. Based upon number of married women: see text.
b. Based upon number of persons aged below 21 years: see text.
c. Minimum probability: see text.
d. Maximum probability: see text.
e. Mean probability: see text.

children ceased to bolster the parental economy at the age at which they married and started to support their own family groups. It proved impossible, however, to calculate the average age of marriage. Moreover, contemporary comment suggested that the assumption was highly arguable, for a rising number of unmarried children, especially girls, sought employment away from home. "The unskilled working girl of our cities," reported the Birmingham Union of Women Workers, "is increasingly becoming a detached unit, not living with parents." The same, it appears, was true in the United States: indeed, Madame Blanc believed that the departure of the "little working-girl" from home epitomized the "desire for independence which may be called a national characteristic."[28]

The rough-but-ready solution was to assume that in both cities, and for both sexes, the age at which children stopped contributing to family income was twenty-one. Based upon this premise, Table 18 contrasts the number of young men and women at work per family unit in Pittsburgh and Birmingham. Captain J. C. Delaney, head of the Pennsylvania Department of Factory Inspection, believed that one of the most evil aspects of child labor was the growing proportion of girls employed, but the situation in Birmingham had progressed much further, the city's youth work force being as dependent upon female labor as upon male.[29] For every Pittsburgh family in which a male under twenty-one years of age was at work, there were 1.3 Birmingham families, but for every Pittsburgh family in which a female under twenty-one years of age was employed, there were 2.0 Birmingham families.

What now had to be estimated was the monetary contribution made by working wives and children to family income. The federal *Census of Manufactures* published annual wages for Pittsburgh workers in 1905, and the Pennsylvania Bureau of Industrial Statistics supplied similar data for the state's manufacturing employees for the period 1908–1912. This information showed that women workers earned about one-half of the income received by male workers: in 1905 females averaged 45.7 percent of the annual wages of men, and between 1908 and 1912, 51.2 percent.[30] These percentages were similar to those estimated for weekly income. Elizabeth Butler concluded that "the ratio between the wages of unskilled workmen and of unskilled workingwomen [was] two to one." Pittsburgh's male laborers in 1907–1908 were paid, she judged, $12 per week, whereas female operatives who had "made themselves valuable by length of service and by familiarity with a certain operation" earned $6.[31] The same ratio prevailed in nearby Homestead: there the weekly income of employed women averaged

48.9 percent of the male wage.[32] And wage rates within Heinz's Pittsburgh factory confirm such evidence. At the beginning of the century, the median wage paid to adult women was $1.06, 48.5 percent of the median rate earned by men ($2.18).[33]

The same wage differential prevailed in Birmingham. A study of working-class Birmingham families in 1908 found that wives employed in the city's factories and workshops received 45.8 percent of the males' weekly income.[34] A subsequent investigation in 1912–1914 estimated that the average weekly wage for females was 49.7 percent that of males in the city's brass industry, 51.7 percent in the jewelery trades, 50.2 percent in electroplate-manufacturing, 55.0 percent in the printing trades, 58.1 percent in brushmaking, and 41.1 percent in the flint glass industry.[35] For both cities, therefore, adult female wages were estimated upon the basis that they equaled 50.0 percent of those paid to men.

An equivalent estimate had to be made of the family income contribution derived from children. Annual income earned by minors under seventeen years of age approximated one-third that received by adult male workers and two-thirds that of adult female employees: mean annual earnings of Pennsylvania minors during 1908–1912 equaled 33.9 percent that of men workers and 66.3 percent that of female workers. Similar figures for Pittsburgh in 1905 support this evidence: juveniles aged under sixteen years earned 32.4 percent of adult male income. A similar estimate for Birmingham's minors appears warranted. There girls aged under eighteen years were engaged in 243 recorded occupations and averaged a weekly wage of 6s. 8d. ($1.63) or 63.2 percent of that paid to adult women workers.[36]

Children, of course, were paid progressively more as they grew older, and there can be no doubt that workers aged nineteen or twenty years earned substantially more than one-third of adult male wages. Certainly by the time they reached their twenty-first birthday, those of Birmingham's young men destined to remain unskilled laborers were approaching their maximum earning capacity.[37] It proved difficult, however, to gauge the rapidity with which the wages of minors approached this adult norm. An estimate was made that assumed that workers aged fifteen years and below averaged one-third of the earnings of adult male employees; that all those aged sixteen and seventeen years received one-half of adult male income; that all those aged eighteen to twenty years earned two-thirds of adult male income; and that all children over that age who still contributed to the family exchequer earned three-quarters of male income. Such an income progression was of course largely informed guesswork, but circumstantial evidence supports such an estimate. Of the 1,562 children who contributed to Pennsylvania family income in 1901, for instance, 331 were less than sixteen years old, 885 were aged sixteen to twenty years, and 346 were dependents twenty-one years of age or older living at home. Calculations based on the above estimates suggested that the average contribution of children to family income would have been 57.2 percent that of their fathers: in fact, the average child's income was 57.0 percent.[38]

Thus far it has been assumed that the wages paid to male and female children were identical. They were not. The initial wage of a Pittsburgh boy in 1907–1908 varied between 75¢ and 90¢ per week. In the suburb of Sharpsburg, boys starting at the glass works or shovel factory received 75¢, and those employed in the iron or tube mills, 90¢; in Pittsburgh's spike, nut and bolt, and steel wire factories, young lads "sat before machines and pickling urns for ten hours and received from 75 cents"; and black youths engaged in the city's Clark steel mill began at a similar daily wage. But the minimum girl's wage—paid within cracker factories—was only 50¢ per week: 60¢ was more normal.[39]

It would appear, then, that the contrast between the wages paid to Pittsburgh's male and female juveniles was less substantial than the difference between the wages paid to adult men and women. The fragmentary evidence available suggests that average weekly earnings of girls were almost as great as those received by boys. Data collected by the federal Department of Commerce and Labor in early 1909 indicated that in six Pennsylvania industries well established in Pittsburgh, female workers under eighteen years earned 85.5 percent of the average weekly income received by male workers of the same age.[40] In fact, as Table 19 shows, the male-female wage differential declined in the early years of employment, only widening from the age of eighteen. Thereafter the differential increased in direct relation to age. A similar phenomenon appears to have prevailed in Birmingham, where the starting pay of girls was generally from 70 to 80 percent that of boys. In 1913 the starting weekly wage for girls was 73.3 percent that of boys in bedstead manufacture, 75.0 percent in brass finishing, 73.1 percent in flint glass production, 81.8 percent in printing, 80.0 percent in the brush trades, and 77.3 percent in enameling.[41]

To make allowance for this chronologically varying sex differential, it was assumed that employed girls aged under eighteen received wages 80 percent of those earned by employed boys; but that those females in the eighteen-to-twenty-year age group received wages only 70 percent of those paid to males.[42] Hence girls under sixteen possessed an earning capacity 29.6 percent that of the adult male, and boys in the same age group a capacity of 37.0 percent (where such workers had an

Table 19

Weekly Earnings of Male and Female Workers: Six Pennsylvania Industries, 1908–1909

Industry	Female Earnings as % of Male Earnings, by Age					
	Under 16	16 and 17	18 to 20	21 to 24	25 and over	16 and over
Nuts, bolts, screws	74.5	89.2	75.3	73.2	53.5	63.9
Cigars	89.9	94.3	74.0	72.8	64.8	65.6
Confectionery	90.7	89.4	83.6	76.5	72.8	66.4
Crackers, biscuits	75.8	70.3	62.0	63.6	57.5	50.2
Paper boxes	94.6	90.3	87.6	44.9	54.6	55.7
Stamped enameled ware	91.6	93.8	74.7	65.8	68.4	65.4
Aggregate[a]	78.2	86.2	76.2	76.5	71.9	61.7[b]

Source: U.S. Department of Commerce and Labor, Report on the Conditions of Women and Child Wage-Earners, 1911, Vol. 18, Table 8.

a. Total workers in all six industries.

b. 1,425 male employees averaged $9.16 per week; 2,785 female employees averaged $5.64 per week.

average capacity of 33.3 percent); girls aged sixteen and seventeen had an earning capacity of 44.5 percent and boys 55.6 percent (where the average was 50.0 percent); and young women aged eighteen to twenty had a capacity of 55.0 percent and young men 78.5 percent (where the average was 66.7 percent). Estimates were then made of the earning capacity of each potential family member, and of the number of such members per family unit. Comparative family earnings were calculated as in Table 20. Two important conclusions emerged from the data.

First, the financial role of wives and children in supporting the family was 67.8 percent greater in Birmingham than in Pittsburgh. If it is postulated that the husband was the major breadwinner in each normal family unit, then it is apparent that in the American city family earnings equaled 1.255 of his income; in Birmingham, 1.428. Thus family members gained just over one-quarter of the husband's income in Pittsburgh but received more than four-tenths of his income in Birmingham. Where the weekly rate of pay of a Pittsburgh working husband was $X, the Birmingham husband would have had to receive only $0.88X for family income to have been identical; conversely, where a Birmingham husband received a weekly wage of $X, a Pittsburgh husband would have needed to earn $1.14X in order to achieve the same family income. In short, when we compare family income of Pittsburgh and Birmingham workers, the relative material living standards enjoyed by Birmingham workers appear improved. Whether or not quality of life improved depends upon whether or not wives and daughters faced a greater financial necessity to work in the British city.

Second, most of the difference in family earnings can be attributed to the comparative importance of working wives. The average contribution of Birmingham wives to family income was 304.3 percent greater than the contribution of wives in Pittsburgh. The financial role of employed daughters was also substantially greater in Birmingham. In that city they contributed, on average, 85.7 percent more to family income than was the case in Pittsburgh. The role of male children, however, was similar, Birmingham sons providing only 23.9 percent more income than those in the American city.

Respectable Income . . . Parasitic Burden

The wife who wished to contribute directly to family income did not necessarily seek paid employment in the work force. An alternative source of revenue was the provision of accommodation—and, perhaps, meals and laundry services—to paying lodgers. Opportunity was particularly strong in Pittsburgh, where the 1900s witnessed a massive

Table 20

Contribution of Wives and Children to Family Income: Pittsburgh and Birmingham, 1910–1911

City	Family Units[a]	Family Member	No. Employed	No. Employed (per Family Unit)	Earning Capacity (Adult Male = 1.000)	Average Contribution to Family Income[b]
Pittsburgh	98,734	Wife	4,542	.046[c]	.500	.023
		Son (under 16)	3,237	.033	.370	.012
		Son (16 and 17)	8,393[d]	.085	.556	.043
		Son (18 to 20)	12,590[d]	.128	.785	.100
		Daughter (under 16)	2,032	.021	.296	.006
		Daughter (16 and 17)	5,508[d]	.056	.445	.025
		Daughter (18 to 20)	8,261[d]	.084	.550	.046
		Aggregate				.255
Birmingham	97,043	Wife	17,940	.185	.500	.093
		Son (under 16)	8,584	.088	.370	.033
		Son (16 and 17)	8,986	.093	.556	.052
		Son (18 to 20)	13,187[e]	.136	.785	.107
		Daughter (under 16)	7,411	.076	.296	.022
		Daughter (16 and 17)	9,062	.093	.445	.042
		Daughter (18 to 20)	13,884[e]	.143	.550	.079
		Aggregate				.428

Sources: Table 18; also see text.

a. Based upon number of wives: see text.

b. (Number employed per family unit) × (earning capacity).

c. Estimate: See Table 18 and text.

d. Estimate: the census stated only the aggregate number of workers of each sex aged between 16 and 20, so it was assumed that those aged 16 and 17 comprised 40 percent of that number, and those aged 18 to 20 comprised 60 percent.

e. Estimate: the number of 20-year-olds had to be calculated, so it was assumed that they equaled the average number of 16-to-19-year-olds employed.

inflow of migrants. Might not the difference between the income contribution made by wives and/or children in Birmingham and Pittsburgh have been at least partially offset by the financial aid American families derived from boarders? Might not the provision of boarding facilities have been an alternative to the wife seeking employment in order to increase family income? Certainly some contemporaries believed so. "Taking in boarders is one of the oldest and most respectable forms of adding to the income," claimed the *Weekly People*. "No one has ever pointed out that taking in boarders is a form of wife labor fully as much to be reckoned with as other forms. It is work done in the home, to be sure, but so are all the tenement trades, such as flower making, finishing garments etc."[43]

There can be little doubt that a large number of Pittsburgh's working families put up boarders. This certainly added to family income, but pressures upon family life were increased commensurately. It was, perhaps, an old and respectable trade, but it was also inconvenient and exhausting. Boarders were nearly always given exclusive use of the best room, while the host family crowded into a single bedroom. Conditions were cramped, privacy destroyed, domestic freedom constrained. Boarders were usually kept by those families having many young children: indeed, "it was because of this presence of many children below the working age . . . that the family was compelled to take in a boarder." The claustrophobic atmosphere that prevailed was sometimes accentuated by "doubling up" boarders; that is, by having workers sleep in shifts. "The foreign laborer who climbs into a bed still warm from the slumbers of the man on the other shift, is not only a proverb in Pittsburgh," reported the headworker of the Woods Run Settlement, Samuel Ely Eliot, in 1912; "he is a great fact."[44]

Few Pittsburgh social investigators failed to comment upon the "fundamental economic problem" of the city's boarding population. Most observers believed that lodgers crowded houses and tenements, placed unforeseen pressure on inadequate toilet facilities, and created serious health dangers. However, they found it difficult to estimate the proportion of families who kept boarders. Byington estimated that 21.0 percent of Homestead families provided paid accommodation; the records of Mrs. Hoyt, Allegheny's probation officer, suggested 24.4 percent; and analysis of the poor Soho district by Abraham Oseroff, a University of Pittsburgh postgraduate, indicated 31.3 percent.[45] The far more comprehensive study of Pennsylvania families in 1901 found that 20.0 percent derived an income from boarders (who were provided with meals) and 2.8 percent from lodgers (who received only accommodation). Table 21A indicates that the percentage of families housing boarders or lodgers was similar for most ethnic groups, although new immigrants—Italians, Russians, and Austro-Hungarians—were more likely to provide boarding facilities than the old.[46]

Estimates of the average number of paying residents each family housed varied enormously (Table 21B). Stern found that only two out of twelve families kept more than one boarder, and Hoyt's data revealed that twenty-one families who let rooms averaged but 1.3 boarders each; on the other hand, Oseroff believed that an average of 3.0 boarders were accommodated by families so engaged. There can be little doubt that this latter estimate included boardinghouses in which the income received from paying residents was the mainstay of family economy rather than a supplement to the husband's earnings. Byington's study, for instance, showed that the nineteen families who took

Table 21
Boarders and Lodgers: Pennsylvania, 1901

A. *Families Deriving an Income from Boarders or Lodgers*

Nativity of Head of Family	Total Families	Families with an Income from Boarders	
		No.	%
United States	2,496	580	23.2
Foreign	1,206	252	20.9
Austria-Hungary	55	14	25.5
England	180	41	22.8
Germany	272	45	16.5
Ireland	460	101	22.0
Italy	23	6	26.1
Russia	70	16	22.9
Scotland	31	7	22.6
Wales	69	13	18.8
Total	3,702	832	22.5

B. *The Number of Boarders or Lodgers Kept*

	No. of Families	No. of Boarders/ Lodgers	No. per Family
Families having boarders	741	1164	1.57
Families having lodgers	104	239	2.30
Families having lodgers and/or boarders	845[a]	1403	1.66

Source: U. S., Eighteenth Annual Report of the Commissioner of Labor, 1903, Pt. 1, Tables 1D, 3A, 3C, pp. 232, 306, 336–37.

a. This number differs from that in Table 21A because in the former case families who kept both boarders and lodgers were counted only once.

in boarders accommodated an average of 3.1 persons, but twelve housed only one or two boarders. In only two of the seven other families was the income derived from boarders merely an addition to the husband's earnings: in one family the son alone was at work; in three cases the husband was intemperate, incapacitated, or aged; in a fifth family, the husband and wife, possessing property in the old country and financial security in the United States, had apparently set up in business as lodging-house keepers. The fourteen remaining families averaged 2.1 lodgers. The more extensive 1901 investigation indicated that those Pennsylvania families who derived an income from boarders or lodgers gave accommodation, on average, to 1.66 persons.[47] It was therefore assumed that 22.5 percent of Pittsburgh's families kept boarders and/or lodgers, and that each family so engaged housed 1.66 paying residents: in effect, including those families who did *not* provide accommodation, there were 0.38 boarders or lodgers per family.

How much did these residents pay for the lodging and domestic services extended? A 1909 investigation of the areas in which many of the city's Poles and Slavs found accommodation concluded that the minimum cost of lodging, for which a man might be expected to share a bed or to sleep in shifts, was $2.50 per month, while the maximum cost was $3.50. Food expenses increased this sum considerably. Boarders were required to pay between $3.50 and $5.00 per fortnight for provisions. However, this latter expenditure resulted in no further gain to the landlady: she simply bought the food for her boarders, and they settled with her later. The Russell Sage survey presented similar estimates. In immigrant lodging houses the price paid for sleeping facilities, and for the landlady's cooking and washing chores, ranged between 75¢ and $1.00 per week. Food was bought on a pro rata basis, the cost averaging about $3.00 each fortnight.[48] Thus the Pittsburgh Survey calculated boarding expenses at between $2.25 and $2.50 per week in 1907–1908; the British *Enquiry* found that costs varied from $2.33 to $3.31 in 1909.[49]

The maximum gain to a family providing accommodation to a boarder, assuming that the food bill resulted in no extra profit, appears to have been $1.00, and the mean number of paying residents housed in such families was 1.66. Therefore the financial advantage that accrued to them totaled $1.66, justifying the claim of Samuel Ely Eliot that boarders were more "parasites on [the] homes of their countrymen" than an important source of income to immigrant families.[50] The additional revenue derived from paying residents did not fundamentally alter the statistical comparison of family income in Pittsburgh and Birmingham presented in Table 20. If there were 0.38 boarders per

Pittsburgh family, and if it is estimated that $1.66 comprised 15.0 percent of the adult male weekly wage, then boarders and/or lodgers accounted for an average of 5.7 percent of the husband's income per family (15.0 percent × 0.380). Thus the estimated contribution made by sources other than the husband to Pittsburgh family income is increased from 0.255 (Table 20) to 0.312.

This latter figure probably reduces the contrast between Pittsburgh and Birmingham too much. First, some families in the English city would also have accommodated paying guests, thereby advancing family income. Second, Table 11 suggests that $1.66 was probably less than 15.0 percent of the average weekly income of the Pittsburgh worker. Third, and most important, not all the fees received for boarding facilities were "profit" to the families who received them. Property owners often exacted "an additional payment of about [50¢] per week for each family taken in, while in the case of professional boarding houses . . . the tenant paid [25¢] per week more for each boarder."[51] This being so, few families could have hoped to gain more than $1.00 per week from paying residents after the deductions required to pay the landlord, and the estimated contribution made by sources other than the husband to Pittsburgh family income is probably more accurately calculated at 0.293 (0.255 + 0.038).

5

Food Prices

Observers on both sides of the Atlantic generally agreed that American manual workers were paid money wages superior to those earned by employees in Britain, but whether these higher rates of pay signified a superior standard of living was earnestly debated. An extreme view was held by that symbol of Pittsburgh industrial life, Andrew Carnegie, who claimed that higher wages for the American employee represented a real improvement in the workers' station and adamantly asserted that if price levels were taken into account, the apparent economic gulf between the British and American worker would be increased. "Of course," Carnegie confidently declared, "all food is cheaper in the United States than in Britain. . . . Tobacco is very much cheaper . . . what the American drinks is cheaper; . . . speaking generally, [fuel] is much cheaper; . . . a pound sterling in the United States today will purchase more of the necessaries of life for the mass of the people than it will in Britain." On this issue he gained unequivocal support from Samuel Gompers, assertive president of the A.F. of L. "Living is cheap to the wage worker in Europe only because he does without what in America soon becomes necessary to him," he informed American unionists. "Food in good quantity and quality, presentable clothes among his aspiring fellow-workmen and their families, and a comfortable furnished home": these epitomized the gains made by pure-and-simple unionism and delineated the comparative advantages in material living standards enjoyed by workers in the United States.[1]

Some Americans exhibited less confidence about the real value of higher wages in their country. The *Pittsburgh Post* expressed the fear that there was "such a thing as boosting [American] standards too high. At least, when living [was] made so costly that the wage earner [could] obtain fewer comforts and benefits on his wage than the European laborer [could] obtain from his lower wage." Others argued that while basic purchase requirements were a little more expensive in the United States, non-necessary commodities were considerably dearer. "To the ordinary traveller who compares the two countries from his experience of hotel life alone, the difference [between the cost of living in the United States and that in Britain] may be three to one," claimed James Fox of the British Association of Iron and Steel Workers. However, "to the ordinary working man, the cost of living is not so much higher in America as we are led to believe." A fellow member of the Mosely Commission, William Dyson, agreed. Food, he believed, was no dearer in the United States, but luxuries were a great deal more expensive. It was with perhaps more than academic interest that he decided to sample such items. Whiskey cost 10¢ to 15¢ a shot and proved "not very palatable at that"; cigars bought for 10¢ were judged "not equal to what [one got] in England for 3d."; and beer was sold at 5¢ a glass, although a superior "bottle of Bass" cost 25¢. Haircuts cost 15¢ and shaves 10¢. "So," Dyson drew his moral, "although the necessaries of life are not much dearer than in England, the luxuries are very much dearer, and therefore, unless a man is very careful, etc., he will very soon spend the difference between the wages earned."[2]

More astute commentators did not believe that so simple a dividing line could be drawn. Food was—perhaps—cheaper in the United States, but nonluxuries such as rent and clothing were assessed by many to be much more costly. George Barnes, who held that the "cost of living in Pittsburgh [was] about up to the American standard," discovered that rent was exorbitant at "about 14s. per week" in that city, while clothing was "nearly double the English price." "Rent, clothes, service, wines, beers, spirits, tobacco, all are cheaper in the English than in the American town," concurred the American Price Collier. However, the prices of meat, vegetables, bread, butter, poultry, and eggs were judged to be "much the same."[3]

Many contemporaries, then, were interested in the comparative cost of living. Yet although they summarized their conclusions with a brazen and cavalier confidence, none can have found it easy to gauge differences in price levels. Certainly the historian's task proved hard; comparison of food prices illustrates the major difficulties awaiting the unwary researcher. First, I found it necessary to standardize units of measurement: while most reference books provided the formulas necessary to convert liquid measures between the American and imperial scales, they were less forthcoming on the poundage in a bushel of potatoes or the cubic capacity of coal contained in a barrel bag. Second, it proved a time-consuming business to verify that the grades of food compared were of similar quality and character: there exist no conversion manuals able to shortcut the effort involved in identifying the beef sirloin sold as roasting joint in Birmingham as the porterhouse steak sold in Pittsburgh, or in establishing that American mutton chops were bought in Britain as cutlets. Third, I had to consider the key factors determining retail price: the type of outlet from which food was sold, the quantities in which items were purchased, and the impact of seasonality. The data presented here—average prices prevailing for goods bought in small quantities at local workingmen's corner stores— are comparable. Whether they are typical is a question to which detailed attention will be paid in the next chapter.

Paying Out the Money Saved before the Raise

In the United States the collection of retail prices was undertaken by the Bureau of Labor Statistics. In Pittsburgh thirteen neighborhood stores "situated in sections of the city occupied by laborers and mechanics" were regularly visited by bureau agents who took prices directly from the stores' books. The figures returned were then "carefully gone over in . . . [the] division of examination and criticism" and if necessary, rechecked before being published.[4] Such care resulted in the presentation of reliable data. However, the number of commodities for which prices were listed varied annually, as Table 22 shows. The 1903 *Annual Report of the Commissioner of Labor* presented retail prices for twenty items for the 1890–1902 period; subsequent Bureau of Labor Statistics bulletins increased this number, until the series temporarily lapsed in 1908; and when the series was retrospectively continued in *Bulletin* 105, only sixteen items were reported.[5] The maximum number of food items for which prices were listed was thirty-six in 1904; therefore I selected that year as the base for Table 23.   ·

Given the varying size and composition of the sample frame construction of a mean price series was complicated. Two indices were calculated, the first based upon all food articles for which price statistics were recorded, the second estimated from the nine commodities for which data were presented in every year. Comparison of the two series in Table 24 indicated a substantial degree of similarity. The variable number index (sixteen to thirty-six observations) suggested that retail food prices rose by 45.6 percent between 1899 and 1913, whereas the constant number index (nine observations) suggested an equivalent figure of 51.7 percent. Conversion to a three-year moving average base also revealed general agreement between the two series, although the smaller frame showed a greater upward movement from 1900 to 1902 and a slightly slower increase from 1911 to 1912. The nine-product series exhibited more fluctuations than the larger sample series, and, unlike the latter index, suggested two periods of actual price decline, from 1903 to 1904 and from 1910 to 1911. Nevertheless, both series indicated that the years from 1899 to 1911 fell broadly into five periods paralleling the movement of wages: a rapid advance in prices from 1899; gradual stabilization from 1902–1903 to 1905; four years of rapidly rising prices until 1909, although with a slowing from 1907 to 1908; another two-year price plateau; and finally acceleration upward once more from 1911.

This statistical profile gains support from circumstantial, qualitative evidence. At the turn of the century, as prices rapidly advanced, many individuals and institutions were hard hit. Robert Pitcairn, for instance, bearing the burden of trying to finance the activities of the city's Western Pennsylvania Hospital, found his task compounded in 1901 by the "extraordinary prices reached by vegetables, provisions and food products generally."[6] From 1902, during the period of price stability, comment was subdued, but the issue of inflation became heated once more in 1906, and by 1907 the Pennsylvania Bureau of Industrial Statistics was reporting that "numerous complaints had been made of excessive profits or extortionate prices in the commodities of life [in Pittsburgh]." The culmination of this agitation was the creation of a joint committee of the state legislature whose appointed task was to ascertain "the true condition of affairs in the Pittsburgh district." Although the five-man committee subpoenaed witnesses from the city in an attempt to discover the reason for the "alarming extent" by which food prices had risen in the previous two years, it published no testimony, collected no retail prices, and the three-page report was little more than a compilation of the investigators' private convictions. "A legislative committee made what purported to have been an investigation," concluded the *Searchlight*. It "accomplished nothing aside from sustaining the fact . . . [that] Pittsburgh residents have been gouged for necessities of life."[7]

Pittsburgh newspapers did not require the report of an official investigation upon which to base their conclusions. The *Gazette-Times* made its own survey, asking readers "what significance [had] prosperity to the army of wage-earners when they [found] it more difficult to procure the necessaries of life than in times of stress?" The *Sun* exposed wastage of fruits and vegetables at the Pittsburgh produce yard and accused retailers of gaining unfair profits, and the *Dispatch* shared this belief, greeting Thanksgiving Day 1907 with the headline: "Reason for Thanks As Seen by Grocer; Consumer Can't See." According to the statement beneath, all holiday delicacies had risen from 10 to 33 percent in price since November 1906. Similarly, milk retailers were accused of seeking unfair profits. "The poor of Pittsburgh," reported the *National Labor Tribune* in January 1907, were "staggered by the . . . advance in the price of milk."[8]

Table 22

Retail Prices of 36 Food Items in Working-Class Stores: Pittsburgh, 1899–1913[a]

Article	1899	1900	1901	1902	1903	1904	1905	1906	1907	1908	1909	1910	1911	1912	1913	1914[b]	Description
Apples					10.0	11.0	12.3	12.8	14.0								Evaporated
Beans	9.4	10.0	10.1	10.0	10.0	10.0	10.0	10.0	10.0								Dried, navy
Beef, chuck	12.1	12.1	12.5	13.8	12.5	12.5	12.3	12.5	13.1								Roast
Beef, rib					17.5	16.3	16.8	17.0	17.8	18.1	18.1	18.7	19.0	20.7	21.6	21.4	Roast
Beef, round					15.0	15.0	15.1	15.9	16.0	16.3	16.7	17.8	18.1	21.0	23.3	23.2	Steak
Beef, sirloin					20.0	19.4	18.9	19.7	20.1	20.5	21.0	21.2	21.4	25.3	25.3	27.5	Steak
Beef, corned	10.0	10.0	10.1	12.0	10.2	10.4	11.8	11.3	11.8								Salted
Bread	5.0	5.0	5.0	5.0	5.0	5.0	5.0	5.0	5.8								White
Butter	27.5	29.7	29.2	31.8	30.2	31.8	31.5	33.0	33.3	34.1	35.5	35.1	34.5	37.9	40.2	39.2	Creamery
Cheese	16.1	16.4	15.8	16.9	17.2	16.5	17.5	18.0	19.0								Full cream
Chicken					16.3	17.2	17.8	19.8	19.0	20.0	25.0	22.2	21.8	23.5	25.2	26.7	Dressed, old
Coffee	12.2	13.4	14.4	12.7	12.7	14.6	15.5	16.7	18.0								
Cornmeal					2.5	2.5	2.4	2.4	2.7	2.8	2.7	2.7	2.8	2.9	2.8	2.9	White/Yellow
Eggs, fresh	22.1	20.1	21.8	24.8	26.8	28.1	26.6	28.9	28.0	27.4	30.9	30.2	30.2	31.1	32.5	37.8	Country
Fish, salmon					11.2	13.2	13.3	13.8	14.0								Lake
Fish, cod					9.0	9.9	10.0	10.0	10.0								Salted
Fish, mackerel					15.2	15.0	15.0	17.5	17.5								Salted
Flour	2.7	2.7	2.4	2.5	2.7	3.4	3.1	2.8	3.2	3.5	3.6	3.5	3.3	3.4	3.2	3.2	Wheat
Lard	8.7	9.4	12.1	13.5	13.2	13.2	12.8	15.8	14.5	14.2	15.5	18.0	14.9	15.3	15.5	15.6	Pure leaf

Commodity	1	2	3	4	5	6	7	8	9	10	11	12	13	14	15	16	Description
Milk, fresh	5.5	6.3	6.4	6.3	6.8	7.0	7.1	7.2	8.0	7.9	8.0	8.2	8.3	8.4	8.8	9.2	Unskimmed
Molasses	14.4	15.0	15.5	15.0	15.0	15.0	13.8	13.8	15.0								New Orleans
Lamb, roast	11.6	11.9	12.1	12.0	12.0												Mutton
Lamb, leg	12.8	14.6	14.0	13.8	14.5	16.2	16.7	16.7	16.2	16.5	16.8	19.2	20.8	20.6			Mutton
Pork, fresh	12.0	12.1	13.9	14.1	15.9	14.7	15.1	15.4	16.3	14.9	16.7	19.0	18.4	20.1	22.2	21.9	Roast
Pork, chops	12.0	12.1	14.6	15.0	18.2	17.9	17.9	17.6	19.9	19.7	22.3	23.0	23.7	25.2	28.7	29.0	
Pork, bacon	13.2	13.7	15.2	16.2	15.5	13.5	13.7	14.1	14.4								Sliced
Pork, dry	14.2	14.0	15.0	15.0	15.0												Salted
Pork, pickled																	
Pork, ham	19.7	19.4	18.4	21.2	22.8	23.2	23.6	23.2	24.8	27.6	28.1	28.5					Sliced
Potatoes	18.8	18.2	23.0	23.6	23.1	20.6	23.0	24.7	27.7	28.0	26.2	29.8	33.0	26.2	28.0		Irish, 60–70 lb.
Prunes	10.0	9.0	9.0	9.0	9.4												
Rice	9.5	9.5	9.5	9.5	9.5	9.5	9.5										Carolina
Sugar, white	5.9	6.4	6.7	6.0	6.0	6.1	6.5	6.5	6.1	6.1	6.1	6.8	6.5	5.6	5.4		Granulated
Tea	60.0	60.0	59.6	55.0	55.0	55.0	55.0	55.0									Oolong/Japan
Veal, cutlet	23.5	22.7	22.4	23.4	22.2												
Vinegar	7.5	6.5	7.5	7.0	6.5												Cider

Sources: U. S., *Eighteenth Annual Report of the Commissioner of Labor*, 1903; U. S. Bureau of Labor, *Bulletin*, Nos. 59, 65, 71, 77, 105 (1905–1912); U. S. Bureau of Labor Statistics, *Bulletin*, Nos. 115, 125, 132, 136, 138, 140 (1912–1914).

a. All prices are cents per pound except milk (per American quart), beans (per quart), potatoes (per American peck), molasses (per quart), eggs (per dozen) and vinegar (per pint).

b. January–March.

Table 23

Index Numbers of Retail Prices of 36 Food Items in Working-Class Stores: Pittsburgh, 1899–1913

Article	1899	1900	1901	1902	1903	1904	1905	1906	1907	1908	1909	1910	1911	1912	1913	1914[a]	Description
Apples					90.9	100.0	100.0	116.4	127.3								Evaporated
Beans	94.0	100.0	101.0	100.0	100.0	100.0	100.0	100.0	100.0								Dried, navy
Beef, chuck	96.8	96.8	100.0	110.4	100.0	100.0	98.4	100.0	104.8								Roast
Beef, rib					107.4	100.0	103.1	104.3	109.2	110.0	111.0	114.7	116.6	127.0	132.5	131.3	Roast
Beef, round					100.0	100.0	100.7	106.0	106.7	108.7	111.3	118.7	120.7	140.0	155.3	154.7	Steak
Beef, sirloin					103.1	100.0	97.4	101.5	103.6	105.7	108.2	109.3	110.3	130.4	138.1	141.8	Steak
Beef, corned	96.2	96.2	97.1	115.4	98.1	100.0	113.5	108.7	113.5								Salted
Bread	100.0	100.0	100.0	100.0	100.0	100.0	100.0	100.0	116.0								White
Butter	86.5	93.4	91.8	100.0	95.0	100.0	99.1	103.8	104.7	107.2	111.6	110.4	108.5	119.2	126.4	123.3	Creamery
Cheese	97.6	99.4	95.8	102.4	104.2	100.0	106.1	109.1	115.2								Full cream
Chicken					94.8	100.0	103.5	115.1	110.5	116.3	145.4	129.1	126.7	136.6	146.5	155.2	
Coffee	83.6	91.8	98.6	87.0	87.0	100.0	106.2	114.4	123.3								
Cornmeal					100.0	100.0	96.0	96.0	108.0	112.0	108.0	108.0	112.0	116.0	112.0	116.0	White/Yellow
Eggs, fresh	78.6	71.5	77.6	88.3	95.4	100.0	94.7	102.8	99.6	97.5	110.0	107.5	107.5	110.7	115.7	134.7	Country
Fish, salmon					84.8	100.0	100.8	104.5	106.1								Lake
Fish, cod					90.9	100.0	101.0	101.0	101.0								Salted
Fish, mackerel					101.3	100.0	100.0	116.7	116.7								Salted

Flour	79.4	79.4	70.6	73.5	79.4	100.0	100.0	91.2	82.4	94.1	102.9	105.9	102.9	97.1	100.0	94.1	94.1	Wheat
Lard	65.9	71.2	91.7	102.3	100.0	100.0	97.0	104.5	100.8	107.6	117.4	136.4	112.9	115.9	117.4	118.2		Pure leaf
Milk, fresh	78.6	90.0	91.4	90.0	97.1	100.0	100.0	101.4	102.9	114.3	112.9	114.3	117.1	118.6	120.0	125.7	131.4	Unskimmed
Molasses	96.0	100.0	103.3	100.0	100.0	100.0	92.0	92.0	100.0									New Orleans
Lamb, roast	96.7	99.2	100.8	100.8	100.0													Mutton
Lamb, leg					91.4	100.0	103.6	115.7	119.3	119.3	115.7	117.9	120.0	137.1	148.6	147.1		Mutton
Pork, fresh	87.0	87.7	100.7	102.2	105.8	100.0												Roast
Pork, chops	81.6	82.3	99.3	102.0	108.2	100.0	102.7	104.8	110.9	101.4	113.6	129.3	125.2	136.7	151.0	149.0		
Pork, bacon	73.7	76.5	84.9	90.5	101.7	100.0	100.0	98.3	111.2	110.1	124.6	128.5	132.4	140.8	160.3	162.0		Sliced
Pork, dry					114.8	100.0	101.5	104.4	106.7									Salted
Pork, pickled						100.0	98.6	105.6	105.6									
Pork, ham	81.4	78.8	99.6	99.6	101.5	100.0	94.8	109.3	117.5	119.6	121.6	119.6	127.8	142.3	144.8	146.9		Sliced
Potatoes					102.2	100.0	89.2	99.6	106.9									Irish
Prunes					111.1	100.0	100.0	100.0	104.4									60–70 lb.
Rice	100.0	100.0	100.0	100.0	100.0	100.0	106.6	106.6	100.0	100.0								Carolina
Sugar, white	96.7	104.9	109.8	98.4	98.4	100.0	106.6	106.6	100.0	100.0				111.5	106.6	91.8	88.5	Granulated
Tea	109.1	109.1	109.1	108.4	100.0	100.0	100.0	100.0	100.0	100.0								Oolong/Japan
Veal, cutlet					103.5	100.0	98.7	103.1	97.8									
Vinegar					115.4	100.0	115.4	107.7	100.0									Cider

Source: See Table 22.

a. January–March.

Others thought that the explanation for rising prices lay further back along the chain of production. The collapse of two of Pittsburgh's most prominent wholesalers in September 1907 was greeted with undisguised delight by the local press. The moral appeared clear: the failure of the dealers was a direct result of increased prices that had depressed purchasing power. Producers too were blamed: farmers sought unjustified price increases. Manufacturers also exploited consumers: bakers, for example, were accused of hiding price rises caused by the "greatly increased" cost of flour by reducing the size of loaves from sixteen to fourteen ounces. Others, such as the "Chicago Combine," subverted market forces on a grander scale, extracting "monopoly" profits from hapless housewives. When meat prices advanced in 1908, the *Tribune* rejected the packers' argument that increases resulted from a shortage of pasture as the "usual glib explanation." The fact that beef and pork prices were rising faster than those of other foodstuffs resulted from "meat trust" activities in restraint of trade, reported the *Dispatch*.[9]

Satan, it is clear, appeared in many guises. The identity of the victims was less controversial—they were the wage earners, who had believed that increased pay packets would bring a superior standard of living. The *National Labor Tribune* was not alone in its belief that the city's workers had derived little real benefit from the years of industrial boom. However, it was able to express its skepticism better than most newspapers:

> The firm increased his salary two years ago last May
> The said increase amounted to just thirty cents a day.
> Since then they've raised the price
> Of sugar, salt and rice,
> Of carrots and of beet,
> Of flour, meal and meat, . . .
> Of hats and socks and coats
> Of all that sinks or floats;
> He's paying out the money that he saved before the raise,
> But—Prosperity's upon us and his heart is full of praise.[10]

After the panic of late 1907, emphasis altered. Comment for the next two years was directed toward the "unprecedented" situation in which food prices continued to advance in spite of the severely depressed economy. The *Pittsburgh Dispatch* editorialized ironically in November 1907, as the city's furnaces were blown out and as the steel mills closed, that at least some comfort could be found in the reduced cost of the "necessaries of life." The previous day the price of lim-

Table 24

Mean Index Retail Price Series for Food: Pittsburgh, 1899–1913

Year	No. of Items	16–36 Food Items			9 Food Items		
		Mean Index No.		3-year moving average	Mean Index No.		3-year moving average
		1904 = 100.0	1907 = 100.0	1907 = 100.0	1904 = 100.0	1907 = 100.0	1907 = 100.0
1899	20	89.0	82.6	—	80.3	76.0	—
1900	20	91.4	84.8	86.1	83.1	78.5	81.2
1901	20	96.2	89.2	89.1	90.7	85.8	85.5
1902	20	98.6	91.5	91.7	93.8	88.7	90.1
1903	35	99.5	92.3	92.8	97.5	92.2	93.0
1904	36	100.0	92.8	93.4	100.0	94.6	94.4
1905	34	100.7	93.4	94.8	98.0	92.7	95.4
1906	34	104.0	96.5	97.2	100.6	95.2	97.2
1907	34	107.8	100.0	100.0	105.7	100.0	100.0
1908	16	109.5	101.6	103.4	106.6	100.9	104.0
1909	16	115.0	106.7	106.1	113.2	107.1	107.1
1910	16	116.4	108.0	108.5	115.2	109.0	110.0
1911	16	117.3	108.8	112.1	115.9	109.6	112.6
1912	16	126.4	117.3	116.2	121.4	114.9	114.7
1913	16	129.6	120.2	—	121.8	115.2	—
1914 (early)	16	132.2	122.6	—	124.7	118.0	—

Source: See Tables 22 and 23.

burger cheese and sauerkraut had been reduced. "What more," questioned the *Dispatch,* could "be asked? Such luxuries as sugar and flour are held almost out of reach, . . . but with limburger and sauerkraut in the cellar the poor man can face the winter without fear." The tone of this editorial was repeated in the *National Labor Tribune,* which reported that the fall in retail food prices had in general been minimal and disputed indications that prices were beginning to move downward with greater celerity. "Diamonds and automobiles can be bought by the working classes . . . very much cheaper than a year ago," the *Tribune* noted bitterly, "but bread and meat cannot." In fact, 1908 saw some prices increase, a phenomenon the *Tribune* declared to be "unnatural," coinciding as it did with unemployment and short time, and with consequent reduced consumer demand. The *Dispatch* agreed. In May 1909, in spite of the lack of employment, prices mounted rapidly, and the editor claimed that the situation was "one that [defied] the usual economic theories. It [was] a law of ordinary conditions that a limitation in consumption by the lessening of the purchasing power of the masses must force reduction in prices of the great staples. But . . . circumstances seemed to override the law both as to meat and to flour." So desperate did the *Tribune* become that it eventually advocated, with apparent sincerity, "Fletcherism." This short-lived panacea was named after its inventor, who had discovered that by chewing each mouthful of food thirty times one could more easily satisfy one's hunger![11]

In short, contemporary comment suggests that prices, like wages, showed little response to the financial crisis that affected the city's industrial activity so adversely in late 1907 and throughout 1908. The recession of 1904, it is clear from Table 24, correlated with a slowdown in the upward movement of prices in the sixteen-to-thirty-six product series and with an actual price decline in the nine-product series. In neither case did prices respond so markedly to the far more severe 1907–1908 depression. Indeed, retail food costs rose faster in the following year than at any time in the previous decade in spite of the fact, well attested to by contemporaries, that the year was one of general industrial inactivity.

This continuing upward movement of retail food prices was of major concern to Pittsburgh, and in 1909 the Chamber of Commerce Committee on Trade and Commerce felt obliged to carry out what proved to be a most unsatisfactory investigation of prices in the city.[12] The British vice-consul in Pittsburgh, C. E. E. Childers, reported that although mercantile business had slowly increased through the year, improvement had been made more difficult by the "serious handicap"

Pittsburgh Dispatch, 6 November 1908

of the high prices that had prevailed, "especially in food products." Seen in this light the critical attention devoted by Pennsylvania's chief factory inspector, J. C. Delaney, to the state's "premature and dema- gogic" child labor agitation appears far more understandable; at "a time . . . when the high cost of living [absorbed] the wages of old and young," a reduction in a family's total earnings would have proved disastrous.[13]

National Labor Tribune, 19 September 1907

But in the following year, concern with the cost of living seems to have abated. In November that self-appointed watchdog of the Pittsburgh consumer, the *Dispatch,* heralded the "glad news" that prices were at long last coming down, an occurrence attributed to the immense corn crop. A large decline in the primary foodstuffs had taken place months before, noted the paper, but only in the final months of the year had meat products shared in the price reductions.[14] Bureau of Labor Statistics data clearly support the *Dispatch's* assertions, and Table 24 indicates a retail price plateau in 1910–1911.

The stabilization was short-lived. The year 1912 saw a reemergence of Pittsburgh concern with food prices. The rapidly increasing cost of living, claimed the *Pittsburgh Index,* was "connected with, if not entirely responsible for, disturbed labor conditions." Certainly the revival of local agitation was not confined to newspaper editorials, although such journalistic comment abounded. J. S. McNeil, superintendent of the city's Bureau of Food Inspection, felt compelled to defend his inspectors against the accusation that vigorous enforcement of food regulation was pushing prices upward. The chamber of commerce again attempted its own investigation, which in the event proved embarrassingly futile. Invitations were sent by its Committee on Food Supply to about a hundred representative retail grocers, but a solitary individual attended the meeting organized. Further letters were then distributed to 2,000 city retailers, but of this number only "about twelve" bothered to meet with the chamber! More successful were the activities of the Pittsburgh Women's Marketing Club, which hired the Alvin Theater in order to stage a forum on the cost of living before a mass audience and arranged two consumer boycotts against "overpriced" goods—in June against the "meat trust" and in November and December against egg retailers.[15]

As in 1907, public clamor was rewarded by the establishment of an official investigation, this time ordained by the city council, authorizing the mayor to "appoint and employ . . . a person or persons to investigate the economic and other conditions of the city." Dr. Holdsworth, a dean at the University of Pittsburgh, was appointed. His investigation was serialized in a number of city newspapers as he progressed and finally published as the *Economic Survey of Pittsburgh.* The report, extremely valuable to the historian, presented no easy solutions to the problem of inflation. By the time of publication, in mid–1913, meat prices were advancing as rapidly as at any time in the previous decade. "All meats are now away up in 'G,' " reported a local retailer. "Scarcity of stock seems to be the cause of the increase." But by that time concern was tempered by the knowledge that the city's factories were working at full capacity once again, and that wage rates were advancing apace. As the retailer informant concluded: "it seems the people do not want anything but nice steaks and chops."[16]

Buying the Necessities of Life: A Comparison

The major surveys of retail food prices in Britain were the two investigations carried out by the Board of Trade in working-class areas of British towns in 1905 and 1912. "Predominant prices" were published for fifty-four food items in Birmingham.[17] Table 25 tabulates the retail price of the listed commodities and calculates the percentage of price movement over the seven years: the price of British meat items rose 6.9 percent; that of cheaper foreign meat cuts 10.2 percent; and for other foodstuffs, including bacon, 12.7 percent. The mean price increase for all food products was 10.0 percent, substantially less than the 23.9–25.5 percent recorded in Pittsburgh during the same period.

Unfortunately, British retail price statistics were not collected with such regularity as in the United States, and it was therefore difficult to compile an accurate measure of annual movements in Birmingham. However, a number of surveys undertaken in the early twentieth century allowed the price series to be extended beyond the 1905 and 1912 benchmarks. The Board of Trade investigated individual family budgets in July and August 1900 and included a small number of returns from the Midlands city. A more comprehensive study, instigated by the American Senate Committee on Wages and Prices, was undertaken overseas by consular officials. In Birmingham the responsible agent was Albert Halstead, who performed a detailed investigation of retail prices charged by provisioners catering to the "medium-quality" and "highest-class" trade: he recorded the prices of English meat in 1903 and 1910, nonmeat food items in 1901 and 1910, and foreign meat in 1910 alone. Finally, in early 1914, Dr. Carver carried out a study for the Birmingham Public Health and Housing Committee in which were listed the "predominant" prices paid for food "as purchased." I have combined these reports, varying in both scope and methodology, to provide an estimate of retail price movements in Birmingham between 1900 and 1914.[18] Four stages were involved.

First, I compared the prices paid by Birmingham families for food items in mid–1900 to the prices that, according to the Board of Trade, prevailed in October 1905. For the twelve commodities presented in both reports, the mean price fell by 2.2 percent. In short, if 1900 is used as the base year (100.0), by 1905 food prices had declined to 97.8.

Straight-line interpolation suggests that in 1901 the index would have been 99.6.

Second, I added to the series the figures garnered by Halstead in February 1910. Prices, "gathered from many sources in the period of five days" but largely obtained, it would seem, from a small number of higher-class storekeepers who had preserved their retail records, were cited for a wide range of food items. The consul's figures suggested that between 1903 and 1910, retail prices increased by 10.6 percent, while between 1901 and 1910, the advance was only 5.5 percent. The deduction made was that the 1901–1903 period witnessed a 4.6 percent price decline: that is, if the 1901 price index was 99.6, it had fallen to 95.0 by 1903 and had increased to 105.1 by 1910.[19]

Third, there were eighteen food items for which both the Board of Trade and Halstead collected prices. These comprised ten English meat cuts (pork leg, pork loin, pork belly, mutton leg, mutton shoulder, mutton breast, mutton chops, beef prime ribs, beef silverside and beef rump steak) and eight other commodities (tea, white granulated sugar, home-cured bacon, eggs, Danish butter, colonial butter, flour and Canadian cheese). According to the Board of Trade the average retail price of those items increased by 8.9 percent between 1905 and 1912. Where the index number for 1905 was 97.8, that for 1912 would have been 106.5.

Fourth, Dr. Carver's study for 1914 was introduced to the price series. Collected from working-class expenditures, the prices gathered were compared both to the Board of Trade investigation for 1912 and to that for 1900. The statistical evidence thus obtained was surprising, for although the two comparisons were based upon a very different range of commodities, estimates of price movement were similar. Between 1912 and 1914 the mean price increase for fourteen comparable food items was 5.1 percent, giving an index number for the latter year of 111.9. For the fourteen-year period, the mean retail price advance for thirteen items was 11.5 percent, giving an index number for 1914 of 111.5.

By such means I found it possible to estimate a retail food price index for Birmingham for 1900–1914 incorporating observations for seven separate years. Table 26 compares these data with those calculated for Pittsburgh. The evidence confirms that food prices, like money wages, advanced far more rapidly in the American city. Whereas prices declined in Birmingham between 1900 and 1903, a sharp increase of from 8.8 to 17.5 percent occurred in Pittsburgh. Only in the final years of investigation, from 1912 to early 1914, did British food prices rise faster. Overall, in the first fourteen years of this cen-

Table 25

Predominant Retail Prices Paid for 54 Food Items: Birmingham, October 1905 and October 1912.

A. Meat Products[a]

Commodity	British Meat			Foreign/Colonial Meat		
	Price Oct. 1905	Price Oct. 1912	% Movement 1905–1912	Price Oct. 1905	Price Oct. 1912	% Movement 1905–1912
Beef						
Ribs, prime cuts	16.3¢	18.4¢	+12.8	10.2¢	10.7¢	+4.9
Ribs, flat or top		12.8	−21.5		9.2	−9.8
Brisket	—	9.2	—	—	6.1	—
Silverside	15.8	17.3	+9.5	11.2	11.7	+4.5
Shin, with bone	—	—	—	4.6	5.1	+10.9
Shin, without bone	12.2	14.3	+17.2	8.2	9.2	+12.2
Steak, shoulder	—	17.3	—	—	12.2	—
Steak, beef	14.3	—	—	10.2	—	—
Steak, rump	22.4	25.5	+13.8	14.3	16.3	+14.0
Thin flank	10.2	10.7	+4.9	6.6	7.1	+7.8
Mutton						
Leg	17.4	17.9	+2.9	10.2	12.1	+10.6
Shoulder	15.8	16.3	+3.2	9.2	10.2	+10.9
Breast	9.7	9.7	±0.0	5.6	6.1	+8.9
Neck, best end	16.8	misprint	—	9.2	10.2	+10.9
Neck, scrag end	12.8	13.3	+3.9	5.6	6.6	+17.9
Chops (trimmed)	20.4	22.4	+9.8	11.2	13.3	+18.8
Pork						
Leg	16.3	18.4	+12.9	—	—	—
Fore loin	16.3	18.4	+12.9	—	—	—
Belly	14.8	16.3	+10.1	—	—	—
Chops	16.3	18.9	+12.9	—	—	—

B. *Other Foods*[a]

Commodity	Price Oct. 1905	Price Oct. 1912	% Movement 1905–1912
Tea	34.7¢	34.7¢	±0.0
Sugar, lump	5.1	4.8	−5.8
Sugar, white granulated	4.1	4.1	±0.0
Sugar, white moist	3.6	3.3	−8.3
Bacon, home-cured	18.4	21.4	+16.3
Bacon, American drafts	14.3	18.4	+28.7
Bacon, roll	16.3	20.4	+25.2
Eggs, Irish dozen	—	32.6	—
Eggs, foreign/Canadian dozen	24.5	27.0	+10.2
Cheese, American Cheddar	14.3	17.3	+21.0
Butter, fresh	—	33.7	—
Butter, Irish salt	26.5	28.6	+7.9
Butter, Danish salt	28.6	30.6	+7.0
Butter, colonial salt	25.5	28.6	+12.2
Potatoes, 7 lb.	5.1	7.9	+54.9
Flour, 7 lb.	20.4	21.4	+4.9
Bread, 7 lb.	9.7	11.2	+15.5
Milk, American quart	5.9	6.8	+15.3

Sources: Great Britain, Board of Trade, *Report of an Enquiry . . . into Working Class Rents, Housing, Retail Prices and Standard Rates of Wages in the United Kingdom, British Parliamentary Papers,* Cd. 3864, 1908, Vol. 53, and Cd. 6955, 1913, Vol. 63.
a. All prices for one-pound units unless otherwise stated.

tury, Birmingham food prices increased by 11.5–11.9 percent, whereas in Pittsburgh prices soared 44.6–50.3 percent.

If the indices of food prices are compared to those for hourly wage rates presented in Table 5, it appears that in both cities the real cost of food remained relatively stable. In Pittsburgh the movement of wages and prices was similar: the period 1900–1912 witnessed a 38.3–45.6 percent improvement in hourly rates and a 38.3–46.4 percent jump in food prices, representing a maximum growth in real prices of 5.9 percent, or a maximum decline in real prices of 5.0 percent. In Birmingham there occurred an advance in real prices: whereas hourly rates increased by 4.7–4.8 percent between 1900 and 1912, food prices escalated 6.5 percent, suggesting a rise in real prices of 1.6–1.7 percent.[20]

Estimation of the movement of Bimingham food prices was necessarily more conjectural than that allowed by the superior Pittsburgh data. There remained fears that some of the suggested fluctuations, in particular the apparent price decline between 1900 and 1903, were untrustworthy. Fortunately, circumstantial evidence validated the quantitative calculations. An inquiry by the British Board of Trade into the prices of bread at Co-operative stores found that the cost of a four-pound loaf in Birmingham fell from 13.9¢ in 1898, to 11.2¢ in 1899, to 10.6¢ in 1900, to 10.4¢ in 1901, and to 10.2¢ in 1902. Furthermore, when the superintendent of St. Mark's Boys' Home in Birmingham wrote to the press in 1911 complaining of the increased cost of living, the year he selected as his base was 1903. It would appear logical for anyone wishing to emphasize rising prices to choose as his time base a year in which prices were at their lowest point in recent history: the above calculations suggest that 1903 was just such a year.

Table 26
Estimated Movement of Retail Food Prices: Pittsburgh and Birmingham, 1900–1914

	Index Number of Prices		
Year	Birmingham	Pittsburgh[a]	Pittsburgh[b]
1900	100.0	100.0	100.0
1901	99.6	105.2	109.3
1903	95.0	108.8	117.5
1905	97.8	110.1	118.1
1910	105.1	127.4	138.9
1912	106.5	138.3	146.4
1914	111.5 – 111.9	144.6	150.3

Sources: See text and Table 24.
a. Based upon variable sample (16 to 36 commodities).
b. Based upon stable sample (9 commodities).

Finally, Halstead unequivocally asserted that 1900 "was the time of a trade boom when prices were necessarily at the highest and after that came a depression with very low prices." By 1910, he noted, business was "only reviving slightly after a second and severe depression, so a comparison of prices between 1910 and 1901 [was] not a fair one as showing the actual advances in . . . prices; the advances [seemed] smaller than they would have been had the year . . . 1902 or 1903, been taken as a basis."[21]

Birmingham food prices appear to have risen most rapidly after 1910, and this marked increase in the rate of price advance evoked "considerable comment" in the local press. By September 1910 Halstead's consular reports were suggesting that meat prices, which always rose in summer, were advancing more than was usual. He attributed this development to the decline in North American beef supplies and the embargo imposed against Argentine cattle in response to the outbreak of foot-and-mouth disease in that country. However, the next year prices continued to increase for a widening range of commodities. Whereas the British summer was, in Halstead's words, "usually wet, with intervals of bright weather," 1911 proved a glorious exception. The sun shone brightly, and the city's bicycle manufacturers did a brisk trade. Farmers, faced with an "unprecedented drought," had less reason to be enthusiastic. Dairymen were forced to stall-feed their cattle because of the lack of pasturage, and milk and butter prices advanced rapidly. So too did the price of cheese, for although New Zealand increased its exports in response to demand, Canadian stocks were below normal. "Something like a famine" occurred in the vegetable market, and crops of English and Irish potatoes were blighted. Fruit dropped early, and the price of both fresh and canned produce climbed; sugar prices did likewise, for the German beet crop was subject to similarly adverse weather conditions. Yet climatic factors alone cannot be blamed for the fact that the closing months of the year witnessed "a steady increase in the cost of some of the principal articles connected with the grocery and provision trades," for those items included tea, coffee, and rice.[22]

Moreover, prices continued to rise for many foodstuffs in 1912. Sugar, bacon, and lard became cheaper, but cheese, milk, and butter prices showed no signs that their upward movement was losing momentum. Public concern grew. In February the General Purpose Committee of the Birmingham Chamber of Commerce reported that "in view of the many, and oftentimes contradictory, statements made respecting the cost of living, [the] Committee proposes to obtain such information as may be available and if deemed necessary, to prepare and submit a report on the matter." Seven months later the committee claimed that investigation was under way and stated that it hoped to publish its conclusions "at an early date." In fact, however, the Birmingham chamber made even less progress than its namesake in Pittsburgh. In the final *Journal* for the year, the committee, which had considered "at several of their meetings the question of the causes of the increased cost of living," beat an inglorious retreat from the problem. The subject had proved "of very wide scope, and . . . extremely complicated, and many months of close investigation would [have been] needed. . . . On these grounds it [was] thought desirable to defer the matter."[23]

The report, not surprisingly, never appeared. But concern continued. The *Daily Post,* for instance, reported that meat cuts now fetched "extravagant prices" from one to four cents per pound beyond "normal." "Very serious indeed is the view Birmingham butchers take of the present position," reported the columnist of "The Domestic Larder" in May. "There is restriction of [meat] supply throughout all departments of the market, even to the lowest grades."[24]

In general, however, agitation against the increasing cost of Birmingham food was less vocal than that in Pittsburgh, even in these later years. Perhaps the thriving condition of Birmingham's industry in the post–1910 period made the rising prices easier to bear. The *Post*'s domestic columnist, while noting the seriousness of price advances, nevertheless believed that retailing trade was "much better" in 1912 than in previous years and noted that the city's shops had "put on their Christmas dress a week or more earlier than usual."[25] It is not too fanciful, perhaps, to imagine that the citizens of Birmingham were celebrating the return of industrial prosperity to the city, a Christmas of full pay packets after a decade of near-stationary wages, underemployment, and winter relief schemes. Wages may not have kept pace with prices, but at least increases were being conceded and, more importantly, work was abundant.

Pittsburgh's retail food prices were, it has been shown, increasing vis-à-vis Birmingham's, at least in money terms. But how did prices in the British Midlands compare with those which prevailed in the Pennsylvania community? Comparison of prices, presented in Table 27, suggests that at each of the three dates for which reliable comparative data could be prepared—1900, 1905, and 1912—food was more expensive for Pittsburgh workers than for their Birmingham counterparts. Staples such as bread and potatoes, tea and sugar, and beef and mutton were 50 to 100 percent dearer, whereas dairy products such as eggs, cheese, butter, and milk were generally less than 25 percent more expensive. Somewhat unexpectedly, given the forceful criticisms of the monopoly practices of American meat-packers, pork and bacon were cheaper in Pittsburgh in 1900 and even by 1912 the price of chops was only 6 percent higher in the American city. The estimated mean price of fifteen food commodities, unweighted for budgetary expenditure, was 25.9 percent higher in Pittsburgh in 1900; but the relative price of Birmingham items fell in the following decade, so that by 1905 the mean price was 37.7 percent greater, and by 1912, 54.3 percent dearer.[26]

However, these calculations almost certainly overestimate the greater cost of food in the American city: tea has been included in the list although Pittsburghers almost without exception drank the cheaper beverage, coffee; Birmingham beef and mutton prices are those charged for foreign cuts, and in terms of quality a fairer comparison would have been with British home-killed meat; and the price of American creamery butter has been compared to that of Birmingham's salt butter rather than to "fresh" butter, for which details are absent. Nevertheless, even if it is assumed that Pittsburgh food prices were only 10 percent higher than those in Birmingham in 1900—a minimum estimate—then they would have been 20 percent more expensive by 1905, and 34 percent more expensive by 1912.[27] Moreover, the greater advance in Pittsburgh retail food prices was general. Of the nine commodities for which prices may be compared in 1900 and 1905, seven became relatively more expensive in Pittsburgh; and of the twelve items for which prices are available in both 1905 and 1912, only one—sugar—had not become relatively dearer there.

Not All the Statistics That the Government Can Invent

It would be extremely pleasant to progress without further ado to a study of rents and dry-goods prices, but such a course would be as unworthy as it is tempting. For as any housewife would readily appreciate, the data thus far presented represent but a fragment of reality, rather like a description of a city based upon the close study of a single street. As a guide to price movements of particular products in a particular type of store, the calculations possess a certain validity; as an account of what working-class consumers actually paid for their food, the material analyzed is decidedly inferior. In short, shopping was—and is—a complex decision-making process in which the shopper faces a wide range of possibilities, not only with respect to the type of commodities bought, but also with regard to the quality and quantity

Table 27

Retail Food Prices: Pittsburgh and Birmingham; 1900, 1905, and 1912

Commodity	1900 Price Bhm (¢)	1900 Price Pgh (¢)	1900 Pgh Price: Bhm = 100.0 (index)	1905 Price Bhm (¢)	1905 Price Pgh (¢)	1905 Pgh Price: Bhm = 100.0 (index)	1912 Price Bhm (¢)	1912 Price Pgh (¢)	1912 Pgh Price: Bhm = 100.0 (index)
Meat products									
Beef ribs[a] lb.	n.s.	n.s.	—	10.2	16.8	164.7	9.9	20.7	209.1
Beef round[b] lb.	n.s.	n.s.	—	11.2	15.1	134.8	11.7	21.0	179.5
Beef sirloin[c] lb.	n.s.	n.s.	—	14.3	18.9	132.2	16.3	25.3	155.2
Mutton leg[d] lb.	n.s.	n.s.	—	10.2	14.5	142.2	12.2	19.2	157.4
Pork chops lb.	14.3	12.1	84.6	16.3	15.1	92.6	18.8	20.1	106.3
Bacon[e] lb.	18.4	13.7	74.5	16.3	17.9	109.8	20.1	25.2	125.4
Dairy products									
Eggs[f] dozen.	21.7	20.1	92.6	24.5	26.6	108.6	27.0	31.1	115.2
Cheese[g] lb.	14.8	16.4	110.8	14.3	17.5	122.4	17.3	n.s.	—
Butter[h] lb.	26.6	29.7	111.7	26.9	31.5	117.1	29.3	37.9	129.0
Milk Amer. qt.	5.1	6.3	123.5	5.9	7.1	120.3	6.8	8.4	123.5

Other foodstuffs

Bread lb.	3.0	5.0	166.7	2.4	5.0	208.3	2.8	n.s.	—
Flour 7 lb.	n.s.	18.9	—	20.4	21.7	106.4	21.4	23.9	111.7
Potatoes 15 lb.	n.s.	18.2	—	10.9	20.6	189.0	16.9	33.0	195.3
Tea lb.	34.7	60.0	172.9	34.7	55.0	158.5	34.7	n.s.	—
Sugar[i] lb.	4.1	6.4	156.1	4.1	6.5	158.5	4.1	6.5	158.5

Mean Index No.	9			15			12		
	commodities 121.5			commodities 137.7			commodities 147.2		
				9					
				commodities 132.9					
				12					
				commodities 131.4					

	Estimate A[j]						*Estimate B*[k]		
Mean Index No.	15			15			15		
	commodities 125.9			commodities 137.7			commodities 154.3		

Sources: See Tables 22, 24 and text.

Note: n.s. = not stated.

a. Mean price of prime cut and top ribs (foreign or colonial) in Birmingham.

b. Price for silverside (foreign or colonial) in Birmingham. According to Halstead, "top side of the round" was priced the same as "silverside."

c. Price for "beef steak" (foreign or colonial) in Birmingham.

d. Price for foreign or colonial mutton leg in Birmingham.

e. Mean price for home-cured sides, American drafts, and roll bacon in Birmingham; for sliced bacon in Pittsburgh.

f. Price for "country fresh" eggs in Pittsburgh; for "foreign eggs" in Birmingham.

g. Price for "full cream" cheese in Pittsburgh; for Canadian or American cheddar in Birmingham.

h. Mean price for Irish, Danish, and colonial salt butter in Birmingham; for creamery in Pittsburgh.

i. Price for white granulated sugar in both cities.

j. Estimate A: $(121.5 \times 137.7)/132.9$

k. Estimate B: $(147.2 \times 137.7)/131.4$

of the items chosen and the time and place of purchase. By contrast, the retail price statistics upon which the historian has in large measure depended are deceptively simple.

The prices presented by the U.S. Bureau of Labor Statistics and the British Board of Trade were collected from a narrow retailing environment and generally referred to a single grade of produce bought in a small quantity. Field-workers for the agencies took no account of whether the transaction was in cash or dependent upon credit facilities, disregarded the social status of the purchaser, and ignored the weekly bargains, leading offers, and other discount or dividend schemes in which stores indulged. Food prices quoted in the bureau's bulletins, for example, were those that prevailed in stores "patronised largely by families of American, English, Irish, German, and Scandinavian wage earners." Shops whose customers were predominantly new immigrants were excluded from the federal investigation. More importantly, information was collected almost exclusively from neighborhood stores. Prices in "so-called 'cut-rate' stores" and in chain stores were specifically disregarded by the bureau, as were those prices current at markets or charged by itinerant hucksters.[28]

Perhaps for this reason contemporaries were decidedly more wary of government investigations than economic historians have been. "Not all the statistics that the government . . . can invent will convince the average housewife that prices have only advanced in the same proportion as wages," declared the *National Labor Tribune* in 1907. While the journal was persuaded that the price of necessities had risen faster than wages, it was unable to explain why the BLS figures, carrying the official imprimatur of government authority, failed to reflect grassroots experience. Nevertheless, skepticism of the statisticians' findings was unrestrained. "We cannot contradict them in set terms," the *Tribune* grudgingly admitted, "but we can tell them that their statistics are not believed." It should not be thought that only workers disputed the BLS series. In the arbitration proceedings between the Pittsburgh Railways Company and the local motormen's union in 1914, it was the labor representatives who presented government data as evidence of the increased cost of living, while the employers challenged the validity of the federal statistics and presented their own material, privately collected from the two largest retail grocers in the Pittsburgh district. Inflation, the company argued, had been much less than the government suggested.[29]

British commentators were equally doubtful of official sources. Dr. Carver's 1914 investigation of working-class diets in Birmingham convinced him that "no one who is not familiar with [shopping realities] knows how cheaply the poor might live." This view was shared by F. J. Cross, who believed it possible—from experience—to live for three pence a day in Southeast London, so long as one bought in quantity, purchased from peddlers, and ate only food in season.[30] These three crucial variables—the amount purchased, type of retailer, and time of year—must be examined in detail.

6
Shopping

Chain Stores and Department Stores: Cut-Rate Emporiums

Prior to the First World War, American retail price statistics referred to commodities sold at local neighborhood stores. Initially, this emphasis appears sound. Even by 1912 Pittsburgh's provisioning trade was shared by no less than 2,500 grocers, of whom the great majority were single shop enterprises. Nevertheless, chain stores and giant food departments played an increasingly important part in the city's retailing structure. In 1909 two important national "multiple" firms were well established in the grocery trade of Pittsburgh and environs, one having twenty-two shops locally and the other nineteen. Moreover, a few local firms had experienced horizontal expansion. At the start of the century, Weldon's possessed a dozen "food markets," and by 1909 at least one other local firm had six branches. Some "of the large general stores [sold] groceries and other foodstuffs," and one of them, Kaufmann's, claimed to "sell more groceries in a day than the average corner grocer [sold] in a month." A number of meat retailers also had more than one shop in the city, and one such had six. These stores often directed their appeals largely to the workingman: P. H. Butler Company, "Cut Price Grocers," for instance, advertised regularly in the *Iron City Trades Journal,* giving examples of their prices and stressing that "there [was] a store near."[1]

The Pittsburgh housewife who budgeted wisely must have been sorely tempted by the lure of the cut-price food stores, for the economic survey undertaken in the city in November 1911 attested to the fact that items bought from such shops were substantially cheaper than those purchased from neighborhood stores. Holdsworth found that retailers "in different sections of the city [showed] no uniform or marked difference in prices," but that between the different types of shop in any locality, prices varied considerably. He distinguished three types of food merchandising establishment: the "workingman's shop," which approximated the neighborhood stores from which the BLS collected data; the "high class store"; and the "chain" or "cut-rate" store. The results of his investigation are presented in Table 28.[2]

It is apparent that the federal statistics must in many cases have overestimated the prices that working-class families paid for their produce. For seventeen grocery food items a mean 9.5 percent price saving could have been made in 1911 by purchasing at the local branch of a chain store. Even the prices charged by high-class provisioners were only 4.5 percent in advance of those that prevailed at working-class corner stores. For ten basic grocery commodities—coffee, white granulated sugar, bread, flour, cheese, butter, eggs, oats, potatoes, and milk—relative prices charged by the local workingman's shop were even higher: the mean price gain achieved by purchasing at a cut-rate store was 10.3 percent.[3] The mean price gain to be derived from shopping at cut-rate meat stores was even greater, twenty-five meat cuts selling at an average of 27.9 percent less than at the local independent butcher. The high-class meat retailer was only 1.8 percent dearer than the workingman's shop for the same items.

Contemporaries were generally agreed that chain and department stores sold groceries at lower prices than neighborhood shops. They were far less forthcoming on the extent to which the movement of retail prices in the cut-rate stores paralleled or deviated from that recorded for the more expensive corner stores. Data are very scanty. Fortunately, one Pittsburgh enterprise, Kaufmann's Department Store, which claimed to possess "Pennsylvania's Biggest Grocery," advertised the prices of its food commodities each week. By collating these statistics for the months of May and November in each year, I was able to construct a time series of food prices that prevailed at the store.[4] Table 29 presents a comparison of this index with that constructed from the prices recorded by the BLS at neighborhood stores. The Kaufmann and BLS series exhibit surprising similarity except in two instances. In each case, first in 1903–1904 and more prominently in 1908–1909, prices recorded by the BLS rose, while those advertised by Kaufmann's declined. Between 1906 and 1907 Kaufmann's prices increased more steeply than did those at corner groceries: in contrast, the department store's prices fell precipitously in the following two years of economic depression, while food prices at the workingmen's stores held firm.

These statistical estimates receive circumstantial support from the comment of contemporaries. Secretary of Labor Charles P. Neill testified that prices in working-class stores were "not susceptible to the same degree of fluctuation" as those in other retailing provisioners. And, as already noted, the arbitration proceedings between the Pittsburgh Railways Company and the union in 1914 focused upon the fact that prices in different types of stores advanced at different rates. Division 85 of the motormen's and conductor's local union (the Amalgamated Association of Street Car Employees of America) presented

Table 28

Food Prices in Neighborhood Stores, High-Class Stores, and Chain Stores: Pittsburgh, November 1911

Commodity	High-Class Store (¢)	Chain Store (¢)	Neighborhood Store (¢)	Price in High-Class Store Compared to Neighborhood Store (% Variation)	Price in Chain Store Compared to Neighborhood Store (% Variation)
Tea (lb)	75.0[a]	47.5[a]	50.0[a]	+50.0	-5.0
Coffee (lb.)	29.0[a]	28.5[a]	31.5[a]	-7.9	-9.5
Condensed milk (lb.)	10.0	10.0	10.0	±0.0	±0.0
White sugar (lb.)	7.0	7.0	8.0	-12.5	-12.5
Brown sugar (lb.)	6.0	6.5	6.0	±0.0	+8.3
Loaf sugar (lb.)	8.0	8.0	10.0	-20.0	-20.0
Large loaf bread	10.0	8.0	9.0	+11.1	-11.1
Winter flour (49lb.)	170.0	155.0	160.0	+6.3	-3.1
American cheese (lb.)	20.0	18.0	20.0	±0.0	-10.0
Creamery butter (lb.)	37.0	32.0[a]	37.0	±0.0	-13.5
Select eggs (12?)	30.0	24.0	30.0	±0.0	-20.0
Rolled oats (lb.)	12.5[a]	10.0	10.0	+25.0	±0.0
Can Peaches	25.0[a]	17.5[a]	10.0	+150.0	+75.0
Can Corn	12.5[a]	10.0	12.5[a]	±0.0	-20.0
Can Peas	15.0	12.5[a]	13.5[a]	+11.1	-7.4
Can Tomatoes	12.5[a]	10.0	12.5[a]	±0.0	-20.0
Salmon (lb.?)	20.0[a]	18.5[a]	17.5[a]	+14.3	+5.7
Potatoes (peck?)	30.0	23.0	30.0	±0.0	-23.3

Beef round roast (lb.)	18.0[a]	16.0[a]	19.0[a]	-5.3	-15.8
Prime ribs (lb.)	20.0	16.0[a]	21.0[a]	-4.8	-23.8
2nd cut ribs (lb.)	12.5	13.8	21.0[a]	-40.5	-34.3
Short ribs (lb.)	—	9.0	25.0	—	-64.0
Round steak (lb.)	20.0	17.5[a]	20.0	±0.0	-12.5
Sirloin steak (lb.)	25.0	19.0[a]	25.0	±0.0	-24.0
Porterhouse steak (lb.)	30.0	19.0[a]	27.5	+9.1	-30.9
Flank (lb.)	18.0	10.0	19.0	-5.3	-47.4
Plate (lb.)	9.0	6.5[a]	7.5[a]	+20.0	-13.3
Lamb leg (lb.)	20.0	13.8[a]	21.5[a]	-7.0	-35.8
Breast (lb.)	12.5	9.5[a]	12.5[a]	±0.0	-24.0
Loin (lb.)	25.0	13.8[a]	22.5[a]	+11.1	-38.7
Chops (lb.)	25.0	13.8[a]	22.5[a]	+11.1	-38.7
Shoulder (lb.)	20.0	8.0	17.5	+14.3	-54.3
Neck (lb.)	10.0	7.0	11.8	-15.3	-40.7
Veal cutlets (lb.)	30.0	20.0	30.0[a]	±0.0	-33.3
Rib chops (lb.)	25.0	15.0	21.5[a]	+16.3	-30.2
Loin chops (lb.)	25.0	15.0	21.5[a]	+16.3	-30.2
Breast (lb.)	15.0	12.5	17.5[a]	-14.3	-28.6
Neck (lb.)	12.5	10.0	15.3[a]	-18.3	-34.6
Pork loin (lb.)	20.0	16.0	17.3[a]	+15.6	-7.5
Spare rib (lb.)	12.5	11.0	11.5[a]	+8.7	-4.3
Shoulder (lb.)	15.0	10.5	14.0[a]	+7.1	-25.0
Chops (lb.)	20.0	16.0	18.3	+9.3	-12.6
Dry salt (lb.)	—	12.0	17.3[a]	—	-30.6
Large hams (lb.)	17.5[a]	13.0	15.8[a]	+10.8	-17.7
Bacon (lb.)	27.5[a]	16.0	26.0[a]	+5.8	-38.5

Source: John T. Holdsworth, *Economic Survey of Pittsburgh* (Pittsburgh, 1914), p. 74.
a. Midpoint of price range.

BLS data as evidence of the increased cost of living in the previous five years. The company, in contrast, presented price material compiled from Charters and another big Pittsburgh grocery chain: brandishing these statistics, the company's representative, Mr. King, could claim that "the increase in the cost of food . . . at retail [was] much less than the Government statistics." Interestingly, the union barely contested this claim but rather contended that most of their members still shopped at neighborhood stores. John O'Connor, Jr., reported that "objection was very properly made by the counsels for the employees to the consideration of Charter's price lists as typical of the ordinary grocery stores of Pittsburgh as those stores must be held to partake of the nature of chain-stores." Congressman Porter, dissenting from the majority opinion in the arbitration report, nevertheless accepted its claim that Charters' prices had risen by about 7 percent since 1910, less than the BLS statistics suggested.[5]

The reasons for the apparent divergence in the price movements of neighborhood stores and the large-scale provisioners are not clear. One undoubted advantage of the department and chain store vis-à-vis the small grocery was their superior purchasing power and greater turnover of stock. "The secret of underselling by chain stores," wrote Holdsworth, "seems to lie in their ability to buy and sell in large quantities." But in at least one Pittsburgh suburb independent food

Table 29
Retail Food Prices in Pittsburgh, 1900–1912: A Comparison of Neighborhood Stores and Kaufmann's Department Store

| | Neighborhood Store Prices[a] | | Department Store Prices[a] | |
Year	Single Year	3-Year Average	Single Year	3-Year Average
1900	78.5	81.2	70.1	—
1901	85.8	85.5	81.0	85.3
1902	88.7	90.1	85.4	90.4
1903	92.2	93.0	83.8	91.3
1904	94.6	94.4	83.9	90.8
1905	92.7	95.4	84.9	91.1
1906	95.2	97.2	84.9	97.0
1907	100.0	100.0	100.0	100.0
1908	100.9	104.0	92.2	100.8
1909	107.1	107.4	87.0	97.2
1910	109.0	110.3	90.2	99.0
1911	109.6	112.9	97.4	103.0
1912	114.9	114.7	98.9	—

Sources: See Table 24, Cols. 6–8, and text.
[a]Retail food price indices, where 1907 = 100.0

retailers had formed a cooperative purchasing association through which to negate the larger stores' advantage in this respect. Furthermore, economies of scale may explain the ability of cut-rate provisioners to sell cheaper than single-store, low-capital grocers, but they hardly provide a satisfactory reason for the different movement of prices.[6]

Neill believed that the less mobile prices found in neighborhood stores were a considered response to working-class demands. "The average [laboring-class] housewife's one desire is that there shall be steadiness of price," he claimed. "The slightest variation upsets her calculations. . . . When prices are going up, the [neighborhood] retailer will let them go up a little before he increases his price, hoping they will drop again. If they drop away down, he does not change his price again, but recoups himself."[7] Statistical estimates for the years 1906 to 1910 appear to confirm the secretary of labor's assertion: workingmen's stores increased their prices less than Kaufmann's did from 1906 to 1907 but "recouped" in 1908 and 1909 while the department store lowered prices. Yet so massive a price divergence as occurred from 1907 to 1909 can be only partially attributed to such behavior. One is left to explain why working-class consumers continued to buy produce at local grocers and butchers in a period when the prices charged by large-scale retailers were becoming relatively cheaper.

The key factor, perhaps, was that neighborhood stores carried a large amount of credit trade, whereas chain and department stores were almost exclusively cash concerns. Marshell's, a grocery with three Pittsburgh outlets, made no secret that this policy allowed it to undersell competitors. "The Cash Grocer Will Save You Money" ran the advertisements. " 'You only get paid once a month. We can't pay cash for our groceries.' This is what one man's wife said. He told her they could try, anyhow. They did try and saved $10.00 the first month. We saved that $10.00 for them. Why not for you?"[8]

The ability to extend credit facilities was a customer requirement reflected in the political activity of the Retail Merchants' Association of Pennsylvania. On the one hand, the association aimed to persuade its members to extend credit cautiously; on the other, it hoped to make the debts of purchasers legally retrievable. In the prosperous days of early 1907, the association introduced a bill at Harrisburg that would have allowed a merchant to garnishee a man's wages for debts contracted for food and clothing, the debtor being required to pay not more than 10 percent of his wages monthly until the account was settled. The governor, unconvinced as to the bill's merits, imposed his veto upon it in August. There can be little doubt that in the years

following the depression many Pittsburgh grocers, as they gazed rue-
fully at the books of unpaid debts incurred by unemployed workers,
must have mourned the failure of their bill to secure legislative
enactment.[9]

John A. Green, secretary of the National Association of Retail
Grocers, commended the members of his organization for their impressive response to the 1907 depression. "The retail grocers of the
United States," he testified before a Senate Select Committee, "extended credit to the amount of millions of dollars, and if it hadn't been
for that credit extended . . . I don't know what would have become of
the wage-earning public."[10] With most of the steel mills silent, with
receivers called in to the Westinghouse machinery plants, and with a
slump in the city's building trades, there can be little question that the
huge army of Pittsburgh unemployed had to depend upon the goodwill
of the neighborhood storekeeper. In such a situation, where small
retailers frequently had to accept good intentions in lieu of coin, price
reductions were unlikely: indeed, it was rather more likely that prices
would be raised so that the grocers could try to recover the inevitable
losses which would accrue from unpaid debts. Stores such as Kaufmann's, which transacted business in cash, did not have to take into
account future difficulty in recouping extended credit. Such stores
were able to lower their prices in response to reduced wholesale costs
and to retain their share of a declining cash market.

According to Joseph Hallsworth and Rhys J. Davies of the Shop
Assistants' Union, the "amount of business done by petty tradesmen"
in Britain in 1910 was "completely outweighed by that of the great
multiple firms and stores."[11] Yet in Birmingham, as in Pittsburgh, the
number of chain grocery retailers was relatively small. The vast majority of provisioners remained single shop enterprises. Kelly's directory
of the city listed 1,152 grocers who possessed two or fewer stores in
1901, and this number fell by about 5 percent to 1,098 a decade later.
The number of food retailers with three or more stores remained
stable over the same period: there were 22 in 1901 and 23 in 1911. The
most significant trend in Birmingham's retailing structure is hidden by
these statisics, however, for it occurred within the latter group of storekeepers. At the turn of the century, R. C. Evans, with three shops in
the city, could still be described as a grocer "in a large way of business." Only 10 Birmingham provisioners owned more than four stores
locally in 1901. Over the next decade the importance of three- or
four-shop grocers declined considerably, and of the 23 firms with more
than three shops in 1911, 17 had five or more. Maypole's, the "largest

retailers of choice quality butter, tea and margarine in the [United] Kingdom," increased the number of stores trading in Birmingham from two in 1901 to ten in 1911, by which time George Mason's had nine local shops, Lipton's eight and Home and Colonial sixteen. Birmingham's Co-operative Society was even better established, but numerically the largest provisioner in the city was G. E. Neale's with eighteen stores in 1901 and twenty-nine a decade later.[12]

In meat provisioning a similar situation existed. The number of retail butchers in Birmingham remained at approximately 650 between 1901 and 1911, and of this number only four had more than three shops locally. But these included very large concerns: Eastman's possessed thirty-nine stores in the city in 1901 and forty-seven in 1911, and James Nelson and Sons owned twenty-seven in 1901 and forty-five in 1911.[13] It would appear that with meat, as with other food products, neighborhood stores remained of overwhelming importance numerically, but that a multiple shop was within walking distance of anybody in the city.

There can be little doubt that, as in Pittsburgh, neighborhood shops were more expensive than the chain stores. Certainly Dr. Carver was scathing in his remarks about those working-class housewives stupid enough to buy at their local shops where the food was both dear and stale. Dr. Robertson, Birmingham's medical officer, agreed, disparaging the retail methods of small grocers and urging the poorer class of purchasers to make use of the city's Co-operative stores.[14]

Unfortunately it was not, as Carver suggested, mere consumer laziness that retained the corner shops' patronage. For the factors assuring the continued existence of higher-priced neighborhood stores in the American city were also present in Birmingham. The power of the small shopkeepers, the "local potentates," derived from their willingness to transact business in small amounts, to work long hours, and to extend credit to known customers.[15] They in turn, were often dependent upon credit facilities extended by wholesalers or manufacturers, further increasing the cost of the articles they sold. Benjamin Lilley, for instance, a leading supplier of Birmingham's milk to grocers, offered "special terms to cash customers."[16]

It was a situation with regard to which R. H. Best, a leading city brass manufacturer, and W. J. Davis, secretary of the National Society of Amalgamated Brassworkers, could share a common platform. Workers in Berlin, they were convinced, were able to purchase the necessities of life more cheaply than could workers in Birmingham because the "system of payment [was] always cash, all clothing, boots and food stuffs [were] paid for by *cash—no credit*" (authors' italics). Yet, as the Birmingham Chamber of Commerce noted, although the city's tradesmen "would no doubt [have welcomed] the universal adoption of a cash system . . . it [was] impracticable and impossible. . . . The credit system [was] of long standing, and [had] been almost universal." Without such a trade the weekly wage earner would have been seriously disadvantaged, for credit facilities were often of the utmost importance "especially in times of severe trade depression."[17]

The amount of trade that each individual grocer could carry "on tick" was probably small. Cadbury's survey of eighty-six corner-store retailers in the city found that the trader was usually the wife of a husband employed elsewhere, and that total family income averaged only 39s. ($9.50) per week. Credit extended was both small-scale and short-term. Inability to retrieve incurred debts swiftly and regularly meant that the local retailers themselves required credit, and they were sometimes forced to pawn temporarily the shop's scales and weights.[18]

The prevalence of credit trading and the precarious profitability of many neighborhood groceries were reflected in the unsuccessful attempt made by Birmingham retailers to stay the passage of the Debtors' Imprisonment Reform Bill. In 1907 the Retail Trades Section of the city's chamber of commerce petitioned the Lord Chancellor, pleading that few traders made unconscionable use of the process of the county courts for the purpose of recovering payment, and arguing that the aim was always to regain money, not to send the debtor to prison. The chancellor, however, remained "convinced that the use made of the Debtors' Act [was] oppressive to an extent which [called] for investigation." Perhaps he was aware that, unconscionable or not, Birmingham traders made extensive use of the act. Indeed, the Birmingham circuit court dealt with more debt plaints than any of the other fifty-eight circuits in England and Wales: in 1907, for example, more warrants were issued (3,532), and more debts claimed ($176,608) than elsewhere in the country.[19] When the promised investigation occurred, and a Parliamentary Select Committee was established, the section made an unsuccessful attempt to present evidence. The committee's chairman, concluded the chamber, was biased; the recommendations preordained; and the reform symbolic of "a distinct vein of weak and sickly sentiment" among certain politicians.[20] Yet many Birmingham workers, bound by credit arrangements to the higher-priced corner store and constantly worried about imprisonment for debt incurred due to illness, industrial accident, or unemployment, must have been grateful for such alleged moral cowardice.

Market Stalls, Hawkers and Hucksters

The competition faced by neighborhood provisioners from large-scale retailers was only part of their difficulties, for they viewed with equal disfavor market stall holders. Although neither the Board of Trade nor the BLS took cognizance of such salesmen, market facilities were an important sector of the food-retailing structure in both Pittsburgh and Birmingham. In the American city there were three main retail markets, housing approximately 150 butcher stalls, 330 vegetable stalls, and a variety of other facilities. In Birmingham there was one major retail market, situated on High Street at the Bull Ring and able to accomodate 600 stall-holders, and from 1897 there was a City Meat Market.[21]

Pittsburghers were convinced that the city's markets enabled perceptive shoppers to purchase food more cheaply than in the corner shop. Although Holdsworth found no uniform difference in the prices charged by the stall-holders of the Diamond Market compared to those current in neighborhood stores, he nevertheless believed that to "the careful buyer able to judge of quality and value the market [offered] undoubted advantages." The marketeer paid a license fee small in comparison to the rent required of a grocer, he incurred no delivery expenses, and—again perhaps most important—trade was strictly cash.[22]

The general belief that cheaper prices prevailed in the markets was reflected in a campaign against facilities judged inadequate. While Pittsburgh's North Side Market was praised as having "a bright, cheerful, cleanly appearance and with its various food products, neatly and nicely arranged, [showed] up like a beautiful department store," the larger Diamond Market was "old, dilapidated, wornout, unsanitary, overcrowded and unhealthy." Many Pittsburghers breathed a sigh of relief when the "generator of evil smells" was badly damaged by fire in December 1909, but in spite of local public agitation and repetitious statements of good intentions by council members, no new building was constructed until 1914. Until then, the market, "disgusting to the eye as well as to the nostril," and increasingly conducted on surrounding pavements, lacked the facilities "necessary for the preservation of the foodstuffs kept there for sale." Moreover, Sunday trading was frowned upon in the American city although, as in Birmingham, the sale of food necessities was allowed. It is not surprising, therefore, to discover that the "business merchants" of the Diamond Market offered "SPECIAL PRICES" on Saturdays.[23]

In Birmingham there seems to have been general satisfaction with the retail market facilities. It was claimed that the Market Hall afforded "ample accommodation for 'buying and selling' upon a scale . . . unequalled in any open market in the Kingdom." There can be little doubt that prices there were often less than the "predominant prices" collected by the Board of Trade. The Birmingham and District Butchers' and Pork Butchers' Trade Association was well aware of the danger posed to their trade by retailing in the market and forlornly hoped that this price-cutting competition could be "remedied."[24] The exact difference in price charged by independent butchers and by market stall-holders is impossible to gauge, however, for market prices altered radically according to the time of week. Moreover, the element of barter still existed, so that prices varied according to the bargaining skill of the purchaser and the amount of time remaining for vendors to sell their wares. Fresh herrings, for instance, which cost 2¢ each on Friday, were reduced to six for 8¢ by Saturday morning and by the evening of that day could be bought at eight for 4¢. Meat, sold not by weight but by piece, was offered by Dutch auction for whatever it would fetch after 8:30 P.M. on a Saturday; veal, for example, varied by as much as 16¢ a pound in one day! "Examples of this kind might be multiplied indefinitely," reported Dr. Carver, who was convinced that those many housewives who availed themselves of the city's market facilities showed far greater budgetary wisdom than those who, "through ignorance and laziness, [were] content to buy at the little shops round the corner, where food [was] neither so cheap nor so fresh."[25]

It is ironic that BLS investigators concentrated upon the gathering of information from stores patronized by Americans and old immigrant groups, for it was persons of these ethnic stocks who made the most substantial use of market facilities. While Pittsburgh's North Side Market and the Diamond Market were both crowded with stall-holders, the South Side market experienced a declining business in the post-1905 period, and by 1912 several leases were vacant. The reasons, believed the director of public works, lay in "the noticeable change taking place in the character of the population, due to a great influx of foreigners, who have opened stores and shops that are patronized by their fellow countrymen."[26] This social phenomenon helps to explain the continuing vigor of small shopkeeping in Pittsburgh compared to Birmingham: in 1911–1912 the American city possessed about two-and-a-half times as many provisioners as did the British town.[27] In the immigrant community, neighborhood stores received a stimulus far beyond those natural advantages derived from their convenient locality and long opening hours, their willingness to trade in small quantities, and their ability to extend short-term credit facilities: to a newcomer, unable to speak the language of his newly adopted country, shops managed by fellow countrymen provided a community in diaspora in which trading was easy and the food items familiar. Moreover, the alternatives to, and price disadvantages of, purchasing at the local grocer were less likely to reveal themselves to the new immigrant, unfamiliar with the city and unable to read the English newspapers. In short, the more recent the immigrant and the greater his ignorance of and alienation from American life, the more likely it was that he patronized the neighborhood store.

In effect, therefore, the persons who paid most for their foodstuffs were the group least able to afford it, the Italians and Slavs who labored in so many of Pittsburgh's unskilled occupations. The BLS series, although based upon stores in American, English, German, and Irish areas, may thus have provided—quite unintentionally—a far better guide to the prices paid by newer immigrants.

There existed, however, another group of retailers, with whom it is quite probable that immigrants, old and new alike, would have traded— the hucksters. These food peddlers were excluded from the BLS price investigation, yet in the summer of 1913 some 1,500 hucksters' wagons in Pittsburgh sold fully 30 percent of the city's consumption of fruit and vegetables. Milk, too, continued to be sold from horse-drawn wagons pulling "brass-bound hogsheads," a means of delivery as unhygienic as it was picturesque. Dr. J. F. Edwards, city superintendent of health, claimed that of the 60,000 gallons of milk drunk daily in Pittsburgh in 1908, one-sixth was still supplied by dairymen adjacent to the city, who sold directly from the wagon to the customer.[28]

There was no doubt among Pittsburghers that the prices charged by these street hawkers were less than those prevalent in grocery stores. "Practically every person agrees with me," wrote the superintendent of the city's Bureau of Food Inspection in 1912, that "the cheapest way to get the produce from the [railway] yard to home is through the medium of the huckster and peddler. These vendors have little expense save that of team and wagon." Others were less enthusiastic about the savings passed on by peddlers. A main objective of the Pittsburgh Retailers' Association was to eliminate what members viewed as unfair competition. But attempts by the storekeepers to make barrow business less profitable were attacked fiercely. "The grocers of Pittsburgh, who have a strong organization, but do not call it a union, oh, no! want to tax the hucksters out of business," commented the *National Labor Tribune*. "We hope this won't come to pass."[29]

The *Tribune* was not exaggerating. The ordinance proposed by the association in early 1907 would have required street peddlers to pay an

annual license fee of $25, together with a yearly charge of $225 for one
horse, $275 for two horses, or $125 for the possession of a handcart.
Unlicensed vendors would have been made to pay a penalty of $25 a
day. The motives of the retailers were quite openly admitted: it was
believed that such a law "would drive [peddlers] out of business."[30]
1907 was a bad year for Pittsburgh's retail food provisioners, however,
for their proposed city ordinance had as little success in reaching the
statute books as did their state garnishee bill.

Street sellers were as popular to the price-conscious "Brum" as they
were to the Pittsburgher. The *Daily Post* praised their contribution
toward reducing the cost of living in 1912, although the paper noted
that the vendors' enterprise was "much resented by the tradesmen,
who [had] rent, rates, lighting charges and servants to pay." The *Post*
was correct. The Birmingham Butchers' Association ineffectually
sought action against the presence of meat peddlers in the city, and the
Grocers' Association was incensed at "women hawking margarine
from door to door."[31]

Lower fixed costs were not the only reason why street peddlers were
able to undersell storekeepers. In November 1912 the *Post* cited a case
of Almera grapes which, from the barrow, cost only 4¢ a pound, in
spite of the fact that if they had been bought wholesale "in the cheapest market," the seller would have been "actually . . . losing money on
their sales." The explanation was that street peddlers were allowed to
buy sample produce from wholesalers, foodstuffs used for showroom
purposes and which, unsaleable in the ordinary way of trade, was sold
to the hawker at approximately half-price. The food thus offered in the
streets was still good although "the bloom [had] gone."[32] That, for
many Birmingham workers, was a small loss to incur for substantially
cheaper prices.

The Co-operative: Greatest Menace of the Day

The criticism of Birmingham's storekeepers was directed not so
much against street salesmen as against the "increased opposition and
unfair competition of the Multiple Shops and Cooperative Trading
concerns." And of these two enemies, it was the latter who incurred
most wrath from independent grocers. "Co-operative Societies," proposed a storekeepers' representative in a 1911 debate held at the local
YMCA, "Unfairly [Competed] with the Ordinary Shopkeeper." The
gist of his presentation was that cooperative stores, by their "accumu-
lation of capital [were] able to crush out the small private trader." This
formal argument was only a mild manifestation of a long and acrimo-

nious fight between the Birmingham Industrial Co-operative Society and the city's neighborhood storekeepers.[33]

Formed by a group of Duddeston railway men, the Birmingham Co-operative opened its first store in 1881 on Great Francis Street. Expansion came fast, with three branch shops and a bakery established in the following year, and the links with the national movement were quickly affirmed. All goods were purchased from the Co-operative Wholesale Society at Manchester, and in July 1882 the local branch paid its first subscription to the Co-operative Union. By the first decade of the twentieth century, the importance of the society in Birmingham's retailing structure was firmly established. When the Co-operative Congress was held in the city in 1906, the host store had twenty-one grocery branches and two butcher departments; by 1913 another seven groceries had been added, together with two more meat departments.[34]

This growth had been achieved in spite of fierce opposition from the city's neighborhood storekeepers, most notably from local members of the Private Traders' Defence Association, from the Retail Trades Section of the Birmingham Chamber of Commerce, and from the Birmingham Grocers' Association. The Co-op fought back. In November 1902, Co-operators granted £200 to the "Boycott Defence Fund," and in 1909 they had 12,000 leaflets printed and distributed to counter attacks in the local press. Such efforts were necessary, for according to the *Searchlight* in 1913, "every manufacturer in Birmingham [was] the deadly foe of co-operation [and] every store-keeper [and] every retail trader [regarded] co-operation as the greatest menace of the day." The Grocers' Association, through a Co-operative Subcommittee, waged a "determined fight against the evil of the Trade," although the nature of its attack precluded much evidence of this activity emerging. Members of the association were informed that their organization was "working quietly but persistently to destroy [the Co-operative Society's] benumbing effects upon trade." "It is a matter that must be done quietly in order that our opposition shall not serve them as an advertisement," continued the association furtively. "Full information cannot be communicated in this report, but can only be imparted to members present at the General Meetings."[35]

The charges against the Co-operative were many and varied. The Retail Trades Section of the Birmingham Chamber of Commerce felt particularly infuriated at the "unjust tax discrimination", whereby the Co-operative was exempted from direct assessment for the income tax. Co-operation was also viewed as a wedge for socialism; a harbinger of economic hardship (by forcing small shops to close, the Co-op was "responsible for more unemployment than any other cause"); and a cause of reductions in the rateable value of the town.[36] But the heart of the matter was that the Co-operatives "unfairly" undersold the individual small-shop retailer either directly or, indirectly, by the return of a substantial dividend every quarter.

Birmingham's independent grocers did indeed have cause for concern. As membership of the Co-operative rose rapidly between 1899 and 1914, the "struggle of the individual trader [got] harder . . . as the larger Co-operatives spread their branches over the ever expanding suburbs." However, to ascribe the Co-operative's success to cheap prices is highly dubious. The store vehemently denied that it was underselling the neighborhood storekeeper, and opponents were "unable to prove that Co-operative societies sold at cutting prices." Not all members were proud of this fact. According to one, Mr. Whitmarsh, the elitist nature of Co-operative membership was a direct result of the store's unwillingness to carry any other than superior grades of produce. "Scarcely without exception [members] belong to the artisan class, the better paid factory employee, and the man in regular employment; in fact the whole of the membership is drawn from these classes," he observed with disappointment. "While they are heartily welcome, we also require as members that multitude of low-paid workers who receive wages varying from £1 to 30s. weekly [but] the class of goods provided are quite beyond his earnings. . . . We should supplement our present trade by retailing a cheaper class of goods."[37]

The advertisements placed by the Co-operative substantiated Whitmarsh's assertion. The butcher departments, for example, sold "Best English Meat Only"; the grocery departments stocked nothing but provisions of "the *Highest Grade.*" Nor did Mrs. F. Stein, secretary of the local Co-operative Educational Committee, contest Whitmarsh's basic argument in her rejection of his conclusions. She accepted that the store traded only in high-grade commodities but dismissed the idea that this persuaded the lower ranks of the working class to shop elsewhere: "even the very poor can deal at the [Co-operative]", she asserted, so long as they could be taught "that a smaller quantity of the best article goes much further than a very cheap article."[38]

Other members shared Whitmarsh's concern that the Co-operative ignored the most needy section of the Birmingham populace. The secretary of the Emergency Fund believed that Co-operators were "a little further removed from the poverty line than sociologists [led him] to believe [was] the case with the working-classes generally." The reason for this de facto exclusion, it has often been argued, was that the Co-operative Society required payment in cash, whereas the small neighborhood stores were willing to trade "on tick." Moreover, in order to qualify for the dividend, customers were required to pay sixpence (12.2¢) entrance fee. An investigation of the situation in Birmingham suggests that perhaps too great an emphasis has been placed upon the significance of these factors.[39]

Although cash trading was usual in markets and with peddlers many workers purchased from these retailers. More significantly, the Co-operative's cash payment prerequisite became increasingly less rigid. Bread, for instance, could be bought on a weekly credit system, and the creation of an Emergency Fund in 1911 allowed customers credit facilities in times of distress due to "sickness, unemployment or other causes." The motives of the Birmingham Co-operative were explicit. "If the societies' cash trading rules were strictly adhered to," reported the *Wheatsheaf,* "members were possibly compelled to go to private traders who were prepared to give credit." To prevent this occurrence, temporary loans, issued in the form of coupons, could be secured so long as the customer in difficulty had been a Co-operative member for at least six months, had spent in excess of £5 in the previous half year, and possessed no withdrawable share capital.[40] Access to the fund claimed the secretary, J. McDowell, was "as easy as possible," with "no unnecessary formalities," and he expressed disappointment that few members made use of the facilities available. Finally, as has been noted, the debate within the membership as to why the poorer working class failed to join the Co-operative centered not upon the issue of cash trading but rather on the grade and price of items offered for sale.

According to the British *Enquiry* of 1909, working people had not organized any cooperative societies in Pittsburgh, although a number of organizations laid claim to such a title. The Leader Department Store, for instance, heralded itself as the "largest co-operative store in America," but it is difficult to discover what was implied by this boast. The shop, formerly Gusky's, appears to have been reorganized in 1904, and through John Cavanagh and Company it offered for sale 50,000 shares of preferred stock at $10 per share together with a bonus of one share of common stock. It was hoped that "every Tradesman, Merchant, Clerk, [and] Craftsman . . . [would] become profit sharers in this great enterprise." Stockholders were entitled to a "special discount on every purchase," but no mention was made either of the degree of control over managerial policy which they were to possess or who were the guiding lights of this enterprise. Just what happened to the store is unclear, although its post–1906 absence from newspaper advertisements leads one to suspect that its growth was less successful than its founders had predicted. Andrew Carnegie also boasted that he was responsible for the creation of a cooperative store at Braddock, just outside the city. In reality it appears to have been primarily a company store, supplied with cost-price coal by Carnegie and managed by a committee of workers. While the reputation of the cooperative retail movement had migrated to the American city, the reality remained firmly rooted in Britain.[41]

Quantity Incentives

In May 1912 Pittsburghers opened their daily newspapers to find advertised the city's newest retailing enterprise: the "Harrison System." The scheme appeared attractive. "JOIN OUR SYSTEM in co-operation with thousands of others and you can buy ONE ARTICLE direct from the factory, through us—at the same price and sometimes lower than your local merchant pays for the same goods." The finer print elaborated the means by which groceries, as well as furniture, clothing, and other dry goods, could be bought directly from manufacturers. Annual membership cost $4.00. Purchase was by mail, with a 25¢ delivery charge for any order under $10.00. Terms were strictly cash. But, explained the accompanying blurb, the system could save the $4.00 fee "on almost any $10.00 order." It is possible that this exaggerated claim had its foundation in truth, but only for members willing to purchase in relatively large amounts. The itemized list of savings instanced referred to goods bought in quantity: for fifteen pounds of sugar, five pounds of rice, or three packets of cereal or yeast.[42]

This emphasis upon quantity purchasing would not necessarily have deterred Pittsburgh workers. Indeed, the British Board of Trade investigation in 1909 expressed surprise at the extent to which the city's food retailers indulged in such practices. "Inducements are held out to customers to buy two or more units of a commodity instead of one unit," reported the board. "It is common to sell two or more pounds of coffee at a considerable reduction on the price of a single pound." Sugar, too, noted the British investigators, was "generally bought in large quantities."[43]

The board saw this as a major contrast to the situation in Britain, where the working class was loath to purchase even in one-pound units. "The poor," it was claimed by exasperated middle-class reformers, bought "their tea by the ounce, or sometimes by the halfpenny-worth; . . . nothing could be more uneconomical." Often no specific vegetable was purchased, but rather "a pennyworth of pot-herbs," a mixed bunch of carrots, turnips, and onions, which were added to stews made from meat "pieces." Others, more sympathetic to those women who "practically made the stores [their] pantry," argued that their shopping reflected not budgetary incompetence but financial stringency: many working-class housewives simply could not afford to buy food for more than one day ahead. Hallsworth and Davies of the Shop Assistants' Union were skeptical. They believed that "frequent buying of small quantities of food [was] not necessarily by reason of tight purses." Certainly other factors appear to have been influential. The general lack of storage space in British homes, the difficulty of protecting food from mice and other vermin, and the necessity to limit the amount of food consumed by the family—all contributed to small-scale purchasing.[44]

Nevertheless, Birmingham housewives willing and able to purchase foodstuffs in quantity could make substantial savings. Budgetary returns from local families in the summer of 1900 revealed that a number of items could be bought relatively cheaply if more than a single unit was purchased. Details are given in Table 30. However, it was families with relatively high weekly income (from $8.77 to $10.24 per week in 1914), the "aristocracy" of Birmingham's laboring classes, who made use of the benefits to be derived from large-scale purchasing. Families in this income group were able to obtain checks from a society of tradesmen that could be presented in full or partial payment to one or more of the retailers forming the society. The family could then pay off the checks by weekly installments. Dr. Carver viewed such schemes with caution, noting the potential dangers to the buyer if income decreased for some reason, but he also accepted that participation in such a credit system allowed consumers to obtain better value for their money by enabling them to buy goods in quantity.[45]

Table 30
Prices for 5 Commodities Bought in Quantity: Birmingham, 1900

| Commodity | Price per lb. (¢) | Price in Quantity | | | Saving per lb[a] (%) |
		Price (¢)	Quantity (lb.)	Price per lb. (¢)	
Oatmeal	6.1	36.7	7.0	5.2	14.3
Potatoes	1.8	6.1	6.0	1.0	43.2
Sugar	3.9	14.3	4.0	3.6	8.9
Jam	10.5	21.4	3.0	7.1	32.3
Syrup	9.2	11.2	2.0	5.6	38.9

Source: Great Britain, Board of Trade, *Report on Wholesale and Retail Prices in the United Kingdom in 1902, With Comparative Statistical Tables for a Number of Years, British Parliamentary Papers,* Cd. 321, 1903, Vol. 68, Pt. 3, "Prices Paid by Certain Families in the United Kingdom, 1900–1901."

a. Calculated from original pence data.

There can be little doubt that Pittsburgh's workers bought in larger quantities than did the laboring force of Birmingham. British observers remarked upon the greater frequency with which items were sold in units of more than one pound in the American city. Coffee and sugar were the goods most often offered as "quantity incentives," but firms advertising in the local labor press presented a wide range of groceries in quantity discounts. Marshell's, for example, offered onions in half-peck units, vinegar in gallons, ketchup in quarts, flour in 49-pound bags, and ginger, cinnamon, and nutmegs in pounds rather than ounces; the Great Atlantic and Pacific Tea Company advertised soup in quarts, cans of milk in threes, and boxes of matches in dozens; Henry Deutschmann's quoted prices for beef ribs, chuck roast, veal chops, and pork sausages in 2-pound units, liver pudding in 3-pound units, and bacon in quantities of from 3 to 5 pounds; Chester's Grocery cited prices for cans of milk in threes; Donahoe's offered special prices on 2-pound packages of roasted coffee; McCann's quoted reduced prices on 3-pound and 5-pound bags of coffee; and Weldon's on 3-pound packs of butter.[46]

Workers who read such advertisements were doubtless tempted by the quantity incentives offered by chain and department stores. One Braddock worker found that by traveling into Pittsburgh "every fourth Saturday afternoon" and buying supplies "for the next month," it was possible to save "one third." Yet the amount that could be gained by purchasing more than a single unit of an item varied enormously, and in some cases the shopper profited not at all. Quantity savings also varied substantially between stores. Analysis of 116 quantity incentives offered at Kaufmann's between 1899 and 1912 showed that 51.7 percent of offers resulted in less than a 6 percent saving (per standard unit) to the purchaser. In contrast, avowed savings at Charters' were generally between 30 and 50 percent (see Table 31). Savings also reflected the quantity purchased. A positive relationship existed between the percentages saved and the increase in the quantity bought. The modal average saving for goods acquired at Kaufmann's in up to three times the normal quantity was from zero to 3.0 percent; the average saving for items that required the shopper to buy from three to six times the amount customarily purchased ranged from 3.1 to 6.0 percent; and the average saving for commodities bought in excess of six times the normal amount was from 6.1 to 12 percent.[47]

Stores employed no neat mathematical formula to calculate quantity offers. This was apparent from analysis of the prices of stocked canned goods at Kaufmann's. Throughout the twelve years of statistics recorded for that store, the price per dozen cans relative to the price of a

single can varied little. Thus twelve 7¢ cans of produce could almost
always be obtained for 75¢, and so on. The complete list of prices for
canned goods, bought individually and in dozens, is given in Table 32.
It shows that the amount saved by purchasing a dozen cans at one time
bore little relation to the price of a single can. The percentage advantage gained by buying in quantity was in general higher for lower-
priced articles (11¢ or less), but there was no clear correlation between

Table 31
Prices for Items Bought in Quantity at S. B. Charters: Pittsburgh, May, 1900

| Product | Per Standard Unit | | In Quantity | | Saving per Unit (%) |
	Price (¢)	Quantity (Unit)	Price (¢)	Quantity (Unit)	
Currants	10.0	lb.	25.0	4 lbs.	37.5
Prunes	12.5	lb.	25.0	3 lbs.	33.3
Prunes	10.0	lb.	25.0	4 lbs.	37.5
Prunes	5.0	lb.	25.0	7 lbs.	28.6
Stove polish (enameline)	5.0	box	10.0	3 boxes	33.3
Soap (laundry)	5.0	bar	25.0	10 bars	50.0
Coffee	20.0	lb.	55.0	3 lbs.	8.4
"Home-made" bread	5.0	loaf	25.0	7 loaves	28.6
Strawberry preserve	10.0	jar	25.0	3 jars	16.7
Bartlett pears	12.5	can	25.0	3 cans	33.3
Baked beans	12.5	can	25.0	3 cans	33.3
Cornstarch	7.0	packet	25.0	7 packets	49.0
Root beer extract	10.0	bottle	25.0	5 bottles	50.0
Lemon extract	10.0	bottle	25.0	6 bottles	58.3
Graham bread	5.0	loaf	10.0	3 loaves	33.3
Canned goods	n.s.		25.0	4 cans	n.c.
Tomatoes	n.s.		13.0	gal. can	n.c.
Rolled oats	n.s.		25.0	11 lbs.	n.c.
Washing soda	n.s.		10.0	10 lbs.	n.c.
Bottled goods	n.s.		25.0	6 bottles	n.c.
Ketchup	n.s.		35.0	gal. jug	n.c.
Doughnuts	n.s.		10.0	15	n.c.
Rhubarb	n.s.		5.0	3 lg. bunches	n.c.
Potatoes	n.s.		50.0	bushel	n.c.
Butter	n.s.		25.0	2 lbs.	n.c.
Eggs	n.s.		25.0	2 doz.	n.c.
Flour	n.s.		98.0	49 lb. bag	n.c.
Macaroni	n.s.		25.0	6 lbs.	n.c.
Cornmeal (yellow)	n.s.		12.0	10 lb. bag	n.c.
Cornmeal (white)	n.s.		25.0	15 lb. bag	n.c.
Matches	n.s.		12.0	2,400 matches	n.c.

Source: Pittsburgh Dispatch, 5 May, 12 May 1900 (advertisements).
Note: n.s. = not stated; n.c. = not calculable

the price of one unit and the price of twelve. The key factor appears to have been Kaufmann's desire to quote neatly rounded prices—divisible by nickel units—for the dozen articles.

The mean financial gain made by buying a dozen of each of the priced cans in Table 32, 6.6 percent, was small considering the outlay required of the purchaser. This may be attributed to the fact that the saving was consistently offered, and it suggests that the far greater savings that could be made by purchasing foodstuffs in quantity at Charters' were related to the limited period for which they were offered. In brief, it appears likely that the more substantial quantity incentives advertised by Pittsburgh's stores were either "leaders" designed to attract customers and/or a means of clearing shelves of slow-moving stock. The most significant savings Kaufmann's offered were for items that were advertised infrequently—for example, rice, marmalade, soup, pickles, sauce, and maple syrup. Those commodities generally selected as quantity incentives—lard, tea, prunes, coffee, and flour—afforded the shopper relatively minor savings.

Seasonality

It was a fact well appreciated by contemporaries that food prices fluctuated with the seasons. "The rich," claimed F. J. Cross in 1912, "eat early strawberries that cost 20/- a pound; early peas at 5/- a pound; and early potatoes at a 1/- a pound; all of which can be bought later in the season at a tenth of the cost or less." Similarly, Albert Halstead noted that early in the season, when tomatoes came from

Table 32
Prices of Canned Goods Bought in Quantity at Kaufmann's: Pittsburgh, 1900–1913

Price per Can (Purchased Singly) (¢)	Price per Dozen Cans (¢)	Price per Can (Purchased in a Dozen) (¢)	Saving per Can (%)
7.0	75.0	6.25	10.7
8.0	90.0	7.50	6.3
9.0	100.0	8.33	7.4
10.0	110.0	9.17	8.3
11.0	120.0	10.00	9.1
12.0	135.0	11.25	6.3
13.0	150.0	12.50	3.8
14.0	160.0	13.30	5.0
15.0	175.0	14.17	5.5
17.0	195.0	16.25	4.4

Source: Pittsburgh Dispatch, 1900–1913 (advertisements).

heated greenhouses, they cost 20¢ per pound, but by mid-September they were selling at Birmingham greengrocers and fruiterers for from 8¢ to 12¢ per pound.[48] Yet no contemporary seems to have made a systematic study of the relationship of retail price to season. For the British city, indeed, no relevant data appear to have survived. Fortunately, after 1907 the BLS quoted prices for every other month, and after 1911 for every month. By employing these Pittsburgh data, I was able to estimate seasonal fluctuations in retail price for ten food commodities for the 1907–1913 period.[49]

Table 33 estimates the seasonal component in price for every second month. It is clear that seasonal upward movement of prices was not experienced concurrently in the various products. In general, the cheapest time of year for food was in January/March, but with butter, eggs, and milk the opposite was true, seasonal factors advancing retail prices in winter and lowering them in summer. Moreover, the degree of price fluctuation that can be attributed to the seasonal component varied enormously from item to item.

This becomes more obvious if, as in Table 34, the seasonal factor (1907–1913) is expressed as a percentage of the 1910 mean retail price. Although dairy products fluctuated in price against the "trend," the variation in their prices was of much greater significance than that of all the other items except potatoes. The seasonal component in the price of mutton and cornmeal was quite marked; that in sugar and

Table 33
Seasonal Component of Food Retail Prices in Cents: Pittsburgh, 1907–1913

Commodity	Quantity	Seasonal Component (¢)					
		Jan.	*Mar.*	*May*	*July*	*Sept.*	*Nov.*
Beef ribs	lb.	−0.13	−0.09	+0.40	−0.11	+0.05	−0.12
Butter	lb.	+4.51	+1.21	−2.10	−2.93	−1.56	+1.88
Cornmeal	lb.	−0.04	−0.04	−0.04	−0.02	+0.02	+0.11
Eggs	dozen	+9.10	−2.96	−5.60	−4.41	−2.05	+5.58
Flour	⅛bbl.	−0.52	−0.39	+0.18	+0.38	+0.06	+0.30
Milk	Amer. qt.	+0.48	+0.41	−0.39	−0.52	−0.41	+0.43
Leg of mutton	lb.	−0.11	+0.16	+0.74	−0.10	−0.17	−0.52
Pork chops	lb.	−0.67	−0.05	+0.14	+0.18	+0.44	−0.05
Potatoes	peck	−0.11	−0.53	+0.95	+4.37	−2.00	−2.67
Sugar	lb.	−0.03	−0.03	−0.17	+0.05	+0.14	+0.09

Source: U. S. Bureau of Labor, *Bulletin*, No. 105 (1912); U.S. Bureau of Labor Statistics, *Bulletin*, Nos. 115, 125, 132, 136, 138, 140 (1912–1914). For the price statistics, see Appendix Table 8.

Note: + Seasonal component increased the price.

− Seasonal component decreased the price.

pork less so; and that in beef and flour scarcely registered at all. For most items, beef ribs being the exception, the price movement attributable to seasonality (SPM) was greater than the average annual price movement from 1907 to 1913 (APM). Thus the seasonal movement in the price of eggs (14.2 percent) was far greater than the secular annual increase (0.8 percent). Expressed differently, the annual rise in the price of eggs due to seasonality represented almost twenty years of secular price movement (based upon 1907 to 1913), while the annual variation in the price of potatoes attributable to seasonality was equivalent to almost thirty years of secular price movement.[50]

Studies of prices are usually dominated by the attempt to establish annual movements in the cost of living. The significance of enormous price variations within each year is too often ignored. Yet from the standpoint of the turn-of-the-century consumer, the price movement within the year may have been, at least for dairy products, potatoes, and cornmeal, as significant as the long-term advance in average annual prices. It follows, given the substantial element of seasonality in food prices before the First World War, that the real grocery expenditure available to Pittsburgh and Birmingham housewives fluctuated considerably from month to month. Shopping decisions—when to buy, in what quantities, from where—presented a complex problem, one that the "official" statistics too easily hid. The historian, like the buyer, must beware.

Table 34
Seasonal Component of Food Retail Prices as Percentage of 1910 Price: Pittsburgh,
1907–1913

Commodity	1910 Mean Price (¢)	(Quantity)	Seasonal Component[a] (Expressed As a % of 1910 Price) Jan.	March	May	July	Sept.	Nov.
Beef ribs	18.7	lb.	−0.7	−0.5	2.1	−0.6	0.3	−0.6
Butter	35.1	lb.	12.9	3.5	−6.0	−11.2	−4.4	5.4
Cornmeal	2.7	lb.	−1.5	−1.5	−1.1	−1.1	0.7	4.0
Eggs	29.7	doz.	30.6	−10.0	−18.9	−14.8	−6.9	18.8
Flour	85.5	⅛ bbl.	−0.6	−0.5	0.2	0.5	0.1	0.4
Milk	8.2	Amer. qt.	5.9	5.0	−4.8	−6.3	−5.0	5.2
Mutton leg	16.5	lb.	−0.7	1.0	4.5	−0.6	−1.0	−3.2
Pork chops	19.0	lb.	−3.5	−0.3	0.7	0.9	2.3	−0.3
Potatoes	26.2	peck	−0.4	−2.0	3.6	16.7	−7.6	−10.2
Sugar	6.1	lb.	−0.5	−1.3	−2.8	0.8	2.3	1.5

Source: See Table 33.
Note: − Monthly price was below 1910 mean price.
a. Seasonal component based upon 7-year period, 1907–1913.

7

Rent

Comparative Rents

Apart from food, rent was the most important item of working-class expenditure in both Birmingham and Pittsburgh, and comparative analysis of the manual workers' standard of living in those cities must incorporate the price tenants had to pay for accommodation. Such a calculation is fraught with difficulty, and the qualifications attached to the estimation of an "average" rental must be explicitly stated. Evidence from the American city, for instance, reveals that it was not merely the quality of the housing that determined the rental charged. Other criteria were influential.

First, rents varied according to the ethnic origin of the tenants, and it would seem that those groups comprising the lower ranks of Pittsburgh's labor force were treated in discriminatory fashion. "The immigrants in general, like the negroes, appear to pay more in rent than Americans or German-Americans for similar accommodation," noted the British *Enquiry* of 1909. There were a number of possible reasons for this. Contemporaries argued that the saleable value of real estate declined in areas in which immigrants became predominant, and that property owners attempted to recoup their losses by increasing the rentable value of their property. Moreover, the higher rents charged new immigrants may have reflected the restraints placed upon the landlords' ability to let property in the future, to the extent that the range of potential tenants for houses or apartments vacated by such immigrants was more limited than for premises vacated by Americans. "When Poles, the poorer immigrants, enter a neighborhood in which English-speaking people live the property depreciates," claimed the visiting British delegation. "Just as in Southern cities houses once occupied by negroes cannot afterwards find white tenants, so in Pittsburgh, houses occupied by Poles and other Slavs or Italians are rarely taken later by American, German, or British-American tenants."[1]

Other factors were also at work. The immigrants' ignorance of the American environment, their strong desire to live in areas in which fellow countrymen predominated, and their wish—given their low income and lack of English—to reside within walking distance of their place of employment made the discriminatory pricing of landlords easier to enforce.

Second, rents varied according to the area of the city in which houses were located. For a similar quality of accommodation, "the lower income classes of Pittsburgh [were] paying relatively higher rents" than their wealthier neighbors. Rents also advanced more rapidly in the Soho-Hill and Lawrenceville-Bloomfield areas (inhabited chiefly by wage workers) than in nearby Shadyside and Squirrel Hill (in which were situated the homes of more prosperous businessmen and professionals).[2] Given such influences upon rent levels, I found it imperative to employ rent data collected from a wide selection of dwelling types located in different areas and housing workers of diverse ethnic origins.

The most useful rent surveys were those undertaken by the British Board of Trade in Pittsburgh in February 1909 and in Birmingham and Sheffield in October 1905 and May 1912. Investigators gathered rent data from working-class areas throughout the city, for residences ranging in size from two to six rooms. Comparison reveals that the cost of rented accommodation in Pittsburgh was far dearer than in either of the British cities. Table 35 indicates that rents in Pittsburgh were almost two-and-a-half times those in Birmingham: the median rent for three rooms was 144.2 percent greater; that for four rooms 158.2 percent greater; that for five rooms 155.7 percent greater; and that for six rooms 136.9 percent greater.[3]

The difference between the levels of rent in the two cities was therefore far wider than that between the levels of food prices, and in many cases the increased money wage received in Pittsburgh would have been insufficient compensation for the higher cost of rented accommodation. A Birmingham building laborer, for example, would have had to work 9.8 hours to pay the median rent for a four-room house in 1909, while his counterpart in Pittsburgh would have been obliged to work 11.6 hours to provide a similar residence; a third-hand baker would have had to labor 11.8 hours in Pittsburgh in order to pay rent on three rooms, but only 9.0 hours in Birmingham.[4]

In Birmingham rents remained static between 1905 and 1912. Indeed, the evidence of Consul Halstead suggests that no upward movement had occurred since 1900. After exhaustive investigations he was convinced that rents in 1910 had been stationary for a decade. "This does not mean that in every district of the city the rents remain the same," he noted. On the contrary, "while in one section they may have risen a little in others they have fallen a little, thus keeping the balance even. . . . This is despite the increase of local taxation for the period." Other contemporary comment emphasized the rent stability of the Midlands city. Evidence submitted to the Birmingham Special Housing Inquiry indicated that the rent for three rooms in 1913 ranged from 3.5 to 5s., identical with the range reported in 1905 and 1912.[5]

Information on the movement of rents in Pittsburgh is scantier, although there exists evidence of similar stability. Certainly the Pittsburgh Railways Company, presenting data secured from four large real estate agents in 1914, claimed that house rents of less than $25 per month had remained static since 1908–1909. This argument was accepted by the majority of arbitrators, who reported that they were "satisfied that during the [previous] few years house rents, as distinct from business rents, [had] not increased in Pittsburgh."[6]

The stability of Pittsburgh rents between 1908 and 1914 paralleled the national trend.[7] Aggregated data suggest that a substantial increase in the cost of America's rented accommodation occurred between 1900 and 1907, and it is likely that this rent inflation was also experienced in the Iron City.[8] If the movement of rents in Pittsburgh had been identical to that estimated for the United States, and if the rent plateau attested to by Birmingham contemporaries was genuine, then the transatlantic difference in the cost of rented accommodation would have been less at the beginning of the twentieth-century than thereafter: based upon such premises, the median rent in Pittsburgh in 1900 was 118.0 percent greater than in Birmingham, compared to 148.8 percent greater in 1909.[9]

Back-To-Backs and Tunnel-Backs

Rents, it is apparent, were considerably higher in Pittsburgh. Yet it is possible that the standard of housing rented in the American city was superior to that of the Birmingham workers, and that the difference in rents reflected, at least to some degree, a difference in the quality of accommodation. Initial investigation warrants such an interpretation. Consul Halstead, for instance, believed that the accommodation available to workingmen in Birmingham was "not really satisfactory and [did] not offer the same conveniences as workmen of the same class in the United States [required]." Samuel Gompers, president of the A.F. of L., echoed Halstead's sentiments. Visiting Britain, he "naturally looked for the counterpart of the neat, convenient, and well-fitted-up bathroom to which so many . . . wage-earners [were] accustomed when living at the American standard." Instead he was shown "in some places a tub sunk in the kitchen flooring and covered with a trap-door, and in others a sort of closet with a cold-water faucet

Table 35

Predominant Weekly Rents for Working-Class Accommodation: Pittsburgh, Birmingham, and Sheffield, 1905, 1909, and 1912

A. Weekly Rents in Pittsburgh, February 1909

Rooms Rented	Rent Range[a]	Midpoint of Range
2	$1.62–$2.08	$1.85
3	$2.08–$3.00	$2.54
4	$2.76–$4.16	$3.46
5	$3.46–$4.62	$4.04
6	$4.16–$5.08	$4.62

B. Weekly Rents in Birmingham and Sheffield, October 1905 and May 1912

	Birmingham 1905		Birmingham 1912		Sheffield 1905		Sheffield 1912	
Rooms Rented	Rent Range[a]	Mid-point	Rent Range[a]	Mid-point	Rent Range[a]	Mid-point	Rent Range[a]	Mid-point
3	$0.85–$1.22	$1.04	as for 1905		$0.91–$1.10	$1.01	$0.85–$1.10	$0.93
4	$1.22–$1.46	$1.34	as for 1905		$1.10–$1.34	$1.22	$1.10–$1.46	$1.28
5	$1.34–$1.83	$1.58	as for 1905		$1.34–$1.64	$1.49	$1.34–$1.58	$1.46
6	$1.58–$2.31	$1.95	as for 1905		not stated		not stated	

C. Rents in Pittsburgh, Birmingham, and Sheffield Compared, February 1909

Rooms Rented	Pittsburgh Rent Compared with Birmingham Rent[b]	Pittsburgh Rent Compared with Sheffield Rent[b]
3	+144.2%	+154.0%
4	+158.2	+176.8
5	+155.7	+173.0
6	+136.9	
3–5[c]	+152.7	+167.9
3–6[c]	+148.8	

Sources: Great Britain, Board of Trade, *Report of an Enquiry . . . into Working Class Rents, Housing and Retail Prices, Together with the Rates of Wages in Certain Occupations in the Principal Industrial Towns of the United States of America. British Parliamentary Papers,* Cd. 5609, 1911, Vol. 88; Great Britain, Board of Trade, *Report of an Enquiry . . . into Working Class Rents, Housing, Retail Prices and Standard Rates of Wages in the United Kingdom, British Parliamentary Papers,* Cd. 6955, 1913, Vol. 63.

a. Rents include rates and local taxes in all cities.

b. Assumes Birmingham rents as in 1905 and 1912, and that Sheffield rents were $1.00 (3 rooms), $1.25 (4 rooms), and $1.48 (5 rooms).

c. Mean of midpoint comparisons.

near the ceiling for a shower, the cement flooring answering for a tub."[10]

To some extent, such comments were valid. Birmingham City Council was acutely aware of the existence of thousands of houses lacking adequate sanitation or ventilation and which failed to provide sufficient privacy for their occupants. Such dwellings, frequently situated amid factories and workshops, meant "that a large proportion of the poor in Birmingham were living under conditions of housing detrimental both to their health and morals." In effect, submitted George Cadbury, Jr., chairman of the Housing and Town Planning Committee, the overcrowded and defective housing conditions in which many of the city's workers lived resulted in an "astounding . . . loss, socially and industrially," to the local community. The strength of the nation and, indeed, of the British Empire was sapped at its heart.[11]

The "bugbear of housing reformers in Birmingham" was the large number of "back-to-back" houses situated in the congested central area of the city. Built, in general, between 1830 and 1875, their construction had been made illegal by the Housing Act of 1909. Yet by 1914 43,000 such dwellings still existed in Birmingham, and they continued to provide the bulk of cheap accommodation. Table 36 shows that in the inner city wards, in which rentals were lowest, the majority of houses were back-to-back.[12]

Typically, the back-to-back comprised one-quarter of a three-story building, with one room on each floor. Most possessed neither hall nor scullery, and as a result the kitchen had to be lived in. No garden was attached but behind the building lay a paved courtyard, entered by a side alley which also provided access to the house. It was here that the toilets and wash-houses were built, often ramshackle wooden constructs giving the appearance of embarrassed afterthoughts. Dingy and dark, back-to-backs became remembered as "a squalid mass of insanitary hovels crowded around sunless courts."[13]

Yet criticism of the back-to-back houses must be qualified. It is true that they provided little through ventilation, that those houses facing north gained no direct sunlight, and that the smallness of the rooms and lack of storage facilities for foodstuffs made living conditions cramped. However, there were compensations. If kept in reasonable repair, they were comfortable and easy to clean; many possessed a cellar in which wood and coal could be stored; and, most importantly, they could be kept warm far more cheaply than any other form of house. "Back-to-back houses should not be condemned because they are back-to-back," argued John Robertson, city medical officer of health. "If the owner likes to keep them in a reasonable state of repair, I do not think I could assert that they are unfit for habitation."[14]

The primary problem of the back-to-back was, as the American consul noted, the communal nature of the washing and sanitary facilities.[15] Few back-to-back houses had running water laid on, and even superior types of accommodation often provided no separate toilet. In four cen-

Table 36
Housing Conditions by Ward: Birmingham, 1913

	Description of Houses				
Ward	Under $1.22 per Week	Back-to-Back	In Courts	No Water in House	No Separate Toilet
St. Mary's[b]	48%	56%	36%	50%	66%
St. Bartholomew's[b]	45	47	29	39	59
St. Martin's and Deritend[b]	44	56	36	51	71
Duddeston and Nechell's[b]	43	40	29	44	62
St. Paul's[b]	49	63	42	58	74
Market Hall[b]	31	54	34	51	68
Ladywood[b]	36	57	35	47	69
Rotton Park	27	31	18	23	41
Aston	20	24	18	19	30
All Saints'	29	34	19	31	45
Soho	7	6	2	9	10
Washwood Heath	8	5	2	8	11
Saltley	6	4	4	6	8
Lozell's	16	25	16	22	28
Sparkbrook	10	10	7	10	15
Small Heath	5	6	3	5	8
Balsall Heath	9	10	6	17	24
Acock's Green	4	0	0	4	2
Selly Oak	5	3	1	3	5
Edgbaston	10	20	11	19	24
Harborne	6	2	0	12	11
Yardley	6	3	0	6	3
Sparkhill	2	0	0	4	2
Sandwell	1	2	1	2	3
Handsworth	2	3	2	4	4
Erdington North	5	1	0	6	6
Erdington South	2	0	0	1	2
Moseley and King's Heath	3	1	0	5	5
Northfield	22[a]	3	1	14	10
King's Norton	5	1	0	6	5

Source: Birmingham, Medical Officer of Health, *Annual Report,* 1913.
a. Largely country cottages.
b. Inner-city wards.

tral wards more than half of the homes had no indoor water supply, and in seven wards more than half had no individual closet.[16] Inevitably, privacy was encroached upon and hygiene endangered.

These shortcomings were accentuated by the deplorable state into which many of Birmingham's outbuildings had lapsed. Some social workers attributed the degeneration of courtyard facilities to the behavior of residents. Arthur T. Wallis, organizing secretary of Birmingham's Adult Schools, suggested that problems began when Jews moved into a building. "Jews will not sit on the same seat as Gentiles," he claimed. "They therefore stand on the seat, and cause an abominable mess." Dr. Robertson noted that numbers of men, unwilling to use the courtyard closets, used the passage to the yard as a urinal. Others, however, stressed the impact of the environment. The fact that courtyards were open to any who chose to enter meant that facilities were far more subject to vandalism, and the continued dependence of many buildings upon pan (rather than water) closets and the insufficient number of closets provided made it extremely difficult to keep toilets clean.[17]

Housing outside the central city area was generally of a higher standard, five-room terrace houses of more recent construction predominating. Known as "tunnel-backs" by virtue of their extended, narrow appearance, such dwellings possessed a front parlor, living room, scullery with sink, and, in the back garden, a coal shed and toilet; above the parlor and living room were situated two bedrooms.[18] Only rarely was the toilet placed within the house, or a bathroom included. Nevertheless, many Birmingham workers, living in back-to-backs, must have aspired to tunnel-back living, for the toilet was private, an interior tap and sink were provided, and the front room could be arranged to display the trinkets and treasures that had been accumulated by the family. As employees gained in economic status, they frequently departed their inner city wards in order to secure superior living accommodations. It was "usual with the Birmingham people, as they [advanced] financially, to move into better houses, and better neighbourhoods," claimed Dr. Carver. There was "none of that clinging to a particular locality, which [was] so noticeable in the Londoner."[19]

Without wishing to appear complacent, one may hypothesize that the housing of Birmingham's working-class families was in general adequate. By contemporary standards, it might well have been classed as superior. Robert Sherard, traveling England in 1899, found that Birmingham's slums were far less horrifying than many he had visited in other urban areas. Birmingham, he suggested, did "not flaunt its vices and its poverty, as [did] so many other cities." The proud boast of

Birmingham's civic leaders that the city had "little to learn as regards the Housing Problem from Continental cities" was not entirely vain-glorious, for the back-to-backs, in spite of their defects, were—as many observers agreed—probably much healthier than the high block tenements found elsewhere. Properly regulated, kept in a decent state of repair, provided with a sufficient number of clean water closets, and with courtyards open to the sun, the back-to-back could provide comfortable accommodation.[20]

And in the early twentieth century, a zealous group of reform councillors, brought together in the city's Housing Committee, provided the regulatory vigor and necessary leadership to improve working-class housing. Although they refused to countenance municipal home construction, on the grounds that it would have been financially unwise and would have deterred private enterprise, they encouraged contractors to build more and better houses. More importantly, in the short term, they exercised considerable power under part 2 of the Housing Act of 1890 and sections 17 and 18 of the act of 1909. Given the authority to close substandard houses until made habitable once more, or, at their discretion, to order demolition, the committee spurred landlords to upgrade the condition of their premises. Where threat was insufficient, the committee acted. Between 1900 and 1912, 3,082 houses were rendered habitable under threat of demolition.[21]

Other substantial improvements accompanied this work. Virtually all the unsanitary pan closets were replaced by water closets: between 1904 and 1913, 20,000–25,000 were removed under pressure from the medical officer of health, and by the latter year only 1,000 remained. Numbers of dark courts were opened to the streets, and small open spaces and playgrounds were created in the more congested areas of the city. Moreover, the Birmingham Corporation (Consolidation) Act of 1883 enabled the council to order landlords to effect relatively minor repairs: at the zenith of activity in 1913, no less than 28,265 houses had drainage and sanitation defects remedied, damp courses put in, windows opened, or roofs mended.[22]

Such activity was, of course, only partially successful. Indeed, the Housing Inquiry of 1914, basing its arguments upon the data presented in Table 37, admitted that in order to provide totally adequate accommodation for Birmingham's working class, the erection of at least 50,000 houses was required. Yet the extent of housing improvement already undertaken impressed most contemporaries. A local taxpayers' association, which viewed critically the actions and expenditure of the city council, "noted with satisfaction [the effort] being made to cope with the Housing Problem of the poorer classes." Halstead, while believing Birmingham's housing to be inferior to that in the United States, nevertheless informed the American Senate that the council was "pursuing an intelligent policy requiring . . . improvements in the houses of the workingmen." The rapid impact of such activity, believed fellow American Lee Galloway, was enormous: visiting the city in 1914, after an absence of nine years, the New York University academic found the people to be healthier, happier and far more vigorous thanks to the benevolent intervention of the " 'directing classes' of Birmingham."[23]

Tenements and Terraces

In Pittsburgh, by contrast, there existed no council body with the necessary drive or sufficient power to wield effective control over the city's housing environment. If conditions had matched the "American standard" suggested by Halstead and Gompers, this might not have been important. But for most Pittsburgh workers housing accommodation appears to have been no better and, perhaps was even worse than for their counterparts across the Atlantic.

Most English travelers to Pittsburgh were rudely shocked by the manner in which the city's workers were housed. It was not just the "higgledy-piggledy buildings of the town" and the "narrow thoroughfares" which dismayed members of the Mosely Commission, nor was it merely the "overhanging dense pall of black and white smoke" continuously emitted from the city's "sulphorous mills and furnaces." The homes themselves appeared unsatisfactory. M. Deller of the National Association of Operative Plasterers claimed that Pittsburgh's slums "would even make some of [Britain's] own look, comparatively speaking, like palaces. Fancy a court, to get through the entrance to which one had to walk sideways; this was my own and companions' experi-

Table 37
Housing Conditions: Birmingham, 1914: an Aggregate Picture

Description of Residence	Number
Houses at rentals under $2.44 per week	149,228
Houses at rentals under $1.40 per week	67,052
Back-to-back residences	43,366
Courtyard residences	27,518
Residences with no inside water supply	42,020
Residences with no separate toilet	58,028

Source: Birmingham, *Report of the Special Housing Committee* (Birmingham, 1914), p. 6.

ence." Arthur Shadwell agreed. Indeed, the extreme grime and squalor of Pittsburgh reminded him of a stage through which English manufacturing towns had already passed. Viewing the "exhibition of modern and recently built slums" in which Pittsburgh's workers lived, he had no hesitation in proclaiming that Sheffield was, in comparison, "a pleasure resort." Even the British Iron Trade Association, generally eulogistic of American working conditions, believed Pittsburgh's housing to be poor and realized that such factors had to be offset against the higher wages earned by the city's employees.[24]

Many Pittsburghers were acutely aware of the inadequacy of much of their city's housing, and organizations to rectify the situation proliferated in the early twentieth century. The Civic Club of Allegheny County, the Pittsburgh Chamber of Commerce, and the Civic Commission all established committees to investigate the problem and make recommendations for action. In 1911 these groups concerted their efforts in a joint group, the Housing Conference, to prepare an effective housing code for the city. Social settlements, too, agitated with vigor. The director of the Kingsley House Settlements, William Matthews, was particularly active in exposing the deficiences of workers' accommodation, and he received support from Samuel Ely Eliot, headworker of the Woods Run Settlement.[25]

A few Pittsburghers were led to try their own remedies. In 1903 a group of citizens established themselves as a stock company, the Tenement Improvement Company, and succeeded in erecting one five-story model building. But they found it difficult to pay the required dividends, and further plans "for building of model tenements on a business basis" lapsed. However, Henry Phipps, the steel magnate, was impressed by such schemes, and in 1908 he constructed a sixty-apartment tenement in order "to furnish comfortable homes for working people at a reasonable rent." The most substantial individual effort was that undertaken by Henry J. Heinz. Aggrieved by the red-light district surrounding his North Side factory, he quietly gained possession of hundreds of the nearby properties in 1909 and 1910, repaired them, and let them out to "decent people." His paternalistic interest probably aroused as much resentment as thankfulness, for he hired private detectives to investigate the credentials of his tenants. "Go back through their records for fifteen years, if necessary . . . so that we'll be sure of every tenant," he is reputed to have told them.[26]

It is clear, then, that many Pittsburghers were concerned with the low quality of much of the city's housing. "Slumming parties" became a popular pastime for those interested in the welfare of the workers, and "one poor old woman, living in a miserable shanty, . . . was visited by at least four such parties in one week." In part such interest resulted from morbid curiosity, and in part from genuine feelings of humanitarianism. But it also reflected, as in Birmingham, a realization of the loss to the community that resulted from inadequate home conditions. The chamber of commerce argued that bad houses, like bad water, sewerage facilities, or air, were "a species of indirect taxation upon business interests, not only as taxpayers but in their effect upon output," and its president, H. D. W. English, a prominent insurance executive, claimed that new manufacturers refused to locate in Pittsburgh because of the poor accommodations for workers. English and an articulate group of fellow business leaders were convinced that the apathetic attitude of many of their colleagues to working-class housing was short-sighted and in marked contrast to their usual attitude toward economic problems. "Pittsburgh manufacturers are noted the world over for their readiness to scrap obsolete machinery in order to *replace with more efficient apparatus*," the chamber's Committee on Housing Conditions reported in 1911. "Why would it not be *just as good investment to scrap obsolete housing* in order to obtain more efficient workmen?" (author's italics).[27]

Yet such agitation bore little fruit. The early twentieth-century bosses William Flinn and Chris Magee paid little heed to the demands of reform groups, and even the weak regulatory powers possessed by the city were enforced only rarely.[28] In 1906, after four years of political chaos, a Democratic reform candidate named George Guthrie was elected mayor of Pittsburgh and there followed a brief period of intensive activity. The divisions of Sanitary Inspection and Tenement House Inspection were, for the first time, adequately staffed and financed and, more importantly, were urged to execute their duties with vigor. The result was remarkable. Privy vault toilets had been illegal since January 1901, but until the appointment of Charles K. Smith as chief sanitary inspector, the law "had never been enforced except in a few instances on complaints received." Under Smith the uniformed sanitary policemen were urged to prosecute offenders: in consequence, whereas only 47 illegal privies were reported in 1905, 7,755 were discovered in 1907.[29]

Although many business leaders supported Guthrie's efforts, workers were less enthusiastic. The *Iron City Trades Journal* led a strong campaign against the mayor in 1909, claiming that "the spectacle of the Mayor's office being run by the Chamber of Commerce and other like institutions [had] been presented to the citizens of Pittsburgh with a vengeance. Pink tea politics," it was scathingly argued, had "been played to a finish and the silk stocking element catered to at the expense of the wage-earners generally." Many workers appear to have thought similarly. In 1909 William Magee, nephew to the previous boss, beat Guthrie in the mayoralty contest, and although the Department of Health continued to gain council support, its early enthusiasm seems to have waned. The Civic Club reported in 1912 that enforcement of the city's sanitary code had "not been very stringent" and that building laws had been "passed with no appropriation to make them effective."[30]

What then were the housing conditions against which Pittsburgh reformers fought? Undoubtedly the majority of informed criticism, and the bulk of housing legislation enacted by state and city government, applied to tenements. Yet Dr. J. F. Edwards, the active superintendent of Pittsburgh's Department of Health and a member of the city's Housing Conference, contended "that Pittsburgh's problem [was] not one of tenements at all, it [was] one of single and 2-family houses."[31]

The paradox is readily explained. Legally, *tenements* referred to buildings specifically designed to accommodate families in self-contained apartments: in such dwellings the city had the authority to ensure that each resident had at least 400 cubic feet of room space and that no resident lived in the cellar. There were few such buildings, although the number constructed increased as the century progressed. More generally, however, tenements were deemed to be buildings that contained three or more families, no matter for what purpose they had originally been constructed. Tenements, in this broader sense, were numerous in Pittsburgh. A census undertaken by the city's Bureau of Health in 1908 revealed the existence of 3,364 such tenements, in which lived 45,899 persons—8.8 percent of the total population. By the end of 1912 their number had risen to 4,311 and, assuming that they possessed the same mean number of residents as in 1908, 10.7 percent of Pittsburgh's population dwelt in them. Virtually all those who lived in tenements were manual workers.[32]

Those tenements not originally designed to hold more than two families, and over which the city held little regulatory power, were the bane of housing reformers. Amid the freight yards and factories of downtown Pittsburgh stood "rows of old-fashioned houses made into forlorn-looking tenements" crowded with the poorer members of the city's working class. Pittsburgh's story is familiar. The demise of proud family residences into squalid, ill-repaired tenements is a recurrent theme in American urban history. In the mid-nineteenth century the flat areas bordering the Allegheny and Monongahela rivers had been sought-after residential zones. But increasingly mills and factories encroached on the districts, and as commercial and manufacturing activity increased, the original residents departed. In their place came an army of workers, eager to live close to their employment. They could scarcely afford to pay the large rentals required for such residences, and still less could they purchase them. As a result, landlords, desirous of attaining maximum income from their properties, subdivided the houses. By the early twentieth century, dwellings originally intended to house one family in elegance housed three or four, "crowded in often without much regard to the sanitary requirements of light, ventilation and toilet accommodations."[33] Such buildings comprised 75.4 percent of Pittsburgh's tenements in 1912.

Thus Soho, situated on the north bank of the Monongahela and once the "garden spot of Pittsburgh," was by 1900 one of the most crowded tenement areas of the city. Decrepit residences vied for space with the sidings of the Baltimore and Ohio Railroad, the mills of the National Tube Company, and the Bessemer converters of Jones and Laughlin. Similarly, the "Strip" an area bordered on the south by the passenger yards of the Pennsylvania railroad and on the north by the Allegheny River, had originally been a middle-class residential section. As the incursion of industry had taken place, construction of new houses had been halted and the large family residences converted into makeshift tenements. By 1915 there was "terrible overcrowding in the one and two family houses" that stood between the mills, factories, and railway sidings. The area had become "the hog trough of Pittsburgh."[34]

Such tenements were generally in a dilapidated state. Property owners, knowing that their houses were situated in declining residential areas, were unwilling to make repairs. Nor did the economics of renting require landlords to make improvements, for "houses which in fact should no longer [have been] considered habitable [were] readily occupied at a comparatively good rental." In tenements actually built to accommodate three or more families, conditions were more satisfactory. Not until 1903 was a law introduced regulating the construction of such buildings, however, and most apartments were as dark, cramped, and ill-ventilated as Birmingham's back-to-backs. Interior rooms had windows opening onto an alley or narrow light shaft, forecourts were practically unknown, and rear yards small. Nevertheless, unlike family residences converted into tenements, in which water and toilet facilities were communal, apartments in these buildings were usually self-contained.[35]

The other common form of worker's dwelling in Pittsburgh was the undetached terraced house. On the north bank of the Monongahela, for example, rows of company houses, wall-to-wall, lined a series of parallel streets running from east to west, each street following the contour of the hillside—the "steppes of Soho." Such houses were not markedly superior to those in Birmingham. Generally possessing three or four rooms of dimensions similar to those in the British city, their water supply and toilets were frequently situated in a small backyard. Typical was the row of twenty-eight houses on Glenwood Avenue, rented to American workmen employed in the nearby railway repair shops. The street door opened directly into the parlor, the residence possessed no yard, and the toilet was placed in a small cellar. Four rooms contained a total of 552 square feet of living space, compared to 598 square feet in the normal Birmingham tunnel-back and 478.5 square feet in the three-story back-to-back.[36]

In Pittsburgh, as in Birmingham, the most pressing housing problem was the inadequate water and sewerage facilities supplied to workers. By 1900 only 110 miles of the city's 450 miles of streets were adequately sewered, and even in 1917 one could still witness raw sewage running through open gutters. Dry closet vaults (equivalent to the English pan closet) abounded in spite of their illegality. Their conditions were, as numerous contemporary critics noted, "indescribable." Emptied rarely, they stank and were difficult to keep clean. In tenements, where such toilet facilities had to be shared, conditions were worst, and the privies acted as a catalyst for contagious diseases with deadly efficiency. Often situated in muddy, unpaved courtyards, the wooden closet sheds were "of the flimsiest character," provided little privacy, were cramped (2.5' by 3.5' was normal), had no lights for use at night, and were often slept in by derelicts.[37]

Under Mayor Guthrie the privy vault nuisance was tackled at last. Nevertheless, even in 1909 Pittsburgh's director of the Department of Public Health, E. R. Walters, could claim that at least 18,000 illegal vaults were still in use. And even when landlords were forced to provide water closets for their tenants they usually installed "only the very cheapest kind" whose cisterns possessed inadequate flushing capacity.[38]

Washing facilities were also inadequate. Frequently the only source of running water was an outside spigot, and in many terraced houses one had to fetch water from a communal tap. Bathrooms may have been the "American standard," but few Pittsburgh manual workers possessed such a luxury. J. Boyd Duff, addressing a meeting of the Pittsburgh Merchants' and Manufacturers' Association in 1906 and citing data gathered by the city's Bureau of Water, claimed that there were only 20,000 bathtubs in the entire city—roughly one for every five premises or one for every twenty-five residents.[39]

Concerned citizens responded to this situation by financing public washing facilities. The city's recorder stressed the "great necessity" of building public baths as early as 1901, but the council responded with typical lethargy, and it was left to private enterprise to set the pace. By 1910 the Civic Club, in conjunction with the city council, operated baths in Soho; the Kingsley House, Woods Run Settlement, Covode House, and Irene Kaufmann Settlement all provided washing facilities for the surrounding neighborhood at certain hours; the Public Wash House and Baths of the Pittsburgh Association ran similar enterprises; and the city's Playground Association provided public baths daily at two of its parks. Yet Kate McKnight, president of the Civic Club, was probably correct when she alleged that many more public baths were needed before one could "feel assured that the laboring classes [were] being even decently cared for in the matter of necessary cleanliness."[40]

In short, Pittsburgh's manual workers did not enjoy toilet and washing facilities superior to those available to their counterparts in Birmingham. The conclusion of the British Board of Trade investigators in Pittsburgh echoes the comments made by Consul Halstead in Birmingham. "Bathrooms are rare in working men's houses, builders having only just begun to put them in dwellings of this class. A water-tap is found in the kitchen in the better houses, but often the only water supply is from a hydrant in the yard, sometimes so placed on the boundary between two houses that it may serve for both."[41] Further, there seems little reason to conclude that the overall quality of accommodation received by Pittsburghers was superior to that afforded to workers in Birmingham. Indeed, there are two reasons why it might be argued that the standard of housing was inferior in the American city.

First, Pittsburgh's manual workers appear to have been more crowded. At least until 1913–1914, the problem that concerned Birmingham's reformers was "the quality rather than the quantity of working men's dwellings." Although more "decent houses" were required, there was, contended Dr. Robertson, practically no overcrowding: there were sufficient houses, distributed throughout the city, to accommodate its population. There existed "no immediate small house famine in Birmingham."[42]

In Pittsburgh crowding presented far more of a problem. The city's commercial and industrial premises, and the workers employed within them, were crammed along the narrow strips of flat land bordering the waterways. In these river wards conditions were dreadfully congested. The greatest concentration of population occurred in wards 7 and 8, the Hill district, where there were "practically no breathing spaces except Washington Park, all available space being occupied for buildings." Workers lived amid the factories on the level plain or hung precariously to the nearby hillside. Theodore Dreiser vividly remembered the steeply climbing side streets, unpaved and muddy, where "one found, invariably, uniform grey houses, closely built and dulled by smoke and grime, and below, on the flats behind the mill, . . . clustered alleys . . . unsightly and unsanitary."[43]

Related to those "three R's in Pittsburgh which [were] not advantages for cheap housing plans . . . ridges, rivers and ravines" was the inferior transportation system available to workers in Pittsburgh. In many areas only an inclined plane could cope with the problem of conveying people up and down the hills dividing the city. Since the "inclines" were a slow and expensive form of transport, most workers preferred to live within walking distance of mills and workshops.[44]

It was not merely the physical characteristics of Pittsburgh that persuaded the city's workers to crowd into such a confined area. The street railway facilities provided by the Pittsburgh Railways Company were, even where they did operate, inferior to the tram service managed by Birmingham City Council. In the British city one could travel long distances for a penny (2¢), and many workers were willing to live in areas removed from their employment. Rents "in the crowded part of the city [had] decreased," it was reported in 1910, "by reason of the construction of street-car lines which [enabled] people to live in less crowded areas." In Pittsburgh, however, the minimum tram fare was substantially more expensive (5¢), and the quality of transportation provided was far worse.[45]

The construction of the street railway lines had been poorly executed, so that cars bumped and rattled over "ill laid metal rails, along the wretchedly made and worse kept roadway." The passenger service extended was clearly unable to meet the demands made upon it. Virtually all visitors to Pittsburgh were astounded by the crowded nature of the city's public transportation. The British unionist T. Jones found that Pittsburghers recognized "no such things as overcrowding: you [hung] on anywhere without let or hindrance." Residents of the city were in apparent accord. Colonel Church, a Pittsburgh eminent, claimed in 1907 that the "present rapid transit system [had] long ceased to be civilized and [was] . . . immoral and . . . rapidly becoming indecent." The *Searchlight* was in agreement, alleging that Pittsburghers were deprived of the public transport they deserved and instead faced an "intolerable method of human freightage." And the *Kingsley House Record* contended that Pittsburgh was "unrivaled in the number of passengers its car conductors [could] crowd into one small car."[46]

Second, working-class houses in Pittsburgh appear to have been less sturdily constructed than those in Birmingham. For all their defects, virtually all houses in the British city were built of brick, whereas many residences in Pittsburgh were wooden. The 1912 census of tenements found that no less than 36.5 percent of the 4,311 buildings were constructed of wood, and in some areas in which manual workers resided, the figure was substantially greater. In Ward 6, 46.1 percent of tenements were wooden; in Ward 16, 55.6 percent; in Ward 17, 53.4 percent and in Ward 24 no less than 82.6 percent. Such dwellings were more predominant in these riverside working-class areas not only because "cheaply constructed wood structures" provided a low-priced form of housing, but also because they were often intended to have only a limited life span. Floods were frequent. "No one referred them to man's criminal folly in deforesting the hills and over-grazing the plains," Mary Roberts Rinehart recorded. "They came, were lived through, and came again." In consequence, "flimsy frame buildings were established on the flats annually inundated by the spring floods." Sometimes their inhabitants were able to tie a skiff to the windowsill, retire to the upper floor, wait for the river to subside, and then return downstairs to shovel out the thick layers of deposited silt; on other occasions substantial rebuilding was required.[47] It was a seasonal activity that Brums, ensconced in their solidly constructed, if dank, brick houses, or walking the footpaths of the city's calm canals, would have found difficult to understand.

8

Fuel, Clothing, Furniture

Coal, Kerosene, and Candles: Gas and Electricity

Black diamonds. That was the term frequently employed to describe the magnificently rich coal resources upon which Pittsburgh's industrial expansion had so largely been based. The city was surrounded by bituminous coalfields 14,000 square miles in area, with ten-foot veins cropping out of nearby hills and banks, and its permanent haze bore somber witness to the relentless speed with which its manufacturers consumed apparently limitless supplies of coal.[1] But it was not only industry that prospered from Pittsburgh's mineral wealth. In an era in which open fires and iron cooking ranges predominated, the cost of coal was an equally significant factor in determining domestic fuel expenditure, and Pittsburgh's locational advantage resulted in retail prices which—by contemporary American standards—were extremely cheap. "Pittsburgh consumers," noted a local coal operator and banker, had "been abundantly supplied with the various grades of coal required at average prices as low or lower than [had] been current in any other consuming market in the United States."[2] In January 1912, to select an example at random, Pittsburghers could buy bituminous coal at $3.53 per ton (2240 pounds). At the time workers in Omaha, Nebraska, paid $6.16 to $7.84; in New Orleans, $7.39 to $7.47; and in Portland, Oregon, $10.64 to $11.20. In New York and Philadelphia, only the more expensive anthracite coal was readily available, in the former city generally selling at $7.28, and in the latter at $6.75 to $7.25.[3]

Both Birmingham and Sheffield experienced similar locational advantages in respect to coal supply, and workers in those cities paid prices for coal far less than those that prevailed in the English capital. Indeed, the relatively low cost of living in Sheffield in 1905 was "largely explained by the cheapness of coal."[4] The crucial question for this study was the comparative cost of coal to the domestic consumer in such "cheap" towns on different sides of the Atlantic.

It was not easy to provide an accurate answer to this question. One problem, for instance, was assessment of the quality of the coal consumed. In both Pittsburgh and Birmingham, bituminous coal was the most widely bought fuel, but within the broad category there existed a large range of possible qualities. In the British city quality varied from Class One coal, known locally as "Cannock Deep," which burned with very little ash, gave forth a great heat, and was "as good a quality bituminous coal as [was] obtainable" to "slack," a poor fuel, slow to ignite, and comparable in quality to coal sold as "run of the mine" in the United States. Fragmentary evidence available suggested that most Birmingham workers purchased a medium grade described as Class Two.[5] The quality of Class Two probably approximated that of the bituminous coal "Pittsburgh Gas," generally used by workers in the American city. Certainly the Pittsburgh coal, sometimes sold as "one-and-one fourth inch Lump," was much superior to the fine screenings bought in times of financial exigency.[6]

Far more than with most commodities, the cost of coal varied according to one's location within the city. In large measure this was because coal, generally sold in 76-pound "bushels" in Pittsburgh and in 112-pound "hundredweights" in Birmingham, had to be delivered to the consumer's residence, and prices were adjusted according to the time and effort involved in this task. In Birmingham, for example, workers able to purchase directly from the local mines could obtain all grades of coal at $1.58 cheaper per ton than those who had to buy from city dealers. Again, coal cost substantially less in the eastern neighborhoods of Sheffield closest to the local pits.[7]

Pittsburgh's hilly topography resulted in a more unusual pricing structure. Coal delivered to homes situated "on the level" sold at 8.2 percent less than coal delivered to workers who lived "on the hill." Moreover, merchants refused to sell quantities of less than fifty bushels "on the hill," although there existed no such limitation for those who resided on the plain beneath. As a result there were in Pittsburgh middlemen who bought wagonloads of coal and then resold their purchase in smaller quantities, permitting consumers to buy any amount from a pail to bushel sack. In winter these vendors, the equivalent of the grocery hucksters, were a familiar sight in Pittsburgh. Many a worker on night shift, attempting to sleep through the day, must have "sworn and fussed over the long drawn cries of the coal vendor with his tiresome but still musical yell of co-le-co-le, as his rickety old wagon [jolted] along the streets and alleys."[8]

Table 38 presents data on the cost of coal in Birmingham for the 1900–1912 period. Price fluctuations were substantial, with sharp increases being followed by equally precipitous decreases.[9] Table 39 reveals that in contrast, Pittsburgh's bituminous coal prices remained stable until increases occurred in 1912–1913.[10] At all times coal cost more in the British cities. Table 42 indicates that in 1912 a ton of bituminous coal, delivered to the door, cost $4.47–$4.87 in Birmingham, and $4.06–$4.87 in Sheffield, whereas in Pittsburgh a similar quantity would have been sold for $3.65: assuming that the midpoint price may be taken as average, coal was 27.9 percent more expensive in Birmingham and 22.5 percent more expensive in Sheffield. Earlier differentials were even greater: in 1907, when Birmingham prices were at their high-water mark, coal was 50.7 percent dearer.

Coal, then, was cheap for the Pittsburgh consumer, relative both to contemporary American and British standards. Nevertheless, most of the city's workers did not use coal for cooking. For not only was Pittsburgh located close to some of the finest coal reserves in the United States, but also the city lay adjacent to another great fuel resource—natural gas. Substantially cheaper than manufactured gas (costing only 25 percent as much in 1907), yet possessing a higher heat content, piped natural gas provided a source of inexpensive fuel and lighting for the majority of Pittsburgh's domestic consumers. Aside

Table 38
Coal Prices: Birmingham, 1900–1912

Date	Type of Coal[a]	Price per Ton[b]	Index[c]
1900	Class one	$5.48–$5.60	
	Class two	$4.87–$4.99	93.1
	Slack	$3.53–$3.78	
1900 (Sept.)	All grades	"extraordinary increase"	
1905 (Oct.)	Class two?	$3.25–$4.06	69.0
1907	Class one	$5.84–$5.96	
	Class two	$5.23–$5.35	100.0
	Slack	$3.65–$3.78	
1908	All grades	Price decline	
1910	Class one	$5.23–$5.35	
	Class two	$4.63–$4.75	88.5
	Slack	$3.05–$3.17	
1911	All grades	Price decline	
1912 (Jan.)	All grades	Price decline	
1912 (Oct.)	Class two?	$4.47–$4.87	88.1

Sources: U. S. Senate, *Wages and Prices Abroad*, 61st Cong., 2nd sess., 1910 (hereafter referred to as Halstead, "Report on Prices"); Great Britain, Board of Trade, *Report of an Enquiry . . . into Working Class Rents, Housing, Retail Prices and Standard Rates of Wages in the United Kingdom, British Parliamentary Papers,* Cd. 6955, 1913, Vol. 63.
a. Bituminous coal
b. Ton of 2240 lbs.
c. Based on class two coal.

from being "cheaper than coal," natural gas was "clean and safe." There was "no coal to carry or ashes to haul away." Women didn't "roast to death cooking in summer."[11]

So manifest were the apparent advantages that by 1900 the city's chamber of commerce Special Committee on Smoke Prevention could claim that there existed "but few households . . . which [used] coal, since natural gas [was] generally used for all domestic purposes." An English visitor noted in some astonishment that "almost every dwelling in Pittsburgh's densely populated districts was furnished with pipes to supply the gas."[12] Yet the future of natural gas did not necessarily burn brightly. Even when the chamber's committee filed its optimistic report, there remained concern that the quantity of gas sent to Pittsburgh would not suffice to meet advancing demand.

As early as 1875 natural gas was being piped seventeen miles from the Harvey well in Butler County to two Pittsburgh manufacturing establishments. But it was the ebullient entrepreneur George Westinghouse who first appreciated the full potential of the gas deposits lying in a vast subterranean semicircle twenty miles to the east of the city. In 1884 he organized the Philadelphia Company to bore wells and pipe the gas to consumers, commercial and private, in Pittsburgh. By the beginning of 1885, he had 7 gas wells in operation; within a year there were 45. By 1900 the company controlled 416 gas wells, serviced 1,000 miles of pipeline, and, having pursued a successful policy of acquiring competitive enterprises, held a commanding position within the local market.[13]

As with petroleum, however, boring proved easier than storing, and huge amounts of released gas were wastefully burned off when demand

Table 39
Coal Prices: Pittsburgh, 1907–1913

Year	Price of coal per ton[a]	Index
1907	$3.51	100.0
1908	$3.51	100.0
1909	$3.51	100.0
1910	$3.51	100.0
1911	$3.51	100.0
1912	$3.65	104.0
1913	$3.73	106.3

Source: U.S. Bureau of Labor, *Bulletin,* No. 105 (1912); U.S. Bureau of Labor Statistics, *Bulletin,* Nos. 115, 125, 136, 138 (1912–1914)

a. Bituminous coal per ton of 2240 lbs.: mean price charged by five coal retailers.

proved insufficient to consume available supplies. The blazing chimneys which, providing a safety valve for excess natural gas, flamed throughout the night and cast an eerie glow across the city, became as familiar to the Pittsburgher as the constant sulfurous smell emitted from the district's steel mills. Such behavior, as prodigal as it was spectacular, meant that the initial discoveries of natural gas were rapidly depleted. As companies had to search farther afield for gas resources, prices rose, and this development, together with the uncertainties of supply which resulted from the greatly fluctuating domestic demand, persuaded many manufacturing enterprises to return to using coal. By the turn of the twentieth century the pall of black smoke, which had lightened somewhat as Pittsburgh's industrial establishments had converted to gas, darkened once more. The short "season of cloudless skies and clean shirt fronts" was over.[14]

To many Pittsburghers it seemed only a matter of time before domestic consumers too would be deprived of the natural gas supplies which they had come to depend upon. The Philadelphia Company, anticipating such an eventuality, acquired Brunot Island in the city to serve as a convenient site for manufacturing gas. However, three factors combined to assure workers that they would continue to enjoy the benefits of natural gas. First, the introduction of compressing stations allowed available gas supplies to be used more effectively; second, the institution of gas metering helped to eliminate undue wastage; and third, new and larger natural gas deposits were discovered in Armstrong, Washington, and Greene counties, and—further removed—in West Virginia. The exploitation of these deposits, together with increased efficiency in production and distribution, enabled the Philadelphia Company to provide an increasing number of domestic consumers with natural gas. In 1900 the company sold 19.9 million cubic feet of gas to 29,000 consumers. By 1910 sales had advanced 82.3 percent, the company's 902 gas wells and more than 2,300 miles of pipeline supplying over 100,000 Pittsburghers; and by 1912 sales exceeded 40.5 million cubic feet to 117,000 consumers.[15]

Birmingham possessed no such supply of natural gas, but the manufactured product was widely used. By the first decade of the twentieth century, fishtail gas jets had become standard fixtures in most houses, the popularity of gas as a lighting agent increasing with the introduction of the incandescent burner. An increasing proportion of the city's manual workers also used gas cookers to supplement their coal ranges.[16]

In large part, the progressive policy of the city's municipally owned Gas Department accounted for the increasing demand for gas from

Birmingham workers. From 1908 the department undertook to clean and adjust gas burners and to fix and supply mantles for a small charge, thereby eliminating many of the difficulties encountered by consumers in servicing their light fittings. Gas cookers were also readily available to working-class consumers. By 1900 workers could either buy a cooker from the department upon an installment plan or else rent a stove for 2¢ to 3¢ a week; and from November 1903 gas cookers were issued free to customers using prepayment meters. This latter development caused the Birmingham Ironmongers' Association considerable chagrin and resulted in a fierce campaign against "municipal trading." A resolution was sent to the city council proclaiming that the association viewed "with alarm the action of the . . . Council in supplying free gas-stoves to householders; it [considered] such a course decidedly detrimental to their interests as hardware tradesmen and ratepayers." The Lord Mayor remained unimpressed, replying that the new policy would effectively increase the ironmongers' trade by creating demand for cooking utensils suitable for gas stoves. The free issuance of cookers to prepayment consumers continued, and such customers comprised an increasing share of the market. By 1913 more than half of Birmingham's domestic gas users were buying their fuel under the "penny-in-the-slot" system.[17]

How then did prices compare in Pittsburgh and Birmingham? In the American city prices, certainly after 1907, were stable. Table 40 indicates that the price of manufactured gas was stationary at $1.00 per thousand cubic feet. Natural gas—far more important to the domestic consumer—advanced slowly in price, following a much-resented price hike by the Philadelphia Company in May 1907. The increase from 25.0¢ to 27.5¢ per thousand cubic feet remained in force until 1914, and the city's smaller competing suppliers slowly fell into line.[18] In contrast Table 41 reveals that the cost of gas fell in Birmingham. Between 1903 and 1912 the price of gas fell by 25.7 percent for consumers supplied via prepayment meters, and by 23.3 percent for consumers supplied direct. Thus the price of gas was becoming cheaper to the Birmingham worker relative to his Pittsburgh counterpart.

Nevertheless, in absolute terms, gas fuel, like coal, remained substantially cheaper to Pittsburghers. Table 42 indicates that in 1907 the price was 134.2 percent more expensive in Birmingham, and in 1912 67.4 percent dearer. It is true that the provision of cookers, installation of fittings, and servicing of equipment was cheaper in the British city. Whereas Birmingham's workers could acquire a gas cooker and fittings free if they were supplied via prepayment meters, workers in Pittsburgh had to pay for such services and equipment. But against this must be weighed the fact that the natural gas enjoyed in Pittsburgh would have had a greater heat content than the manufactured gas supplied in Birmingham, so that if comparison were made of thermal units (rather than of cubic feet of gas), the difference in price would appear even greater.

Although coal and gas provided the mainstay of heating and lighting requirements in both cities, kerosene remained an important item in the fuel bill. In Birmingham most families paid 16.3¢ per gallon for Daylight Petroleum in 1900, but a superior grade, White Rose Petroleum, cost 24.4¢. By 1910 the price of Daylight had risen by 12.5

Table 40
Gas Prices: Pittsburgh, 1899–1913

Year[a]	Natural Gas Mean Price[b]	Natural Gas Domestic Price[b]	Manufactured Gas Price[b]	Natural Gas Domestic Price (index numbers)	Manufactured Gas Price (index numbers)
1899	12.5¢				
1900	13.0				
1901	13.3				
1902	13.3				
1903	14.1				
1904	14.7				
1905	14.2				
1906	14.3	25.0¢		96.2	
1907	16.2	26.0	100.0¢	100.0	100.0
1908	16.2	26.5	100.0	101.9	100.0
1909	16.0	26.5	100.0	101.9	100.0
1910	n.c.	27.5	100.0	105.8	100.0
1911	17.3	27.5	100.0	105.8	100.0
1912	16.7	27.9	100.0	107.3	100.0
1913		27.9	100.0	107.3	100.0

Sources: Prices have been calculated from U.S. Bureau of Labor, *Bulletin*, No. 105 (1912); U. S. Bureau of Labor Statistics, *Bulletin*, Nos. 125, 132, 138 (1912–1914); Philadelphia Company, *Annual Reports of the Board of Directors . . . to the Stockholders*, No. 15 (year ending 31 Mar. 1899) through No. 30 (year ending 31 Mar. 1914); [Pittsburgh] *Searchlight*, 1 Oct. 1907.

Note: n. c. = not calculable. The mean price of natural gas in Pittsburgh included the sale of large quantities to industrial and commercial enterprises; to the extent that the price movement of "industrial" gas varied from the movement of "domestic" gas, and to the extent that the sales ratio of "industrial"/"domestic" gas altered, then so far did the mean price trend vary from the domestic price trend.

a. For the mean price of natural gas the year refers to the twelve months ending March 31 following the year specified; for the domestic price of natural gas and for manufactured gas the year refers to April 15 of the year stated, and in 1912–1913, refers to the price charged in both April and October of the year stated.

b. Price per 1,000 cubic feet.

percent to 18.3¢, while the price of White Rose had fallen by 16.7 percent to 20.3¢.[19] In Pittsburgh in 1909, kerosene cost 17.4–21.6¢.[20] Thus, as Table 43 indicates, the cost of kerosene was almost identical in the two cities.

Other components of the fuel bill were of relatively little domestic significance in the 1900s. Birmingham workers still purchased half-penny candles (1.0¢) or, more economically, bought wax to manufacture their own candles at 10.2¢ per pound.[21] However, candles were by now subsidiary to paraffin lamps and fishtail gas jets as a source of lighting; essentially they provided a means of illuminating one's way up narrow, creaking stairways to the bedroom, or of lighting one's nightly trips to the outside toilet.

Although candles were of declining significance, electricity was of increasing importance as a source of power. In Birmingham the Electrical Supply Department, which had become municipalized at the beginning of the century, posed a potential threat to the Gas Department,

Table 41
Gas Prices: Birmingham, 1899–1913

Year	Gas Price				Index Number			
	A	B	C	D	A	B	C	D
1899	60.9¢	56.8¢			100.0	93.3		
1900	67.0	62.9	84.6¢		110.0	103.3	108.6	
1901	67.0	62.9	84.6		110.0	103.3	108.6	
1902	60.9	62.9	84.6		110.0	103.3	108.6	
1903	60.9	60.9	78.1	65.5¢	100.0	100.0	103.0	100.0
1904	60.9	60.9	78.1	65.5	100.0	100.0	100.0	100.0
1905	60.9	60.9	78.1	65.5	100.0	100.0	100.0	100.0
1906	60.9	60.9	78.1	65.5	100.0	100.0	100.0	100.0
1907	60.9	60.9	78.1	65.5	100.0	100.0	100.0	100.0
1908	56.8	56.8	72.5	61.5	93.3	93.3	92.8	93.9
1909	56.8	56.8	72.5	61.5	93.3	93.3	92.8	93.9
1910	56.8	56.8	72.5	61.5	93.3	93.3	92.8	93.9
1911	52.8	52.8	65.5	68.9	86.7	86.7	83.9	88.5
1912	46.7	46.7	58.0	52.0	76.7	76.7	74.3	79.4
1913	46.7	46.7	58.0	52.0	76.7	76.7	74.3	79.4

Sources: Charles Anthony Vince, *History of the Corporation of Birmingham*, Vol. 4, "1900–1915" (Birmingham, 1923), pp. 400, 415; *Birmingham Magazine of Arts and Industries*, 3, No. 2 (1901).

Note: A. Price per 1,000 cubic feet when under 25,000 cubic feet used.

B. Price per 1,000 cubic feet when 25,000–50,000 cubic feet used.

C. Price per 1,000 cubic feet for prepayment meter customers (if gas department supplied fittings free).

D. Price per 1,000 cubic feet for prepayment meter customers (if fittings provided by customer).

especially as the price of supply became increasingly competitive. In
1900–1901 the average price per unit (presumably per kilowatt) was
8.9¢; by 1906–1907, 4.6¢; and by 1912–1913, only 2.4¢. In spite of the
substantial reduction in prices, supply remained largely confined to
industrial users, and prior to 1914 the municipal Gas Department
"gained far more by the increased use of . . . gas cooking-stoves, and
by the introduction of gas into houses rented by the week under the
penny-in-the-slot system, than it had lost by the development of electric lighting."[22]

Table 42

Comparative Costs for Fuel and Lighting: Pittsburgh, Birmingham, and Sheffield, 1907
and 1912

| Commodity | Year | Price | | | Price in Pittsburgh Compared to | |
		Pgh	Bhm	Shfd	Bhm	Shfd
Coal[a]	1907	$3.51	$5.23–5.35	$4.06–4.87	66.4%	78.5%
	1912	$3.65	$4.47–4.87	$4.06–4.87	78.2	81.7
Gas[b]	1907	26.0¢	60.9¢		42.7	
	1912	27.9¢	46.7¢		59.7	
Kerosene[c]	1905–1910[d]	17.4–21.6¢	18.3–20.3¢	16.2¢	101.0	120.4

Sources: See Tables 38, 39.

a. Bituminous coal, per ton of 2240 lbs.

b. Natural gas in Pittsburgh, manufactured gas in Birmingham: per 1,000 cubic feet.

c. Kerosene price in Pittsburgh, paraffin price in Birmingham and Sheffield.

d. Price in Pittsburgh, February 1909; price in Birmingham 1910; maximum price in
Sheffield, October 1905.

Pittsburgh's privately owned electricity supply companies likewise
benefited from increasing demand and, in contrast to Birmingham,
domestic consumers comprised an important share of the market. At
the turn of the century there were about 7,000 customers in Pittsburgh,
mostly domestic users, and this number advanced with the development of electrical home appliances, particularly the electric iron. Many
of the installations were made to low-income families in high-density
housing areas. For their supply in 1909 they paid 10.3¢ per kilowatt,
suggesting that electricity was one source of domestic power that was
substantially cheaper in Birmingham.[23]

Suits, Skirts, Socks, and Shoes

In 1910 the American commissioner of labor, Charles Neill, was
closely questioned by the Senate Select Committee on Wages and
Prices. The evidence is chastening to the historian.

Senator SIMMONS.   Do these [Bureau of Labor Statistics] investigations extend to anything except food products? Do they include clothing?

Mr. NEILL.   Not in the case of retail prices; . . . we have not
gone outside of foodstuffs in retail prices because of the difficulty of getting a standard.

Senator SIMMONS.   Can you not get a standard of cotton goods
and a standard of woollen goods?

Mr. NEILL.   No; you can not. You can get that for the wholesale
price, but not for the retail price; . . . when you come to the
retail price, showing the actual cost of living and the actual cost
of clothing, you can not get a standard. Men buy ready-made
clothing. . . . If you go to any store, you will find that they
have no standard. . . . You can not possibly tell whether the
goods are selling this year for $10 or $12 a suit are the same
standard or of a poorer standard of cloth than they sold the
year before.

Senator SMOOT.   It may be a tricot one year, a cheviot the next,
and a cashmere the next, according to the styles.

Mr. NEILL.   Or it may be the same kind of cloth each year.

Senator SMOOT.   Made up in different styles.

Mr. NEILL.   And you can not tell to what extent cotton and wool
are mixed in it.[24]

If it was difficult for the contemporary consumer to assess the standard of clothing or judge the extent to which effective price increases
were hidden by reductions in quality, it is so much harder for the
historian.[25] The problem is accentuated by the fact that prices were
consciously stabilized in line with consumer expectations, the standard
of an item being decreased in direct proportion to an advance in the
cost of manufacture and/or distribution. American shoe manufacturers
were well aware that there was "almost an agreed price at which a
good shoe [was] expected to be turned out." By 1910 Utz and Dunn
manufactured Dr. Edison ladies' oxford shoes to retail at $3.50 or
$4.00 (patent colt) and boots to sell at $4.00 or $4.50 (patent colt);
Krohn-Fechheimer, with a retail outlet in Pittsburgh, charged identical
prices for its Red Cross shoes; and Hamilton, Brown produced American Lady shoes to retail at $3.00, $3.50, and $4.00. Kaufmann's did not
even bother to state the brands stocked in its shoe department: ladies'
shoes were simply advertised for sale at $3.50 and $4.00.[26]

Similar price stability existed for other garments. Kaufmann's consistently advertised men's suits and overcoats in a set range of price

categories. Throughout the 1899–1912 period, the store's cheapest (nonsale) suit sold for $10: these were manufactured, it was claimed, from "the most dependable American woolens." Other superior models cost $15 ("better grades than the $10 lines"); $20 ("excellent workmanship all through"); $25 ("imported woolens, carefully selected"); and upward to $40. Other stores had similar price categories, although the price of the cheapest suit varied. Joseph Horne's, for example, had a $12 "strictly all-wool" suit at the bottom of its range. The two Pittsburgh branches of Arnfield's and National's both offered a low-price man's suit or overcoat for $7.50. However, these garments were deemed much inferior to the $10–$12 lines. "You, as a reader of the [*National Labor*] *Tribune*, have seen summer clothes advertised at $6.00 . . . a suit," warned Horne's. "Your intelligence must certainly tell you that such suits are PRINCIPALLY MADE OF COTTON materials, and are . . . of no account whatever."[27]

Price stability also prevailed in Birmingham. Consul Halstead noted that "the prices at which such goods [sold] at retail [were] a fixed quantity, and manufacturers in selling wholesale and stores in selling at retail [calculated]their profits so as not to increase the price to consumers." He judged that clothing "with shoddy and the cheapest qualities" had not advanced in price between 1900 and 1910. Rather, the difference had been "taken out of the quality."[28]

Undeterred, Halstead approached manufacturers and wholesalers who supplied clothes to Birmingham retailers. From their statements he made estimates of the price "increases" that had occurred between 1900 and 1910 to determine whether those increases had actually been passed on to the ultimate consumer, or whether they had been accounted for by a reduction in product quality. He calculated that in spite of apparent price stability, boots and shoes had effectively risen by 7.5–10 percent; men's suits and overcoats by 10–12 percent; men's superior grade socks, underwear, shirts, and hats by 15 percent; and equivalent inferior grades by 15–25 percent.[29]

The difficulty in judging product quality was as crucial to the assessment of comparative prices as it was to the calculation of price movements. Tables 43 and 44 present evidence of clothing prices in Pittsburgh and Birmingham. Educated guesses, based upon fragmentary evidence, suggested that these were items bought by manual workers, and that they were of similar quality on both sides of the Atlantic.[30] Consul Halstead actually noted whether garments were purchased by "workmen," "laborers," or "skilled mechanics," and analysis of the advertisements placed in the Birmingham press indicated general agreement with his categorization.

Table 43
Cost of Clothing: Birmingham, 1900–1910

Clothing	Quality	Price[a]	
Man's			
Boots/shoes	Cheapest	$ 2.56	
	Medium quality	3.29	
Suit	Cotton, ready-made, cheapest	2.90	
	Cotton, ready-made, medium quality	3.41	
	Cotton/wool mix, ready-made, cheapest	4.22	
	Wool, ready-made, "good cut"	8.12	
	Cotton, made-to-measure, cheapest	4.87	
	Wool, made-to-measure, "good cut"	7.30	
	Wool, made-to-measure, "excellent"	19.47	
Overcoat	Cotton, ready-made, cheapest	3.73	
	Cotton, made-to-measure, cheapest	4.87	
	Wool, made-to-measure, "good cut"	7.30	
	Wool, made-to-measure, "excellent"	17.03	
Socks	Cotton, rough seams, cheapest[b]	0.13	
	Cotton, medium quality	0.19	
	Cotton/wool mix, coarse, ribbed[c]	0.24	
	Wool, cheapest	0.25	
	Mercerized cotton, cheapest	0.37	
Underwear	Heavy wool[b]	0.47	
	Wool, "good quality"[c]	0.61	
Shirt	Coarse cotton, colored, cheapest[b]	0.47	
	Coarse cotton, colored, medium quality	0.55	
	Wool, "good quality"[c]	1.44	
	White linen, cheapest	0.71	
	White linen, medium quality	0.95	
Handkerchief	Cotton, cheapest[b]	0.05	
Woman's			
Boots/shoes	Cheapest	2.17	
	Medium quality	2.56	
Skirt	Made-to-measure (Co-operative)	2.17	
Coat	Made-to-measure (Co-operative)	3.90	
Suit	Made-to-measure (Co-operative)	5.60	
Clothing material	Flannel, cheapest	0.17	(1900)
		0.21	(1910)

Sources: Halstead, "Report on Prices," pp. 40–41; *Wheatsheaf,* May 1911, p. iv.
a. Expressed to the nearest cent.
b. Worn by laborers and workmen.
c. Worn by skilled mechanics.

Hipps, the "Public Benefit Tailoring Company," with "branches everywhere" in the Birmingham metropolis, offered made-to-measure overcoats from $4.02 and suits from $4.51, somewhat less than Table 43 indicates. Hipps, however, was the exception. Smart's, whose city department store claimed to possess the "World's Largest Mail Order Business," sold ready-to-wear Chesterfield (single-breasted) suits for $4.75 and Lincoln (double-breasted) suits for $5.12. Thomas Harrison, a local tailor fond of urging Brums to "SUPPORT YOUR OWN PEOPLE," made up suits from $4.87, and Wallace Lines charged the same price for made-to-measure overcoats. Some retailers urged Birmingham workers to buy even more expensive clothing. Dixon and Parker, the "Grand CLOTHING EMPORIUM" of the city, who advertised on the front cover of the local tramway workers' maga-

Table 44
Cost of Clothing: Pittsburgh, 1900–1910

Clothing	Quality	Price Range
Man's		
Suit	Ready-to-wear, cotton	$7.50
Suit	Ready-to-wear, wool	$10.00, $12.00, $15.00, $20.00–40.00
Suit	Made-to-measure	$11.75, $18.00.
Overcoat	Ready-to-wear, cotton	$7.50
Overcoat	Ready-to-wear, wool	$10.00, $12.00, $15.00, $20.00–40.00
Overcoat	Made-to-measure	$11.75, $18.00.
Trousers	Ready-to-wear	$1.98, $3.00, $4.50, $11.00+
Suspenders		$0.50
Belt	Leather	$0.39
Shirt	Cotton	$1.00, $1.50–3.50
Gloves	Wool	$0.25–1.50
Underwear	American "silk"	$0.75
Underwear	Fleeced wool	$1.00, $1.50
Socks	Mercerized cotton	$0.50
Boy's suit	Ready-to-wear, wool	$3.00, $5.00, $7.50+
Woman's		
Suit	Ready-to-wear, wool	$10.00, $15.00, $16.75+
Cape	Wool	$4.50, $5.00
Jacket	Wool	$4.50, $5.00
Skirt	Wool	$5.00, $10.00–22.50
Vest	Half-wool, half-cotton	$0.75
Underpants	Half-wool, half-cotton	$0.75
Petticoat	Cotton	$0.65, $1.00
Shoes	Leather	$3.50, $4.00, $5.00+
Clothing material	Flannel, cheapest	$0.35

Sources: Advertisements in the *National Labor Tribune,* 1907–1908, and *Pittsburgh Dispatch,* each November, 1900–1910.

zine, charged $5.28 for ready-to-wear coats and $7.31 for tailored garments.[31]

Halstead's data on boots and shoes also appear reliable, although the cheaper grades he noted were not widely advertised. Manfield and Sons, "one of the leading shoe stores in Birmingham," offered shoes at $4.02, $5.12, and $6.09. These shoes were similar to those produced in the United States, for they were manufactured in Northampton upon recently installed American machinery and with American lasts. The "leading American shoe store in Birmingham," the Walk-Over, which had two branches, sold shoes at $4.02 and $4.51. John Bird stocked K shoes in box calf from $3.78, and in glazed kid and willow calf for $4.02. And the newly amalgamated Saxone Shoe Company, "sole agency in Britain for the famous American 'Sorosis' shoes," sold men's and women's shoes at $4.02 and $3.90, respectively.[32]

Equivalent Pittsburgh prices were derived from a study of advertisements placed in the *National Labor Tribune* each week in 1907–1908, checked against analysis of advertisements appearing in the *Pittsburgh Dispatch* in every November for the period 1899–1913. All refer to stores that took space in the local labor press and periodically couched their appeal to "Mr. Workingman." Was this tabulation as reliable as the price data presented for Birmingham? I encountered two major problems.

First, clothes, perhaps more than any other commodity, were frequently sold at sales, and it is possible that the advertisements fail to give a true indication of normal prices. In Pittsburgh as in Birmingham, late December and January witnessed the annual winter sale, and July and August the summer sale. But sales were a far more important feature of the American retail trade than they were in England. British Board of Trade investigators in Pittsburgh noted that in "the interest of a quick turnover of their stock retailers [resorted] not only to . . . season sales, but also to special day or even special hour sales."[33] By 1905 Rosenbaum's department store frequently advertised five-hour sales, lasting from 10 A.M. to 3 P.M. on a single day; Kaufmann's organized one-hour sales at which, throughout the day, each hour brought reductions in a different variety of goods; and Frank and Seder's ran a constant sale on clothing, both new and seconds, in their "bargain basement."[34]

Fortunately, sale goods were clearly designated in advertisements, and it was therefore not difficult to exclude such items from incorporation in the data set. Nevertheless, it should be appreciated that although sale items have been eliminated from the sample frame, many workers would have actually paid less for their clothing than Tables 43 and 44 suggest. In Birmingham discerning consumers could have gained substantial savings either by buying during sale periods or by purchasing second-hand clothing. Reconditioned overcoats, for instance, could be bought for $1.22: retailers "[pressed] these things and [made] them look like new." Such reconditioning, alternatively, allowed consumers to extend the life of their own garments. Similarly, many workers would have paid for shoe-mending, in spite of its relative dearness: by 1914 the average price to sole and heel ladies' boots was 42.6¢ per pair "for medium class work" and 67.1¢ per pair for men's boots.[35]

In the United States, because of the greater frequency of retail sales, there existed even more opportunity to purchase clothes cheaply, and there can be no doubt that many housewives made considerable use of such facilities.[36] Women were not the only ones to derive such economies. James R. Cox, later to achieve fame as the "pastor of the poor" who led the march of the unemployed to Washington, D.C., in 1932, was in 1904 a struggling student at the Holy Ghost College in Pittsburgh. His diary exultantly recorded his success in securing a new suit in Kaufmann's summer sale that year for only $6.30, "a 30% reduction . . . sale suit was 9$\frac{00}{}$": celebrating his astuteness, he promptly spent $1.49 of his "savings" on a debonair straw hat at Solomon's![37]

The second criticism that might be lodged against the Pittsburgh data is that although many workers purchased clothing from department stores, those who continued to buy from specialized retail tailors would have paid markedly different prices. Yet this assumption, too, appears incorrect. It is true that their prices were somewhat more expensive than those in department stores. But whereas the department stores directed patrons' attention toward their stock of ready-to-wear coats, suits, trousers, and skirts, clothiers emphasized their tailoring expertise and advertised made-to-measure garments. Lyons' Tailors, for instance, charged $11.75–$18.00 for made-to-measure men's suits and overcoats; and London Woolen Mills company made similar clothes "to order" at $12.50, $15.00, and $18.00: both enterprises directed their appeal to Pittsburgh's manual workers.[38]

Table 45 summarizes the comparative cost of clothing in Birmingham and Pittsburgh and suggests that garments of equivalent quality were considerably more expensive in the American city. In most instances the retail price of clothes in Birmingham was only 40–50 percent of that in Pittsburgh. A similar price differential prevailed for materials with which the adept housewife could herself manufacture clothes for her family. The popular and cheap cotton-wool mix, flannel, was only about one-half the cost in Birmingham that it was in the

American city. If fuel was comparatively cheap in Pittsburgh, clothing was comparatively dear.

Chairs, Carpets, and Curtains; Crockery and Cutlery

It proved as difficult to estimate the comparative cost of furniture, furnishings, and the various domestic hardware and utensils required in

Table 45
Cost of Clothing: Pittsburgh and Birmingham, 1900–1910

	Price		Bhm. Price Compared to
Item/Quality	*Pittsburgh*	*Birmingham*	*Pgh. Price*
Man's suit/overcoat			
Ready-to-wear, lowest quality[a]	$ 7.50	$ 2.90	38.7%
Ready-to-wear, medium quality[b]	10.00	4.22	42.2
Ready-to-wear, good cut[c]	20.00	8.12	40.6
Excellent quality[d]	40.00	19.47	48.7
Made-to-measure, lowest quality[e]	11.75	4.87	41.5
Man's underwear			
Wool, cheapest[f]	1.00	0.467	46.7
Wool, good quality[g]	1.50	0.609	40.6
Man's shirt			
Cotton, cheapest[h]	1.00	0.467	46.7
Man's socks			
Mercerized cotton[i]	0.50	0.365	73.0
Woman's suit			
Medium quality[j]	15.00	5.60	37.3
Woman's skirt			
Medium quality[k]	5.00	2.17	43.4
Woman's shoes			
Medium quality	3.50	2.56	73.1
Clothing material			
Flannel, cheapest	0.35	0.173–0.213	49.4–58.0

Sources: See Tables 43 and 44.

a. Cotton.

b. Cotton/wool (Bhm); "all wool" (Pgh).

c. Wool, "good cut" (Bhm); wool, "excellent workmanship" (Pgh).

d. Wool, made-to-measure, "excellent" (Bhm); wool, ready-made, highest quality (Pgh).

e. Cotton.

f. Heavy wool (Bhm); "balbriggan" (Pgh).

g. Wool, "good quality" (Bhm); wool, "union suits" (Pgh).

h. Coarse cotton, colored (Bhm); cheapest (Pgh).

i. Cheapest (Bhm); cheapest, half-hose (Pgh).

j. Made-to-measure (Bhm); ready-to-wear (Pgh).

k. Made-to-measure (Bhm); ready-to-wear broadcloth (Pgh).

a home as it had been for clothing: as hard to assess the quality of a chair, curtain, carpet, or colander as it had been to judge the grade of a garment. For instance, the wood employed in the construction of furniture, like the fabric used in the manufacture of garments, could not easily be identified even from the most detailed advertisements. Manufacturers and retailers engaged in the early twentieth-century furniture trade were well aware that there existed "a soft wood, known as bass wood, which [was] easy to stain to any requisite shade . . . used to imitate other woods in furniture . . . of the cheaper kind. But it [had] no wear in it and [was] therefore worthless." A suitable solution of chromate of potash converted such a wood into a "mahogany" that only the more reputable stores would admit to be imitation; "ebony" was often sycamore or pear tree, doctored with a mixture of logwood chips, vinegar, and steel filings; and even the more expensive "brown oak" was frequently a lighter variety darkened with fumes of ammonia.[39] Thus the conscientious historian, just as much as the contemporary consumer, may all too easily be lured into false assumptions.

To complicate matters, furniture and hardware, like shoes and clothing, had a well-established price range. Consequently, the usual response to increased costs was to reduce production standards. Workers desired the maintenance of stable prices for household items, and manufacturers and retailers alike felt obliged to meet consumer expectations. "A certain class of people [made] a practice of never paying more than 6½d. [13.2¢] for small domestic goods. Whenever they [wanted] brooms, kettles, saucepans, hammers, choppers, and, indeed, all kinds of tools, they always [asked] for something about 6d. [12.2¢]," bemoaned the *Searchlight of Greater Birmingham.* Others had "an idea that the humble penny [was] quite enough to pay for practically any ordinary household article. For instance, ironmongers [did] a substantial trade in penny saucepans, penny hammers, penny cake tins, and dozens of other cheap and nasty articles."[40]

The problem posed by established prices, fixed by convention, was enormous. To minimize the possibility that transatlantic price differentials reflected quality differentials, I selected items that avoided extremes which pointed "on the one hand, toward short-sighted economy, and on the other hand toward extravagance." The goods chosen sold at "moderate prices" from "reliable firms whose names stood for sound worth." Birmingham prices were those that prevailed for items retailed at Britain's Co-operatives, checked against the bottom-range merchandise offered at London's Army and Navy Stores; in Pittsburgh prices were those commonly advertised by Taylor Brothers, the Hardware and Home Supply Company, and the city's department stores, checked against the minimum American prices suggested in a survey for newlywed couples carried out by *Harper's Bazaar*.[41] While such prices, presented in Tables 46 and 47, may have been higher than those generally paid by manual workers, they provided a fairly satisfactory measure of relative prices for commodities of comparable quality. However, given the greater imprecision of these estimates compared to those constructed for foodstuffs, rents, and fuel products and the necessity to include data from beyond city limits, it seemed fairer to present them as intercountry estimates. Table 48 compiles these statistics and, given the wider range of approximation, represents a fair comparison of prices for furniture, fittings, and domestic hardware that prevailed in Pittsburgh vis-à-vis Birmingham and Sheffield in 1907.

Wooden furniture was far cheaper to the British consumer. Howe's Patent Household bedstead cost only 50 percent of the price of a similar item sold in the United States; and dining chairs were only 41

Table 46
Prices of Home Furnishings: British
Co-operative Stores, 1914

Item	Price[a]
Oilcloth, yard	$0.50
Blankets, pair (wool?)	4.47
Sheets, each (linen?)	1.44
Towels, each	0.18–0.20
Plates, six	0.37
Cups, six	0.54
Saucers, six	0.55
Knives, six	1.24
Broom	0.18–0.37
Scrubbing-brush	0.13
Lamp glasses (chimneys?)	0.07
Chairs, six (dining?)	6.21
Washboard	0.13
Bucket	0.15
Enamel bowl	0.85
Clothes basket	0.13
Frying-pan	0.09–0.13
Saucepan, large	0.73
Meat tins, set	0.13

Source: Trades Union Congress, Joint Committee on the Cost of Living, *Final Report* (London, 1920), checked against Army and Navy Stores Catalogues.

a. Prices of items under $0.50 expressed to nearest cent.

Table 47
Prices of Home Furnishings: The United States, 1907

Item	Cheapest Prices	Other Prices	Prices in Pittsburgh
Oilcloth	$ 0.35	$ 0.39	$ 0.45
Linoleum, printed	0.50		0.75
Carpet, ingrain	0.65	0.75–2.00	0.29–0.85
Curtains, bobbinet	0.35	0.62	
Tablecloth, linen (2 × 2½ yds.)	2.00	3.50	
Napkins, linen (12)	2.00	3.00	
Sheets, cotton (2)	0.47	1.25	
Sheets, linen (2)	2.00	8.00	
Blankets, all wool (2)	6.50	10.00	
Towels, hand	0.50		
Dinner set, English china (100 pc)	16.00		
Lunch set, English china (55 pc)	10.00		
Cutlery, silver plate (12 pc)	1.70	4.00–7.00	
Tumblers, glass (12)	0.50		
Carpet-sweeper	1.35	3.00	2.50
Scrubbing-brush	0.35	0.50	
Broom	0.45	0.55	
Gas fitting (double fixture)	6.00	20.00	
Gas fitting (single fixture)	3.00	15.00	
Lamp shade, glass	1.50	7.00	
Morris chair, oak	15.00		15.00
Dining chair, oak	2.50	5.00	1.95–5.00
Sideboard, oak	10.00	30.00	13.75
Bedstead, iron	5.75	16.00	3.75–21.00
Bedstead, brass	26.00	40.00	33.00
Mattress, cotton	5.50		5.00
Mattress, felt	15.00		8.75
Kitchen range, coal	25.00		15.00
Kitchen range, gas	2.40	13.75	10.00–11.50
Washboard, wood	0.45	0.70	
Tub, cedar	0.75	1.25	
Rolling pin, holly wood	0.25		
Colander	0.20		
Saucepan, agate	0.35	0.40	
Frying-pan	0.06	0.60	0.75–1.25
Tea kettle	1.05		

Sources: Cols. 1 and 2: Martha Cutler, "The Cost of Home Furnishings—A Review," *Harper's Bazaar,* 41 (1907); col. 3: Taylor Bros. and/or Pittsburgh Hardware and Home Supply: nonsale prices advertised in *National Labor Tribune,* 1907–1908.

percent of their cost in America. An English oak washstand was relatively dearer, retailing at 90 percent of the American model, but the former item included a 15-inch earthenware basin, plug, and chain. Wooden household utensils were also substantially dearer in the United States. The price of a broom in Britain was only 31 percent of the cost in America; and the equivalent figure for a scrubbing brush was 29–40 percent; for a laundry washboard, 29 percent; for a wooden washing tub, 24 percent; and for potato mashers and rolling pins, 36 percent.

It was harder to compare the prices of metal domestic hardware. Some products, such as eggbeaters, pails, kettles, and dustpans, appeared cheaper in England, while others, such as colanders and mixing bowls, seemed similarly priced. My major difficulty was to correctly identify the material of which utensils were composed, for prices varied according to whether the item was made of tin, wrought iron, enamel, copper, or aluminum, and according to whether the metal had been japanned, planished, or plated. A common alloy for American utensils was agate (enameled iron) which stood "half-way between the ordinary tin and enamel, on one hand, and aluminum and copper on the other."[42] Whereas agate cookpots were priced upward of 50¢ in the United States, a cast-iron pan in England (probably of similar quality) cost 51¢. Cheaper than agate was tin: colanders manufactured from this metal sold for about 20¢, identical to the English price. Aluminum ware, on the other hand, was twice as expensive as agate: aluminum saucepans cost between 70¢ and 80¢ in the United States but retailed from 81¢ in England. Thus whether the comparison be made between

Table 48
Prices for Home Furnishings, 1907

Item	English Price As % of American Price
Domestic utensils, wooden	25–35
Furniture, wooden	40–50
Bedding, mattresses	40–50
Crockery, china, earthenware	45–55
Bedding and toweling, linen	45–55
Light fixtures	50–60
Glassware	70–80
Domestic utensils, metal	95–105
Cutlery, silver plate	95–105
Floor covering, oilcloth	110–120
Bedding and toweling, cotton	150–160

Sources: See text.

utensils of tin, agate/cast iron, or aluminum, the statistical picture which emerges is one of similar prices: in contrast, articles of wood appear to have been three times as expensive in America.

Tableware too was generally cheaper in England. Glass products such as tumblers cost only 73 percent of their retail price in the United States, and earthenware and chinaware items were likewise relatively less expensive. A 55-piece china dinner set cost in excess of $10.00 in America, while the Army and Navy Stores sold a 52-piece service of silicon china for $5.36 and a set of Minton earthenware for $5.05. The stores also advertised cheaper services "suitable for kitchen and nursery"; a dark blue willow pattern cost $4.51, and a white stone china set could be bought for only $4.38. Crockery, in short, seems to have been somewhat less than half its American price. However, cutlery—at least the superior, silver-plated variety—was similarly priced.

The comparative price of bedding and table linen varied according to the material examined. Mattresses stuffed with woolen shreds (flock in Britain, felt in the United States) retailed in England for only 39 percent of the cost in America, and pure hair mattresses were 44 percent of the American price. Genuine linen goods were likewise cheaper in England: the price of a pair of linen sheets ranged from $2.00 to $8.00 in the United States, but the Army and Navy Stores offered a superior quality for $2.80; and linen pillowcases cost only 44 percent of the price charged in America, damask napkins 51 percent, and damask tablecloths 70 percent. Woollen goods were also less expensive in England. A pair of Witney white wool blankets, for instance, cost less than half the price for which they were sold in the United States. In marked contrast, the cheaper cotton bedclothes, which most manual workers would have purchased, were probably dearer in England. Plain cotton sheets cost between 47¢ and $1.25 in America, whereas the cheapest grade advertised by the Army and Navy Stores cost $1.44; and cotton pillowcases, which sold at from 14 to 26¢ in America, were retailed at 22¢ by the London enterprise. Similarly, white cotton Turkish bath towels cost $1.07 in England compared to 13¢ to $1.00 in the United States.

The wide range of carpet qualities made it impossible to calculate comparative prices with any degree of accuracy. Woollen rugs were almost certainly cheaper in Britain, but the floor covering favored by working-class consumers, oilcloth, was somewhat cheaper in America. Co-operative stores sold such material for 50¢ per yard as compared to the American price of between 35¢ and 39¢.

Light fittings, on the other hand, were substantially dearer in the United States. A single brass wall fixture for gas lighting, bought in

England, cost only 64 percent of the price of a similar item in America, and a double fixture was 54 percent less. Oil-burning brass table lamps could be purchased in England for only 53 percent of the price across the Atlantic. Small lighting accessories were likewise considerably more expensive in America. Cheaper quality glass lampshades cost between 22¢ and 39¢ in England, barely 20 percent of the price in the United States; and a large silk shade sold for but 37 percent of its American equivalent.

The overall statistical picture that emerged was confused. Yet sufficient evidence was accrued by which to make the informed "guesstimate" of price differences summarized in Table 48. It is probable that additional, more sophisticated analysis would improve the accuracy of these educated estimates. Nevertheless, if, as seems likely, national prices for furnishings fairly represented prices in the cities of Pittsburgh and Birmingham, then the figures provide a satisfactory basis for comparative investigation. It can justifiably be claimed that a light, however weak, has been shed on an area that previously lay in almost total darkness.

9

Expenditure

The Food Budget

The major item of working-class expenditure in the United States was food. It was conceded by all parties in the Pittsburgh Railways Company arbitration case of 1914 that food products accounted for about "two-fifths of the expense of living," and this estimate was confirmed both by studies of 3,702 Pennsylvania families in 1901 and of 90 Homestead families in 1907–1908.[1] However, the fraction was not constant. Although the absolute sum spent upon foodstuffs increased as the decade progressed, the percentage of total expenditures devoted to the purchase of food slowly declined. In 1901 the Pennsylvania family spent $6.00 per week upon food, or 43.5 percent of average income; in 1907–1908 the Homestead family spent $6.27, but this amount represented only 40.4 percent of weekly earnings.

In England the purchase of food accounted for a larger share of the worker's pay packet. Expenditure upon viands accounted for 58.2 percent of the mean income of 262 working-class families who resided in towns in the British Midlands in 1904. The actual weekly expenditure of these families was $5.25. In the northern towns, including Sheffield, the equivalent outlay was $5.57, or 57.6 percent of the mean income of 439 families studied. Comparison of these data with those collected from 40 healthy, working-class Birmingham families in 1914 suggests that, as in America, the percentage of income expended upon food declined as the First World War approached. When the mean food expenditure was calculated by weighting equally the five income groups presented in Table 49, then the disbursement upon food in Midland towns in 1904 represented 59.8 percent of income, compared to only 54.5 percent in Birmingham in 1914.[2]

Engel's law of consumption, formulated in 1857 and based upon a survey of Belgian workers' family budgets, states that the poorer a family, the greater the proportion of its total expenditure that has to be devoted to the provision of food.[3] Statistical evidence from both sides of the Atlantic supports this thesis. Table 49 reveals that absolute expenditure for food in England increased, if unsteadily, as family earnings rose. However, expenditure, expressed as a percentage of income, fell from 59.4 percent for Birmingham families with a weekly income of less than $6.09 in 1914 to 49.7 percent for families with a weekly income in excess of $10.23.

A similar situation prevailed in Pennsylvania. Table 50 illustrates the manner in which disbursement upon food advanced less substantially than annual earnings, so that purchases of food occupied a decreasing portion of total expenditure. Families receiving less than $300 per annum in 1901 spent 47.7 percent of their budget upon food, whereas families receiving more than $1,100 per annum devoted only 36.3 percent of expenditure to the purchase of food.

American data suggest that nativity as well as income had an impact upon the family food budget. Table 51 shows that itemized food expenditure varied enormously, exhibiting little relation to the mean income of the ethnic group. Pennsylvania's Russian-born families annually earned, on average, only $571.96 and, as might have been ex-

Table 49

Expenditure for Food per Family, by Income: Midland and Northern English Towns, 1904, and Birmingham, 1914

Family Weekly Income	No. of Families	Food Expenditure $	%[a]
Midlands, incl. Birmingham, 1904			
$ 6.08 or less	27	3.30	64.2
6.09–7.30	35	4.13	62.7
7.31–8.51	61	4.57	58.2
8.52–9.73	49	5.10	57.4
9.74 and over	90	6.72	56.7
North of England, incl. Sheffield, 1904			
6.08 or less	55	3.27	64.4
6.09–7.30	61	4.18	62.8
7.31–8.51	64	4.98	64.4
8.52–9.73	90	5.25	58.5
9.74 and over	169	7.14	54.0
Birmingham, 1914			
6.08 or less	8	3.17	59.4
6.09–7.30	6	3.48	53.4
7.31–8.51	8	4.44	56.9
8.52–10.22	7	4.89	52.8
10.23 and over	11	6.67	49.7

Sources: Great Britain, Board of Trade, *Report of an Enquiry . . . into Working Class Rents, Housing, Retail Prices, and Standard Rates of Wages in the United Kingdom, British Parliamentary Papers,* Cd. 3864, 1908, Vol. 53, pp. 11, 14; A. E. Carver, *Dietary of the Labouring Classes of Birmingham, with Special Reference to its Bearing upon Tuberculosis* (Birmingham, 1914), pp. 16–30.

a. Food expenditure as a % of family income.

pected, spent a large proportion of that income, 52.6 percent, upon food. On the other hand, the state's Italian families received an even smaller annual income, $539.20, but used only 41.6 percent of that total to buy food—less than any other ethnic group.

From the 3,702 Pennsylvania families studied in 1901, detailed expenditure data were collected for 398 families. Disaggregated analysis of these figures (Table 52) indicates that the food preferences of native- and foreign-born families were generally similar. Meat products accounted for 25.7 percent of food expenditure, and fresh beef was by far the most important single purchase, requiring just over 15 percent of the food outlay of both natives and immigrants. The major difference between these two groups occurred in the "other meat" category, families with foreign-born heads expending 3.1 percent of their food budget upon such items (primarily mutton), while families with native-born heads spent only 2.3 percent. The percentage of expenditure upon dairy products was virtually identical for foreign- and native-born, the mean outlay being 23.8 percent. Of this total 9.8 percent was spent upon butter, 6.8 percent upon eggs, 6.3 percent upon milk, but only 0.9 percent upon cheese. Additionally, 10.0 percent of the worker's food purse was devoted to the purchase of vegetables, of which potatoes accounted for almost one half. Immigrants spent more upon potatoes than native-born Americans, but the latter group spent

Table 50
Expenditure for Food per Family by Income: Pennsylvania, 1901

Annual Income Category	No. of Families	Food Expenditure $	Food Expenditure %[a]
$ 200–299	19	179.32	47.7
300–399	117	186.60	46.1
400–499	298	218.48	46.8
500–599	388	246.03	46.2
600–699	342	272.53	44.6
700–799	249	291.83	42.2
800–899	113	315.09	41.1
900–999	75	325.71	40.2
1,000–1,099	38	322.94	38.1
1,100 and over	25	377.02	36.3

Source: U.S., *Eighteenth Annual Report of the Commissioner of Labor,* 1903, Pt. 1, Table 5C, p. 556.

Note: Families in this sample were "normal," i.e., the husband was at work; there was a wife; there were not more than five children and none over 14 years of age; and there were no dependents, boarders, lodgers, or servants.

a. Food expenditure as % of family income.

Table 51

Expenditure for Food per Family by Ethnicity: Pennsylvania, 1901

Ethnic Group[a]	No. of Families in Sample	Average Yearly Income	Average Yearly Expenditure	Average Yearly Food Expenditure	Food Expenditure as % of Total Expenditure	Food Expenditure as % of Total Income
Native-born	2,496	$717.93	$672.89	$305.61	45.4%	42.6%
Foreign-born[b]	1,206	716.92	685.01	325.07	47.5	45.3
Scotland	31	834.45	782.95	351.95	45.0	42.2
Germany	272	759.11	707.26	330.04	46.7	43.5
England	180	738.86	604.78	321.57	46.3	43.5
Wales	69	722.59	665.01	305.84	46.0	42.3
Ireland	460	713.62	692.47	338.47	48.9	47.4
Austro-Hungary	55	639.65	604.86	280.38	46.4	43.8
Russia	70	571.96	613.94	300.77	49.0	52.6
Italy	23	539.20	517.94	224.05	43.3	41.6
Aggregate	3,702	717.60	676.84	311.95	46.1	43.5

Source: U.S., Eighteenth Annual Report of the Commissioner of Labor, 1903, Pt. 1, Table 3C, p. 336.

a. Nativity of head of family.

b. Only ethnic groups consisting of over 20 families have been listed separately.

Table 52

Itemized Expenditure for Food: Pennsylvania Families, 1901

Food Item	Families Having Expenditure			Average Yearly Expenditure[a]			Proportion of Food Budget on Each Item		
	Native-born (%)	Foreign-born (%)	Total (%)	Native-born ($)	Foreign-born ($)	Total ($)	Native-born (%)	Foreign-born (%)	Total (%)
Fresh beef	100.0	99.1	99.8	46.38	50.34	47.51	15.3	15.5	15.3
Salt beef	21.8	22.1	21.9	1.35	1.11	1.28	0.4	0.3	0.4
Fresh pork	68.1	70.8	68.8	8.34	9.98	8.73	2.7	3.1	2.8
Salt pork	90.2	84.1	88.4	14.00	15.23	14.35	4.6	4.7	4.6
Other meat	53.7	66.4	57.3	7.13	10.02	7.96	2.3	3.1	2.6
Poultry	89.5	78.3	86.4	6.81	6.32	6.67	2.2	1.9	2.1
Fish	78.6	77.9	78.4	5.30	6.18	5.55	1.7	1.9	1.8
Eggs	99.7	97.4	99.0	20.47	22.99	21.18	6.7	7.1	6.8
Milk	96.8	98.2	97.2	19.47	20.25	19.69	6.4	6.2	6.3
Butter	100.0	98.2	99.5	30.19	30.70	30.34	9.9	9.5	9.8
Cheese	71.6	74.3	72.4	2.68	3.41	2.89	0.9	1.1	0.9
Lard	99.0	98.2	98.7	10.63	9.47	10.30	3.5	2.9	3.3
Tea	82.8	94.7	86.2	4.07	6.91	4.87	1.3	2.1	1.6
Coffee	99.0	90.3	96.5	10.99	10.52	10.86	3.6	3.2	3.5
Sugar	100.0	100.0	100.0	16.18	17.47	16.55	5.3	5.4	5.3
Molasses	65.6	55.8	62.8	1.63	1.29	1.53	0.5	0.4	0.5
Flour and meal	97.5	99.1	98.0	14.70	18.71	15.84	4.8	5.8	5.1
Bread	80.7	69.0	77.4	12.90	13.05	12.95	4.2	4.0	4.2
Rice	83.5	86.7	84.4	1.65	2.08	1.77	0.5	0.6	0.6
Potatoes	100.0	100.0	100.0	12.39	14.80	13.07	4.1	4.6	4.2
Other vegetables	100.0	100.0	100.0	18.41	18.09	18.32	6.0	5.6	5.9
Fruit	97.5	93.8	96.5	17.67	14.82	16.86	5.8	4.6	5.4
Vinegar, pickles, condiments	100.0	100.0	100.0	3.51	3.91	3.62	1.1	1.2	1.2
Other foods	98.6	99.1	98.7	18.47	16.69	17.96	6.1	5.1	5.8

Source: U.S., Eighteenth Annual Report of the Commissioner of Labor, 1903, Pt. 1, Tables 3, 4B, 4E, pp. 430–31, 481–85.

Note: "Native-born" and "foreign-born" apply to head of household.

a. Includes families who did not purchase an item.

more upon other vegetable products. Pennsylvania workers disbursed 5.4 percent of total food outlay upon fruit, but the foreign-born expended significantly less than the native-born: 4.6 percent contrasted with 5.8 percent. Bread comprised 4.2 percent of the Pennsylvanian's food budget, less than the 5.1 percent spent upon flour and meal. Indeed, these provisions were considerably more important to immigrant families. They devoted 5.8 percent of their food budget to their acquisition, compared to 4.8 percent by native-born Americans, a difference which suggests a greater effort by foreign families to bake their own bread and cake. Expenditure for beverages (5.1 percent of the average food budget) also varied significantly between the foreign- and native-born worker, the latter purchasing more tea than the former but less coffee. Sugar—primarily the white, granulated variety—absorbed 5.3 percent of the sum spent upon food; lard 3.3 percent; and poultry and fish 3.9 percent. Other items of food bought were, individually, of minor importance.[4]

At least some of the ethnic differences in budgetary expenditure resulted from immigrants' retention of dietary patterns acquired before their arrival in the United States. Perhaps out of conscious preference for traditional foodstuffs, perhaps because of habit, the European migrant adapted only slowly to his new environment. In Pittsburgh coffee was the "almost universal domestic drink of the working-class, tea being little consumed even by Russians."[5] Yet Pennsylvania statistics indicate that English, Welsh, and Scottish migrants retained their affinity for tea in spite of the very different price situation that prevailed in America. In Pittsburgh in 1901 tea, at 60¢ per pound, was more than 300 percent more expensive than coffee, whereas in Birmingham the cheapest brand of unblended tea sold at 28.6¢ per pound, only 40 percent dearer than the cheapest variety of French coffee. Nevertheless, British migrants had only partially adjusted to the radically altered price conditions, spending considerably more for tea than American workers ($6.46 compared to $4.07), and less upon coffee ($8.92 compared to $10.99). Irish families too retained traditional food habits in the United States. Bread and potatoes, long the staple diet of the Irish laborer, continued to dominate food expenditure even after migration. While the American family bought only $12.90 worth of bread per annum, and $12.39 worth of potatoes, the Irish family expended $25.52 and $19.19, respectively.[6]

It was not only the migrant who showed conservatism with regard to diet. British workers were equally unresponsive to changing price structures, and many middle-class reformers believed working-class dietary practice to be both economically and nutritionally irrational. The traditional predilection of Birmingham families for certain foodstuffs was deemed to resemble "the fashions in dress more than any other phenomenon, and in a similar way hit hardest those who [were] poorest in purse and originality." Tastes changed slowly, and diet remained "the slave of convention."[7]

Comparison of Tables 52 and 53 reveals that budgetary expenditure in Birmingham was substantially different from that in Pennsylvania. Whereas the Pennsylvania family expended 5.4 percent of its total food budget upon fruit, the Birmingham working-class family spent only 1.7 percent—and a substantial portion of that outlay was devoted to the purchase of dried articles such as currants and raisins.[8] Families in Pennsylvania also disbursed a greater percentage of their food expenditure upon fresh vegetables. Excluding potatoes, the Birmingham family spent only 3.3 percent of its food purse upon vegetables, primarily cabbage, compared to 5.9 percent in Pennsylvania.[9] In marked contrast, Birmingham families spent 14.4 percent of their total food allowance upon bread, while Pennsylvania families spent a mere 4.2 percent, but the 5.1 percent devoted to the purchase of flour and meal in the American state was substantially greater than the 1.6 percent disbursed in Birmingham. Perhaps the most surprising fact was that the percentage of total food outlay devoted to the purchase of meat and fish was greater in the British city: 33.6 percent compared to 29.6 percent.

Diet

Expenditure figures tell but part of the story. Fundamental queries remain: What did monetary expenditure upon food items mean in terms of quantity? How much bread was eaten? How much meat consumed? Unfortunately, the statistical evidence necessary to answer such questions proved scanty. Dr. Carver failed to record the quantity of foodstuffs eaten by Birmingham families, although the 1904 Board of Trade investigation did publish information for a limited range of products. The commissioner of labor's 1901 survey of American expenditure likewise provided little dietary information. However, data were presented for a selected group of 213 "normal" Pennsylvania families. In addition, it proved possible to estimate consumption by relating the expenditure data gathered from 398 Pennsylvania families (detailed in Table 52) to the price of various foodstuffs in Pittsburgh in 1901 (detailed in Table 22).

But before comparison could be made, another factor had to be taken into account—family size. The consumption level of each family

Table 53
Itemized Expenditure for Food: Midland Families, 1904, and
Birmingham, 1914

	% of Total Food Expenditure	
Food Item	Midland towns, 1904	Birmingham, 1914
Meat and fish	31.4	33.6
Beef	n.s.s.	12.4
Fresh pork	n.s.s.	3.3
Ham	n.s.s.	0.7
Bacon	5.6	5.5
Mutton, lamb	n.s.s.	6.1
Rabbit	n.s.s.	1.4
Veal	n.s.s.	0.9
Sausage	n.s.s.	0.9
Liver	n.s.s.	0.5
Poultry	n.s.s.	0.4
Fish	n.s.s.	1.3
Other meat	n.s.s.	0.2[a]
Dairy produce	19.4	17.3
Eggs	4.0	2.4
Fresh milk	4.9	6.2
Cheese	2.8	2.4
Butter	7.7	6.3
Vegetables and fruit	9.5	9.2
Potatoes	3.8	4.2
Cabbage	n.s.s.	1.3
Other vegetables	5.7	2.0[b]
Fruit	n.s.s.	1.7
Flour and bread	16.0	16.0
Flour	n.s.s.	1.6
Bread	n.s.s.	14.4
Rice, tapioca and oatmeal	1.5	1.6
Rice	n.s.s.	0.4
Tapioca	n.s.s.	0.6[c]
Oatmeal	n.s.s.	0.6
Beverages and condiments	8.2	10.3
Tea	5.2	n.s.s.
Coffee and cocoa	1.7	n.s.s.
Condiments and pickles	1.4	n.s.s.
Sugar	4.8	4.7
Jam, marmalade, treacle, and syrup	1.8	1.4
Marmalade and jam	n.s.s.	1.2
Treacle and syrup	n.s.s.	0.2
Other foods	7.5	6.0
Lard	n.s.s.	1.5
Margarine	n.s.s.	1.3
Dripping	n.s.s.	0.9

Food Item	% of Total Food Expenditure	
	Midland towns, 1904	Birmingham, 1914
Biscuits and cake	n.s.s.	1.3
Condensed milk	n.s.s.	0.9
Total (error due to rounding)	100.1	100.0

Sources: See Table 49.
Note: n.s.s. = not separately stated.
a. Tripe, suet, kidneys, sheeps' heads.
b. Peas were the next most important vegetable purchased.
c. Included small amount of semolina.

varied, of course, according to the number of members within it, and it was therefore imperative to relate consumption to some standardized unit. According to the commissioner of labor, the relative consuming powers of the different members of a family were as follows: husband (100 units); wife (90 units); child, 11–14 years inclusive (90 units); child, 7–10 years inclusive (75 units); child, 4–6 years inclusive (40 units); child, 3 years and under (15 units).[10] I assumed that these relative weightings, decided "after careful comparison and study," were correct, and that they were as valid for England as for the United States. It was then possible to estimate weekly consumption per adult male worker.

Table 54 indicates that the British male adult worker consumed less of almost every article than his American counterpart. The major exception was bread, "the staple article of diet among the [Birmingham] laboring classes," which was consumed voraciously. Bread was eaten at all meals and served all purposes. Three slices of bread and butter/margarine/dripping for both breakfast and tea was the norm for the city's working girls in 1904. School children consumed substantial quantities. Dietary reformers were aghast at the hordes of children who played in the streets, greedily clutching slabs of bread in their hands, and many took it as an indication that they had received no cooked dinner at home. More careful observers derided such suggestions. Working-class children demanded "a slice of bread and butter as a finish to their meal of meat and vegetables—just as middle class children expected pudding—and . . . they ate this in the street, being glad to escape into the open air as soon as possible." Bread was also distributed to children much in the same way as are cookies or chocolate bars today. When a child felt hungry, or was especially troublesome, he was "given a 'piece', on which some lard or butter was hastily dabbed, and he ate it walking about the town." Indeed the "Birmingham child [preferred] 'a length of bread' to any other article of food . . . and the only way to tempt him more [was] to spread it with cod liver oil and malt." And when the boy grew to adulthood, the dedication to bread remained. The Midlander ate almost as much bread in one day as the Pennsylvanian did in five: 7.60 pounds weekly, compared to only 1.54 pounds.[11]

Table 54

Weekly Consumption of Foodstuffs per Adult Male Worker: The Midlands and North of England, 1904, and Pennsylvania, 1901

Food Item	Quantity	Pa. 1901[a]	Pa. 1901[b]	Midlands 1904	North of England 1904
Meat	lbs.	3.11	3.21	2.24	1.94
Fresh beef	lbs.	1.74	1.81	n.s.s.	n.s.s.
Salt beef	lbs.	0.07	0.05	n.s.s.	n.s.s.
Fresh pork	lbs.	0.37	0.40	n.s.s.	n.s.s.
Bacon	lbs.	0.54	0.61	0.47	0.39
Mutton, lamb	lbs.				
Veal	lbs.	0.39	0.34	n.s.s.	n.s.s.
Other	lbs.				
Fish	lbs.	0.30	0.29	n.s.s.	n.s.s.
Poultry	lbs.	0.25	0.20	n.s.s.	n.s.s.
Dairy products					
Fresh milk	Amer. pints	3.65	3.15	2.47	2.80
Cheese	lbs.	0.11	0.11	0.25	0.17
Butter	lbs.	0.62	0.59	0.39	0.61
Eggs	no.	6.90	6.20	2.6(e)	n.s.s.
Vegetables					
Potatoes	lbs.	5.06	5.57	3.10	3.47
Bread, flour, meal	lbs.	5.46	5.09	8.28	7.34
Bread	lbs.	1.54	1.22	7.60	n.s.s.
Flour, meal	lbs.	3.52	3.87	0.69	n.s.s.
Lard	lbs.	0.51	0.52	n.s.s.	n.s.s.
Rice	lbs.	0.11	0.12	0.40	0.48
Molasses	Amer. qts.	0.06	0.10	n.s.s.	n.s.s.
Beverages	lbs.	0.50	0.31	0.22	0.21
Tea	lbs.	0.05	0.05	0.16	0.14
Coffee	lbs.	0.45	0.26	0.06	0.07
Sugar	lbs.	1.47	1.39	1.43	1.42

Sources: U. S., *Eighteenth Annual Report of the Commissioner of Labor*, 1903, Pt. 1, Tables 6A, 4B, 4E, pp. 610–14, 430–31, 481–85; Board of Trade, *Enquiry into Working Class Rents, Housing, Prices and Wages in the U.K.*, 1908, pp. 11, 14.

Note: n.s.s. = not separately stated; e = estimate (see text).

a. Quantities estimated from expenditure data of 398 Pennsylvania families.

b. Quantities for 213 "normal" Pennsylvania families.

Bread was less popular elsewhere in Britain. Consumption of flour and bread was 0.94 pounds less in northern towns, and the regional difference was probably greater with respect to bread alone. Certainly there was far more likelihood of the Sheffield family baking its own bread than was the case in Birmingham. Even by 1905 the amount of ready-baked bread sold in Sheffield was less than 10 percent of the total amount consumed. In Birmingham, in contrast, hardly any home baking was performed: the city's workers, "unlike the Northerners, [had] no facilities for baking their bread at home; hence flour [was] only used in small quantities for puddings, cakes and pastry."[12]

In Pittsburgh, as in Sheffield, most families generally baked their own loaves. Indeed, there was a certain disgrace attached to purchasing bread. Mr. Riley, research chemist at Heinz, remembered that if his mother "wanted to buy a loaf of bread from the baker [in 1900] she would send [him] around to the back door so the neighbors wouldn't see."[13] Thus consumption of bread and flour in Pittsburgh was probably closer to the Sheffield pattern than to that of Birmingham. In the latter city consumption of flour represented only 17.6 percent the amount used in Pennsylvania.

As Birmingham children grew up and went to work, their taste for bread pieces developed—much to the chagrin of dietary reformers—into a desire for the sweet confectionery that a handful of small change could buy. The majority of the city's working girls spent their dinner money "unprofitably, choosing tarts, buns, and ginger-beer in preference to more nourishing foods." They also developed a taste for strong pickles to accompany their meals. However Tables 52 and 53 suggest that such accompaniments were as popular in Pennsylvania as in the Midlands, for the portion of the food budget devoted to such items was similar: 1.2 and 1.4 percent, respectively. Certainly Pittsburgh's working girls possessed preferences in food similar to those of women employed in Birmingham. At the Heinz factory in Pittsburgh, newspaper bundles were unwrapped at lunchtime to reveal dried preserve sandwiches, pickles, cold fried oysters, jam, cake, and occasionally "a piece of stringy cold meat"—a fare that their Birmingham sisters would willingly have shared.[14]

It was generally believed that the workers' addiction to strong tastes, to pickles and "tasty kippers," jam and buns, resulted from a jaded appetite. "I am beginning to understand why the meager lunches of preserve-sandwiches and pickles more than satisfy the girls whom I was prepared to accuse of spending their money on gewgaws rather than on nourishment," wrote one of the few middle-class observers to experience Pittsburgh factory life firsthand. "It is fatigue that steals the appetite. I can hardly taste what I put in my mouth; the food sticks in my throat. . . . I crave sours and sweets, pickles, cake, anything to excite my numb taste." Working girls in Birmingham, equally exhausted from their labor, responded similarly, seeking to stimulate lunchtime appetite "with strong tea, pickled cabbage, tinned fish and vinegar, or by sucking lemons."[15]

Table 54 indicates that oats, like bread, was one of the few products of which more was eaten in England. Estimates suggest that the adult male Midlands workers consumed 0.24 pounds of oats or oatmeal each week, whereas expenditure upon oats in Pennsylvania was insufficient to warrant separate categorization. Yet reformers remained frustrated at how few Birmingham workers included such a cheap and protein-rich item in their diet, "and the poorer the family the greater their distaste for it." Yet the reasons for working-class antipathy to oatmeal porridge were well founded. The time needed for cooking, and the constant stirring required, made it difficult for the mother intent upon getting her husband, children—and perhaps herself—out of the house; lack of culinary utensils meant that the mixture acquired the flavors of food previously cooked in the saucepan; and the addition of sugar and milk were required to make the gruel acceptable. But the major reason was "entirely a question of taste." Many Birmingham women would have echoed the response of a Lambeth housewife to a social worker intent upon converting her to porridge breakfasts: "Besides, my young man 'e say, Ef you gives me that stinkin' mess, I'll throw it at yer."[16]

That other great staple of the workers' diet, the potato, was used extensively on both sides of the Atlantic. Consumption was, as with rice, tapioca, and oatmeal, higher in Britain's northern towns than in the Midlands, but in both areas the quantity of potatoes eaten was second only to the amount of bread and flour. It was generally agreed that in Britain vegetable greens and butter might go, and meat "diminish almost to vanishing-point, before potatoes [were] affected."[17] Yet potato consumption in the British towns was significantly lower than in Pennsylvania, the quantity eaten per adult male worker in the Midlands being just 61.3 percent of that eaten in the American state. However aggregate consumption of the starchy, carbohydrate foods—bread, flour, potatoes, rice, tapioca, oatmeal—was higher in the British towns. The total quantity eaten per adult male worker was 11.78 pounds in the Midlands, 11.29 pounds in the north of England, and 10.52 pounds in Pennsylvania.

American workers, in contrast, enjoyed a greater quantity of most dairy products. Cheese was eaten in far larger amounts in the Midlands: 25 pounds compared to 11 pounds. However, eggs, fresh milk, and butter were all consumed less. Estimates suggest that 10.25 eggs were eaten weekly by Midland families, or 2.62 eggs per adult male. This was only 37.9 percent of consumption in Pennsylvania. Yet some medical authorities believed that even the relatively small number of eggs purchased in Birmingham constituted one of the "greatest extravagancies" of the city's workers. That they were so widely bought reflected not so much a fondness for their taste as a common belief in their magical properties, and in their efficacy in curing illness. "The result was that if a child [was] not feeling well or '[was] off his food' the mother immediately [sent] out for a fresh egg for his tea." Dr. Carver reported that he had "often been asked if it [was] safe to eat more than one egg a day, the idea of the questioner being that an egg [contained] some very potent elixir of life."[18] Greater quantities of butter and fresh milk were also eaten in Pennsylvania compared to the British Midlands, but this is not necessarily an indication that the American worker had a superior diet. The Birmingham worker had cheaper, readily available substitutes for both items, and the alternative foodstuffs were by no means inferior in terms of protein, vitamins, or caloric value.[19]

Most Birmingham families consumed condensed milk in addition to fresh milk: it kept longer, required no additional sugar to sweeten cups of tea, and could be used as a spread in place of jam. It was also significantly richer in protein, fat, carbohydrates, and vitamins than fresh milk.[20] More importantly, unless the more expensive, hygienically produced grade was purchased, consumption of fresh milk was fraught with danger. Milk was the "dirtiest food" on sale in Birmingham. Not only were there insufficient safeguards against tubercular cows, but also the milk was progressively contaminated and adulterated "on its way from the udder to the mouth."[21]

Similar circumstances prevailed in Pittsburgh. From 10 to 15 percent of the dairy cattle supplying the city had tuberculosis in 1907, and this, combined with unhygienic milking, insufficient pasteurization, and dirty retailing conditions, meant that Pittsburgh's milk supply was a commodity to be treated with extreme caution. The Pennsylvania Department of Health, lacking the facilities to properly inspect the production of milk, admitted that the state's supply was often a "filthy, disease-breeding fluid." Informed Pittsburghers concurred in this judgment. The Pittsburgh Bureau of Health bluntly asserted that impure milk was the chief cause of infant mortality. Certainly diarrheal diseases, attributable to such milk, took a horrific toll of the city's babies. In 1907, for instance, 612 children under one year of age succumbed to such illness: in the same period only 8,724 births had been recorded.

As Dr. J. F. Edwards, superintendent of the bureau, emphasized, this effectively meant "that one out of every 13 babies died before it reached the age of one year because of impure milk." Although many attempts were made to introduce "pure" milk to the city, progress was painfully slow. The Allegheny County Medical Society established a commission to fix hygiene standards for certified milk, the under-staffed Bureau of Health made valiant attempts to increase inspection of milk handling and retailing establishments, and city authorities aided the charitable Milk and Ice Association in the distribution of good milk to the poor. Too many distraught mothers, however, re-mained hopelessly ignorant of milk's harmful effects. As a result, few were "willing to pay an increased cost for 'cleanliness' in milk; the quality of cleanliness [was] not apparent, and hence it [had] no com-mercial value."[22] Unfortunately, while many Birmingham families used condensed milk as a substitute, few tins were sold in Pittsburgh.

Birmingham workers also sought a substitute for butter. Margarine, or oleomargarine, as the product was known in the United States, was widely eaten in the city. It is true that although margarine cost less than one half the price, butter—especially Danish—was still preferred. This prejudice was believed to be a hangover from the nineteenth century when margarine possessed "a not altogether agreeable flavor of its own." But by the early twentieth century, purified margarine was "if anything rather nicer than cheap butter," possessed similar amounts of fats, proteins, and carbohydrates, and was frequently substituted for that product. Estimates suggest that by 1914, for every pound of butter bought by the Birmingham worker, 0.40 pounds of margarine were purchased. Dripping was also in common use among the city's workers, although only in small quantities: probably 0.28 pounds of dripping were consumed for every pound of butter. More important was the "custom prevalant among the [Birmingham] poor of using lard rather than butter as a relish to their bread": families purchased 0.36 pounds of lard for each pound of butter.[23]

In Pennsylvania relatively little margarine was bought. The butter substitute was available to the Pittsburgh consumer, but its widespread production had been considerably impeded by legislation enacted at the behest of American dairy interests. At the federal level, oleomar-garine manufacture was heavily taxed, and those who produced or retailed the product had to pay substantial license fees.[24] Pennsylvania state laws were even more suppressive. In 1885 oleomargarine manu-facture had been banned in Pennsylvania, but in 1898 this prohibition was declared unconstitutional. Instead, in 1899, a new law was passed allowing the manufacture and sale of oleomargarine free from coloration but prohibited tinting the product yellow. At the same time stringent financial conditions were imposed: the manufacturer had to pay an annual fee of $1,000, the wholesale dealer a fee of $500, and the retailer a fee of $100.[25]

Such legal discrimination angered many Pittsburghers. Oleomargarine was, as the *Pittsburgh Bulletin* noted, "the poor man's butter" and, when properly made, was a nutritional substitute for the more expensive spread. Yet little was eaten. Supply of the product was severely limited by state and federal tax imposts levied against those who made or sold it, while demand was restrained by an artificially high price level attributable to taxation, and by the inability of manufacturers to color the product in line with consumer expectations. It was a situation against which the *National Labor Tribune* fought vigorously, claiming that there was "no more reason why the people should not be permitted to buy cheap butter than there would be in denying them the privilege of buying cheap clothing." The "Shameless Legislative Truckling to Dairy Trust Shown in Pennsylvania" was, headlined the *Tribune,* a disgrace: anti-oleo laws represented "class legislation of an inexcusable character." With over a hundred Allegheny County oloemargarine dealers facing prosecution by mid–1907, the journal called for the repeal of the repressive legislation.[26]

In spite of such forceful opposition, the laws remained on the statute books. As a result the "considerable demand among certain sections of the workpeople" for butter substitutes had to be met by other products.[27] It seems likely that a much greater amount of lard was eaten in Pennsylvania than in Birmingham or Sheffield. Unfortunately, the nutritional value of lard (manufactured from the fat of pigs), as of dripping, was extremely limited, consisting primarily of fat. Oleomargarine was far superior.

Meat purchase accounted for the largest percentage of working-class food expenditure in the Midlands and, in terms of quantity eaten, was the third most important item of diet. As with other foodstuffs, however, the amount of meat consumed by British workers varied enormously from region to region. Residents of Midland towns ate significantly more than did those who dwelt in the north of England, and consumption in Birmingham was probably higher than in most Midland towns by virtue of the fact that the city was a key distributing center for both British and imported meat. Moreover, meat consumption in the city was increasing. By 1906 "better food—more meat at any rate—[was being] eaten."[28]

The amount of meat purchased per adult male worker in the Midlands, 2.24 pounds per week, provides a reliable indicator of the quantity actually consumed, for Birmingham women were "always shy of bones with their meat, and in buying beef, they nearly always [refused] to have a piece with any bone in it." Meat from the ribs was invariably stripped and rolled as a joint before being offered for sale.[29] It is not known if Pittsburgh's butchers also sold their meat boned. If they did, Table 54 indicates that Pennsylvanians consumed 63.4 percent more meat (including fish and poultry) than Midlanders. If bones were included in the estimates of meat consumption in the American state, this differential is overstated. However, there can be little doubt that far more meat was eaten in America.

This was not necessarily because the English worker ate meat less frequently: in fact, most Birmingham girls partook of meat at least once a day, stews, "faggots" (balls of chopped meat pieces) and "pig's fry" (internal organs of pig, for frying) predominating. The lower consumption appears to have been the result of the British worker eating less per meal.[30] Nor was the major meat preference of British and American workers different. In Birmingham, as in Pennsylvania, beef held "pride of place" among the working population. "Pieces," ideal for stews and pies, were customarily purchased, although "flank" provided the majority of Sunday joints.[31] Nevertheless, estimates suggest that the male adult Midlands worker ate only 77.4 percent of the amount of beef eaten by his counterpart in Pennsylvania.[32]

Mutton was the second most popular meat in Birmingham. Neck was the cut most commonly bought and, boiled with potherbs, it provided an alternative to the Sunday roast beef. What was left was served throughout the week: midweek dinners "[rang] the changes on cold neck," and it could replace or supplement the traditional Wednesday stew of beef pieces.. Only the more well-to-do of Birmingham's work force ran to the expense of purchasing loin chops, the next favorite mutton cut.[33] In contrast, pork was the second most consumed fresh meat in Pennsylvania, and the importance of mutton to the American diet was not considered worthy of separate mention by the commissioner of labor. Certainly consumption was comparatively low: estimates suggest that for every pound of mutton eaten per adult male in Pennsylvania, 2.7 pounds were consumed in the British Midlands.

Although Birmingham's Co-operative stores sold only home-grown meat, "the best procurable . . . PRIME HEREFORD BULLOCK AND HEIFER BEEF and the CHOICEST SHROPSHIRE MUTTON," most of the meat eaten by the city's workers was imported frozen or chilled. Pork was the exception. The large pork shops that abounded in Birmingham, and did "a continuous flourishing business," dealt almost exclusively in domestically produced meat. "The love of the pig as an article of diet," noted Dr. Carver, explaining the pork butchers' success, was "almost characteristic of the Anglo-Saxon race."[34] Yet the amount of fresh pork eaten in the British city was less than in Pennsylvania, in part, no doubt, because it was one of the few items to actually cost more in Birmingham than in Pittsburgh. Calculations indicate that for every pound of fresh pork eaten by the male adult worker in Pennsylvania, only 0.71 pounds were eaten in the Midlands. However, consumption of salt pork such as bacon and ham was similar, in spite of the fact that the most popular rashers in Birmingham were cut from unsmoked drafts imported from the United States.[35]

In summary, the adult male Midlander consumed about two-thirds the amount of meat eaten in Pennsylvania. But equally significant were the differences in relative meat consumption. While he ate considerably more mutton and about the same quantity of salt pork products, he ate less fresh pork and beef.

The final important components of working-class diet were the non-alcoholic beverages, predominantly tea in England and coffee in America. Total purchases of tea and coffee were greater in Pennsylvania, but a pound of dried tea, of course, infused a much greater amount of water than did a pound of dried coffee. Even the poorest English could afford tea, it was argued, for one received "a lot of pleasure out of two ounces; . . . at least a gallon of liquid [could] be brewed from it (double if [one was] content to have it weak)." This assertion was supported by the culinary wisdom of Mrs. Beeton, who calculated that a pound of tea could provide six times as much beverage as an equivalent amount of coffee. Whereas half an ounce of beans (a tablespoon) was needed to brew enough coffee for a single person, only one-twelfth of an ounce of tea leaves (a teaspoon) was required to provide a like amount of tea. Translation of the quantities estimated in Table 54 into cupfuls of consumed liquid suggests that the Pennsylvania male adult worker drank, on average, 16.3 cups of coffee each week, and supplemented this with 9.6 cups of tea. The Midland worker, in contrast, drank only 1.9 cups of coffee, but no less than 30.7 cups of tea—almost four and a half cups a day. This substantiates the claims made by contemporary investigators that two cups of tea usually accompanied the bread-and-butter breakfast eaten by most Birmingham workers, and that a further two cups washed down the evening meal. Moreover, tea was frequently brewed at the workplace, and some of the city's most stringently enforced factory rules concerned the times at which the teapot could make its appearance. Assuming each cup contained half a British pint, it appears the adult male weekly consumption totaled 18.4 American pints.[36]

Not surprisingly, many middle-class observers were worried by the British workers' "addiction" to tea. Dr. Carver, doubtful if the Birmingham worker knew the taste of water, attributed the prevalence of dyspepsia to such unrestrained tea consumption. "Alcohol may slay its thousands," he solemnly intoned, "but tea tortures its tens of thousands."[37] The city's workers turned a deaf ear to the warning.

The Budget for Rent, Fuel, Clothing, and Furniture

In 1914 Birmingham families devoted 54.5 percent of income to the purchase of food. Table 55, categorized by income group, suggests that at the same time families devoted an average of 17.7 percent of income to the payment of rent and 5.9 percent to the provision of fuel and lighting. "Thrift," totaling 3.3 percent, presumably comprised the portion of income that workers subscribed to friendly societies, trade unions, burial funds, or industrial insurance policies. "Surplus," representing 17.7 percent, probably included all income not immediately consumed. In part such sums were banked or hoarded for those financial exigencies that loomed in the future. But surplus also referred, one surmises, to income accumulated for a more definite purpose: to purchase, perhaps, a new pair of boots, an easy chair, a new set of crockery, a trip to the music hall, or a cheap day railway excursion; or, in some instances, it was a sum painstakingly saved in order to buy one of the new durable luxuries to which Birmingham workers could aspire— a gramophone or a bicycle. It was expenditure, in short, made only irregularly, and therefore rarely captured in short-term investigations.

It is true that many of Birmingham's manual workers bought clothes and shoes, furniture and luxuries through regularly contributing to clubs formed for that purpose, or acquired such items upon extended credit facilities by paying weekly installments. The city's "average working girl," for example, purchased "almost all her clothing through clubs." The clubs were managed by a colleague at the workplace, and their organization was attractively simple. Perhaps twenty girls would contribute sixpence (12.2¢) to a boots club for twenty consecutive weeks: each payday lots would be drawn, and the lucky winner could spend 10s. ($2.45) upon new boots.[38] Other families made their own credit arrangements with stores providing "lay-by" deposit schemes or holding out alluring "buy now, pay later" terms. Even among low-income groups, a "large proportion of families" purchased a gramo-

phone for from \$12 to \$17, "obtained on the hire purchase system."
Many others, eager to travel to work cheaply and increase recreational
opportunities, bought bicycles. Indeed, Birmingham had an army of
small dealers who assembled frames for as little as \$18 and sold upon
partial or deferred terms.[39] Credit even came door-to-door. "Foggers"
traveled the city's streets, persuading unwary housewives to buy wares
upon extended purchase arrangements.

Many others, fearful of the "usurious rates" charged for credit facili-

Table 55
Expenditure for Nonfood Items: Birmingham, 1914, and Sheffield, 1860–1892

A. *Birmingham, 1914*

| Family | Expenditure Category | | | | | | | |
| | Rent | | Fuel | | Thrift | | Surplus | |
Weekly Income	Amt.	%	Amt.	%	Amt.	%	Amt.	%
\$6.08 or less	1.26	23.5	0.37	7.0	0.24	4.4	0.30[a]	5.6
6.09–7.30	1.17	17.9	0.41	6.3	0.20	3.1	1.26	19.3
7.31–8.51	1.47	18.8	0.44	5.6	0.21	2.7	1.24[b]	15.9
8.52–10.22	1.42	15.3	0.55	6.0	0.29[c]	3.1	2.12	22.9
10.23 and over	1.72	12.8	0.61	4.5	0.41	3.0	4.03	30.0

B. *Birmingham, 1914, and Sheffield, 1860–1892*

| | % Outlay | |
Expenditure Category	Bhm 1914[d]	Shfd 1860–92[e]
Food	54.5	57.8[f]
Rent	17.7	15.0
Fuel/Lighting	5.9	5.6
Clothing	?	13.0
"Thrift"	3.3	?
"Surplus"	17.7	?

Sources: Carver, *Dietary of the Labouring Classes of Birmingham*, pp. 16–30; Sidney
Pollard, "Real Earnings in Sheffield, 1851–1914," *Yorkshire Bulletin of Economic and
Social Research*, 9 (1957), 59. Mean for 6 families: the breadwinner identified as "Cutler,
1889" was excluded as the data appeared inaccurate.

a. 1.24/- was misprinted as 2.25/- (presumably because families with a deficit, rather
than a surplus, were excluded).

b. 5.10/- was misprinted as 5.35/- (presumably because families with a deficit, rather
than a surplus, were excluded).

c. 1.18/- was misprinted as 1.13/- (presumably because of typographical error).

d. Percentage of income. Mean of five income categories presented in Tables 49 and
55A.

e. Percentage of expenditure.

f. Includes expenditure for tobacco, beer and soap.

ties and believing foggers to represent "the worst vermin of the parasitic class," eschewed such methods of payment.[40] For them the Chesterfield suit or Morris chair, the Standard gramophone or Wonder bicycle, were objects to be bought only after months of calculated thrift. And it is certain that Dr. Carver's generic umbrella, "surplus," included both the temporary savings preceding purchase and the regular installments that followed. The central question was the proportion of surplus devoted to the provision of clothing and furnishings. Upon that Dr. Carver, like the majority of his contemporary investigators, remained silent.

There can be little doubt that the bulk of surplus would have been ultimately committed to the purchase of clothing rather than to furniture, hardware, liquor, tobacco, newspapers, or recreation. Among Birmingham's working girls the mean percentage of expenditure upon clothing was 13.3 percent.[41] This is in line with a collection of Sheffield budgets for the 1860–1892 period. The Sheffield data, presented in Table 55, are similar to the Birmingham figures with respect to food, rent, and fuel, and it seemed fair to assume that the Sheffield clothing estimate—13 percent of expenditure—also bore close relation to the Birmingham experience. Pollard, using the budgets as his guide, estimated that 12 percent of working-class expenditure went to purchase clothing, and this educated guess appeared the best approximation for the present study.[42]

The percentage of income devoted to the purchase of furniture, accessories, and hardware proved equally difficult to gauge. George Barnsby, analyzing the standard of living in the English Black Country in the nineteenth century, postulated that a family would have needed to spend 1s. (24.4¢) per week to provide furnishings and domestic hardware, or 4 percent of expenditure.[43] However, the lack of empirical evidence makes this calculation dubious, especially since the demand for such items would have been more elastic than for those components of the cost-of-living index previously discussed, and weekly expenditure would have been correspondingly more irregular. It is interesting to note that a study by the Economic Club in the depression of the early 1890s suggested that outlays for furniture in British urban centers averaged only 1.6 percent of total expenditure, although this was admitted to be on the low side as a result of incomplete enumeration.[44]

As will be seen shortly, in 1901 the Pennsylvania family spent 2.6 percent of its budget for furniture. In the absence of other data, and insofar as this accorded with the maximum-minimum parameters indicated above, it seemed justifiable to assume that Birmingham manual workers would have set aside a similar proportion of expenditure for furniture.

The 1901 study of the budgets of 3,702 Pennsylvania families, previously referred to, noted the yearly income devoted to rent, fuel, lighting, and clothing (as well as to food) and elaborated the percentage of expenditure in detail for a selected group of 398 of those families: see Tables 56 and 57.[45] The budgetary profile of Pittsburghers probably matched that of the state at large. Certainly a 1907–1908 survey, presented in summary form in Table 58, suggests that the expenditure of Homestead workers was in percentage terms, very similar to that recorded for the Pennsylvania families.[46]

The surveyed foreign- and native-born families received similar mean annual incomes and had similar budgets. Somewhat unexpectedly, immigrant workers were more likely than their native-born colleagues to pay union subscriptions: 49.6 percent of foreign-born families contributed an average of $11.49 to labor organizations, whereas 40.4 percent of native-born families spent an average of $13.24. However, immigrants, in accordance with contemporary and historical comments, do seem to have been willing to live at a lower standard than native-stock Americans, spending less on rent, adult clothing, and furniture. Homestead's Slavic families generally lived in "poorly furnished, unattractive home[s]," whereas native-born Americans, both black and white, frequently resided in "neat and well furnished" rooms. The major surprise was that Pennsylvania's foreign-born spent proportionately more upon children's clothing, but this was probably attributable to the fact that the immigrant families surveyed were larger than were those of the natives: 5.23 members compared to 4.72 members. Evidence indicated that for families with the same number

Table 56
Expenditure for Rent, Fuel, Lighting, and Clothing: Pennsylvania Families, 1901

	Mean Yearly Expenditure ($)			% of Total Expenditure			% of Total Income		
Item	N	F	A	N	F	A	N	F	A
Rent	131.17	122.01	128.31	19.2	17.5	18.7	18.3	17.0	17.9
Fuel	28.09	27.87	28.02	4.1	4.0	4.1	3.9	3.9	3.9
Lighting	6.28	6.54	6.36	0.9	0.9	0.9	0.9	0.9	0.9
Clothing	82.75	86.81	84.07	12.1	12.4	12.2	11.5	12.1	11.7
Other[a]	128.71	129.92	129.10	18.9	18.6	18.8	17.9	18.1	18.0

Source: U.S., *Eighteenth Annual Report of the Commissioner of Labor*, 1901, Pt. 1, Tables 3B, 3C, pp. 317, 336–37.
Note: N = Native-born head of family (2,496 families).
F = Foreign-born head of family (1,206 families).
A = Aggregate: total native and foreign (3,702 families).
a. Excludes expenditure upon food.

of children, the foreign-born spent less upon clothing than did the native-born.[47]

Immigrants also disbursed more, both relatively and absolutely, upon liquor. More foreign-born families admitted to purchasing alcoholic beverages (60.2 percent compared to 45.2 percent), and those

Table 57
Detailed Expenditure Pattern: Pennsylvania Families, 1901
(Except Food)

Item	Average Yearly Expenditure[a]			% of Total Expenditure		
	N $	F $	A $	N	F	A
Rent	133.11[c]	118.30[c]	129.01[c]	19.1	16.7	18.4
Fuel	28.73	28.75	28.73	4.1	4.1	4.1
Lighting	6.76	6.89	6.80	1.0	1.0	1.0
Clothing						
Men's	29.01	26.58	28.33			
Women's	20.55	17.75	19.76	12.1	13.5	12.4
Children's	34.94	49.84	39.16			
Taxes	4.53	5.46	4.79	0.6	0.8	0.7
Insurance						
Property	1.21	1.03	1.16	2.7	2.7	2.7
Life	17.54	18.13	17.71			
Organizations						
Labor	3.41	3.34	3.39	1.7	1.4	1.6
Other	8.50	6.61	7.96			
Religion	6.80	8.44	7.27	1.0	1.2	1.0
Charity	2.53	2.00	2.38	0.4	0.3	0.3
Furniture/Utensils	20.92	12.67	18.57	3.0	1.8	2.6
Books/Newspapers	6.45	5.18	6.09	0.9	0.7	0.9
Amusements	11.30	8.10	10.40	1.6	1.1	1.5
Liquor	5.46	14.78	8.11	0.8	2.1	1.2
Tobacco	10.00	9.29	9.80	1.4	1.3	1.4
Sickness/Death	19.93	15.80	18.76	2.9	2.2	2.7
Other[b]	30.36	37.49	32.38	4.3	5.3	4.6
Subtotal[b]	393.35	382.58	390.29	56.3[d]	54.1[d]	55.7[d]

Source: U.S., *Eighteenth Annual Report of the Commissioner of Labor,* 1903, Pt. 1, Tables 4D, 4E, 4F, pp. 430–1, 446–47, 464–5.

Note: N = Native-born head of family.
      F = Foreign-born head of family.
      A = Aggregate: total U.S. and foreign families.

a. Includes families who had no expenditure.
b. Excludes expenditure for food.
c. Based only on those families who paid rent: i.e., 87.2% of sample.
d. Includes families who did not pay rent.

who did drank more freely than their native-born colleagues. Immigrant drinkers spent, on average 47¢ a week upon liquor, enough to buy more than nine pints of beer or half a quart bottle of whiskey.[48] But it would be incautious to interpret such figures as evidence of dipsomanic indulgence. To many foreigners the local saloon represented one of the few cathartic escapes from working life, while native-born Americans were able to derive greater leisure satisfaction from the music hall and nickelodeon, from picnic excursions and baseball games, and from reading. Thus the native workers spent, on average, 39.5 percent more than immigrants upon officially designated amusements, and 24.8 percent more upon books and newspapers.

Fashion

Table 59 summarizes the comparative expenditure schedules of Birmingham and Pittsburgh manual workers in the first decade of the twentieth century. The American employee devoted substantially less

Table 58
Expenditure of Homestead Families, 1907–1908

Item	Mean Weekly Expenditure	Share of Total Expenditure
Food	$6.27	39.5%
Rent	2.99[a]	18.8
Fuel	0.63	4.0
Clothing	1.86	11.7
Furniture	0.33	2.1
Household expenses	0.38	2.4
Insurance	1.00	6.3
Tobacco	0.06	0.4
Liquor	0.28	1.8
Health	0.36	2.3
Other	1.73	10.9
Total	15.89	100.2[b]

Source: Margaret Byington, *Homestead: The Households of a Mill Town* (New York, 1910), Appendix 11, pp. 206–13.

Note: Reworking of the date disclosed several errors, *viz.*, family 19 expenditure totaled $9.53, whereas stated as $9.35; family 31 expenditure totaled $5.90, whereas stated as $10.90; family 37 expenditure totaled $15.96, whereas stated as $15.93; and family 86 expenditure totaled $19.83, whereas stated as $19.80.

a. Based on the 77 families who paid rent: i.e., 85.6% of sample of 90 families.

b. Error due to rounding.

of his total budget to food, as has already been noted, but slightly more to paying rent and local property taxes. In short, to feed and house a family required just over 60 percent of the Pittsburgher's purse but approximately 75 percent in Birmingham.

Fuel and lighting together accounted for 6 percent of expenditure in the British city. In Pennsylvania fuel and light required only 5 percent of the total budget, although the exigencies of climate would have required the American family to consume greater quantities of coal, wood, and gas in order to warm the house through bitter winter months. The explanation of the greater expenditure in Birmingham lies in the comparative price structures. If all fuel and lighting requirements had been met from the purchase of bituminous coal, the Pittsburgher could, in 1901, have acquired 2.1 tons for each ton bought in Birmingham: if, instead, all such needs had been met by the purchase of gas, the Pittsburgher could have purchased 3.3 cubic feet for every foot consumed in the British city.[49]

Coal, gas, and kerosene would have comprised the basic ingredients of the fuel and lighting bill on both sides of the Atlantic. I estimated that three-quarters of lighting expenditure went to purchase kerosene and one-quarter to buying gas. Similarly, I calculated that the fuel bill was split evenly between providing the house with warmth and supplying the heat with which to cook. It was assumed that coal performed the former function. Clearly, this was inaccurate insofar as workers in both Pittsburgh and Birmingham complemented their coal resources by purchasing bundles of wooden tinder and by burning logs: hawkers of wood were a common sight in early twentieth-century Birmingham.

Table 59

Expenditure for Food, Rent, Fuel, Lighting, Clothing, and Furnishings: Pittsburgh and Birmingham, 1900–1910

	% of Total Income		% of Total Expenditure	
Item	*Birmingham*	*Pittsburgh*[a]	*Pittsburgh*[a]	*Pittsburgh*[b]
Food	54.5	43.5	46.1	44.3
Rent	17.7	17.9	18.7	18.4
Fuel	} 5.9	3.9	4.1	4.1
Lighting		0.9	0.9	1.0
Clothing	12.0	11.7	12.2	12.4
Furniture/Utensils	2.6	n.s.s.	n.s.s.	2.6

Sources: See Tables 51, 55, 56, 57 and text.
Note: n.s.s. = not separately stated.
a. Based on a sample of 3,702 Pennsylvania families.
b. Based on a sample of 398 Pennsylvania families.

But the lack of statistical data on wood/fuel prices prevented the incorporation of this item into the fuel index. In Pittsburgh natural gas was extensively used for cooking, and by 1909 gas ranges were "probably more used than coal ranges." In the British city, too, families increasingly employed gas as a cooking agent. The provision of free equipment by the local council convinced workers to convert to gas stoves, although many families retained their coal ranges as well. In both cities, then, I gauged that half the cooking bill was devoted to the purchase of coal and half to the purchase of gas. In brief, I estimated that 60 percent of the total outlay for fuel and lighting went to purchase coal, 25 percent to buy gas, and 15 percent to buy kerosene.[50]

Furniture and domestic utensils accounted for only a small percentage of total budget in both Britain and the United States. However, expenditure upon such items increased as family income rose. The Birmingham family receiving less than $6.09 a week generally possessed little furniture. A table dominating the center of the floor, around it clustered a number of plain Windsor chairs, a couch pushed against the side wall, and a chest-of-drawers placed opposite the window—such was the typical living-cum-dining room. On top of the chest stood, perhaps, a cheap glass vase sprouting artificial flowers, an array of china ornaments, and a few tinted photographs. A couple of colored prints hanging on the walls, a sticky flypaper dangling from the ceiling, oilcloth on the floor, and patchwork rug in front of the hearth were the only other accessories. Upstairs rooms were barer still. Bedrooms were "simply . . . not furnished; an iron bedstead, with flock mattress and flannelette coverings" represented the sum total of domestic possessions. As disposable income increased, the starkness of empty rooms was deftly transformed into that overpowering combination of ornateness and gentility beloved by the Edwardian housewife. The neatly arranged, if overly furnished, front room, replete with rocking chair and china cabinet, frilled cloths and lacework antimacassars, was used to entertain visitors; and in the bedrooms appeared mirrors, washbasins, and chamberpots.[51]

In the United States too, expenditure upon furnishings increased in direct relation to family income. In Homestead those workers who earned less than $12.00 per week spent a mere 9¢ on furniture, and only 15¢ upon household utensils, while those with an income of $20.00 or more expended 80¢ and 66¢, respectively. Moreover, there exists little evidence that workers in America enjoyed a standard of home furnishings much superior to that which existed in England. Although Homestead families aspired to a cozy front room with "fresh curtains, a couch, and an occasional carpet" and longed to possess luxuries such as sewing machines and pianos, not many could achieve their ambitions even with the assistance of installment plans. Pennsylvania's foreign-born spent, on average, $12.67 per year upon furniture and utensils, while the native-born expended $20.92. Contemporaries estimated that $10.00 was required annually simply to replace worn linen, frayed curtains, and soiled carpets, so that there could have been few with the financial resources to furnish the home according to the ideal. Homestead employees rarely enjoyed the "American standard" to which Samuel Gompers made loving reference. Only among the the top echelon of manual workers, in families earning more than $20.00 a week, did there exist sufficient funds to satisfy "the reasonable ambitions of an American who puts his life into his work . . . with the children fed and housed in such a fashion as to maintain physical well-being."[52]

Table 59 suggests that workers in Pittsburgh and Birmingham also devoted similar portions of their expenditure to the purchase of clothing. While total expenditure was larger in America, the additional disbursement would have compensated for the comparative dearness of clothing. The statistical evidence, in brief, indicated that British workers were buying more and/or superior quality clothing.

This was an unexpected finding, for contemporaries generally agreed that Americans were more fashion-conscious than their English counterparts. Like many of his compatriot travelers, Douglas Knoop, Gartside scholar to the United States in 1906, was impressed by the attire worn by American workers. Witnessing cotton operatives leaving Newark textile factories at the conclusion of their labors, he noted that they "would be ashamed to be seen on the streets in their working clothes, and consequently [they changed] before commencing and after finishing work. They [kept] overalls or old clothes at the factory, and they [dressed] like any other American citizen. The clogs, the shawls, the mufflers, the corduroy or other working suits" with which Knoop was familiar in Lancashire were "unknown in America."[53]

Such concern with clothing convinced European visitors, unconsciously following in the footsteps of Alexis de Tocqueville, that American democracy created its own tyrannical imperatives. Manual workers in the United States, it was argued, spurred by the opinions of their peers and keen to equal the garb worn by social superiors, felt obliged to dress in fashionable splendor. Many travelers, with nuances of aristocratic disdain, contended that no nation in the world was in such bondage to fashion. American "men and women, young and old, [wore] boots that [narrowed] to a sharp point, like skates, two inches beyond the toes; they [tinkered] at their faces with complexion-washes and nose-machines as zealously as some people in England [tinkered] at their souls."[54]

It was not merely upper- and middle-class travelers who commented in such vein. Terence Flynn who, as a representative of the Amalgamated Society of Tailors, possessed both the reason and the ability to examine the question with critical zeal, was convinced that Americans displayed more interest in clothing style than workers in England. And to many immigrants the adjustment to American fashion proved traumatic. Typical, perhaps, was the painful experince of one English shop girl. "When I first came in at the door of this [mercantile] house, and registered, one of the other shop-girls here was standing at the desk," she remembered. "I had on a heavy winter coat, just a plain, rough-looking coat but it's warm. That girl gave me such a look, a sort of sneering look—oh, it made me hot! But that's the way American shop-girls are."[55]

The interesting aspect of this poignant memory is the clear implication that fashion was not synonymous with quality. It is true that Samuel Gompers believed that many workers in Great Britain had "tattered clothing, and unshod feet," epitomizing the "poverty and misery" that abounded. Fellow American Lee Galloway found Birmingham's slum dwellers repulsive, as they accosted him with "their dishevelled hair, their dirty faces, and their medley costumes, of which no two garments [belonged] together." Yet British visitors to Birmingham were certain that there existed "no rags and no bare feet" in the city.[56]

Two points need to be noted about such qualitative evidence. First, most statements referred to slum children and adult beggars and therefore gave little indication of normal working-class attire. Second, emphasis was not upon clothing quality per se, but upon the carelessness of dress appearance and the dirtiness of those parts of the body that exposed themselves to view. Even in 1905 Galloway admitted that Birmingham's working girls, in spite of their hopeless sense of fashion, and in spite of their apparent aversion to washing, spent money on luxury items: they wore "ragged bits of lace as adornment on their unclean necks, and, as further accessories, old brass brooches and tawdry necklaces." By 1914 he was more impressed: in the city's streets he found "young men neatly attired . . . [and] young women stylishly dressed."[57]

American workers were more fashionable. They possessed a greater quantity of clothes. Few Americans would have followed the English practice of wearing the same small collection of articles throughout the year. But their wardrobes were not necessarily superior. Pittsburghers might have appeared more flamboyantly dressed, but a closer examination rapidly disclosed the tawdry nature of much of their attire. Factory girls employed at the Heinz plant typically wore "coarse woolen garments, a shabby felt sailor hat, a cheap piece of fur, a knitted shawl and gloves." They shared with Birmingham girls the love of inexpensive ornamentation. "Almost all the girls [wore] shoes with patent leather and some or much cheap jewellery, brooches, bangles, and rings."[58] Moreover, not all American workers spent valuable time and money following the dictates of fashion. The magnificent photographs of steelworkers and child factory operatives that Lewis Hine contributed to the Pittsburgh Survey bore testimony to the fact that many laborers wore clothes that were as shabby, soiled, and shapeless as those in which Birmingham employees customarily went to work.

Certainly it would be unwise to attribute the alleged shabbiness of English clothing habits to lack of expenditure. Birmingham workers consciously defied the vagaries of fashion, preferring instead restrained, individually tailored items, capable of withstanding the passing seasons. Unnecessary show was abhorred. A Birmingham man, noted Consul Halstead, did "not like to have his clothes in cut or fit such as to attract attention," and he depised the conspicuous broad shoulders, heavy seams, and large pocket flaps that captured the imagination of Americans. Manual workers in the United States were in "the habit of buying many articles of poor quality, instead of few articles of better quality": in England the reverse was true. "*Wear your own Costume!*" the Birmingham Co-operative Society urged men and women alike. "Not necessarily because you bought and paid for it, but more especially from the fact that it was MADE TO FIT YOU, embodying the many little individualisms that constitute the really high-class MADE TO MEASURE costume." And the city's workers apparently responded. Ready-made clothing was "not greatly purchased in Birmingham," according to the American consul. There existed "many tailors who [made] the cheapest clothing to order, and there [was] a large demand for this on the theory that suits and overcoats that [were] made to order [were] better."[59]

Quality rather than quantity; warmth and comfort rather than fashion; durability rather than style—these were the major differences in the English and American attitudes toward the purchase of clothes. The variety and flamboyance of American attire was not, per se, an indication of a superior living standard. Indeed, the habit of buying many cheap clothes was, contended the National Consumers' League, "not a matter of choice but of necessity. The cheap, hand-to-mouth buying which [proved] paradoxically so expensive in the end [was] no doubt often caused by the simple fact that the purchaser [had] not, at the time the purchase [was] made, any more money to offer."[60] It is, at the least, a possibility that must be seriously considered.

10
The Standard of Living

It has been noted in previous chapters, with a determined repetitiveness that has probably proved frustrating, that qualifications must be appended to virtually all the quantitative evidence presented. Such statistical diffidence indicates a perhaps fastidious desire for accuracy. It also reflects the belief that the disaggregation of industry-wide and nationwide wage and earnings data, and the breakdown of price and cost-of-living indices into their component parts, reveals the scale of error inherent in many cliometric exercises. In surveys of real wages, knowledge of occupational wage levels, skill differentials, standard hours of work, and of the contribution of wives and children to family income is just as relevant as aggregate indices of work payment. This is true whether comparison is temporal or spatial and irrespective of whether the compiled indices aim to measure payment per unit of work done or earnings over a set period of time. Similarly, the manner in which prices vary according to retailing environment, seasonal factors, and purchasing behavior and the manner in which expenditure patterns respond to changes in income and nativity are as significant to the economic historian as are the aggregate indices generally presented. In short, the qualificatory estimates attached to measures of real income may tell as much about comparative living standards as the indices themselves.

In this concluding chapter, the numerous reservations attached to apparently definitive statistical statements will be shelved, and categorical estimates will be made of the comparative standard of living of manual workers in Pittsburgh, Birmingham, and Sheffield. Nevertheless, a brief note of warning must be inserted. The reader must not only heed the cautions previously expressed, but must also remain aware of the narrow definition of standard of living here employed. The standard refers to the "basket of goods" that workers could buy for an hour of labor, or that families could purchase from weekly earnings. It is real income, assessed in terms of the material resources that could be bought, but the standard of living is but one measure of a wider, more significant, less quantifiable, and extremely subjective concept—the quality of life.

Real Hourly Wages

The bases from which to assess comparative hourly rates of pay, family earnings (for a full-time work week), commodity retail prices, and expenditure schedules have already been presented. From such data it was a straightforward task to calculate relative real wages or, more accurately, to estimate the real cost of a common composite unit of consumables in the British and American cities, expressed in terms of the hours of labor required to purchase it. The major decision involved which budgetary profile to select as the foundation upon which to construct the composite unit of consumables—a unit which, in turn, dictated the respective weights to be attached to commodity prices. I had to decide whether to use the Pennsylvania worker's expenditure schedule as the guide to the comparative cost of living in Pittsburgh, or whether it would be more valid to base analysis upon the Birmingham pattern.

The theoretical issue was complex. It was unlikely that the Birmingham worker who migrated to Pittsburgh would have spent exactly the same percentage of income upon items as he had previously done at home: no matter how strong the force of habit, and no matter how great his commitment to previous lifestyle, the difference in relative price levels would probably have changed his consumption behavior, albeit slowly, toward a purchasing profile more akin to that of the native Pittsburgher. Yet even had the Birmingham worker been willing to alter his expenditure pattern in response to his new environment, the question remained as to whether it was justifiable to use the Pittsburgher's budget as a guide to comparative living costs. Perhaps the Birmingham employee had derived greater satisfaction from his Midlands diet than he did from the American diet which the change in prices persuaded him to adopt. If so, then the transference incurred a real (nonquantifiable) psychic cost, and in consequence it might have been fairer to base the comparative cost of living upon the assumption that the immigrant retained his previous expenditure pattern in his adopted country.

Indeed, the implications for comparative analysis run even deeper. It might be posited that consideration of psychic costs make the quantification of the standard of living impossible, while a conceptual definition so narrow as to include only the measurement of material satisfaction is meaningless. This was precisely the possibility that E. H. Phelps Brown and Margaret Browne faced, and their considered response was well reasoned:

It may be that we ought really to stand on this ground, and say that for all we know, the Indian wage-earner is more content with his ricebowl than the American with his steak, "for East is East and West is West, and never the twain shall meet." Evidently there is a sense in which this is true: we cannot measure content-ment. But if our aim be only to measure the command of mate-rial resources, and we introduce evaluation only in order to place basketfuls of different physical composition in a common scale, then the assumption may be permitted that consumers in differ-ent countries, though creatures of different habits, are potentially alike.[1]

Certainly it seemed fair to assume that Pittsburgh and Birmingham consumers, if not Indian and American, shared sufficient material de-sires and cultural mores that comparison was meaningful. But the means of comparison remained unresolved. Statistical theory provided no ready-made, incontrovertible solution. In time series there exist two methods of calculating changes in prices or quantities: the first, devised by Laspeyre, uses weights appropriate to the earlier date; the second, by Paasch, incorporates weights appropriate to the later. Estimates derived from these two procedures define the upper and lower limits of the variations over time, and the applied statistician frequently, if arbi-trarily, employs the geometric mean of the two calculations as the basis of comparison. A similar technique might justifiably be used in spatial comparison, although it should be noted that the two weighted esti-mates are not conflicting: rather, they should be treated as "alternative evaluations in alternative scales" of assessment.[2]

It is fortunate, given these difficulties, that practical application of the alternative weighting techniques resulted in remarkably similar es-timates. Table 60 shows that the monetary cost of living, based upon a composite unit of consumables derived from Birmingham budgetary behavior (1914), was 67.1 percent greater in Pittsburgh than in the English Midlands city in 1905, whereas the cost, based upon a compos-ite unit of consumables derived from Pennsylvania expenditure prac-tice (1901), was 65.3 percent higher. It is true that not all items of expenditure were included in the budgetary weightings. Phelps Brown, whose comparative price data on Britain and the United States incor-porated only the cost of the food and accommodation, rightly declined to call his statistical conclusion a cost-of-living index. The present study, however, covers a far more extensive range of commodities comprising 82.8 percent of the Pennsylvania worker's expenditure and

Table 60

Estimates of the Comparative Cost of Living: Pittsburgh and Birmingham, 1901–1914

	1	2	3	4	5
	% Outlay			Weighted Price Index	
Item	Bhm Income (1914)	Pa. Expenditure (1901)	Pittsburgh Price Index 1905 (Bhm = 100.0)	For Bhm budget (col. 1 × col. 3)	For Pa. budget (col. 2 × col. 3)
Food	54.4	44.3			
Beef	6.7	6.8	143.9[h]	964.13	978.52
Pork	1.8	1.2	92.6[i]	166.68	111.12
Mutton	3.3	1.2[f]	142.2[j]	469.26	170.64
Bacon	3.0	2.0	109.8	329.40	219.60
Other meat[a]	3.4	1.9[g]	126.2[k]	429.08	239.78
Eggs	1.3	3.0	108.6	141.18	325.80
Milk	3.4	2.8	120.3	409.02	336.84
Cheese	1.3	0.4	122.4	159.12	48.96
Butter	3.4	4.3	117.1	398.14	503.53
Potatoes	2.3	1.9	189.0	434.70	359.10
Flour	8.9	2.3	106.4	95.76	244.72
Bread	7.8	1.9	208.3	1624.74	395.77
Tea	2.8[e]	0.7	158.5	443.80	110.95
Coffee	0.5[e]	1.6	54.2[l]	27.10	86.72
Sugar	2.6	2.3	158.5	412.10	364.55
Other food	9.9	10.0	134.3[m]	1329.57	1343.00
Rent	17.7	18.4	252.7	4472.79	4649.68
Fuel/Light[b]	5.9	5.1			
Coal	3.5	3.0	66.4[n]	232.40	199.20
Gas	1.5	1.3	42.7[m]	64.05	55.51
Kerosene	0.9	0.8	101.0[n]	90.90	80.80
Clothing[c]	12.0	12.4			
Clothes	9.0	9.3	212.8[o]	1915.20	1979.04
Shoes	3.0	3.1	136.8[p]	410.40	424.08

Furniture[d]	1.3	1.3	22.2	288.86	288.86
Home utensils[d]	1.3	1.3	129.0[q]	167.70	167.70
Subtotal	92.6	82.8		15476.08	13684.47

Relative cost of a composite unit of consumables	Based on Bhm budget	Based on Pa. budget
Formula	Birmingham = 100.0	Birmingham = 100.0
	subtotal col.4	subtotal col. 5
	subtotal col.1	subtotal col. 2
Calculations	15476.08/92.6	13684.47/82.8
Final estimate	Pittsburgh = 167.1	Pittsburgh = 165.3

Sources: See tables in chapters 6, 8, and 9.

a. Includes fish and poultry.

b. Assumes that fuel and lighting expenditure was, as suggested in chapter 8, divided between coal, gas, and paraffin in the ratio 60:25:15.

c. Assumes that clothing expenditure was divided between clothes and shoes in the ratio 75:25.

d. Assumes that expenditure on furniture and home utensils was divided between the two in the ratio 50:50.

e. Based on food expenditure in Midland towns, 1904.

f. Assumes that the "other meat" category referred to mutton.

g. Expenditure on salt beef, poultry, and fish.

h. Based on relative prices of beef ribs, round, and sirloin.

i. Based on relative prices of pork chops.

j. Based on relative prices of mutton leg.

k. Mean unweighted price index for beef, pork, and mutton.

l. Based on the price charged for ground mixed and French coffee in "high" and "medium" class Birmingham stores.

m. Mean unweighted price index for all ten listed (nonmeat) food items.

n. Based on the relative prices of coal, gas, and paraffin in 1907.

o. Based on the mean unweighted price index for man's suit, man's overcoat, man's underwear, man's shirt, man's socks, woman's suit, and woman's skirt.

p. Based on relative prices of woman's shoes.

q. Based on the mean unweighted price index for wooden domestic utensils, mattresses, crockery, linen bedding and toweling, light fixtures, glassware, metal domestic utensils, cutlery, floor covering, and cotton bedding and toweling.

92.6 percent of the Birmingham family's income. Thus it appeared warranted to treat the cost of these composite units of consumables as acceptable substitutes for an index incorporating all components of the cost of living.[3]

I then compared these relative cost of living indices (RCLI) to the relative money wage indices (RMWI) paid to various occupations in Pittsburgh and Birmingham in 1906. By dividing the latter index by the former, I could estimate a relative real wage index (RRWI) for each job category. The derived quotients, presented in Table 61A suggest that while all Pittsburgh occupations gained hourly rates of pay superior, in real terms, to those in Birmingham, the difference at the unskilled level was small. Table 61B, which compares Pittsburgh with Sheffield, confirms the analysis. Laborers engaged in Pittsburgh's engineering and bakery trades, and those in public employment, all had real hourly rates less than 10 percent in advance of those of their counterparts in Birmingham. At least two Sheffield occupations—those of the engineering laborer and foundry blacksmith—actually earned a lower real hourly wage in the United States. Moreover, the largest single occupational group in Pittsburgh, steel mill laborers,

Table 61

Comparative Real Hourly Wages by Occupation: Pittsburgh, Birmingham, and Sheffield, 1906

A. *Real Hourly Wages in Pittsburgh and Birmingham*

Occupation	Pittsburgh R.M.W.I. (Bhm = 100.0)	Pittsburgh R.C.L.I. (Bhm = 100.0)	Pittsburgh R.R.W.I. (Bhm = 100.0)
Engineering laborer	171.7	165.3–167.1	102.8–103.9
Foundry blacksmith	175.7	165.3–167.1	105.1–106.7
Public laborer	178.7[a]	165.3–167.1	106.9–108.1
Third-hand baker	179.6	165.3–167.1	107.5–108.7
Second-hand baker	187.0	165.3–167.1	111.9–113.1
Boilermaker	190.8	165.3–167.1	114.2–115.4
Machinist	191.5	165.3–167.1	114.6–115.8
Compositor, b.&j.	201.9	165.3–167.1	120.8–122.1
First-hand baker	202.2	165.3–167.1	121.0–122.3
Bookbinder	204.0	165.3–167.1	122.1–123.4
Patternmaker	207.4	165.3–167.1	124.1–125.5
Public rammer	207.5[b]	165.3–167.1	124.2–125.5
Building laborer	218.2	165.3–167.1	130.6–132.0
Machine woodworker	226.6	165.3–167.1	135.6–137.1
Carpenter	226.9	165.3–167.1	135.8–137.3
Painter	246.2	165.3–167.1	147.3–148.9
Compositor, m.n.	257.0	165.3–167.1	153.8–155.5

Occupation	Pittsburgh R.M.W.I. (Bhm = 100.0)	Pittsburgh R.C.L.I. (Bhm = 100.0)	Pittsburgh R.R.W.I. (Bhm = 100.0)
Plumber	259.1	165.3–167.1	155.1–156.7
Stonemason	270.9	165.3–167.1	162.1–163.9
Plasterer	277.3	165.3–167.1	165.9–167.8
Bricklayer	326.9	165.3–167.1	195.6–197.8
Public paver	347.2[b]	165.3–167.1	207.8–210.0

B. Real Hourly Wages in Pittsburgh and Sheffield

	Pittsburgh R.M.W.I. (Shfd = 100.0)	Pittsburgh R.C.L.I. (Shfd = 100.0)	Pittsburgh R.R.W.I. (Shfd = 100.0)
Foundry blacksmith	159.3	165.3	96.4
Engineering laborer	164.6	165.3	99.6
Steel mill laborer	168.7[c]	165.3	102.1
Machinist	173.6	165.3	105.0
Bookbinder	185.5	165.3	112.2
Boilermaker	185.6	165.3	112.3
Public laborer	187.2	165.3	113.2
Compositor, b.&j.	195.8	165.3	118.5
Patternmaker	201.7	165.3	122.0
Tram conductor	238.2[d]	165.3	144.1
Carpenter	239.3	165.3	144.8
Machine woodworker	242.0	165.3	146.4
Building laborer	255.6	165.3	154.6
Compositor, m.n.	267.6	165.3	161.9
Plumber	273.2	165.3	165.3
Painter	280.3	165.3	169.6
Stonemason	285.0	165.3	173.4
Plasterer	307.7	165.3	186.1
Bricklayer	326.9	165.3	197.8

Sources: See Tables 10, 12, and 60.

Note: Data for bakers and tram conductors refer to 1907; data for engineering laborers and public rammers refer to 1905; data for public pavers refer to 1909. R.M.W.I. = relative money wage index. R.C.L.I. = relative cost of living index, defined as the relative cost of a composite unit of consumables: the minimum figure refers to the relative cost of a composite unit based on a Pennsylvania budget; the maximum figure refers to the relative cost of a composite unit based on a Birmingham budget. R.R.W.I. = relative real wage index, i.e., 100 (R.M.W.I./R.C.L.I.). B.&j. = book-and-job; m.n. = morning newspaper.

a. Assumes that Birmingham public laborer worked 48.0 hours.

b. Assumes that Birmingham and Pittsburgh pavers/rammers worked the same number of weekly hours.

c. Based on mean hours worked in Sheffield (54.7), not on standard week.

d. Assumes that Sheffield and Pittsburgh tram conductors worked the same number of weekly hours.

gained only 2.1 percent more, in real terms, than their colleagues in Sheffield.[4] At the other extreme, certain skilled workers gained rates very much higher: morning newspaper compositors, for example, were paid more than half as much again in Pittsburgh as in Birmingham; bricklayers and pavers, twice as much.

In some sectors, such as the engineering and bakery trades, Pittsburgh hourly wages were comparatively low. In other areas, notably the construction trades, real rates were extremely high. In general, however, Birmingham's unskilled workers tended to be better off, vis-à-vis their Pittsburgh equivalents, than were the city's skilled employees. Table 62 suggests that unskilled laborers in the American city's engineering, baking, and building trades, and those engaged in public employment, earned mean real hourly wages only 12 to 13 percent greater than their Birmingham counterparts; while skilled manual em-

Table 62

Comparative Real Hourly Wages by Level of Skill: Pittsburgh, Birmingham and Sheffield, 1906[a]

Category	Occupation	Pittsburgh R.R.W.I. (Bhm and Shfd = 100.0)
Birmingham		
Unskilled	Engineering laborer Public laborer Third-hand baker Building laborer	112.0–113.1
"Semiskilled"	Foundry blacksmith Public rammer Second-hand baker Carpenter	119.2–120.7
Skilled	Patternmaker Public paver First-hand baker Bricklayer	162.1–163.9
Sheffield		
Unskilled	Engineering laborer Public laborer Steel mill laborer Building laborer	117.4
Skilled	Patternmaker Compositor, m.n. Bricklayer	160.6

Sources: See Table 61.

Note: R.R.W.I. = relative real wage index; compositor, m.n. = morning newspaper compositor.

a. For occupations for which 1906 was not the year of comparison see Table 61.

ployees in the same industrial sectors, namely patternmakers, first-hand bakers, bricklayers and public pavers, gained real rates 62 to 64 percent higher than employees in similar occupations in Birmingham.

The implications of this analysis became evident when the comparative wage data were placed within an extended chronological framework. When the real hourly wage ratios were linked to national indices of real wage rates, it was possible to view the final estimates for 1906 within a wider historical perspective.[5] Such a statistical technique was, of course, as rough as it was ready. The existing time series possessed all the defects of aggregation heretofore noted: the wage data hid changes in the occupational, sex, and regional components of the work force; the price statistics were derived from dubiously small sample frames; and the expenditure weights incorporated into the cost of living indices were fixed by the infrequent dates at which national budgetary surveys had been conducted. Furthermore, the linking procedure was based upon two primary assumptions: that the movement of real wages estimated for the nation was paralleled in the individual cities; and that the movement of wages occurred equally in all occupations.[6]

The movement of skill differentials in the late nineteenth and early twentieth centuries was sufficiently restrained to suggest that the second assumption was substantially correct. The more debatable question was whether the long-run secular movement of real wage rates paid in the individual cities varied markedly from the national aggregate series. The local material from which to estimate movements in monetary wages and the cost of living, and thereby to construct a regional real wage series, was fragmentary. Nevertheless, it proved possible to check the national series against city data. Circumstantial evidence has already been presented to suggest that the advance in American rents calculated by Rees appears to have been mirrored in Pittsburgh, and Table 63 indicates that the movement of food and bituminous coal prices in the Pennsylvania city, and the increase in hourly wages, likewise matched the national pattern. However, the price at which natural gas was supplied to Pittsburgh consumers rose in the post–1905 period, whereas the price of manufactured gas produced in most American cities declined: as a result, a composite fuel and light index for Pittsburgh would have diverged markedly, over time, from the national one.

More significantly, the present analysis has cast severe doubts on the reliability of Rees's clothing and furniture indices. It has been argued that the recorded price "plateau" might well have been a statistical illusion, insofar as decreases in product quality often hid real increases in commodity prices. Consequently, it is quite possible that Douglas's indices, based upon wholesale price data, are more accurate. This is a crucial issue. Phelps Brown was aware that if he had derived his American real wage series from Douglas rather than from Rees, his statistical conclusions would have been fundamentally altered.[7] It therefore seemed necessary to estimate alternative time series, one comparing the United Kingdom index with Rees's data and the other comparing that same index with Douglas's estimates.

It was also possible that the United Kingdom series were in error. Certainly the fact that the price indices constructed by Bowley were derived almost exclusively from London data raised doubts as to the general applicability of the series. Table 64 compares the statistical

Table 63
American Wages and Prices; 1900, 1905, and 1913: A Comparison of National and Regional Trends

Index	Source	1900	1905	1913	Basis
Hourly wages	Table 6	Not calculable	100.0	128.2	Pittsburgh
	Table 5[a]	84.7	100.0	127.9	Pittsburgh
	Rees, Table 44	87.8	100.0	128.5	U.S.A.
Food prices	Table 24[b]	90.9	100.0	127.0	Pittsburgh
	Table 24[c]	90.8	100.0	124.3	Pittsburgh
	Rees, Table 44	91.0	100.0	124.4	U.S.A.
Bituminous coal prices	Table 39	Not calculable	100.0	106.3	Pittsburgh
	Rees, Table 44		100.0	105.3	U.S.A.
Gas prices	Table 40[d]	Not calculable	100.0	111.6	Pittsburgh
	Table 40[e]	Not calculable	100.0	100.0	Pittsburgh
	Rees, Table 44		100.0	90.1	U.S.A.
Rent	Ch. 7, text	(circumstantial evidence suggests that Rees' index is correct)			
	Rees, Table 44		100.0	103.1	U.S.A.
Furnishings	Ch. 8, text	(circumstantial evidence suggests that Rees' index fails to indicate changes in product quality)			
	Rees, Table 44	109.2	100.0	112.6	U.S.A.
Clothing	Ch. 8 text	(circumstantial evidence suggests that Rees' index fails to indicate changes in product quality)			
	Rees, Table 44	112.5	100.0	105.2	U.S.A.

Sources: See tables as indicated in column 2; and Albert Rees, *Real Wages in Manufacturing, 1890–1914* (Princeton, 1961), Table 44, p. 120.

a. Based on estimate ii in Table 5(A).
b. Based on 16–36 food items.
c. Based on 9 food items.
d. Based on the price of natural gas: price appears to have been stable 1905–1906.
e. Based on the price of manufactured gas: price appears to have been stable 1905–1906.

evidence from Birmingham with the Bowley series. Both the stability in Birmingham rents between 1900 and 1912 and the increase in clothing prices between 1900 and 1910 echoed the national trend. Bowley indicated neither the components included in his fuel index nor the manner in which they were weighted, and this made comparison with Birmingham data difficult. However, when coal and gas were weighted as suggested in chapter 9, the composite Birmingham indices closely matched those for the United Kingdom as a whole: prices declined precipitously between 1900 and 1905, but rose substantially in the ensuing seven-year period.[8]

The major variations between the Birmingham series and the national series occurred with respect to food prices and wage rates. Evidence from the Midlands city suggested that hourly wage rates rose very slightly between 1900 and 1905 and advanced by 3 percent between 1905 and 1912. Bowley, in contrast, estimated that wages fell in the first five-year period but rose by 10 percent in the following seven years. The overall trend, however, appeared similar. The national ser-

Table 64

British Wages and Prices, 1900, 1905, 1910, and 1912: A Comparison of National and Regional Trends

Index	Source	1900	1905	1910	1912	Basis
Wages	Table 5[a]	99	100		103	Birmingham
	Table 5[b]	99	100		103	Birmingham
	Bowley, Table 7	106	100		110	U.K.
Food prices	Table 26	102	100		109	Birmingham
	Bowley, Table 7	97	100		111	U.K.
Fuel prices						
coal	Table 38[c]	135	100		128	Birmingham
gas	Table 41[d]	110	100		77	Birmingham
coal + gas	Estimate[e]	128	100		113	Birmingham
all fuel	Bowley, Table 7	128	100		110	U.K.
Rent	Table 40	100	100		100	Birmingham
	Bowley, Table 7	100	100		100	U.K.
Clothing	Ch. 8, text	100		≅108–115		Birmingham
	Bowley, Table 7	100		111		U.K.

Sources: See tables as indicated in col. 2; and A. L. Bowley, Wages and Income in the United Kingdom since 1860 (Cambridge, 1937), Table 7, p. 30, and Appendix D, pp. 114–26.

a. Based on estimate i in Table 5A.
b. Based on estimate ii in Table 5A.
c. Based on Class Two bituminous coal.
d. Based on estimate A in Table 41.
e. Coal weighted 71, gas weighted 29. For explanation see text.

ies exhibited a 4 percent increase between 1900 and 1912, while the Birmingham series showed a rise of 4 to 5 percent. The more significant difference between the two series occurred in the movement of food prices. Bowley's index numbers, derived from London statistics, indicated that the unweighted mean cost of food items advanced between 1900 and 1905, whereas both quantitative and qualitative evidence from Birmingham indicated that prices declined.[9] Between 1905 and 1912 price movement was more similar, the national index rising by 11 percent and the Birmingham index by 9 percent. For the entire twelve-year period national prices rose 13 percent, while Birmingham prices increased only by 7 percent.

This variation in food prices is certainly significant, and it underlines the necessity for historians to construct a more widely based cost-of-living index for the United Kingdom. Short-term price fluctuations varied considerably from city to city. Yet for the 1900–1912 period as a whole, the movement of wage rates, rents, and fuel and clothing prices was similar in Birmingham and the nation. Food prices rose by 6 percent more in the United Kingdom (London-based) series than in the Birmingham series, but this represented only a 3 percent variation in the cost-of-living index. While Bowley estimated that real wages declined by 6 percent between 1900 and 1912, the Birmingham data indicated a decrease of 3 percent. Nevertheless, although the movement of real wages in the United Kingdom varied from that in Birmingham, it seemed justifiable to use Bowley's data as at least a rough pathway to a broader historical perspective.

The linking of the localized data to the national series is performed in Table 65. The wage paid to the engineering laborer was taken to represent the minimum comparative rate paid in Pittsburgh, and that of public paver the maximum. The data, presented in summary form in Graph 4, indicate that when the Rees index was used as the basis of comparison, 1906 emerged as the first year in the post–1890 period in which the real wage of the engineering laborer rose higher in the American than the British city; and the statistical evidence forcibly suggested that in most unskilled occupations, real wages were as low in Pittsburgh as they were in Birmingham, and in many instances lower. In short, the conclusion which Phelps Brown found "most remarkable," namely that "not until after 1900 . . . did the real wage in the U.S.A. draw ahead of the British," appears to be substantially correct.[10] On the other hand, skilled workers in high-wage industries were paid substantially superior rates.

When, in contrast, the Douglas index was employed as the basis of comparison, the British:American wage ratios appeared to have remained relatively stable over time, veering only slightly from the 1906 relationship. Nevertheless, the data suggest that for a considerable period unskilled laborers received real hourly rates of pay in the United States (Pittsburgh) which were not much superior to those which their counterparts received in the United Kingdom (Birmingham, Sheffield). Rates were no more than 15 percent greater. At the other end of the wage spectrum, skilled manual workers in the American city were paid real rates up to the twice as large as those which British employees received.

Real Weekly Income

Having calculated comparative hourly rates of pay, it was also necessary to estimate real weekly earnings.[11] This involved a subtle reemphasis in analytical framework, insofar as interest was no longer centered on the difference in real earnings for a given (timed) amount of work but upon the variance in real income irrespective of hours of labor required to gain it. For this reason it seemed sensible to incorporate within the calculations of weekly earnings estimates of the income derived from wives and children, for the financial accruements thereby derived would have improved the material standard of living, just as would increases in the hours of employment.

This concentration upon the end standard, rather than upon the means by which it was achieved, begs key questions. The relative weekly earnings of many Pittsburgh workers were increased (vis-à-vis Birmingham employees) by the longer hours demanded of them, but it is uncertain whether the widening of the earnings gap that resulted indicated a genuine advance in the Americans' comparative standard of living. It is a least possible that the manual worker in the British city placed a higher value upon leisure time than upon the ability to consume more material goods and/or to accumulate greater savings. Conversely, the Birmingham employee's earnings were, to a much greater extent than in Pittsburgh, bolstered by the wage labor of his wife, and this reduced the Anglo-American differential in family income. But did this signify a narrowing of the difference in family standard of living? Might it not be just to view longer hours of labor and the greater employment of working wives as alternative means of increasing material lifestyle?

It is questions such as these, which require that levels of contentment and degrees of satisfaction be assessed, that can least satisfactorily by resolved by quantitative analysis. All that can be asserted is that, given the longer hours worked in many Pittsburgh industries, and

Table 65
Comparative Real Hourly Wages: Pittsburgh and Birmingham, 1890–1913

Year	U.K. R.W.I.	U.S.A. R.W.I.[a]	U.S.A. R.W.I.[b]	Pittsburgh R.R.W.I.[a]		Pittsburgh R.R.W.I.[b]	
				Min. Bhm=100.0	Max. Bhm=100.0	Min. Bhm=100.0	Max. Bhm=100.0
1890	95	77	92	84	169	100	202
1891	94	77	96	84	171	105	213
1892	94	77	96	84	171	105	213
1893	96	82	98	88	179	105	213
1894	100	80	99	82	167	102	207
1895	102	81	99	82	166	100	203
1896	102	84	99	85	172	100	203
1897	100	82	97	85	171	100	203
1898	101	81	97	83	168	99	201
1899	106	86	98	84	170	95	193
1900	105	87	98	85	173	96	195
1901	104	90	97	89	181	96	195
1902	103	94	98	94	191	98	199
1903	101	95	97	97	197	99	201
1904	99	92	98	96	194	102	207
1905	99	95	100	99	201	104	211
1906	100	100	100	103	209	103	209
1907	103	99	98	99	201	98	199
1908	103	98	99	98	199	99	201
1909	102	99	100	100	203	101	205
1910	100	102	97	105	213	100	203
1911	99	103	95	107	217	99	201
1912	99	104	99	108	220	103	209
1913	99	110	100	114	232	104	211

Sources: See Table 61A for estimates of comparative real hourly wages in 1906. The time series were derived as follows: U.K.R.W.I.—Bowley, *Wages and Income in the United Kingdom*, Table 7, p. 30, converted to base year 1906; U.S.A.R.W.I. (a)—Rees, *Real Wages in Manufacturing*, Table 44, p. 120, converted to base year 1906; U.S.A.R.W.I. (b)—Paul H. Douglas, *Real Wages in the United States, 1879–1926* (Boston, 1930). Table 24, p. 108, converted to base year 1906.

Note: U.K.R.W.I. = United Kingdom Real Wage Index: based upon the average earnings for a normal week of all wage earners in the United Kingdom, divided by a cost-of-living index.

U.S.A.R.W.I.^{a} = United States Real Wage Index (estimate a): based upon average hourly earnings in all manufacturing industries in the U.S.A., divided by a cost-of-living index.

U.S.A.R.W.I.^{b} = United States Real Wage Index (estimate b): based upon average hourly earnings in all manufacturing industries in the U.S.A., divided by a cost-of-living index.

Pittsburgh R.R.W.I.^{a} = Pittsburgh Relative Real Wage Index (estimate a) i.e., [U.S.A.R.W.I.^{a}/U.K.R.W.I.] × 103 (minimum) or 209 (maximum).

Pittsburgh R.R.W.I.^{b} = Pittsburgh Relative Real Wage Index (estimate b) i.e., [U.S.A.R.W.I.^{b}/U.K.R.W.I.] × 103 (minimum) or 209 (maximum).

Min. = Minimum relative real wage (engineering laborer).

Max. = Maximum relative real wage (public paver).

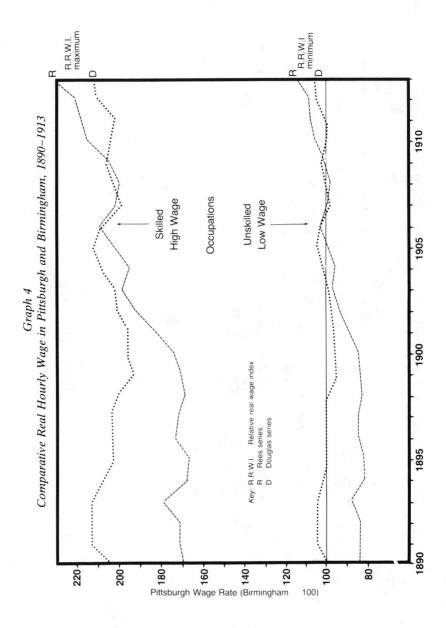

Graph 4

Comparative Real Hourly Wage in Pittsburgh and Birmingham, 1890–1913

Skilled
High Wage

Occupations

Unskilled
Low Wage

R.R.W.I.
maximum

R.R.W.I.
minimum

Key: R.R.W.I.   Relative real wage index
     R   Rees series
     D   Douglas series

Pittsburgh Wage Rate (Birmingham   100)

1890   1895   1900   1905   1910

80   100   120   140   160   180   200   220

given the greater propensity for wives to enter the paid work force in Birmingham, the resulting difference in comparative weekly real earnings was—for most occupations—less substantial than the differences in hourly rates.

Table 66 suggests that the unskilled worker in full-time employment in Birmingham received a family income which allowed him to enjoy a standard of living almost as high as that of his colleague in Pittsburgh in 1906. Laborers employed by the Birmingham Council or engaged in the city's engineering industry had at their disposal greater real earnings, while building laborers had only 3 to 4 percent superiority in Pittsburgh, and third-hand bakers 8 to 9 percent. Few Pittsburghers

Table 66
Comparative Real Weekly Family Earnings: Pittsburgh and Birmingham, 1906

Occupation of Husband	Weekly Earnings (incl. family contribution)[a]		Pittsburgh R.M.E.I. (Bhm = 100.0)	Pittsburgh R.R.E.I. (Bhm = 100.0)
	Birmingham	Pittsburgh		
Engineering laborer	$ 6.95	$11.41	164.2	98.3–99.3
Foundry blacksmith	12.50	22.20	177.6	106.3–107.4
Public laborer	8.40	13.19	157.0	94.0–95.0
Third-hand baker	8.35	15.10	180.8	108.2–109.4
Second-hand baker	9.40	17.54	186.6	111.7–112.9
Boilermaker	13.25	24.31	183.5	109.8–111.0
Machinist	12.50	23.20	185.6	111.1–112.3
Compositor, b.&j.	12.02	22.16	184.4	110.4–111.6
First-hand baker	11.14	22.60	202.9	121.4–122.7
Bookbinder	11.14	20.73	186.1	111.4–112.6
Patternmaker	13.25	25.51	192.5	115.2–116.5
Public rammer	9.08	16.57	182.5	109.2–110.4
Building laborer	10.57	18.20	172.2	103.1–104.2
Machine woodworker	13.34	26.57	200.7	120.1–121.4
Carpenter	14.05	26.38	187.8	112.4–113.6
Painter	13.95	25.66	183.9	110.1–111.3
Compositor, m.n.	15.65	35.30	225.6	135.0–136.5
Plumber	14.88	30.12	202.4	121.1–122.4
Stonemason	14.78	33.13	224.2	134.2–135.6
Plasterer	15.65	33.91	216.7	129.7–131.1
Bricklayer	14.88	38.01	255.4	152.8–154.5
Public paver	12.50	38.13	305.0	182.5–184.5

Sources: See Tables 11, 20, and 60.

Note: R.M.E.I.=Relative Money Earnings Index; R.R.E.I.=Relative Real Earnings Index: 100(R.M.E.I./165.3) or 100(R.M.E.I./167.1). See Table 60.

a. Family contribution estimated at 0.428 of the adult male wage for each Birmingham occupation, and at 0.255 for each Pittsburgh occupation. See Table 20.

had a real family income more than 15 percent greater than their counterparts in Birmingham, and it was only skilled tradesmen such as first-hand bakers, morning newspaper compositors, pavers, brick-layers, and plasterers who had a standard of living more than 20 per-cent in advance of their English colleagues.

In conclusion, whether comparison was made between hourly rates of pay or weekly family earnings, and regardless of whether the American or English budgetary schedules were used to determine the cost-of-living index, the emerging statistical pictures were remarkably similar. The American manual worker's standard of living was not as much in advance of the English worker's as most contemporary com-ment suggested. The skilled Pittsburgh tradesman, it is true, received an income which, judged by the composite unit of consumables it could buy, was 50 to 100 percent greater than that received in an equivalent occupation in Birmingham. But the unskilled Pittsburgh worker gained a real wage that was the same as, or very little better than, that paid to the laborer in Birmingham or Sheffield.

Conclusion

One may criticize Sombart's belief that American socialism had been shipwrecked on shoals of apple pie and roast beef from two distinct perspectives. First, one may challenge the evidence presented to char-acterize the early twentieth-century American worker as a grateful beneficiary of unparalleled economic prosperity; second, one may criti-cize the assertion that high material living standards lead to a bour-geois political mentality. It is best to consider these two aspects sepa-rately and, in so doing, to suggest a new perspective from which to view the development of American labor organization during its for-mative period.

Roast beef . . . For whom?

Sombart's fragmentary statistical measures were insufficient to sus-tain his thesis that American workers enjoyed comparative affluence. At the very least, doubts remain. In a foreword to the recent English edition of *Why Is There No Socialism in the United States?* Michael Harrington expressed surprise that the "evidence, incredible as it may seem, is still in dispute." Yet the observations of the volume's editor, C. T. Husbands, that American workers appeared to receive a much wider range of wage incomes than their German counterparts have been amply justified in this study.[12]

Comparison of real wage rates and real family income in Pittsburgh,

Birmingham, and Sheffield indicates that assertions of relative American affluence must be severely qualified. Unskilled workers experienced similar levels of material welfare in Britain and the United States in the 1900s, and it is quite possible that English laborers actually enjoyed a higher standard of living during the last quarter of the nineteenth century. The dominant characteristic of the American labor force was not comparative income superiority, but the much greater inequality of wage distribution. The most highly paid manual employees, primarily skilled workers, earned substantially larger incomes than those in equivalent English occupations, whereas low-paid workers received incomes similar to those in England. In short, the fruits of economic growth, the benefits of emergent corporate capitalism, were far more unevenly distributed among wage earners in the United States than in England.

Pittsburgh's highly inegalitarian income structure was reflected in substantial variations in workers' lifestyle. At the top of the wage pyramid were those high-skilled, high-income workers able to purchase their own homes, to wash in indoor bathrooms, buy hand-rolled stogies or the *National Labor Tribune,* or, occasionally, watch the Pirates at Forbes Field or arrange an excursion to Kennywood Park—families able to enjoy the "American standard" of which Samuel Gompers boasted so proudly. At the broad base of the pyramid was the city's large laboring population, crowded into hastily converted tenements and rapidly deteriorating wooden constructs, sharing outside toilet facilities and a communal faucet, living next to the noise, glare, and stench of the mills and furnaces. Here were children fighting imaginary battles along the unpaved streets and open sewers and workers to whom leisure was sleep, to whom recreation was a half hour at the nickelodeon, or a drink in the saloon after work, to whom contentment was a full pipe of tobacco, or a Sunday afternoon spent gambling at cards. There were two worlds among Pittsburgh's manual workers: a world of $10 Chesterfield suits and $5 Elton jackets, Red Cross shoes and embroidered antimacassars, and a world of collarless shirts and patched overalls, made-up flannelette and paste jewelery.

This division, far clearer than in Birmingham or Sheffield, was not simply a consequence of wide income differences. It was exaggerated by ethnic divisions. Pittsburgh's unskilled poor were largely new immigrants—Italians and Slavs, Poles and Austro-Hungarians—whose distinctive lifestyles reflected not only low income but also different social values and cultural mores. Such recent arrivals brought with them very little except a willingness to undertake hard work. It is possible that their European backgrounds led them to accept a lower standard of living than Americans. Far more importantly, their attitude toward consumption was not the same as that of native-born Americans or well-established old immigrants. They had a much greater propensity to save, a much greater willingness to forsake immediate material satisfaction for future gain. They hoarded or banked or remitted overseas the maximum amount from their meager incomes and lived a penurious existence in order to dream of a triumphant return home as American big-shots, of bringing friends and relatives to join them, of giving their children a secure future. The unskilled American Pittsburgher—probably black—led a life of the same material standard as his counterpart in Birmingham. The unskilled immigrant Pittsburgher often chose to lead a far worse life. He labored long hours, sleeping as well as working in shifts, spending the bare minimum on accommodation and furniture, even skimping on food.

We do not know to what extent the low wage status of Pittsburgh's unskilled immigrant workers resulted from discrimination. Recent evidence has suggested that ability to speak English, level of skill, and length of residence in America explain most of the ethnic variations in income in the 1900s. On the other hand, there exists circumstantial evidence that discrimination did prevail with regard to rents and access to educational and welfare facilities. More significant, but too often hidden by the impressive battery of statistical tests and regression equations that now throw doubt on whether discrimination occurred in the marketplace, was the widespread prejudice against "Dagos" and "Polacks" in the street. "I am a Hunkie," visitors to the Kingsley House dance were required to announce at the door: an insensitive jest, reflecting the racial stereotyping not only of middle-class settlement workers but of the older established upper working class. Whether or not there existed a dual labor market in fact, there certainly existed one within the minds of Pittsburgh's native-stock Americans and old immigrants. John Griswold, the Scotch-Irish furnace boss, surely articulated the feelings of many of his skilled colleagues when he described the unskilled laborers over whom he wielded control as ignorant muscle, as brute strength, as scarcely human. "They don't seem like men to me hardly": sentiments so often expressed, yet rarely recorded for posterity. To Griswold there were two distinct labor markets, two classes of blue-collar workers, separated by an immense gulf of skill, income, and ethnicity, sharing little common ground either in material lifestyle or in cultural background. In Birmingham, by contrast, income variations were far less extreme and ethnic variations relatively insignificant. It is not surprising to find greater consciousness of working-class status, political strength, and underlying unity in the English city.

The fact that most of Pittsburgh's laborers were from southern or eastern Europe might lead the cautious reader to question the validity of comparing their lot with that of Birmingham's unskilled workers. Certainly the unskilled Englishman migrating to the United States in the early twentieth century would have gained more than the tabulated conclusions might suggest. Leaving Liverpool unskilled, the English worker, by a miraculous Atlantic sea-change, arrived in New York with a skill—the ability to speak English—that would have enhanced chances of finding of a job, increased remuneration, and opened the doors to occupational mobility. Similarly, the unskilled Italian or Pole migrating to the United States probably would have gained substantial comparative benefit by gaining employment as a laborer in Pittsburgh.

However, while comparison of the American and English standard of living may seem artifical in terms of explaining migration, it is certainly not so in terms of understanding American labor history, society, and culture. Initially, it is true, the immigrant would have compared the new world of Pittsburgh and his old world in Cracow or Naples. No doubt the dangerous and backbreaking labor of loading and lifting, digging and filling, heaving and shoveling was viewed as an opportunity for material advance. But as length of residence in American increased, the basis of comparison would have changed. Relative affluence vis-à-vis friends still back home would have become less significant, and relative poverty vis-à-vis colleagues at work correspondingly more important. The migrant would have become aware of the wide distribution of wage earners' income in the United States and increasingly concerned about the barriers of language, skill, and prejudice that hindered his climbing the widely spaced rungs of America's economic ladder. He would soon have learned of, and in his wildest dreams aspired to join, the city's millionaire elite. Yet the vast wealth of an Oliver or Carnegie, a Heinz or Westinghouse, the elegant mansions of Shadyside and rising skyscrapers of the Point, were ultimately less frustrating than the high wage, the comfortable home, and the ill-concealed contempt of a John Griswold. If one could but struggle up those first few rungs—from railway hand to locomotive engineer, from excavator to bricklayer, from street laborer to paver, from cinderman to furnace boss—what unprecedented wage rewards awaited! And yet, for the vast majority of Pittsburgh's unskilled immigrants, that progression must have seemed as distant as Carnegie's Skibo Castle.

Apple Pie . . . a Bourgeois Taste?

Sombart's model suggested that individual affluence resulted in ideological conservatism and, more specifically, that American workers had been "embourgeoised" by the high living standards they enjoyed. Economic well-being, it was argued, acted as a deterrent to class awareness, reformist action, or dedication to the creation of a socialist world. Yet while "it may be claimed with great plausibility that a revolutionary consciousness has established itself most strongly in those capitalist countries which were relatively backward and had a low *per capita* income," the relationship between political stance and material welfare is not obvious.[13] Recently the embourgeoisement thesis, at least in its vulgar form, has been comprehensively attacked. In a thoughtful commentary upon Sombart's work, Adolph Sturmthal rejects a straight monotonic functional relationship between the attractiveness of socialist ideas and living standards: he notes, correctly, that apathy rather than radicalism has generally flourished among the very poor; and that it has been well-paid skilled artisans and intelligentsia who have often provided the leadership for socialist organizations.[14]

If one rejects the notion that the conservatism of American labor derived from high levels of real wages, how is one to explain the A. F. of L.'s emphasis on bread-and-butter gains for a craft membership? The present study reveals a few worthwhile leads. It has been argued that the comparative real income of American manual workers was not as high as generally suggested, and that it would therefore be foolish to keep explaining the conservatism of American labor—or, indeed, the whole of American cultural history—in terms of material superiority. It may "[approach] the commonplace . . . to observe that the factor of relative abundance is, by general consent, a basic condition of American life."[15] It is not, however, the unqualified truth. Rather, it is a commonplace derived from our love of averages. The statistical prowess born of baseball and gridiron is not an adequate basis for historical analysis. If one moves beyond measures of central tendency and considers instead measures of range and distribution, then new doors of understanding begin to open.

Thus the embourgoisement thesis is crude and unconvincing precisely because it infers behavior not from the varied material characteristic of a wide range of human beings, but from a statistical illusion, "Mr./Ms. Average." If one seeks a solution to the "peculiar" behavior of American workers, it is to be found not in a calculation of their mean income, but rather in the wide material and ethnic divisions that separated them. By the early twentieth century, there existed in America a political environment in which universal male suffrage had long provided the basis for participatory democracy; in which egalitarian rhetoric provided the framework for debate; and in which, in Sombart's phrase, a high level of "civic integration" had been achieved by

American workers. It was a society in which geographical mobility—if not social—was much greater than in Europe. Within this world the profound socioeconomic divisions stunted the growth of any mass movement based upon the concept of a united working class. It is the comparative inequality of wage rewards in the United States, an income gulf widened by ethnic heterogeneity and racial prejudice, that must provide the socioeconomic context within which to analyze the American labor movement. American workers found it profoundly difficult to perceive their very diverse lifestyles as the product of a common exploitation. It was not a high average standard of living that dictated how they behaved. Rather, in a supreme historical paradox, it was the combination of a uniquely egalitarian ideology—"Americanism"—with extravagant inequality of material circumstance. Here, surely, lies the basis of the craft-conscious job control, apolitical action, business unionism, and emphasis upon immediate gains within capitalism that characterized the American "pure-and-simple" approach to labor organization.

As we have seen, the major feature that distinguished the status of labor in Pittsburgh from that in Birmingham was not affluence per se, but the wider distribution of incomes. This ranged from the high wages paid to a skilled minority of the American city's workers (which were much greater than the wages earned by their Birmingham counterparts) to the low wages paid to the unskilled majority (which were similar to the wages paid in Birmingham). Additional characteristics that set labor conditions in Pittsburgh apart from those in Birmingham were the greater dependence upon common labor, the wider variation in occupational hours, the substantially lower incidence of female participation in the work force and more frequent contribution to family income from boarders and lodgers, the comparatively high cost of rent and clothing and low cost of fuel and lighting, and the lower percentage of expenditure for food and concomitantly greater expenditure upon luxuries.

These conclusions, boldly stated, derive from the preceding pages of detailed analysis. They represent, it is hoped, a rather unfair summary of the study: the slow digressive path towards statistical assertiveness has revealed far more of the qualitative dimensions of the standard of living, of the material realities of working-class life in Pittsburgh and Birmingham, than the most precise quantitative comparison. And yet so much remains buried. First, one needs to test the conclusions reached here. Would comparison of other English and American towns substantially revise these conclusions? How much superior were workers' real incomes in the United States compared with those in

Ireland or Scandinavia, Italy or Poland? Were the much smaller in-equalities in wage distribution evident in England and Germany typical of European conditions? Second, one needs to expand the analytical parameters. It is quite possible that if the definition of standard of living were extended, one might make a forceful argument that the Birmingham laborer experienced a decidedly better life than did his counterpart in Pittsburgh.

It is probable that the opportunity for upward social mobility was greater in America, although the very sparse evidence on comparative mobility rates remain inconclusive.[16] However, it appears likely the levels of unemployment were lower in England. While unemployment among nonfarm workers averaged 10 percent in the United States between 1904 and 1913, the rate of unemployment among British trade unionists averaged only 5 percent. It would be foolhardy to attach too much weight to such a dubious comparison. But equally significant, and far clearer, is the fact that the extent of annual unemployment varied far more in America. Cyclical movements in business activity were much wider, and fluctuations in unemployment concomitantly larger. In short, it is likely that the years of prosperity probably wit-nessed lower rates of unemployment in Pittsburgh than in Birming-ham, but that years of depression were marked by significantly greater unemployment.[17]

In nearly all other respects, evidence—both quantitative and qualita-tive—indicates that the Birmingham worker experienced more sub-stantial benefits in the early twentieth century. He generally had longer leisure time, enjoying (as did few Pittsburgh workers) a half-day on Saturday; he was less likely to be killed or maimed while at the workplace; and he labored under less pressure. He was almost cer-tainly provided with superior social services and facilities—hospital accommodation, city-based unemployment benefits, garbage collec-tion, park space, and so on.[18] It is areas such as these to which the historian must now turn attention.

Appendix Tables

Notes

Index

Appendix Table 1

Occupational Wage Rates: Pittsburgh and Birmingham, 1899–1913

A. Pittsburgh

Occupation	1899	1900	1901	1902	1903	1904	1905	1906	1907	1908	1909	1910	1911	1912	1913	Sources
Building trades																
Bricklayer	72.3	76.9	92.3	92.3	92.3	92.3	100.0	97.1	100.0	100.0	100.0	100.0	100.0	100.0	107.7	C, B
Carpenter	57.1	67.7	74.0	88.0	88.8	88.4	89.0	89.0	100.0	101.6	101.6	101.6	101.6	101.6	111.8	C, B
Plumber	76.8	79.2	81.6	90.6	98.6	98.4	100.0	100.0	100.0	100.0	112.6	112.6	112.6	125.0	125.0	C, B
Painter	78.4	80.0	82.6	94.6	100.0	100.0	100.0	100.2	100.0	100.0	100.0	100.0	117.6	123.5	129.4	C, B
Inside wireman	45.0	50.0	67.6	100.0	100.0	100.0	100.0	100.0	100.0	100.0	100.0	100.0	100.0	100.0	115.0	C/L, B
Iron worker	55.0	55.0	80.0	95.0	95.0	100.0	100.0	100.0	100.0	112.6	112.6	112.6	112.6	112.6	125.0	C/L
Plasterer		93.3	93.3	93.3	93.3	93.3	93.3	100.0	100.0	100.0	100.0	111.0	111.0	111.0	111.0	B
Tile layer		90.9	90.9	100.0	100.0	100.0	100.0	100.0	100.0	109.1	109.1	109.1	109.1	109.1	125.1	C/L
Tile layer's h.		84.7	84.7	100.0	100.0	100.0	100.0	100.0	100.0	111.4	111.4	111.1	111.1	111.1	125.1	C/L
Elevator constructor			62.6	87.6	93.8	93.8	100.0	100.0	100.0	100.0	100.0	112.6	112.6	125.0	125.0	C/L
Elevator constructor's h.				63.2	87.9	87.9	87.9	100.0	100.0	100.0	100.0	105.3	105.3	105.3	112.4	C/L
Stonecutter (ss.)				100.0	100.0	100.0	100.0	100.0	100.0	100.0	100.0	100.0	100.0	100.0	100.0	C.L, B
Stonecutter (g.)						100.0	100.0	100.0	100.0	100.0	100.0	100.0	100.0	100.0	114.2	B
Hod carrier					93.8	95.6	92.0	88.5	100.0	110.9	110.9	110.9	110.9	110.9	110.9	B
Laborer							71.6	91.2	100.0	100.0	100.0	100.0	100.0	100.0	100.0	B
Steam fitter				100.0	100.0	100.0	100.0	100.0	100.0	100.0	100.0	100.0	100.0	112.6	112.6	C/L, B
Steam fitter's h.									100.0	112.4	112.4	112.4	112.4	125.2	125.2	B
Marble setter									100.0	100.0	100.0	111.0	111.0	111.0	111.0	B
Stonemason									100.0	100.0	100.0	100.0	100.0	100.0	100.0	B
Sheet metal worker									100.0	100.0	100.0	111.1	111.1	111.1	125.1	B
Bakery occupations																
First hand	66.8	85.9	85.9	85.9	85.9	85.9	85.9	85.9	100.0	100.0	100.0	100.0	100.0	120.2	120.2	C/L, B
Second hand	66.7	100.0	100.0	100.0	100.0	100.0	100.0	100.0	100.0	100.0	100.0	100.0	100.0	137.7	137.7	C/L, B
Third hand	60.0	100.0	100.0	100.0	100.0	100.0	100.0	100.0	100.0	100.0	100.0	100.0	100.0	150.3	150.3	C/L, B

Appendix Table 1A (Continued)

Occupation	1899	1900	1901	1902	1903	1904	1905	1906	1907	1908	1909	1910	1911	1912	1913	Sources
Planing-mill trades																
Sawyer								103.4	100.0							B
Machine woodworker					91.1	91.8	91.8	94.0	100.0							B
Carpenter						96.7	96.9	100.7	100.0							B
Laborer							89.6	95.0	100.0							B
Metal trades																
Manufacturing shop																
Blacksmith	79.1	82.8	86.8	90.9	95.3	92.9	93.6	98.0	100.0	110.1	110.1	100.1	110.1	110.1	119.8	C, B
Blacksmith's h.									100.0	124.7	124.7	124.7	124.7	124.7	157.9	B
Machinist	74.8	79.7	83.1	85.2	89.2	91.7	88.6	97.2	100.0	100.0	100.0	116.7	116.7	116.7	116.7	C, B
Patternmaker	76.4	79.5	87.7	90.8	91.6	83.2	86.6	95.3	100.0	100.0	100.0	100.0	100.0	105.0	112.5	C, B
Locomotive works																
Blacksmith									100.0	100.0	118.2	118.2	118.2	118.2	118.2	B
Blacksmith's h.									100.0	100.0	122.2	122.2	122.2	122.2	125.0	B
Jobbing shop																
Patternmaker									100.0	100.0	100.0	100.0	100.0	100.0	111.1	B
Coremaker									100.0	100.0	92.8	100.0	100.0	107.2	114.1	B
Bench & floor																
Iron molder	68.3	74.7	79.2	83.1	93.4	87.9	86.5	90.8	100.0	100.0	92.8	100.0	100.0	107.2	114.1	C, B
Shopman																
Boilermaker	72.6	72.9	80.2	82.0	96.0	100.0	98.8	101.8	100.0	100.0	100.0	100.0	104.9	114.3	114.3	C, B
Boilermaker's h.									100.0	100.0	100.0	100.0	112.6	112.6	112.6	B
Outside man																
Boilermaker									100.0	100.0	100.0	100.0	111.1	111.1	111.1	B
Boilermaker's h.									100.0	100.0	100.0	100.0	109.0	116.3	116.3	B

Railroad shop																
Boilermaker									100.0	100.0	100.0	100.0	100.0	100.0	110.8	B
Engineering laborer	84.9	87.2	86.6	86.0	90.7	89.0	91.9	94.2	100.0							B
Printing trades																
Newspaper																
Compositor (night)	94.2	94.2	94.2	94.2	104.1	104.3	104.3	100.3	100.0	100.0	109.1	109.1	109.1	109.1	109.1	C, B
Compositor (day)									100.0	100.0	110.0	110.0	110.0	110.0	110.0	B
Linotyper (night)	93.4	93.4	93.4	93.4	103.1	103.2	103.2	100.0	100.0	100.0	109.1	109.1	109.1	109.1	109.1	C, B
Linotyper (day)									100.0	100.0	110.0	110.0	110.0	110.0	110.0	B
Stereotyper	69.1	72.9	75.0	79.5	88.7	87.7	83.5	88.9	100.0	103.1	103.1	103.1	103.1	105.9	110.4	C, B
Web press operator[a]									100.0	111.9	111.9	146.8	146.8	153.9	153.9	B
Book & job																
Compositor						98.5	98.5	99.4	100.0	100.0	100.0	106.3	112.6	118.9	118.9	B
Linotyper									100.0	100.0	100.0	100.0	100.0	104.6	104.6	B
Press Feeder									100.0	112.6	112.6	112.6	112.6	122.1	122.1	B
Pressman									100.0	112.6	112.6	112.6	112.6	112.6	125.2	B
Electrotyper[b]									100.0	116.6	116.6	116.6	123.4	130.5	130.5	B
Proofreader	100.0	100.0	100.0	100.0	100.0	100.0	100.0	100.0	100.0	100.0	105.1	105.1	105.1	105.1	105.1	C/L
Bookbinder				105.3	100.0	100.0	100.0									B
Railway occupations																
Engineer (yard)	84.8	84.8	84.8	90.6	90.6	90.6	90.6	100.0	100.0	100.0	100.0	127.2	127.2	127.2	127.2	C/L
Fireman (yard)	67.9	67.9	67.9	81.4	81.4	81.4	81.4	100.0	100.0	100.0	100.0	127.1	127.1	127.1	127.1	C/L
Conductor (yard)	68.6	68.6	68.6	84.9	84.9	84.9	84.9	100.0	100.0	100.0	100.0	107.1	107.1	108.6	108.6	C/L
Brakeman (yard)	60.0	60.0	60.0	77.0	77.0	77.0	70.0	100.0	100.0	100.0	100.0	113.3	113.3	116.7	116.7	C/L
Engineer (road)[c]									100.0	100.0	100.0	131.9	131.9	141.7	141.7	C/L
Fireman (road)[c]									100.0	100.0	100.0	130.4	130.4	147.7	145.7	C/L
Conductor (road)[c]									100.0	100.0	100.0	122.5	122.5	138.5	138.5	C/L
Brakeman (road)[c]									100.0	100.0	100.0	112.5	112.5	125.0	125.0	C/L
Flagman (road)[c]									100.0	100.0	100.0	112.0	112.0	120.0	120.0	C/L
Engineer (road)[d]									100.0	100.0	100.0	111.8	111.8	114.1	114.1	C/L
Fireman (road)[d]									100.0	100.0	100.0	107.1	107.1	114.3	114.3	C/L
Section hand									100.0	100.0					144.4	C/L

Appendix Table 1A (Continued)

Occupation	1899	1900	1901	1902	1903	1904	1905	1906	1907	1908	1909	1910	1911	1912	1913	Sources
Street railway occupations																
Motorman (min.)	80.0	80.0	82.0	86.0	90.0	92.0	(94.7)	(97.3)	100.0	98.0	98.0	100.0	92.0	94.0	94.0	C/L
Motorman (max.)	74.1	74.1	81.5						100.0	98.1	98.1	105.6	109.3	111.1	111.1	C/L
Motorman (median)	77.1	77.1	81.8	(85.8)	(89.8)	(91.8)	(94.5)	(97.1)	100.0	98.1	98.1	102.8	100.7	102.6	102.6	C/L
Police																
Lieutenant	84.7	84.7	84.7	100.0	100.0	100.0	100.0	100.0	100.0							A
Patrolman	83.5	83.5	83.5	100.0	100.0	100.0	100.0	100.0	100.0							A
Brewery trades																
Wash-house man									100.0	100.0	100.0	100.0	109.6	109.6	109.6	C/L
Brew-house man									100.0	100.0	100.0	100.0	105.9	105.9	105.9	C/L
Bottle-house man									100.0	100.0	100.0	100.0	100.0	100.0	100.0	C/L
Chief engineer									100.0	100.0	100.0	100.0	100.0	100.0	100.0	C/L
Engineer									100.0	100.0	100.0	100.0	105.0	105.0	105.0	C/L
Pipe-fitter									100.0	100.0	100.0	100.0	105.6	105.6	105.6	C/L
Pipe-fitter's h.									100.0	100.0	100.0	100.0	106.7	106.7	106.7	C/L
Route driver									100.0	100.0	100.0	100.0	104.3	104.3	104.3	C/L
Bottled beer d.									100.0	100.0	100.0	100.0	105.5	105.5	105.5	C/L
Wholesale dealers' driver									100.0	100.0	100.0	100.0	102.8	102.8	102.8	C/L
Driver's h.									100.0	100.0	100.0	100.0	100.0	100.0	100.0	C/L
Stableman									100.0	100.0	100.0	100.0	106.6	106.6	106.6	C/L
Municipal employment																
Laborer/Garbageman	75.2	87.6	87.6	87.6	87.6	87.6	87.6	87.6	100.0	100.0	100.0	100.0	100.0	100.0	112.4	A,C/L, E
Driver	89.0	89.0	89.0	100.0	100.0	100.0	100.0	100.0	100.0	100.0	100.0					A, E
Teamsters																
Cab driver					64.4	100.0	100.0	100.0	100.0							C/L
Hearse driver					66.8	100.0	100.0	100.0	100.0							C/L

Table A (continued):

Occupation	1899	1900	1901	1902	1903	1904	1905	1906	1907	1908	1909	1910	1911	1912	1913	Sources
General Driver (one-horse)										100.0	100.0	100.0				C/L, E
General Driver (two-horse)									100.0	100.0	100.0					C/L, E
Riverboat employment																
Mate						100.0	100.0	100.0	100.0	100.0						C/L, NLT
Deckhand						100.0	100.0	100.0	100.0	100.0						C/L, NLT
Miscellaneous																
Outside Wireman				92.2	92.2	92.2	92.2	92.2	92.2	92.2	92.2	116.1				C/L
Steel mill occupations																
Laborer			90.5	98.5	98.5	89.0	93.6	93.6	100.0	100.0	100.0	106.4	106.4	106.4	119.0	C/L

B. Birmingham

Occupation	1899	1900	1901	1902	1903	1904	1905	1906	1907	1908	1909	1910	1911	1912	1913	Sources
Building trades																
Bricklayer	94.8	100.0	100.0	100.0	100.0	100.0	100.0	100.0	100.0	100.0	100.0	100.0	100.0	105.2	105.2	
Carpenter	100.0	100.0	100.0	100.0	100.0	100.0	100.0	100.0	100.0	100.0	100.0	100.0	100.0	100.0	105.2	
Plumber	100.0	100.0	100.0	100.0	100.0	100.0	100.0	100.0	100.0	100.0	100.0	100.0	100.0	100.0	107.8	
Painter	93.6	93.6	100.0	100.0	100.0	100.0	100.0	100.0	100.0	100.0	100.0	100.0	100.0	100.0	105.8	
Plasterer	95.1	95.1	100.0	100.0	100.0	100.0	100.0	100.0	100.0	100.0	100.0	100.0	100.0	100.0	102.5	
Stonemason	95.1	95.1	100.0	100.0	100.0	100.0	100.0	100.0	100.0	100.0	100.0	100.0	100.0	100.0	100.0	
Slate roofer	100.0	100.0	100.0	100.0	100.0	100.0	100.0	100.0	100.0	100.0	100.0	100.0	100.0	100.0	105.5	
Mason's laborer	100.0	100.0	100.0	100.0	100.0	100.0	100.0	100.0	100.0	100.0	100.0	100.0	100.0	100.0	107.8	
Bakery occupations																
First hand				100.0	100.0	100.0	100.0	100.0	100.0	100.0	100.0	100.0	100.0	100.0	106.3	
Second hand				100.0	100.0	100.0	100.0	100.0	100.0	100.0	100.0	103.3	103.3	103.3	107.1	
Third hand				100.0	100.0	100.0	100.0	100.0	100.0	100.0	100.0	108.3	108.3	108.3	113.0	

Appendix Table 1B (Continued)

Occupation	1899	1900	1901	1902	1903	1904	1905	1906	1907	1908	1909	1910	1911	1912	1913	Sources
Police																
Constable (min.)	95.6	95.6	95.6	95.6	100.0	100.0	100.0	100.0	100.0	100.0	100.0	100.0	100.0	100.0	108.0	Vince
Sergeant (min.)	96.8	96.8	96.8	96.8	100.0	100.0	100.0	100.0	100.0	100.0	100.0	100.0	100.0	100.0	108.2	Vince
Metal trades																
Foundry/Machine shop																
Machinist	97.1	97.1	97.1	97.1	97.1	97.1	97.1	97.1	100.0	100.0	100.0	100.0	100.0	102.9	102.9	
Patternmaker	97.8	97.8	97.8	97.8	97.8	97.8	97.8	97.8	100.0	100.0	100.0	100.0	100.0	103.4	103.4	
Blacksmith	97.1	97.1	97.1	97.1	97.1	97.1	97.1	97.1	100.0	100.0	100.0	100.0	100.0	102.9	102.9	
Iron founder	100.0	100.0	100.0	100.0	100.0	100.0	100.0	100.0	100.0	100.0	100.0	100.0	100.0	100.0	105.7	
Borer/Slotter	96.1	96.1	96.1	96.1	96.1	96.1	96.1	96.1	100.0	100.0	100.0	100.0	100.0	103.9	103.9	
Gun/Ammunition shop																
Machinist	97.8	97.8	97.8	97.8	97.8	97.8	97.8	97.8	100.0	100.0	100.0	100.0	100.0	103.4	103.4	
Boilermaker																
Heavy plater	100.0	100.0	100.0	100.0	100.0	100.0	100.0	100.0	100.0	100.0	105.7	105.7	105.7	105.7	100.0	
Light plater	100.0	100.0	100.0	100.0	100.0	100.0	100.0	100.0	100.0	100.0	106.1	106.1	106.1	106.1	100.0	
Riveter	100.0	100.0	100.0	100.0	100.0	100.0	100.0	100.0	100.0	100.0	100.0	100.0	100.0	100.0	100.0	
Holder-up									100.0	100.0	100.0	100.0				
Farrier's fireman	98.1	100.0	100.0	100.0	100.0	100.0	100.0	100.0	100.0	100.0	100.0	100.0	100.0	100.0	100.0	
Electrical engineer	97.1	97.1	97.1	97.1	97.1	97.1	97.1	97.1	100.0	100.0	100.0	100.0	100.0	102.9 (102.9)	100.0 (102.9)	
Drophammer forger	97.2	97.2	97.2	97.2	97.2	97.2	97.2	97.2	100.0	100.0	100.0	100.0	102.8	102.8 (102.8)	102.8 (102.8)	
Printing trades																
Newspaper																
Compositor (m.)	96.1	96.1	96.1	100.0	100.0	100.0	100.0	100.0	100.0	100.0	100.0	100.0	100.0	100.0	100.0	
Compositor (w.)	95.9	95.9	95.9	95.9	95.9	95.9	95.9	95.9	100.0	100.0	100.0	100.0	100.0	101.8	101.8	
Lithographer	92.7	92.7	92.7	100.0	100.0	100.0	100.0	100.0	100.0	100.0	100.0	100.0	100.0	101.8	101.8	
Bookbinder	93.3	93.3	93.3	100.0	100.0	100.0	100.0	100.0	100.0	100.0	100.0	100.0	100.0	102.0	102.0	

Woodworking trades															
Cabinetmaker	93.6	100.0	100.0	100.0	100.0	100.0	100.0	100.0	100.0	100.0	100.0	100.0	100.0	100.0	105.8
Upholsterer		100.0	100.0	100.0	100.0	100.0	100.0	100.0	100.0	100.0	100.0	100.0	100.0		106.8

Electrical manufacturing trades

Instrument/Switch maker								100.0	100.0	100.0	106.8	106.8	106.8		109.3
Armature winder								100.0	100.0	100.0	100.0	100.0	100.0		102.2
Electrical fitter								100.0	100.0	100.0	100.0	100.0	100.0		102.3

Municipal employment

Gas stoker						100.0	100.0	100.0	100.0	100.0	100.0	100.0	100.0		
Gas laborer	91.8	95.9	95.9	95.9	95.9	95.9	100.0	100.0							

Brass trades

Brass finisher	97.1	97.1	97.1	97.1	97.1	97.1	100.0	100.0	100.0	100.0	100.0	102.9	102.9		
Brass laborer	(100.0)	100.0	100.0	100.0	100.0	100.0	100.0	100.0	123.1	123.1	123.1	Best			

Sources: For Pittsburgh: A—Allegheny Council, *Municipal Report*, 1898–1899 to 1906–1907; B—Bureau of Labor, *Bulletins*, Nos. 59, 65, 71, 77 (1905–1908); Bureau of Labor Statistics, *Bulletins*, Nos. 131, 143, 175 (1907–1914); C—U. S. Department of Commerce and Labor, *Nineteenth Annual Report of the Commissioner of Labor*, 1904; C/L—John R. Commons and William Leiserson, "Wage-Earners of Pittsburgh," in Paul U. Kellogg, ed., *Wage-Earning Pittsburgh* (New York, 1914); E—Great Britain, *Enquiry into Working Class Rents, Housing and Retail Prices in the U. S. A.*, 1909; NLT—National Labor Tribune. For Birmingham: Vince—Charles Anthony Vince, *History of the Corporation of Birmingham*, Vol. 4, "1900–1915" (Birmingham, 1923); Best—R. H. Best, W. J. Davis and C. Perks, *The Brass Workers of Berlin and of Birmingham: A Comparison* (London, 1905). All other wage information from Birmingham is from Great Britain, *Annual Abstract of Labour Statistics of the United Kingdom*, 1898–1899 to 1913; Great Britain, *Annual Report on Changes in Rates of Wages and Hours of Labour in the United Kingdom*, 1899–1913; Great Britain, *Report on Standard Time Rates of Wages in the United Kingdom*, 1900, 1906, 1909, 1910, 1912–1913, 1914; Great Britain, Board of Trade, *Report of an Enquiry . . . into Working Class Rents, Housing, Retail Prices and Standard Rates of Wages in the United Kingdom*, 1908 and 1913.

Note: h. = helper; ss. = soft stone; g. = granite; m. = morning newspaper; w. = weekly newspaper.

a. Mean of head pressman and four assistants.

b. Mean of battery man, builder, finisher, and molder.

c. Local freight.

d. Through freight.

239

Appendix Table 2
Hourly Wage Rates in 1907

A. *Pittsburgh*

Occupation	Wage (¢ per hour)	Occupation	Wage (¢ per hour)
Building trades		*Outside man*	
Bricklayer	65.0–60.0	Boilermaker	45.0
Carpenter	49.2–43.8	Boilermaker's h.	34.4
Plumber	50.0	*Railroad shop*	
Painter	42.5	Boilermaker	32.5
Inside wireman	50.0	Engineering laborer	17.2
Structural iron worker	50.0		
Plasterer	56.3	*Printing Trades*	
Tile layer	55.0	*Newspaper*	
Tile layer's h.	28.1	Compositor (night)	58.4–55.0
Elevator constructor	50.0	Compositor (day)	50.0
Elevator constructor's h.	35.6	Linotyper (night)	58.9–55.0
Stone-cutter (ss.)	50.0	Linotyper (day)	50.0
Stone-cutter (g.)	43.8	Stereotyper	42.4–42.5
Hod-carrier	33.8–37.5	Head pressman	36.7
Laborer	25.0	First assistant	30.6
Steam-fitter	50.0	Second assistant	25.0
Steam-fitter's h.	25.0	Third assistant	22.2
Marble setter	56.3	Fourth assistant	22.2
Stonemason	55.0	*Book & Job*	
Sheet metal worker	45.0	Compositor	32.9–33.3
		Linotyper	45.8
Bakery occupations		Press feeder	22.2
First hand	27.7	Pressman	33.3
Second hand	16.2–21.5	Battery man	22.2
Third hand	11.5–18.5	Builder	27.8
		Finisher	33.3
Metal trades		Molder	38.9
Manufacturing shop		Proofreader	35.2
Blacksmith	29.6–27.8	Bookbinder	30.6
Blacksmith's h.	17.8		
Machinists	32.5–30.0	*Planing-mill trades*	
Patternmaker	38.1–40.0	Sawyer	41.0
Locomotive works		Machine woodworker	41.7
Blacksmith	27.5	Carpenter	42.1
Blacksmith's h.	18.0	Laborer	20.1
Jobbing shop			
Patternmaker	45.0	*Street railway occupations*	
Coremaker	38.9	Motorman (min.)	25.0
Bench & floor		Motorman (max.)	27.0
Iron molder	37.9–38.9		
Shopman		*Police*	
Boilermaker	32.8–35.0	Lieutenant	40.6
Boilermaker's h.	22.2	Patrolman	37.5

Appendix Table 2 (Continued)

Occupation	Wage (¢ per hour)	Occupation	Wage (¢ per hour)
Railway occupations		*Steel-mill occupations*	
Engineer[a]	34.2	Laborer (J.L.)	15.0
Fireman[a]	22.1	Laborer (USSC)	16.5
Conductor[a]	35.0		
Brakeman[a]	30.0	*Blast furnace (Pgh. "District")*	
Engineer[b]	36.0	Stocker	17.3
Fireman[b]	23.0	Bottom filler	18.2
Conductor[b]	32.5	Top filler	21.7
Brakeman[b]	24.0	Larryman	19.0
Flagman[b]	25.0	Larryman's h.	16.5
Engineer[b]	42.5	Skip operator	19.2
Fireman[b]	28.0	Blower	31.3
Section hand	13.5	Blowing engineer	25.8
		Blowing engineer's asst.	20.5
Brewery trades		Stove tender	19.0
Wash-house man	33.3	Keeper	23.1
Brew-house man	35.4	Keeper's h.	17.3
Bottle-house man	31.3	Iron handler	41.8
Chief engineer	49.1	Pig-machine man	16.5
Engineer	35.7	Cinder man	18.9
Pipe-fitter	30.4	Laborer	15.2
Pipe-fitter's h.	26.8		
Route driver	34.9	*Bessemer converter (Pgh. "District")*	
Bottled beer driver	32.7	Stocker	27.5
Wholesale dealers' driver	32.7	Cupola melter	56.0
Driver's h.	25.5	Cupola tapper	39.6
Stableman	27.2	Blower	65.8
		First regulator	43.7
Municipal employment		Second regulator	43.5
Laborer/Garbage man	25.0	Vessel man	78.1
Driver	28.1	Vessel man's h.	52.0
		Cinder pitman	21.2
Teamsters		Bottom maker	43.7
Cab driver	23.3	Bottom maker's h.	28.3
Hearse driver	25.0	Ladle liner	41.5
General driver (one-horse)	16.7	Ladle liner's h.	22.6
General driver (two-horse)	20.0	Stopper maker	31.9
		Stopper setter	56.8
Riverboat employment		Steel pourer	75.6
Mate	19.2	Mold capper	37.2
Deckhand	13.7	Ingot stripper	35.7
		Laborer	15.6
Miscellaneous trades			
Outside lineman	36.1		

Appendix Table 2 (Continued)

B. *Birmingham*

Occupation	Wage (¢ per hour)	Occupation	Wage (¢ per hour)
Building trades		Farrier's doorman	13.2
Bricklayer	19.3	Electrical engineer	17.0
Carpenter	19.3	Drop hammer forger	14.2
Plumber	19.3	*Printing trades*	
Painter	17.3	*Morning newspaper*	
Plasterer	20.3	Compositor	22.8
Stonemason	20.3	*Weekly newspaper*	
Slate roofer	18.3	Compositor	16.9
Mason's laborer	13.2	Lithographer	16.4
Bakery occupations		Bookbinder	15.0
First hand^c	14.4	*Woodworking trades*	
Second hand^c	12.2	Cabinetmaker	17.3
Third hand^c	10.8	Upholsterer	16.2
Metal trades		*Police*	
Foundry/Machine Shop		Constable (min.)	11.3
Machinist	17.0	Sergeant (min.)	15.8
Patternmaker	17.9	*Electrical manufacturing*	
Blacksmith	17.0	*trades*	
Iron-Founder	17.5	Instrument/Switchmaker	16.2
Borer/Slotter	15.2	Armature winder	18.3
Gun/Ammunition Shop		Electrical fitter	17.3
Machinist	17.9	*Municipal Employment*	
Boilermaker		Gas stoker	16.0
Angle iron smith	17.5	Gas laborer	12.2
Heavy plater	17.5	*Brass Trades*	
Light plater	16.5	Brass finisher	17.0
Riveter	14.6	Brass laborer	9.1
Holder-up	12.0		
Farrier's fireman	15.4		

Sources: See Appendix Table 1. Where Bureau of Labor, *Bulletins*, Nos. 77 and 131 give different estimates for Pittsburgh wages, both have been noted.

Note: h. = helper; ss. = soft stone; g. = granite; J. L. = Jones and Laughlin Steel Corporation; USSC = U. S. Steel Corporation.

a. Yard.

b. Road, local freight.

c. Night shift.

Appendix Table 3
Estimate of the Number of Male Workers Engaged in Specified
Occupations: Pittsburgh, 1907–1910

Occupation	No. of Males Employed	Source of Information
Bricklayer	1250	E1
Carpenter	3999	C
Plumber	635	E2
Painter	1845	C
Inside wireman	252	E3
Structural ironworker	189	C
Plasterer	459	C
Tile layer	72	E4
Tile layer's helper	72	E4
Elevator constructor	75	E5
Elevator constructor's helper	75	E5
Stonecutter	295	C
Hod-carrier Building laborer }	8230	C
Steam-fitter	318	E2
Steam-fitter's helper	317	E2
Marble setter	?	
Stonemason	417	E1
Sheet metal worker	360	E6
First-hand baker	305	E7
Second-hand baker	305	E7
Third-hand baker	305	E7
Blacksmith	1310	C
Blacksmith's helper	317	C1
Machinist	5345	C
Patternmaker	485	C
Iron molder	1790	C
Coremaker	?	
Engineering laborer	6280	C2
Boilermaker	526	C
Boilermaker's helper	?	
Compositor	458	E8
Linotyper	457	E8
Stereotyper	22	E9
Electrotyper[a]	21	E9
Pressman	226	E
Press feeder[b]	318	E10
Proofreader	?	
Bookbinder	?	
Sawyer	45	C
Machine woodworker[c]	70	C
Planing-mill laborer	78	C
Street railway motorman	1759	C
Policeman[d]	960	C

Appendix Table 3 (Continued)

Occupation	No. of Males Employed	Source of Information
Brewery worker[e]	1439	E11
Railway conductor	698	C
Railway engineer	853	C
Railway fireman	632	C
Railway brakeman	1246	C
Railway flagman	?	
Railway yardman[f]	115	C
Railway section hand	3011	C
Municipal laborer[g]	1200	C
Municipal paver[h]	798	E12
Cab driver[i]	795	C3
General driver	3868	C4
Riverboat mate[j]	122	C
Riverboat deckhand	181	C
Outside lineman	190	C
Steel mill laborer	19686	C

Sources:

C   Number stated in U.S.A. *Census*, 1910, Vol. 4, Table 3.

C1   Based upon the number of forgemen, hammermen, and welders who worked with blacksmiths.

C2   Based on the number of laborers employed in automobile factories (21), car and railroad shops (1332), wagon and carriage shops (38), and iron and steel works, excluding furnaces and rolling mills (4889).

C3   Based on the number of carriage drivers, hack drivers, and chauffeurs.

C4   Based on the number of draymen, teamsters, and express-men.

E1   The *Census* of 1910 indicated that there existed 1667 bricklayers and stonemasons, while Commons and Leiserson, "Wage-Earners of Pittsburgh," stated that there were 1500 bricklayers and 500 masons in the Pittsburgh "District" in 1907–1908. Assuming that the same 3:1 ratio prevailed in the city in 1910 it is estimated that there were 1250 bricklayers and 417 stonemasons.

E2   Commons and Leiserson (C/L) estimated the number of bricklayers, painters, plasterers, and plumbers in the Pittsburgh "District" in 1907–1908, estimates which were, on average, 39 percent higher than the 1910 *Census* data for the city indicated, i.e., +56.0, +22.0, +52.5, +25.9. C/L suggest that there were 400 master plumbers, 700–800 plumbers, 750–800 steamfitters. If it is assumed that these ratios prevailed in Pittsburgh in 1910, and that the "District" estimates were 39 percent greater than the *Census* data, it would appear that there were 318 master plumbers; 635 plumbers, and 635 steamfitters, of whom half were probably helpers.

E3   C/L stated that there were 350 inside wiremen in the Pittsburgh "District" in 1907–1908. If it is assumed that this number was 39 percent greater than in the city in 1910 (see E2) it would appear that there were 252 wireman.

E4   C/L stated that there were 200 tile layers and helpers in the Pittsburgh "District" in 1907–1908. If it is assumed that this number was 39 percent greater than in the city in 1910 it would appear that there were 144 tile layers, of whom half were probably helpers.

E5   C/L stated that there were 150 elevator constructors in the Pittsburgh union in 1907–1908, and that there were virtually no nonunionized workers. It has been assumed that half of these constructors were helpers.

E6   C/L stated that there were 500 sheet metal workers in the Pittsburgh "District" in 1907–1908. If it is assumed that this number was 39 percent greater than in the city in 1910 it would appear that there were 360 workers.

E7   The *Census* of 1910 stated that there were 915 bakers in manufacturing in 1910. It was assumed that they were equally divided between first, second, and third hands.

E8   The *Census* of 1910 stated that there were 915 compositors, linotypers, and typesetters in 1910. It was assumed that they were split equally (458:457) between the former two categories.

E9   The *Census* of 1910 stated that there were 43 stereotypers and electotypers in 1910. It was assumed that they were split equally (22:21) between the specified occupations.

E10   The *Census* of 1910 stated that there were 245 semiskilled press operatives and 73 press laborers in 1910. It was assumed that these 318 workers comprised press feeders and assistants.

E11   C/L stated that there were 2000 brewery workers in the Pittsburgh "District" in 1907–1908; if it is assumed that this number was 39 percent greater than in the city in 1910 it would appear that there were 1430 employees—although it is possible that this included females.

E12   The *Census* of 1910 stated that there were 1596 road workers, and it has been assumed that these were pavers and rammers. It has been further assumed that half were employed by the municipality.

a. Includes batteryman, builder, finisher, and molder.

b. Includes pressman's assistant.

c. Includes planing-mill carpenter.

d. Includes police patrolman and police lieutenant.

e. Includes twelve occupations in brewery and bottle-house.

f. Not including switchman or flagman.

g. Includes garbageman.

h. Includes rammer.

i. Includes hearse driver.

j. Includes captain, master, and pilot.

Appendix Table 4
Hourly Wage Differentials: Birmingham and Pittsburgh, 1899–1913

A. *Pittsburgh, 1899–1907*

Industry	Less Skilled Wage as % of More Skilled Wage								
	1899	1900	1901	1902	1903	1904	1905	1906	1907
Engineering	50.2	49.5	44.6	42.8	44.7	48.3	47.9	44.6	45.1
Coal mining[a]	68.3	68.3	68.3	67.4	67.4	67.8	67.4	67.4	67.4
Building					52.8	53.8	47.8	47.4	52.0
Baking	37.3	48.3	48.3	48.3	48.3	48.3	48.3	48.3	48.3
Printing	53.3	56.2	57.8	61.3	61.8	61.1	58.1	64.3	72.6
Steam railway	51.7	51.7	51.7	58.1	58.1	58.1	58.1	64.6	64.6
Woodworking							46.0	48.7	48.2
Municipal park service	60.1	70.0	70.0	70.	70.0	70.0			
Police	91.0	91.0	91.0	92.4	92.4	92.4	92.4	92.4	92.4

Note: Occupations compared: engineering (patternmaker: laborer); mining (undercutter: underground laborer); building (bricklayer: hod carrier); baking (first hand: third hand); printing (morning newspaper compositor: stereotyper); steam railway (yard engineer: yard fireman); woodworking (machine woodworker: laborer); municipal park service (gardener: laborer); police (lieutenant: patrolman).
   a. Pittsburgh "District."

B. *Pittsburgh, 1907–1914*

Industry	Less Skilled Wage as % of More Skilled Wage							
	1907	1908	1909	1910	1911	1912	1913	1914
Engineering	67.2	69.0	69.4	73.6	74.2	72.3	72.9	73.1
Coal mining[a]	82.3	82.3	82.3	82.2	82.2	82.1	82.1	82.1
Building	57.8	56.0	56.0	56.0	56.0	56.2	53.5	54.2
Baking	70.9	70.9	70.9	72.0	72.0	79.2	79.7	78.5
Printing	63.9	64.2	62.9	67.0	67.8	70.9	71.7	69.7
Steam railway	64.8	64.8	64.8	63.7	63.7	65.9	65.9	65.9
Brewing	82.8	82.8	82.8	82.8	84.2	84.2	84.2	87.8
Steel manufacturing[a]	60.6	65.7	63.8	63.4	65.4	62.1	63.9	70.7
blast furnace	(69.0)	(71.0)	(70.9)	(70.2)	(72.4)	(70.9)	(73.6)	(74.9)
Bessemer converter	(52.2)	(60.4)	(56.6)	(56.9)	(58.4)	(53.3)	(54.1)	(66.5)

Note: Occupations compared: engineering (blacksmith: blacksmith's helper—manufacturing shop)/(blacksmith: blacksmith's helper—locomotive shop)/(boilermaker: boilermaker's helper—shop work)/(boilermaker: boilermaker's helper—outside work); mining (pick-miner: underground laborer)/(undercutter: underground laborer)/(tracklayer: tracklayer's helper); building (steamfitter: steamfitter's helper)/(bricklayer: hod-carrier)/(bricklayer: laborer)/(structural ironworker: scaffolder)/(tile-layer: tile-layer's helper)/(elevator constructor: elevator constructor's helper); baking (first hand: third hand—German union)/(first hand: third hand—Hebrew and Polish union); printing (moulder: battery man—book-&-job electrotyping)/(head pressman: fourth assistant—web press)/(morning newspaper compositor: stereotyper)/(morning newspaper compositor: book-&-job compositor); steam railway (engineer: fireman—yard)/(engineer: fireman—local freight)/(engineer: fireman—through freight); brewing (first man: laborer—wash house)/(first man: laborer—cellar)/(fireman: fireman's helper)/(chief engineer: engineer)/(route-driver: stableman)/(wholesale dealer's driver: wholesale dealer's driver's helper); steel manufacturing (larryman: larryman's helper—blast furnace)/(blower: blowing engineer's assistant—blast furnace)/(keeper: keeper's helper—blast furnace)/(blower: laborer—blast furnace)/(bottom maker: bottom maker's helper—Bessemer converter)/(ladle liner: ladle liner's helper—Bessemer converter)/(steel pourer: laborer—Bessemer converter)/(vessel man: vessel man's helper—Bessemer converter).

a. Pittsburgh "District."

Appendix Table 4 (Continued)

C. Birmingham, 1899–1913

| | Less Skilled Wage as % of More Skilled Wage | | | | | | | | | | | | | | |
	1899	1900	1901	1902	1903	1904	1905	1906	1907	1908	1909	1910	1911	1912	1913
Building	68.3	68.3	68.3	68.3	68.3	68.3	68.3	68.3	68.3	68.3	68.3	68.3	68.3	70.0	70.0
Baking				75.0	75.0	75.0	75.0	75.0	75.0	75.0	75.0	81.3	81.3	81.3	79.7
Metal trades	83.4	83.4	83.4	83.4	83.4	83.4	83.4	83.4	84.9	84.9	84.9	84.9	84.9	85.4	85.4
Printing	63.9	63.9	63.9	65.8	65.8	65.8	65.8	65.8	65.8	65.8	65.8	65.8	65.8	67.1	67.1
Police	70.6	70.6	70.6	70.6	71.5	71.5	71.5	71.5	71.5	71.5	71.5	71.5	71.5	71.5	71.3
Municipal gas works		73.1	73.1	73.1	73.1	73.1	76.3	76.3	76.3	76.3	76.3				
Brass trades	55.2	55.2	55.2	55.2	55.2	55.2	55.2	55.2	53.5	53.5	53.5	65.9	65.9	64.0	64.0

Note: Occupations compared: building (bricklayer: mason's laborer); baking (first hand: third hand); metal trades (patternmaker: borer/slotter); printing (morning newspaper compositor: bookbinder); police (sergeant: constable); municipal gas works (stoker: laborer); brass trades (brass finisher: laborer).

248

Appendix Table 5
Weekly Hours in Pittsburgh and Birmingham, 1899–1913

A. Birmingham

Occupation	1899	1900	1901	1902	1903	1904	1905	1906	1907	1908	1909	1910	1911	1912	1913	Year in Which Weekly Hours Were Changed
Building trades																
Bricklayer	54.0	54.0	54.0	54.0	54.0	54.0	54.0	54.0	54.0	54.0	51.0	51.0	51.0	51.0	50.5	1909, 1913
Carpenter	51.0	51.0	51.0	51.0	51.0	51.0	51.0	51.0	51.0	51.0	51.0	51.0	51.0	51.0	50.5	1913
Plumber	54.0	54.0	54.0	54.0	54.0	54.0	54.0	54.0	54.0	54.0	54.0	54.0	54.0	54.0	50.5	1913
Painter	56.5	56.5	56.5	56.5	56.5	56.5	56.5	56.5	56.5	56.5	56.5	56.5	56.5	56.5	56.5	—
Plasterer	54.0	54.0	54.0	54.0	54.0	54.0	54.0	54.0	54.0	54.0	51.0	51.0	51.0	51.0	50.5	1909, 1913
Stonemason	51.0	51.0	51.0	51.0	51.0	51.0	51.0	51.0	51.0	51.0	51.0	51.0	51.0	51.0	50.5	1913
Slate roofer	54.0	54.0	54.0	54.0	54.0	54.0	54.0	54.0	54.0	54.0	54.0	54.0	54.0	54.0	54.0	—
Bakery[a]																
First, second and third hands				54.0	54.0	54.0	54.0	54.0	54.0	54.0	54.0	54.0	54.0	54.0	54.0	—
				60.0	60.0	60.0	60.0	60.0	60.0	60.0	60.0	60.0	60.0	60.0	60.0	—
Metal trades																
Machinist[b]	53.0	53.0	53.0	53.0	53.0	53.0	53.0	53.0	50.5[c]	50.5[c]	50.5[c]	50.5[c]	50.5[c]	50.5[c]	51.5[f]	1907, 1913
Pattern-maker[b]	53.0	53.0	53.0	53.0	53.0	53.0	53.0	53.0	53.0	53.0	53.0	53.0	53.0	53.0	53.0	—
Blacksmith[b]	53.0	53.0	53.0	53.0	53.0	53.0	53.0	53.0	50.5[c]	50.5[c]	50.5[c]	50.5[c]	50.5[c]	50.5[c]	51.5[f]	1907, 1913
Iron-founder[b]	53.0	53.0	53.0	53.0	53.0	53.0	53.0	53.0	53.0	53.0	53.0	53.0	53.0	53.0	53.0	—
Borer/slotter[b]	53.0	53.0	53.0	53.0	53.0	53.0	53.0	53.0	50.5[c]	50.5[c]	50.5[c]	50.5[c]	50.5[c]	50.5[c]	51.5[f]	1907, 1913
Angle ironsmith[b]	53.0	53.0	53.0	53.0	53.0	53.0	53.0	53.0	53.0	53.0	53.0	53.0	53.0	53.0	53.0	—
Heavy plater	53.0	53.0	53.0	53.0	53.0	53.0	53.0	53.0	53.0	53.0	53.0	53.0	53.0	53.0	53.0	—
Light plater	53.0	53.0	53.0	53.0	53.0	53.0	53.0	53.0	53.0	53.0	53.0	53.0	53.0	53.0	53.0	—
Riveter	53.0	53.0	53.0	53.0	53.0	53.0	53.0	53.0	53.0	53.0	53.0	53.0	53.0	53.0	53.0	—
Farrier's fireman	56.5	55.5	55.5	55.5	55.5	55.5	55.5	55.5	55.5	55.5	55.5	55.5	55.5	55.5	56.5	1900, 1913
Farrier's doorman	56.5	55.5	55.5	55.5	55.5	55.5	55.5	55.5	55.5	55.5	55.5	55.5	55.5	55.5	56.5	1900, 1913

Appendix Table 5A (Continued)

Occupation	1899	1900	1901	1902	1903	1904	1905	1906	1907	1908	1909	1910	1911	1912	1913	Year in Which Weekly Hours Were Changed
Electrical engineer	53.0	53.0	53.0	53.0	53.0	53.0	53.0	53.0	50.5[e]	50.5[e]	50.5[e]	50.5[e]	50.5[e]	50.5[e]	51.5[f]	1907, 1913
Drop hammer forger	53.0	53.0	53.0	53.0	53.0	53.0	53.0	53.0	50.5[e]	50.5[e]	50.5[e]	50.5[e]	50.5[e]	50.5[e]	51.5[f]	1907, 1913
Printing Trades																
Compositor[c]	50.0	50.0[c]	50.0	48.0	48.0	48.0	48.0	48.0[g]	48.0	48.0	48.0	48.0	48.0	48.0	48.0	1902
Compositor[d]	52.0	52.0	52.0	52.0	52.0	52.0	52.0	52.0	52.0	52.0	52.0	52.0	52.0	51.0	51.0	1912
Lithographer	52.0	52.0	52.0	52.0	52.0	52.0	52.0	52.0	52.0	52.0	52.0	52.0	52.0	51.0	51.0	1912
Bookbinder	52.0	52.0	52.0	52.0	52.0	52.0	52.0	52.0	52.0	52.0	52.0	52.0	52.0	51.0	51.0	1912
Wood-working Trades																
Cabinetmaker	54.0	54.0	54.0	54.0	54.0	54.0	54.0	54.0	54.0	54.0	54.0	54.0	54.0	54.0	54.0	—
Upholsterer	54.0	54.0	54.0	54.0	54.0	54.0	54.0	54.0	54.0	54.0	54.0	54.0	54.0	54.0	54.0	—
Brass Trades																
Brass finisher		53.0	53.0	53.0	53.0	53.0	53.0	53.0	50.5[e]	50.5[e]	50.5[e]	50.5[e]	50.5[e]	50.5[e]	51.5[f]	1907, 1913

Sources: See Appendix Tables 1 and 2.
a. Bakers worked 54.0 hours when employed at night, 60.0 when employed during the day.
b. Employees in foundries and machine shops.
c. Morning newspaper compositor.
d. Weekly newspaper compositor.
e. Some workers had a 48.0-hour week, others a 53.0-hour week.
f. Some workers had a 50.0-hour week, others a 53.0-hour week.
g. The *Annual Abstract of Labour Statistics* stated that the morning newspaper compositor worked a 48.0-hour week, although the *Report(s) on Standard Time Rates* indicated that 52.0 hours comprised a full-time week.

B. Pittsburgh

Occupation	1899	1900	1901	1902	1903	1904	1905	1906	1907	1908	1909	1910	1911	1912	1913	Years in Which Weekly Hours Were Changed
Building trades																
Bricklayer	54.0	54.0	48.0	48.0	48.0	48.0	48.0	48.0	44.0	44.0	44.0	44.0	44.0	44.0	44.0	1901, 1907–08
Carpenter	54.0	54.0	48.5	48.0	48.0	48.0	48.0	48.0	48.0	48.0	48.0	48.0	44.0	44.0	44.0	1901–02, 1911
Plumber	53.0	51.5	51.5	48.0	48.0	48.0	48.0	48.0	48.0	48.0	48.0[a]	48.0[a]	48.0[b]	44.0	44.0	1900, 1902, 1912
Painter	54.0	54.0	49.0	48.0	48.0	48.0	48.0	48.0	48.0	48.0	48.0	48.0	44.0	44.0	44.0	1901–02, 1911
Inside wireman	60.0	60.0	48.0	48.0	48.0	48.0	48.0	48.0	48.0	48.0	48.0	48.0	48.0	48.0	48.0	1901
Structural iron worker	60.0	60.0	54.0	48.0	48.0	48.0	48.0	48.0	48.0	48.0	48.0	48.0	48.0	44.0	44.0	1901–02, 1912
Plasterer	48.0	48.0	48.0	48.0	48.0	48.0	48.0	48.0	48.0[c]	48.0[c]	48.0[c]	44.0	44.0	44.0	44.0	1910
Stonemason			48.0	48.0	48.0	48.0	48.0	48.0	48.0	48.0	48.0	48.0	48.0	44.0	44.0	1912
Laborer[d]					48.0	48.0	48.0	48.0	44.0	44.0	44.0	44.0	44.0	44.0	44.0	1907–08
Bakery trades																
First hand									65.0	65.0	65.0	65.0	65.0	54.0	54.0	1912
Second hand									65.0	65.0	65.0	65.0	65.0	54.0	54.0	1912
Third hand									65.0	65.0	65.0	65.0	65.0	54.0	54.0	1912
Planing-mill trades																
Machine woodworker					54.0	54.0	54.0	54.0	54.0							
Metal trades																
Blacksmith[c]	59.5	59.5	56.0	58.0	58.0	59.0	58.0	61.0	54.0	54.0	54.0	54.0	54.0	54.0	48.0	Pre-1907 erratic, 1907, 1913
Blacksmith's helper[e]															48.0	1913
Patternmaker[e]	58.5	58.5	55.5	56.0	56.0	58.5	56.0	56.0	54.0	54.0	54.0	54.0	54.0	54.0	54.0	Pre-1907 erratic, 1907
Iron molder[f]	57.5	57.5	55.5	55.0	55.5	58.0	56.5	55.5	54.0	54.0	54.0	54.0	54.0	54.0	54.0	Pre-1907 erratic, 1907
Boilermaker[g]	59.5	59.5	54.0	54.0	54.0	57.5	58.0	58.0	54.0	54.0	54.0	54.0	54.0	54.0	54.0	Pre-1907 erratic, 1907
Boilermaker's helper									54.0	54.0	54.0	54.0	54.0	54.0	54.0	—

Appendix Table 5B (Continued)

Occupation	1899	1900	1901	1902	1903	1904	1905	1906	1907	1908	1909	1910	1911	1912	1913	Year in Which Weekly Hours Were Changed
Engineering laborer	60.0	62.0	60.0	61.0	61.5	59.5	57.5	57.5	56.0							Erratic decrease 1900–07
Printing trades																
Compositor[h]	54.5	54.5	54.5	54.5	54.5	47.5	47.3	48.0	48.0	48.0	48.0	48.0	48.0	48.0	48.0	1904, 1906
Linotyper[h]	54.0	54.0	54.0	54.0	54.0	47.5	47.5	48.0	48.0	48.0	48.0	48.0	48.0	48.0	48.0	1904, 1906
Stereotyper[h]	53.0	53.0	53.0	53.0	53.0	52.5	52.5	56.0	56.0	48.0	48.0	48.0	48.0	48.0	48.0	1904, 1907–08
Compositor[i]						54.0	54.0	54.0	54.0	48.0	48.0	48.0	48.0	48.0	48.0	1907–08
Pressman[i]								54.0	54.0	48.0	48.0	48.0	48.0	48.0	48.0	1908
Proofreader	54.0	54.0	54.0	54.0	54.0	54.0	54.0	54.0	54.0	54.0	54.0	54.0	54.0	54.0	54.0	—
Brewery trades																
Brew-house man								54.0	48.0	48.0	48.0	48.0	48.0	48.0	48.0	1907
Bottle-house man								51.0	48.0	48.0	48.0	48.0	48.0	48.0	48.0	1907
Engineer								84.0	56.0	56.0	56.0	56.0	56.0	56.0	56.0	1907
Municipal employment																
Laborer	48.0	48.0	48.0	48.0	48.0	48.0	48.0	48.0	48.0	48.0	48.0	48.0	48.0	48.0	48.0	—
Steel mill occupation																
Laborer								72.0	72.0	72.0	72.0	72.0	72.0	72.0	72.0	—

Sources: See Appendix Tables 1 and 2.

Note: BLS *Bulletins* Nos. 77 and 131, both of which presented data for 1907, sometimes disagreed as to the hours worked. Thus the hourly decrease (apparently genuine) is, in such instances, dated 1907–1908.

a. Plumbers worked 44.0 hours from June to September.
b. Plumbers worked 44.0 hours from June to December.
c. Plasterers worked 44.0 hours from May to October.
d. Laborer = hod carrier.   e. Employees in manufacturing shops.
f. Bench and floor iron molders.   g. Shopmen.
h. Newspaper employees; compositors working at night.
i. Book and job employees.

Appendix Table 6
Occupations in Each Industrial Sector, 1900–1901 and 1910–1911

Industrial Sector	Occupations
Agriculture	Farming, dairying, agricultural labor, gardeners, lumbering and fishing occupations.
Mining	Mining and quarrying occupations.
Professional	Actors, actresses, architects, artists, clergy, dentists, electricians, engineers, surveyors, journalists, lawyers, literary and scientific persons, musicians, government officials, physicians, surgeons, police, armed forces, and, most importantly, teachers.
Domestic/Personal service	Barbers, barmaids, boarding house and lodging-house keepers, hotel-keepers, housekeepers, janitors, laundry workers, restaurant keepers, nurses, midwives, saloon keepers, charwomen, servants, and waiters/waitresses.
Transportation	Boatmen and sailors, teamsters and drivers, steam railroad employees, and street railway and tram employees.
Trade/Commerce	Agents, bankers, brokers, bookkeepers, accountants, commercial travelers, hostlers, hucksters, peddlers, merchants, retail and wholesale dealers, messengers, packers, shippers, undertakers. Most important, however, were clerks, office workers, telegraph and telephone operators, typists, and shop assistants.
Manufacturing	All the normal manufacturing occupations, together with bakers, butchers, paper and printing employees, photographers, manufacturing officials, and laborers (not specified).
Construction	All those engaged in building and construction activity.

Appendix Table 7
Retail Prices in Birmingham, 1900–1914

A. *1900–1905*

Commodity	Price July/Aug. 1900	Price Oct. 1905	Price Movement 1900–1905	Description
Eggs (dozen)	20.9¢	24.5¢	+17.2%	{ 1900 unstated 1905 "foreign"
Milk (Amer. qt.)	5.1	5.9	+15.7	Fresh
Pork chops (lb.)	14.3	16.3	+14.0	British[a]
Pork loin (lb.)	16.3	16.3	± 0.0	British[a]
Bacon (lb.)	20.4	20.4	± 0.0	{ 1900 dearest[b] 1905 dearest (home-cured)
Tea (lb.)	34.7	34.7	± 0.0	
Sugar (lb.)	4.1	4.1	± 0.0	White, granulated[a]
Cheese (lb.)	14.8	14.3	− 3.4	{ 1900 unstated Can./Amer. 1905 Cheddar
Butter (lb.)	26.6	25.5	− 4.1	{ 1900 cheapest 1905 cheapest (colonial)
Beef round/ silverside (lb.)	18.4	15.8	−14.1	British[a]
Bread (lb.)	3.0	2.4	−20.0	
Mutton shoulder (lb.)	13.3	9.1	−31.6	Foreign
Mean price decrease			− 2.2	

a. Assumed for 1900, but almost certainly correct.
b. Cheapest bacon (American drafts) also remained stationary in price.

B. *1900–1914*

Commodity	Retail Prices		Price Movement 1900–1914
	1900[a]	*1914*[b]	
Rice (lb.)	5.8¢	8.2¢	+41.4%
Raisins (lb.)	9.6	12.2	+27.1
Currants (lb.)	8.2	10.2	+24.4
Lard (lb.)	13.6	16.3	+19.9
Jam (lb.)	10.5	12.2	+16.2
Milk (Amer. qt.)	5.1	5.9	+15.7
Bacon (lb.)	18.0	20.4	+13.3
Syrup/Treacle[c] (lb.)	8.2	9.2	+12.2
Cheese (lb.)	14.8	16.3	+10.1
Cod (lb.)	8.2	8.2	± 0.0
Sugar (lb.)	4.1	4.1	± 0.0
Bread (4 lbs.)	11.9	10.2	−14.3
Potatoes (lb.)	1.8	1.5	−16.7
Mean price increase			+11.5

a. Mean prices paid by seven families.
b. "Predominant price . . . as purchased."
c. 1900 syrup; 1914 treacle.

Appendix Table 7 (Continued)

C. *1901–1910*

Commodity	Retail Prices		Price Movement 1901–1910
	1901	*1910*	
Tea (unblended)	53.0¢	50.0¢	− 5.7%
Tea (China)	46.9	61.2	
Tea (India)	55.1	49.0	
Tea (Ceylon)	53.0	51.0	+ 2.6
Tea (green)	79.6	77.5	
Tea (scented)	61.2	61.2	
Coffee (whole berries)	36.7	36.7	
Coffee (ground, pure)	66.7	66.7	
Coffee (ground, mixed)	28.6	28.6	± 0.0
Coffee (French)	28.6	28.6	
Cocoa (finest nibs)	36.7	38.8	
Cocoa (rock)	24.5	24.5	+ 1.9
Cocoa (roasted shells)	8.2	8.2	
Chocolate powder	28.1	30.1	+ 7.1
Chocolate	49.0	49.0	± 0.0
Bacon (smoked Wiltshire)	18.4	20.4	
Bacon (smoked Canadian)	not stated	18.9	+ 7.0
Bacon (home-cured)	16.8	17.3	
Hams	17.9	18.4	
Hams (American)[a]	16.3	20.4	+23.1
Hams (English)[a]	24.5	24.5	
Lard	14.3	17.3	
Lard (English)[a]	16.3	20.4	+23.1
Lard (American)[a]	not stated	18.4	
Suet (beef)	16.3	20.4	+25.2
Sugar	5.6	5.6	± 0.0
Sugar (fancy)	10.2	10.2	
Eggs (Irish, 10)[a]	24.5	24.5	± 0.0
Tapioca	7.1	9.2	+29.6
Rice	6.6	7.1	+ 7.6
Sago	6.1	9.7	+42.6
Cheese	18.4	18.4	
Cheese (Stilton)	26.5	26.5	+ 5.1
Cheese (Canadian)[a]	15.3	18.4	
Cheese (English Cheddar)[a]	22.4	22.4	
Apples (dried/evaporated)	20.4	22.4	+ 9.8
Apricots (dried/evaporated)	20.4	20.4	± 0.0
Apricots (tinned, in syrup)	32.6	32.6	
Baking powder	49.0	49.0	± 0.0
Biscuits	27.5	27.5	± 0.0
Bottled fruit (for tarts)	25.5	23.5	− 7.8
Breakfast cereals	12.2	12.2	± 0.0
Tomato catsup (12 oz. bottles)	21.4	21.4	± 0.0
Currants	18.4	10.2	−44.6
Raisins	15.3	13.3	−13.1

Appendix Table 7 (Continued)

Commodity	Retail Prices 1901	Retail Prices 1910	Price Movement 1901–1910
Flour (household, 7 lbs.)	24.5	30.6	
Flour (fine pastry, 7 lbs.)	28.6	34.7	
Flour (Hungarian, 7 lbs.)	36.7	44.9	+20.3
Flour (whole-meal, 7 lbs.)	24.5	30.6	
Flour (self-raising, 5 lbs.)	24.5	26.5	
French plums (bottled)	18.4	33.7	+83.2
Fruits (tinned, 3 lbs.)	32.6	28.6	−12.3
Jam (pot, 3 lbs.)	28.6	28.6	± 0.0
Macaroni	10.7	12.2	+14.0
Condensed milk (tin)	7.7	11.7	+51.9
Oats (2 lbs.)	11.7	11.2	− 4.3
Oatmeal (2 lbs.)	10.2	10.2	± 0.0
Paysandu	61.2	49.0	−19.9
Bellies (English home-cured)[a]	24.5	24.5	+15.0
Bellies (Canadian sides)[a]	20.4	26.5	
Butter (Danish)	32.6	30.6	+ 0.9
Butter (Argentina)[a]	26.5	28.6	
Mean price increase[b]			+ 5.4

Note: All prices are for one-pound units unless otherwise stated.
a. "Highest class trade" items: all other items "medium quality".
b. Excludes the luxury items paysandu and bottled French plums.

D. *1912–1914*

Commodity	Retail Prices 1912	Retail Prices 1914	Price Movement 1912–1914	Description
Mutton breast (lb.)	6.1¢	9.2¢	+50.8%	Foreign/Colonial[d]
Potatoes (7 lbs.)	7.9	10.7	+35.4	
Beef flank (lb.)	7.1	8.2	+15.5	Foreign/Colonial[d]
Beef steak (lb.)[a]	14.3	16.3	+14.0	Foreign/Colonial[d]
Beef ribs (lb.)[b]	9.9	10.2	+ 3.0	Foreign/Colonial[d]
Bacon (lb.)[c]	20.1	20.4	+ 1.5	
Flour (7 lbs.)	21.4	21.4	± 0.0	
Sugar (lb.)	4.1	4.1	± 0.0	White, granulated
Pork chops (lb.)	18.9	18.4	− 2.6	British[d]
Cheese (lb.)	17.3	16.3	− 5.8	Canadian/Amer. cheddar
Mutton leg (lb.)	12.2	11.2	− 8.2	Foreign/Colonial[d]
Bread (lb.)	11.2	10.2	+ 8.9	
Mutton shoulder (lb.)	10.2	9.2	− 9.8	Foreign/Colonial[d]
Milk (Amer. qt.)	6.8	5.9	−13.2	
Mean price increase			+ 5.1	

a. (Carver) beef "steak," type not stated; (Board of Trade) mean of "shoulder steak" and "rump steak."
b. (Carver) beef "ribs," type not stated; (Board of Trade) mean of "prime cut" ribs and "flat or top" ribs.

Appendix Table 7 (Continued)

c. (Carver) "bacon," origin not stated; (Board of Trade) mean of "home-cured sides," "American drafts" and "roll" bacon.

d. In no case does Carver specify the country of origin, but in the context of his investigation of working-class diet, it seems almost certain that the mutton and beef prices quoted referred to the cheaper colonial and foreign meat.

E. *1903–1910*

| Commodity | Retail Prices | | Price Movement |
	1903	1910	1903–1910
Beef			
Sirloin	19.4¢	20.4¢	+ 5.2%
Ribs (chine)	19.4	20.4	+ 5.2
Topside of round/silverside	18.4	18.4	± 0.0
Rump steak	15.3	17.3	+13.1
Aitch bone (lower round)	17.3	18.4	+ 6.4
Shoulder	15.3	16.3	+ 6.5
Neck (stickings)	8.2	18.4	+124.4 (?)
Brisket (breast)	12.2	16.3	+33.6
Hip-bone steak (best rump)	26.5	26.5	± 0.0
Stew steak	18.4	18.4	± 0.0
Mutton			
Legs	19.4	20.4	+ 5.2
Shoulder	17.3	18.4	+ 6.4
Loins (whole)	20.4	21.4	+ 4.9
Neck	17.3	18.4	+ 6.4
Cutlets (Amer. chops)	22.4	24.5	+ 9.4
Breast (lower ribs)	10.2	10.2	± 0.0
Liver	16.3	16.3	± 0.0
Pork			
Legs	15.3	18.4	+20.3
Loin	16.3	18.4	+12.9
Neck	15.3	17.3	+13.1
Belly	12.2	16.3	+33.6
Veal			
Legs	17.3	18.4	+ 6.4
Filet or tenderloin	20.4	21.4	+ 4.9
Shoulder	14.3	18.4	+28.7
Cutlet	26.5	26.5	± 0.0
Mean price increase[a]			+ 9.3

Sources: Prices for 1900: Great Britain, *Report on Wholesale and Retail Prices in the U.K. in 1902;* prices for 1901: Halstead, "Report on Prices"; prices for 1903: Halstead, "Report on Prices"; prices for 1905: Great Britain, *Enquiry by the Board of Trade into Working Class Rents, Housing, Retail Prices and Wages;* prices for 1910: Halstead, "Report on Prices"; prices for 1912: Great Britain, *Enquiry by the Board of Trade into Working Class Rents, Housing, Retail Prices and Wages;* prices for 1914: Carver, *Dietary of the Labouring Classes of Birmingham.*

a. Excludes the apparently phenomenal price increase for beef neck (stickings). The price stated for 1903 was probably a typographical error.

Appendix Table 8
Monthly Retail Price of 10 Food Items: Working-Class Stores in Pittsburgh, 1907–1913

A. *1907*

	Jan.	Mar.	May	July	Sept.	Nov.
Beef ribs (lb.)	17.7¢	17.7¢	17.7¢	17.3¢	18.7¢	18.0¢
Leg of mutton (lb.)	17.0	17.0	16.3	15.7	17.0	17.0
Pork, loin chops (lb.)	15.3	15.3	15.7	15.7	17.0	18.7
Corn meal (lb.)	2.71	2.71	2.63	2.71	2.78	2.91
Fresh eggs (dozen)	32.0	28.5	26.5	24.5	26.3	31.0
Creamery butter (lb.)	36.5	36.3	31.8	28.5	30.8	36.3
Fresh milk (qt.)	8.8	8.8	7.5	7.3	7.3	8.3
Flour (⅛ bbl.)	77.5	77.0	78.3	80.8	81.3	80.8
Irish potatoes (peck)	24.5	23.8	23.8	26.3	25.0	25.0
White sugar (lb.)	6.1	6.1	6.1	6.1	6.1	6.1

B. *1908*

	Jan.	Mar.	May	July	Sept.	Nov.
Beef ribs (lb.)	18.0¢	18.0¢	18.0¢	18.0¢	18.0¢	18.7¢
Leg of mutton (lb.)	17.0	17.0	17.3	16.0	16.7	17.0
Pork, loin chops (lb.)	15.0	15.0	15.0	15.0	14.3	15.0
Corn meal (lb.)	2.71	2.71	2.71	2.71	2.83	2.83
Fresh eggs (dozen)	33.3	25.3	22.3	23.8	24.5	33.3
Creamery butter (lb.)	38.0	35.0	33.3	29.5	31.8	37.0
Fresh milk (qt.)	8.3	8.3	7.8	7.5	7.5	8.3
Flour (⅛ bbl.)	84.5	84.5	84.5	83.3	84.0	87.0
Irish potatoes (peck)	26.3	27.5	27.5	32.5	27.5	25.0
White sugar (lb.)	6.1	6.1	6.1	6.1	6.1	6.1

C. *1909*

	Jan.	Mar.	May	July	Sept.	Nov.
Beef ribs (lb.)	18.0¢	18.0¢	18.7¢	18.0¢	18.0¢	18.0¢
Leg of mutton (lb.)	16.3	16.3	16.3	15.7	16.0	16.3
Pork, loin chops (lb.)	16.3	16.3	16.3	17.0	17.0	17.0
Corn meal (lb.)	2.71	2.71	2.71	2.71	2.71	2.83
Fresh eggs (dozen)	37.7	28.6	26.3	27.3	29.3	33.3
Creamery butter (lb.)	38.5	36.8	33.5	32.5	35.5	36.0
Fresh milk (qt.)	8.3	8.3	7.8	7.8	7.8	8.3
Flour (⅛ bbl.)	85.5	86.8	89.5	88.8	86.3	86.3
Irish potatoes (peck)	28.8	28.8	28.8	31.3	25.8	25.0
White sugar (lb.)	6.1	6.1	6.1	6.1	6.1	6.1

D. *1910*

	Jan.	Mar.	May	July	Sept.	Nov.
Beef ribs (lb.)	18.5	18.5	19.0	18.5	18.5	19.0
Leg of mutton (lb.)	16.0	16.3	17.0	17.0	16.5	16.3
Pork, loin chops (lb.)	18.8	19.5	19.5	19.5	18.3	18.5
Corn meal (lb.)	2.71	2.71	2.71	2.71	2.71	2.83
Fresh eggs (dozen)	40.0	28.2	24.4	24.2	26.4	35.0
Creamery butter (lb.)	39.2	35.7	31.8	32.3	34.7	36.8
Fresh milk (qt.)	8.6	8.6	7.6	7.6	8.0	8.8
Flour (⅛ bbl.)	86.0	84.6	86.0	85.0	84.6	86.0
Irish potatoes (lb.)	27.0	24.0	26.0	29.0	26.0	25.0
White sugar (lb.)	6.1	6.1	6.1	6.1	6.1	6.1

Appendix Table 8 (Continued)

E. 1911

	Jan.	Feb.	Mar.	Apr.	May	June	July	Aug.	Sept.	Oct.	Nov.	Dec.
Beef ribs (lb.)	19.5¢	19.5¢	19.5¢	19.0¢	19.0¢	19.0¢	18.5¢	18.5¢	19.0¢	19.0¢	19.0¢	19.5¢
Leg of mutton (lb.)	16.3	16.3	16.3	16.8	17.8	17.3	17.3	17.0	16.0	16.0	15.0	16.0
Pork, loin chops (lb.)	18.0	18.0	18.3	18.8	18.5	19.5	19.5	19.3	19.3	18.5	16.0	16.0
Corn meal (lb.)	2.71		2.71		2.71		2.71		2.71		2.96	
Fresh eggs (dozen)	38.5	30.2	26.6	20.4	22.0	21.4	22.6	23.0	25.6	28.0	36.0	45.0
Creamery butter (lb.)	38.2	34.7	34.3	32.0	30.8	30.7	30.5	31.8	33.5	35.0	38.5	43.7
Fresh milk (qt.)	8.8	8.8	8.8	8.6	7.6	7.6	7.6	7.6	8.0	8.0	8.8	8.8
Flour (⅛ bbl.)	83.6	83.6	81.6	78.6	78.6	78.6	80.0	81.0	83.2	83.6	85.2	84.8
Irish potatoes (lb.)	27.0	25.0	24.0	23.0	25.0	37.0	44.0	34.0	28.0	27.0	31.0	33.0
White sugar (lb.)	6.1	6.1	6.1	6.1	6.1	6.3	7.3	7.5	7.9	7.8	7.5	7.0

F. 1912

	Jan.	Feb.	Mar.	Apr.	May	June	July	Aug.	Sept.	Oct.	Nov.	Dec.
Beef ribs (lb.)	19.5¢	19.0¢	19.5¢	19.8¢	21.8¢	22.3¢	21.8¢	21.4¢	21.4¢	21.0¢	20.6¢	20.4¢
Leg of mutton (lb.)	16.8	17.3	18.0	20.0	21.6	21.0	19.0	19.0	19.5	19.5	18.8	19.5
Pork, loin chops (lb.)	17.2	15.8	17.8	19.8	20.6	20.2	20.2	22.8	23.4	24.0	22.2	17.6
Corn meal (lb.)	2.87		2.89		2.89		2.93		2.97		2.94	
Fresh eggs (dozen)	41.0	39.5	24.9	24.4	23.7	23.8	25.7	26.7	29.5	34.0	40.3	39.3
Creamery butter (lb.)	44.7	41.3	36.8	38.3	36.6	33.1	33.4	33.6	35.7	38.2	39.8	43.7
Fresh milk (qt.)	9.0	9.0	9.0	9.0	7.8	7.8	7.8	7.8	7.8	8.0	9.0	9.0
Flour (⅛ bbl.)	84.0	84.3	85.2	85.2	86.7	86.7	86.7	85.5	83.0	81.7	78.3	76.7
Irish potatoes (lb.)	36.0	39.0	39.2	46.7	44.2	44.2	31.7	28.7	23.8	23.3	21.2	21.7
White sugar (lb.)	6.9	6.8	7.0	6.8	6.4	6.3	6.3	6.2	6.2	6.2	6.2	6.1

G. 1913

	Jan.	Feb.	Mar.	Apr.	May	June	July	Aug.	Sept.	Oct.	Nov.	Dec.
Beef ribs (lb.)	20.4¢	20.6¢	21.3¢	21.5¢	21.8¢	22.0¢	21.8¢	22.5¢	22.2¢	21.7¢	21.7¢	21.8
Leg of mutton (lb.)	21.3	21.5	22.1	22.0	21.2	25.0	20.8	19.7	20.0	20.0	20.3	20.7
Pork, loin chops (lb.)	19.4	20.0	21.1	23.2	22.0	22.0	23.0	23.5	25.2	23.2	22.5	28.0
Corn meal (lb.)	2.60		2.71		2.74		2.77		2.85		2.96	
Fresh eggs (dozen)	37.6	28.4	25.4	24.1	24.1	25.5	27.1	28.9	34.8	38.0	46.3	49.2
Creamery butter (lb.)	41.9	43.5	43.4	42.6	37.2	36.7	35.7	35.6	39.3	39.7	40.5	45.9
Fresh milk (qt.)	9.0	9.0	8.8	8.8	8.6	8.6	8.6	8.6	8.6	8.8	9.2	9.2
Flour (⅛ bbl.)	74.3	76.2	76.3	77.3	76.7	78.8	79.8	78.9	79.2	78.5	78.1	77.6
Irish potatoes (lb.)	22.5	23.6	22.2	22.5	24.0	25.0	27.2	28.9	31.4	28.1	30.0	28.9
White sugar (lb.)	6.0	5.8	5.5	5.4	5.5	5.5	5.4	5.6	5.8	5.8	5.7	5.5

Source: U.S. Bureau of Labor Statistics, *Bulletins*, Nos. 115, 125, 132, 136, 138, 140 (1912–1914).

Appendix Table 9
Estimates of Comparative Meat Consumption: Pittsburgh and Birmingham, 1901–1914

The formula by which comparative meat consumption was estimated in chapter 9 is stated below.

(1)
$$\frac{[(E^{b.1914}/E^{m.1914})(E^{m.1904})][(P^{b.pbh.1905}/P^{b.bhm.1905})]}{(E^{b.pa.1901}/100)} = Q^{md.f} ,$$

(2)
$$Q^{md.f}/(S^{md.f}/S^{pa.f}) = Q^{md.a} ,$$

where

$E^{b.1914}$ is weekly expenditure for beef (mutton, pork) in Birmingham, 1914;

$E^{m.1914}$ is weekly expenditure for meat in Birmingham, 1914;

$E^{m.1904}$ is weekly expenditure for meat in the Midlands, 1904;

$E^{b.pa.1901}$ is weekly expenditure for beef (mutton, pork) in Pennsylvania, 1901;

$P^{b.bhm.1905}$ is the price of beef (mutton, pork) in Birmingham, 1905;

$P^{b.pbh.1905}$ is the price of beef (mutton, pork) in Pittsburgh, 1905;

$Q^{md.f}$ is the estimated quantity of beef (mutton, pork) eaten weekly per family in the Midlands stated as a percentage of the quantity of beef (mutton, pork) eaten weekly per family in Pennsylvania;

$S^{md.f}$ is the size of Midlands families (in consumer units);

$S^{pa.f}$ is the size of Pennsylvania families (in consumer units);

$Q^{md.a}$ is the quantity of beef (mutton, pork) eaten weekly per adult male worker in the Midlands stated as a percentage of the quantity of beef (mutton, pork) eaten weekly per adult male worker in Pennsylvania.

1. Calculations for beef consumption are as follows:
   (a) [(40.69/92.15) (66.25)] [(143.9)*] = 42.13 pence
   = 85.52 cents
   85.52/(91.4/100) = 93.6
   (b) 93.6/(391.6/323.7) = 77.4 (i.e., Birmingham consumption = 77% Pittsburgh consumption).
   Note: (143.9)* is calculated from the mean price difference ($P^{b.bhm.1905}/P^{b.bhm.1905}$) on beef ribs, round, and sirloin, i.e., 1.647, 1.348, and 1.322.

2. Calculations for mutton consumption (i) are as follows:
   (a) [(19.91/92.15) (66.25)] [(14.5/12.8)*] = 16.21 pence
   = 32.91 cents
   32.91/(10.2/100) = 322.6
   (b) 322.6/(391.6/323.7) = 266.6 (i.e., Birmingham consumption = 267% Pittsburgh consumption).

   Calculations for mutton consumption (ii) are as follows:
   (a) [(19.91/92.15) (66.25)] [14.5/12.8] = 16.21 pence
   = 32.91 cents
   32.91/(15.3/100) = 215.1
   (b) 215.1/391.6/323.7 = 177.8 (i.e., Birmingham consumption = 178% Pittsburgh consumption).
   Note: (i) is based on the assumption that two-thirds of Pennsylvanian's "other meat" expenditure went to purchase mutton;
   (ii) is based on the assumption that all of Pennsylvanian's "other meat" expenditure went to purchase mutton; (14.5/12.8)* is based on the prices of mutton leg in Pittsburgh and Birmingham.

3. Calculations for pork consumption are as follows:
   (a) $[(10.81/92.15)\ (66.25)]\ [(15.1/16.3)^*] = 7.15$ pence
   $= 14.5$ cents

   $14.5/(16.8/100) = 86.3$
   (b) $86.3/(391.6/323.7) = 71.3$ (i.e., Birmingham consumption $= 71\%$ Pittsburgh consumption).
   Note: $(15.1/16.3)^*$ is based on the prices of pork chops in Pittsburgh and Birmingham.

Appendix Table 10
Exchange Rates, 1899–1913

Throughout the 1899–1913 period the prevailing international exchange rate was $4.87 = £1.00.
The reader may find the following conversion table useful:

1¢ : 0.5d (0.2p)	1d (0.4p) = 2.0¢
5¢ : 2.4d (1.0p)	1/- (5p) = 24.4¢
10¢ : 4.9d (1.9p)	10/- (50p) = $ 2.44
50¢ : 2/0½ (10.2p)	£ 1 (100p) = $ 4.87
$ 1.00 : 4/1 (20.4p)	£ 5 = $24.35
$ 5.00 : £1:0:6½ (£1.03)	£10 = $48.70
$10.00 : £2:1:1 (£2.05)	

Notes

Chapter 1: Introduction

1. Dorothy Crook, "Perspectives—An Interview with Thomas Cochran," *Economic Impact*, No. 3 (1975), 60.

2. J. Potter, " 'Optimism' and 'Pessimism' in Interpreting the Industrial Revolution: An Economic Historian's Dilemma," *Scandinavian Economic History Review*, 10 (1962), 259.

3. E. Rothbarth, "Causes of the Superior Efficiency of U.S.A. Industry As Compared with British Industry," *Economic Journal*, 56 (1946), 383–90; H. J. Habakkuk, *American and British Technology in the Nineteenth Century* (Cambridge, 1962). Habakkuk, pp. 11–14, accepts the view that "industrial money wages were substantially higher than they were in England" and suggests, more cautiously, that "American workers enjoyed better nutrition and more spacious working and living conditions."

4. See, for example, Peter Temin, "Labor Scarcity and the Problem of American Industrial Efficiency in the 1850's," *Journal of Economic History*, 26 (1966), 277–98, and "Labor Scarcity in America," *Journal of Indisciplinary History*, 1 (1971), 251–64; Robert W. Fogel, "The Specification Problem in Economic History," *Journal of Economic History*, 27 (1967), 283–308; Ian M. Drummond, "Labor Scarcity and the Problem of American Industrial Efficiency in the 1850's: A Comment," *Journal of Economic History*, 27 (1967), 383–90.

5. Paul A. David, *Technical Choice, Innovation and Economic Growth* (Cambridge, 1975), p. 26n. Noting, p. 20, that "not the least of difficulties with the entire subject is that its empirical outlines at present are so hazy, and so inadequately corroborated even in their grossest imprecisions," David explores the realities of the nineteenth-century American technological environment. He does not, however, examine the cost of labor per se. A recent economic history text by Susan Praviant Lee and Peter Passell, *A New Economic View of American History* (New York, 1979), asks: "Where does this leave the [technology] debate? In need of more detailed empirical information about . . . returns to capital and labor" (p. 104).

6. Daniel Bell, "The Background and Development of Marxian Socialism in the United States," in Donald Drew Egbert and Stow Persons, eds., *Socialism and American Life* (Princeton, 1952), 1:217.

7. For a traditional overview of the various factors that restrained the development of socialism within the United States, see G. D. H. Cole, *A History of Socialist Thought* (London, 1956), 3, Pt. 2, 775–819.

8. Philip Taft, *The A. F. of L. in the Time of Gompers* (New York, 1957), p. xvii; and his "The Philosophy of the American Labor Movement," in William Haber, ed., *The Vista of American Labor* (Washington, D.C., 1966), p. 148. See also Taft's "Theories of the Labor Movement," in Industrial Relations Research Association, *Interpreting the Labor Movement* (Madison, Wis., 1952), pp. 35–37. "Let those who are concerned about American labor's lack of philosophy engage in a bit of comparative analy-

sis," he suggests. The superior standard of living gained by American workers indicates that "there is really no reason why anyone should assume that European labor represents the ideal and the American movement only a distortion of the true type."

9. Warren B. Catlin, *The Labor Problem in the United States and Great Britain* (New York, 1926), p. 156. According to Catlin, "The average wages paid in the United States [were] still more than double those paid in Great Britain."

10. Henry Pelling, *American Labor* (Chicago, 1960), pp. 216 and 126. Daniel J. Boorstin, in his editor's preface, shares this view, suggesting that one of the "unique characteristics" of American labor has been the high wages paid (p. v).

11. Henry Pelling, *America and the British Left, from Bright to Bevan* (London, 1956), p. 79.

12. John H. M. Laslett, *Labor and the Left: A Study of the Socialist and Radical Influences in the American Labor Movement, 1881–1924* (New York, 1970), pp. 302 and 308n.

13. Howard H. Quint, *The Forging of American Socialism: Origins of the Modern Movement* (Columbia, S.C., 1953), p. 5; Marc Karson, *American Labor Unions and Politics, 1900–1918* (Carbondale, Ill., 1958), pp. 286–88. Such views are not new. Robert Franklin Hoxie, *Trade Unionism in the United States* (New York, 1917), pp. 159–60, believed that economic conditions had "for generations been such that workers *could* see hope ahead in gradual betterment through constructive industrial and political action."

14. International Labour Office, *The Trade Union Situation in the United States* (Geneva, 1960), p. 15.

15. Philip Foner, *History of the Labor Movement in the United States,* (New York, 1964), pp. 14, 20.

16. Melvyn Dubofsky, *We Shall Be All: A History of the Industrial Workers of the World* (New York, 1969), pp. 7, 481.

Chapter 2: Methodological Considerations

1. Edward Aveling and Eleanor Marx Aveling, *The Working-Class Movement in America* (London, 1888), p. 23.

2. Eugene Debs, *Debs: His Life, Writings and Speeches* (Chicago, 1908), p. 105; Charles Edward Russell, *Why I am a Socialist* (New York, 1910), p. 166. According to Russell, "Nothing [can] be more fallacious than the continual assumption from the platform and in the newspapers that [the U.S.A., is] a country of general prosperity; . . . it is evidently a country of general poverty" (p. 146).

3. For a valuable account of the early twentieth-century debate on American conditions among European socialists, see R. Laurence Moore, *European Socialists and the American Promised Land* (New York, 1970), esp. Ch. 5.

4. Quoted in Goetz A. Briefs, *The Proletariat* (New York, 1937), p. 193.

5. *International Socialist Review,* 7 (1906–1907), 425; Morris Hillquit, *History of Socialism in the United States* (New York, 1903), p. 153; William Z. Foster, "The Basis of American Syndicalism," in *American Trade Unions. Principles and Organization, Strategy and Tactics* (New York, 1947), p. 51.

6. Great Britain, *The Parliamentary Debates (Official Report), House of Commons,* 1912, Vol. 34, col. 100. The *Official Reports* are hereafter referred to as Hansard.

7. *Ibid.,* cols. 126, 136–37.

8. *Ibid.,* cols. 783–86, 795, 831–32.

9. Great Britain, Board of Trade, *Report of an Enquiry . . . into Working Class Rents, Housing and Retail Prices, Together with the Rates of Wages in Certain Occupa-*

tions in the Principal Industrial Towns of the United States of America, British Parliamentary Papers, Cd. 5609, 1911, Vol. 88.

10. Hansard, 1909, Vol. 2, cols. 1224, 1626; 1910, Vol. 15, cols. 336–37; 1910, Vol. 18, cols. 338, 1232–33; 1911, Vol. 21, cols. 883, 1428, 2048; 1911, Vol. 23, cols. 1357–58, 1811; 1911, Vol. 25, cols. 14–15.

11. *Ibid.*, 1911, Vol. 21, cols. 333, 3281; 1912, Vol. 34, cols. 137, 158.

12. The "Pittsburgh Survey" was a major social investigation undertaken by the Russell Sage Foundation in 1907–1908. Six reports were eventually published under the editorship of Paul Underwood Kellogg: Elizabeth R. Butler, *Women and the Trades, Pittsburgh 1907–1908* (New York, 1909); Crystal Eastman, *Work Accidents and the Law* (New York, 1910); J. A. Fitch, *The Steel Workers* (New York, 1910); Margaret F. Byington, *Homestead: The Households of a Mill Town* (New York, 1910); Paul Underwood Kellogg, ed., *The Pittsburgh District Civic Frontage* (New York, 1914); and Paul Underwood Kellogg, ed., *Wage-Earning Pittsburgh* (New York, 1914).

13. Individual analyses changed according to the topic under discussion. The Labour party spokesman, arguing against the introduction of tariff barriers, denied that the American worker was much better off than his British counterpart. Yet Labour member William Thorne contradicted this line in 1911 when he announced that the United States employee experienced far superior economic conditions as a result of "powerful trade unions" (Hansard, 1911, Vol. 25, cols. 14–15).

14. *Mosely Industrial Commission to the United States of America, October to December, 1902. Report of the Delegates* (Manchester, 1903). For a brief account of the commission and its major conclusions, see Vivian Vale, "Watching Americans Work," *Durham University Journal*, 47 (1955), 119–28.

15. Mosely Industrial Commission, *Report*, pp. 33, 90–91, 113, 169.

16. Mosely Industrial Commission, *Report*, pp. 171, 237. For other statements skeptical of the superiority of American life, see the testimony of H. R. Taylor (*Ibid.*, pp. 180–81), M. Deller (*Ibid.*, pp. 187, 189), and William Dyson (*Ibid.*, p. 215). The conclusion of Henry Pelling in *America and the British Left, from Bright to Bevan* (London, 1956), that trade unionists on the Mosely Commission were impressed with "the fact that in most of the areas they visited in the industrial North [of the U.S.], the American workers were . . . better off than the British, in spite of a higher cost of living" (p. 81) is much too cavalier.

17. U. S. Senate, *Wages and Prices Abroad*, 61st Cong., 2nd sess., 1910, Document No. 477 contains the consular data. The Select Committee's conclusions, together with additional information, may be found in U. S. Senate, *Reports of the Select Committee on the Wages and Prices of Commodities*, 61st Cong., 2nd sess., 1910, Document No. 912. The *Majority Report* is part 1, the *Minority Report*, part 2. There are also two volumes of testimony, a topical digest of evidence, and various memoranda.

18. E. Levasseur, *The American Workman* (Baltimore, 1900), p. 294.

19. E. H. Phelps Brown and Margaret Browne, *A Century of Pay: The Course of Pay and Production in France, Germany, Sweden, the United Kingdom, and the United States of America, 1860–1960* (London, 1968). Earlier evidence was published by E. H. Phelps Brown and Sheila V. Hopkins in "The Course of Wage-Rates in Five Countries, 1860–1939," *Oxford Economic Papers*, n. s., 2 (1950), 226–91.

20. Phelps Brown and Browne, *Century of Pay*, Table 2, p. 46.

21. U.S. Department of Commerce and Labor, Bureau of Labor, *Bulletin*, No. 59, (1905), p. 5. The truth of this statement has only slowly been appreciated by the economic historian. Nathan Rosenberg, "Anglo-American Wage Differences in the 1820's," *Journal of Economic History*, 27 (1967), 225, 229, concludes that "much more attention

ought to be focused on particular categories of labor rather than dealing with such highly aggregated concepts as 'skilled' and 'unskilled.' " He suggests that "high priority ought . . . to be attached to . . . research which will provide more reliable information on the nature of these differentials."

22. Arthur Shadwell, *Industrial Efficiency: A Comparative Study of Industrial Life in England, Germany and America* (London, 1906), 1:2–4.

23. Leo Wolman, "American Wages," *Quarterly Journal of Economics*, 46 (1932), noted that wage rates "rarely reflect actual changes in the rate of wages and, particularly during periods of depression, they can be regarded as no more than nominal rates which conceal the true movement of wages" (401–02). However, this divergence over time between rates and earnings is less significant for the pre-First World War period. Albert Rees, *Real Wages in Manufacturing, 1890–1914* (Princeton, 1961), agreed that wage rates are "likely to vary less with the trade cycle than do actual payments for the unit of input" but believed such variations were "not of much account before 1914." Prior to that date, premiums for overtime or shift work were rare.

24. A. P. Kirkland, "Pittsburgh, With Its Black Diamonds," *Engineers' Society of Western Pennsylvania Proceedings*, 15 (1899), 215, citing a speech made by William Graham in the House of Representatives.

25. John Newton Boucher, *William Kelly: A True History of the So-Called Bessemer Process* (Greensburg, Pa., 1924), p. 224; John Duffy, "Smoke, Smog and Health in Early Pittsburgh," *Western Pennsylvania Historical Magazine*, 45 (1962), 97; Lincoln Steffens, "Pittsburgh: A City Ashamed," *McClure's Magazine*, 21 (1903), 24.

26. If I had intended to calculate average wage rates or earnings received in the two cities, then their comparative economic bases would have been of crucial importance. That average wages paid in city X were larger than in city Y may, for example, have reflected the fact that the former had a higher percentage of skilled workers, a greater dependence upon high-wage industries, or a smaller proportion of female employees.

27. F. W. Lawrence, *Local Variations in Wages* (London, 1899), pp. 17–18; M. Ada Beney, *Differentials in Industrial Wages and Hours in the United States* (New York, 1938), pp. 19, 22; Lonny L. Wilson, "Intercity Wage and Cost-of-Living Differentials in the United States, 1889–1939" (Ph.D. diss., University of Iowa, 1973).

28. E. H. Hunt, *Regional Wage Variations in Britain, 1850–1914* (Oxford, 1973).

29. Philip R. P. Coelho and James F. Shepherd, "The Impact of Regional Differences in Prices and Wages on Economic Growth: The United States in 1890," *Journal of Economic History*, 39 (1979), 69–86.

30. Great Britain, *Census*, 1901, Vol. 9, Table 35, and 1911, Vol. 10, Pt. 2, Table 13, give the population of Birmingham as 522,204 (1901) and 525,833 (1911), and of Sheffield as 380,793 (1901) and 454,632 (1911). According to the U.S. Bureau of the Census, *Census*, 1900, Vol. 2, Table 32; and Special Report, "Occupations at the Twelfth Census," Table 42; and *Census*, 1910, Vol. 1, Table 49 and Vol. 4, Table 3, the population of Pittsburgh was 451,512 (1900) and 533,905 (1910). Throughout this study, the city of Allegheny, incorporated as Pittsburgh's North Side in 1906, is included in the Pittsburgh figures.

31. The economic growth of Pittsburgh may be traced, if sketchily, in a number of doctoral dissertations registered at the University of Pittsburgh. See Catherine E. Reiser, "Pittsburgh's Commercial and Industrial Development, 1800 to 1859" (1941); George L. Davis, "Greater Pittsburgh's Commercial and Industrial Development, 1850–1900 (With Emphasis on the Contributions of Technology)" (1951); and James H. Thompson, "A Financial History of the City of Pittsburgh, 1816–1910" (1949). Other accounts, of varying reliability, include: Samuel Hardin Church, *A Short History of*

Pittsburgh, 1758–1908 (New York, 1908); American Historical Society, *History of Pittsburgh and Environs* (New York, 1922), Vol. 3, Chs. 23–28; Frank C. Harper, *Pittsburgh: Forge of the Universe* (New York, 1957); and Stefan Lorant, ed., *Pittsburgh: The Story of an American City* (New York, 1964).

32. Roy Lubove, *Twentieth-Century Pittsburgh: Government, Business and Environmental Change* (New York, 1969), p. 5, suggests that the city had, by the early 1900s, "an over-specialization in a limited range of heavy industrial enterprises."

33. Elizabeth Ledwidge, "The Pittsburgh Sesqui-Centennial, 1908," *Western Pennsylvania Historical Magazine*, 41 (1958), 125.

34. *Ibid.*

35. U.S. *Census*, 1910, Vol. 9, Table 1.

36. *Ibid.*, p. 1053.

37. Great Britain, *Enquiry into Working Class Rents, Housing and Retail Prices in the U.S.A.*, p. 337.

38. For a particularly good study of the relationship between Birmingham's industrial difficulties and development of tariff-reform sentiment within the city, see Asa Briggs, "Borough and City 1865–1938," in *History of Birmingham* (Oxford, 1952), 2:33–37.

39. "About the Making of Birmingham's 3,000,000 Guns," *Birmingham Magazine of Arts and Industries*, 3 (1902), 105.

40. U. S. Department of Commerce and Labor, Bureau of Manufactures, *Daily Consular and Trade Reports*, Oct.–Dec. 1911, Vol. 4, p. 828; Apr.–June 1912, Vol. 2, p. 970. Hereafter referred to as U.S. *Consular Reports*. See also W. T. Pike, ed., *Birmingham at the Opening of the Twentieth Century: Contemporary Biographies* (Brighton, 1905), p. 21; and Birmingham Chamber of Commerce, *Report of the Council . . . for the Year 1900* (Birmingham, n. d., pp. 37–38), for evidence as to the decline in the gun industry.

41. J. R. Roche, *The History, Development and Organization of the Birmingham Jewellery and Allied Trades* (Birmingham, 1927), p. 49.

42. Great Britain, Fair Wages Committee, *Minutes of Evidence, British Parliamentary Papers*, Cd. 4423, 1908, Vol. 34, pp. 144, 178. The Birmingham Chamber of Commerce described the state of the local harness and saddlery trade as "simply wretched" in 1904. See their *Journal*, 31 Jan. 1906, p. 2.

43. Birmingham Chamber of Commerce, *Journal*, 30 Jan. 1904, p. 3.

44. Peter R. Shergold, "Wage Rates in Pittsburgh During the Depression of 1908," *Journal of American Studies*, 9 (1975), 167–69, esp. Table 1.

45. Birmingham Chamber of Commerce, *Journal*, 31 Jan. 1907, p. 1.

46. John R. Commons and William Leiserson, "Wage-Earners of Pittsburgh," in Kellogg, ed., *Wage-Earning Pittsburgh*, p. 118.

47. Steel data from University of Pittsburgh, Bureau of Industrial Research, Statistical Handbooks, No. 2, *Industrial Databook for the Pittsburgh District* (Pittsburgh, 1936), pp. 29–35. Statistics as to new building permits were derived from three sources [City of] Allegheny Department of Public Safety, Bureau of Building Inspection, *Annual Reports*, 1899–1906; Pittsburgh Executive Department, *Annual Report for 1912–13*, Statistical Appendix, p. 30; Pittsburgh Board of Trade, *Year Book*, 1909, p. 30. Railway earnings data were published annually in the *Commercial and Financial Chronicle*, "Railway and Industrial Section."

48. Statistics on the consumption of natural gas in Pittsburgh were derived from the Philadelphia Company, *Annual Report of the Board of Directors to the Stockholders*, No. 16 (year ending 31 Mar. 1900) through No. 30 (year ending 31 Mar. 1913). The quotation is from No. 21 (year ending 31 Mar. 1905), p. 6. It should be noted that the name of

the Philadelphia Company is misleading—it was a Pittsburgh enterprise. Data on the number of street railway passengers carried by the Pittsburgh Railways Company were published each year by the Pennsylvania Department of Internal Affairs, Pt. 4, *Annual Report of the Bureau of Railways.* Information as to the sale of beer (by Pittsburgh's two major breweries, the Independent Brewing Company and the Pittsburgh Brewing Company) were published in the *Commercial and Financial Chronicle,* 28 Nov. 1906, p. 1418; 12 Nov. 1910, p. 1325.

49. *New York Times,* 2 Dec. 1907, p. 10; 21 Nov. 1907, p. 13; 25 Nov. 1907, p. 12; *Commercial and Financial Chronicle,* 10 Oct. 1908, p. 934.

50. *New York Times,* 15 Nov. 1907, p. 16; 2 Dec. 1907, p. 10; *Commercial and Financial Chronicle,* 22 Feb. 1908, p. 481; 23 May, 1908, p. 1249; 28 Nov. 1908, p. 417; U.S. *Congressional Record,* Vol. 42, 60th Cong., 1st sess., Pt. 3, 25 Feb. 1908, p. 2485.

51. *New York Times,* 3 Nov. 1907, p. 9; 8 Dec. 1907, p. 4; *Pittsburgh Sesqui-Centennial Celebration Official Account* (n. p., n. d.), p. 92.

52. Parish of Birmingham, *Interim Report: Presented to the Board, October 21, 1908, by the Special Committee Appointed on April 15, 1908 to Investigate the Whole System of Administering Out-door and In-door Relief in the Parish* (Birmingham, 1908), p. 5; E. V. Birchall, "The Conditions of Distress," *Economic Review,* 20 (1910), 26; Birmingham Chamber of Commerce, *Journal,* 30 Jan. 1909, p. 1. See also Birmingham Trades Council, *Annual Report and Balance Sheet,* No. 44 (1909), p. 7, which described "the ever-increasing problem of unemployment" in the winter of 1908.

53. Birmingham Labour Church, *Minute Books,* Vol. 6, p. 286; Birmingham Right-to-Work Committee, *Annual Report,* 1 Oct. 1908–30 Sept. 1909, p. 4; Annie G. Evans to the Birmingham Chief Librarian, 27 Oct. 1912, letter in the possession of Birmingham Public Library.

54. U.S. *Consular Reports,* July–Sept. 1910, Vol. 1, p. 680; Birmingham Chamber of Commerce, *Journal,* 31 Jan. 1910, p. 1; 31 Jan. 1913, p. 1; Birmingham and Midland Counties Grocers' Protection and Benevolent Association, *Annual Report and Balance Sheet,* No. 36 (1909), p. 25.

55. Sidney Pollard, *A History of Labour in Sheffield* (Liverpool, 1959), p. 182.

Chapter 3: Wage Rates

1. Details of the occupations for which hourly wage rates were identified and the sources of that information are presented in Appendix Tables 1 and 2.

2. For the hourly rates paid to individual occupations in each year, see Peter R. Shergold, "The Standard of Life of Manual Workers in the First Decade of the Twentieth-Century: A Comparative Study of Birmingham, U.K., and Pittsburgh, U.S.A." (Ph.D. diss., London School of Economics, 1976), Table 2.1, pp. 37–47 (index numbers) and Appendix A, pp. 637–53 (cents per hour). Individual copies of these data are available from the author on request.

3. Estimates of the number of adult male workers engaged in each occupation are compiled in Appendix Table 3.

4. Occupations were based on two criteria; first, wage data had to be available for each year; second, the number of workers engaged in each occupation had to be estimated with some degree of accuracy. The earliest year for which a mean index could be calculated had to be 1901, so that I could include data on steel mill laborers, numerically the most important occupation; it was only from that year that reliable wage statistics were collected.

5. Based on Table 5A, estimate iii: estimate i indicates an upward movement in

hourly wage rates of 57.6 percent in Pittsburgh compared to 8.3 percent in Birmingham; estimate ii suggests advances of 64.7 percent and 7.1 percent, respectively.

6. Sidney Pollard, *A History of Labour in Sheffield* (Liverpool, 1959), p. 179.

7. A. L. Bowley, *Wages and Income in the United Kingdom Since 1860* (Cambridge, 1937), p. 6, Table 1.

8. Albert Rees, *Real Wages in Manufacturing, 1890–1914* (Princeton, 1961), p. 4.

9. United States Steel Corporation, *Annual Report*, No. 4 (1905), pp. 24–25.

10. *Iron Age*, 7 Nov. 1907, p. 1134; *New York Times*, 15 Nov. 1907, p. 6.

11. *Iron Age*, 19 Dec. 1907, p. 1774; *National Labor Tribune*, 19 Dec. 1907, p. 1; *New York Times*, 14 Dec. 1907, p. 3.

12. *Commercial and Financial Chronicle*, 22 Feb. 1908, p. 442.

13. *New York Times*, 17 Nov. 1907, p. 6.

14. *Commercial and Financial Chronicle*, 21 Mar. 1908, p. 691. For other comments in a similar vein, see also 23 Nov. 1907, p. 1301; 1 May 1909, p. 1092.

15. *Ibid.*, 25 July 1908, p. 196; 7 Aug. 1909, p. 319.

16. Harry Jerome, *Migration and Business Cycles* (New York, 1926), p. 35, Table 1, p. 105, Table 22. Officially recorded male immigration was, in thousands, 613.1 for the year ending 30 June 1903; 549.1, 1904; 724.9, 1905; 764.5, 1906; 930.0, 1907; 506.9, 1908; and 520.0, 1909. Equivalent figures for departing male steerage passengers were 132.9, 1903; 209.2, 1904; 210.3, 1905; 179.9, 1906; 215.0, 1907; 378.2, 1908; and 199.9, 1909.

17. *New York Times*, 21 Nov. 1907, p. 1; 22 Nov. 1907, p. 1. The correspondent estimated that a similar number would depart in December. See also *National Labor Tribune*, 20 Aug. 1908, p. 1; Peter Roberts, "Immigrant Wage-Earners," in Paul U. Kellogg, ed., *Wage-Earning Pittsburgh* (New York, 1914), p. 34.

18. *National Labor Tribune*, 20 Aug. 1908, p. 1; *New York Times*, 21 Nov. 1907, p. 1.

19. John A. Fitch, *The Steel Workers* (New York, 1911), p. 148.

20. *Iron City Trades Journal*, 18 Sept. 1908, p. 2; *National Labor Tribune*, 20 Aug. 1908, p. 1.

21. *New York Times*, 18 Nov. 1907, p. 6; John R. Commons and William Leiserson, "Wage-Earners of Pittsburgh," in Kellogg, ed., *Wage-Earning Pittsburgh*, p. 118; *National Labor Tribune*, 21 Nov. 1907, p. 1.

22. Gustav Cassel, *The Theory of Social Economy* (London, 1923), 2: 545–57, contended that the availability of immigrant labor in times of industrial boom allowed employers readily to enlarge the scope of their operations, and the resulting unbridled expansion increased the intensity of the subsequent depression. This could provide one explanation for the more pronounced movement of the economic cycle in Pittsburgh vis-à-vis Birmingham.

23. The terms employed are from Alexander D. Noyes, "A Year After the Panic of 1907," *Quarterly Journal of Economics*, 23 Feb. 1909, pp. 186, 189.

24. Harry Ober, "Occupational Wage Differentials, 1907–1947," *Monthly Labor Review*, 67 (1948), 127–34; Gerhard Bry and Charlotte Boschan, "Secular Trends and Recent Changes in Real Wages and Wage Differentials in Three Western Industrial Countries: The United States, Great Britain and Germany," in *Deuxième conférence internationale d'histoire économique* (Paris, 1965), pp. 175–208; K. G. J. C. Knowles and D. J. Robertson, "Differences Between the Wages of Skilled and Unskilled Workers, 1880–1950," *Bulletin of the Institute of Statistics*, 13 (1951), 109–27.

25. Julius Issacs, *Economics of Immigration* (London, 1947), p. 201; Joseph Rayback, *A History of American Labor* (New York, 1966), p. 260.

26. Ober, "Occupational Wage Differentials," p. 313, Table 3; Bry and Boschan,

"Secular Trends," p. 186; Earl E. Muntz, "The Decline in Wage Differentials Based on Skill in the United States," *International Labour Review*, 71 (1955), 577.

27. Harry Jerome, *Mechanization in Industry* (New York, 1934), p. 349.

28. U.S. Industrial Commission, *Report*, 1901, vol. 13, pp. 460, 503. Fitch, *Steel Workers*, pp. 153 and 155–67, noted that whereas the wages paid to Pittsburgh's rollers and heaters had declined substantially between 1892 and 1907, day laborers had seen their hourly rate increase from 14¢ to 15–16.5¢.

29. J. Stephen Jeans, "General Report on American Industrial Conditions," in British Iron Trade Association, *American Industrial Conditions and Competition. Report of the Commissioners* (London, 1902), p. 317. Wage behavior in the Pittsburgh district steel industry reflected that in the nation at large. U.S. Department of Commerce and Labor, *Report on Conditions of Employment in the Iron and Steel Industry in the United States*, 62nd Cong., 1st sess., 1913, Vol. 1, concluded that the wages of skilled workmen "were only slightly increased or actually reduced between 1900 and 1910," whereas the wages of unskilled laborers had "been most largely increased."

30. For a far more detailed analysis of the reduction in percentage wage differentials in Pittsburgh, see Peter R. Shergold, "Wage Differentials Based on Skill in the United States, 1899–1914: A Case Study," *Labour History*, 18 (1977), 163–88. Two recent articles have expressed doubts as to whether the narrowing of wage differentials in Pittsburgh was reflected in the nation at large. Stan Vittoz, "World War I and the Political Accommodation of Transitional Market Forces: The Case of Immigration Restriction," *Politics and Society*, 8 (1978), presents no new quantitative material to substantiate his claim that "all the operative forces of economic expansion from approximately the mid-1870s on . . . had a broadening effect on the wage . . . structure of American industry" (57). Andrew Dawson, "The Paradox of Dynamic Technological Change and the Labor Aristocracy in the United States, 1880–1914," *Labor History*, 20 (1979), 327–37, presents evidence which appears to indicate that the wage gap between the "labor aristocracy" and "unskilled labor" widened in prewar years. However, he employs highly aggregated data, so that apparent variations in differentials may reflect changes in the geographical and/or industrial composition of the two groups. Moreover, the vital statistical basis (Table III, p. 333) seems to compare payroll earnings in manufacturing with wage rates for the labor aristocracy, which represent two quite distinct measures of material reward.

31. Shergold, "Wage Differentials Based on Skill in the United States," Graph 1, reveals that the movement of Pittsburgh food prices was reflected in changes in interoccupational wage structure: as prices increased, percentage skill differentials narrowed.

32. R. Perlman, "Forces Widening Occupational Wage Differentials," *Review of Economics and Statistics*, 40 (1958), 110–11; Knowles and Robertson, "Wages of Skilled and Unskilled Workers," pp. 109–27.

33. Pittsburgh Christian Social Service Union, *The "Strip": A Socio-Religious Survey of a Typical Problem Section of Pittsburgh, Pennsylvania* (Pittsburgh, 1915), p. 19.

34. The Pearsonian coefficient of correlation (*r*) for perfect negative correlation = −1.000. Had the wage spectrum been identical in both cities, i.e., had the wage relationship between the different Pittsburgh/Birmingham occupations remained constant, the linear regression line in Graph 3 would have been perfectly horizontal.

35. There are certain statistical weaknesses inherent in making one variable a ratio of the second variable; that is, by allowing for the "effect" of *x* by forming the ratio *y/x*. See, for instance, W. Allen Wallis and Harry V. Roberts, "Hazards of Ratios," in *Statistics: A New Approach* (London, 1957), pp. 546–49. Within the present context,

however, the method employed appears to be acceptable so long as the following qualifications are carefully headed:

a. The regression of y/x on x does not imply a causal relationship.

b. Observations may not be extrapolated beyond the sample range.

c. The statistically high linear coefficient of correlation between y/x and x does *not* indicate a similar relationship between y and x. Indeed Graph 3 suggests a nonlinear relationship, for it would appear that the best fit of y on x would take the form of a curved line from the bottom left-hand corner to the top right-hand corner, the slope becoming progressively less steep.

For a defense of ratio correlations against the charge that they yield spurious results, see A. MacMillan and R. L. Daft, "Administrative Intensity and Ratio Variables: The Case against Definitional Dependency," and John D. Kasarda and Patrick D. Nolan, "Ratio Measurement and Theoretical Inference in Social Research," both in *Social Forces*, 58 (1979), 212–48.

36. A similar relationship was apparent if Sheffield, rather than Birmingham, was compared to Pittsburgh. Regressional analysis based upon all seventeen comparable occupations listed in Table 10 shows that $y/x = 71.63 - 0.66x$ and $r = -0.855$. If the selected sample base included only those sixteen occupations for which data were available for both British cities, regression analysis achieved the following results: Birmingham: $y/x = 66.52 - 0.54x$, and $r = -0.951$; Sheffield: $y/x = 72.95 - 0.69x$, and $r = -0.854$.

37. Herbert N. Casson, *The Romance of Steel. The Story of a Thousand Millionaires* (New York, 1907), p. 267; William Lucien Scaife, "A Glimpse of Pittsburgh," *Atlantic Monthly*, 87 (Jan. 1901), 84.

38. Pittsburgh Christian Social Service Union, "The Strip," pp. 32–33; Pittsburgh Association for the Improvement of the Poor, *Annual Report for the Year Ending November 1906*, No. 31 (Pittsburgh, n.d.), pp. 4–5; Commons and Leiserson, "Wage-Earners of Pittsburgh," p. 119n.

39. Arthur Shadwell, *Industrial Efficiency: A Comparative Study of Industrial Life in England, Germany and America* (London, 1906), 1: 333.

40. Thirza Potts, "Information Bureaux for Elementary School Children," in *Women Workers: The Quarterly Magazine of the Birmingham Ladies' Union of Workers Among Women and Children*, 17 (1907), 53. Hereafter referred to as *Women Workers*.

41. *Women Workers*, 23 (1914) 82–87; Joseph Wright, ed., *The English Dialect Dictionary* (Oxford, 1960), Vol. 4; Eric Partridge, *A Dictionary of Slang and Unconventional English* (1937; rpt. London 1970), Vol. 1.

42. Victor S. Clark, *History of Manufacturers in the United States* (Washington, D. C., 1929), 1: 392; H. J. Habakkuk, *American and British Technology in the Nineteenth Century* (Cambridge, 1962), pp. 21, 23, 151–52. In a case study, Roland Gibson, *Cotton Textile Wages in the United States and Great Britain: A Comparison of Trends, 1860–1945* (New York, 1948), p. 57, agrees, believing wage differentials had been "slightly less" in America. However, Table 11, p. 49, indicates that in 1910 the skilled/semiskilled gap was narrower in Britain. No unskilled comparisons were available for that year.

43. Nathan Rosenberg, "Anglo-American Wage Differences in the 1820's," *Journal of Economic History*, 27 (1967), has suggested that, contrary to Habakkuk's hypothesis, the "data do not show a significant over-all difference in the wage differentials between skilled and unskilled labor in the two countries" in the early nineteenth century (p. 226). If this is true, what is being explained in the text is not a reversal, but simply a change

from roughly equal skill differentials in the 1820s to much wider skill differentials in the United States in the 1900s. Interestingly, E. H. Phelps Brown and Margaret Browne, *A Century of Pay: The Course of Pay and Production in France, Germany, Sweden, the United Kingdom and the United States of America 1860–1960* (London, 1968), conclude that in 1773, as in 1909, skill differentials were wider in America (p. 163).

44. Fitch, *Steel Workers*, p. 12; Commons and Leiserson, "Wage-Earners of Pittsburgh," pp. 117, 120.

45. Great Britain, *Census*, 1901, Vol. 8, Tables 35, 37; 1911, Vol. 10, Pt. 2, Table 13; 1911, Vol. 9, Table 3; also, U.S. *Census* 1900, Special Report, "Occupations at the Twelfth Census," Table 43; 1900, Vol. 2, Table 32; 1910, Vol. 1, Table 49; and 1910, Vol. 4, Table 8.

46. See, for example, Robert Higgs, "Race, Skills and Earnings: American Immigrants in 1909," *Journal of Economic History*, 31 (1971), 420–28; Peter J. Hill, "Relative Skill and Income Levels of Native and Foreign-Born Workers in the United States," *Explorations in Economic History*, 12 (1975), 47–60; Peter R. Shergold, "Relative Skill and Income Levels of Native and Foreign-Born Workers: A Re-Examination," *Explorations in Economic History*, 13 (1976), 51–61.

On the other hand, Paul F. McGouldrick and Michael B. Tannen, "Did American Manufacturers Discriminate Against Immigrants Before 1914?" *Journal of Economic History*, 37 (1977), 723–24, estimate that "southeast" European workers earned $1.07 less per week than "northwest" Europeans as a result of discrimination. They concluded that in early twentieth-century America there existed "moderate but certainly non-negligible discrimination."

47. Paul G. Keat, "Long-run Changes in Occupational Structure," *Journal of Political Economy*, 68 (1960); 593–94. A classic presentation of the argument that the "enormous influx of immigrants maintained a great supply of unskilled labor and kept down its rate of pay" may be found in F. W. Taussig, *International Trade* (New York, 1927), pp. 58–60.

48. Great Britain, Board of Trade, *Report of an Enquiry . . . into Working Class Rents, Housing and Retail Prices, Together with the Rates of Wages in Certain Occupations in the Principal Industrial Towns of the United States of America*, British Parliamentary Papers, Cd. 5609, 1911, Vol. 88, pp. xv–xvi. E. Levasseur, *The American Workman* (Baltimore, 1900) had no doubt that "wages [were] in general high in the United States (compared to France)" (p. 322). His conclusion was, however, qualified: "There are exceptions, of course, rates cannot be high in all classes because immigration continually supplies a mass of low-grade labor, and there is a multitude of day laborers who have no special skill."

49. Commons and Leiserson, "Wage-Earners of Pittsburgh," pp. 116–17.

50. E. V. Birchall, "The Conditions of Distress," *Economic Review*, 20 (1910), 39; Frank Tillyard, "Poverty in Birmingham," *Women Workers*, 15 (1906), 76, and Frank Tillyard, "Three Birmingham Relief Funds—1885, 1886, and 1905," *Economic Journal*, 15 (1905), 505–20.

51. Birmingham Distress Committee, *Report upon the Proceedings of the Distress Committee from November, 1906 to June, 1907* (Birmingham, 1907), p. 10. Compare this with the situation in the Pittsburgh steel industry where, during the 1907–1909 depression, unemployed skilled and semiskilled workers were given laboring jobs, and even replaced those men already so employed. See Fitch, *Steel Workers*, p. 148.

52. Birchall, "Conditions of Distress," p. 35. Levasseur, *American Workman*, noted that labor was "in general, more mobile in America than in France" (p. 382).

53. Clarence D. Long, *Wages and Earnings in the United States, 1860–1890* (Princeton, 1960), pp. 97–104.

54. Great Britain, *Enquiry into Working Class Rents, Housing and Retail Prices in the U.S.A.,* p. v.

55. These calculations assume that bricklayers, masons, carpenters, painters, plumbers, and laborers comprised the total construction force in all three cities. In Pittsburgh (1910), the aforementioned skilled trades totaled 9,100 workers, and building laborers, 8,345. In Birmingham (1911), there were 1,609 bricklayers, 2,859 painters, 855 plumbers, 2,016 carpenters' laborers, 178 masons, and masons' laborers, 1,651 building laborers, and 825 navvies. If it is assumed that 50 percent of the carpenters and carpenters' laborers were unskilled, and that the same percentage of masons and masons' laborers were unskilled, the number of skilled tradesmen can be estimated at 6,420 and the number of laborers at 3,573. In Sheffield (1911), similar calculations suggest that there were 5,170 skilled workers in the building force and 3,791 laborers. See Great Britain, *Census,* 1911, Vol. 10, Pt. 2, Table 13; U.S. *Census,* 1910, Vol. 4, Table 11.

56. Fitch, *Steel Workers,* Appendix 4, "Wage Statistics of Representative Departments in a Typical Steel Company of Allegheny County, October 1, 1907," pp. 301–05; Great Britain, Board of Trade, *Report on an Inquiry . . . into the Earnings and Hours of Labour of Workpeople of the United Kingdom,* Vol. 6, "Metal, Engineering and Shipbuilding Trades in 1906," *British Parliamentary Papers,* 1911, Vol. 88, pp. 36–38. The latter is hereafter referred to as "Metal, Engineering and Shipbuilding Trades in 1906."

57. The stability of full-time hours in Birmingham was not unique. Analysis of national aggregate net changes in normal weekly hours of work reveals a similar situation. Between 1890 and 1919, aggregate net reduction of weekly hours in Britain was insignificant: M. A. Bienefeld, *Working Hours in British Industry: An Economic History* (London, 1972), pp. 145–61.

58. Charles A. Gulick, Jr., *Labor Policy of the United States Steel Corporation* (New York, 1924), pp. 26–27.

59. Albert H. Gary, James A. Farrell, and Percival Roberts Jr., *Statement as to Wages, Hours and Other Conditions of Labor among Employees of the United States Steel Corporation and Subsidiary Companies* (n.p., 1914) p.2; U.S. Department of Labor, Bureau of Labor Statistics, *Bulletin,* No. 151 (1914), "Wages and Hours of Labor in the Iron and Steel Industry in the United States, 1907 to 1912," Table 3, pp. 62–71, 137–43, 192–6. In 1912, hours were increased.

60. Great Britain, *Enquiry into Working Class Rents, Housing and Retail Prices in the U.S.A.,* pp. 346–48; Commons and Leiserson, "Wage-Earners of Pittsburgh," pp. 121–26, 130–32; *The Motorman and Conductor,* 6, No. 1 (Feb. 1900), 2; No. 3 (Apr. 1900), 7; *Pittsburgh Railways Company Arbitration,* p. 51; *Magazine of the International Brotherhood of Teamsters,* 3 (Mar. 1906), 1–2.

61. "Metal, Engineering and Shipbuilding Trades in 1906," p. 50. The mean full-time hours for the United Kingdom as a whole were 54.4.

62. Great Britain, Board of Trade (Labour Dept.), *Report on Changes in Rates of Wages and Hours of Labour in the United Kingdom, British Parliamentary Papers,* Cd. 5324, 1910, Vol. 84, p. 86; and *Annual Abstracts of Labor Statistics of the United Kingdom;* Charles Anthony Vince, *History of the Corporation of Birmingham* (Birmingham, 1923), 4: 508.

63. William E. Benswanger, "Professional Baseball in Pittsburgh," *Western Pennsylvania Historical Magazine,* 30 (Mar. 1947), 9–14; *Pittsburgh Bulletin,* 26 May 1900, p. 3;

Great Britain, *Enquiry into Working Class Rents, Housing and Retail Prices in the U.S.A.*, p. 341. Sunday baseball was prohibited in Pittsburgh until 1935.

64. *Mosely Industrial Commission to the United States of America, October to December, 1902. Report of the Delegates*, p. 118; Price Collier, *England and The English from an American Point of View* (London, 1912), p. 199.

65. Mosely Industrial Commission, *Report*, p. 149.

66. Standard weekly rates of pay are quite distinct from weekly earnings. The former estimate income for a full-time week, while the latter fluctuate according to the extent to which workers were underemployed and/or were required to work overtime.

Chapter 4: Family Income

1. A. E. Carver, *An Investigation into the Dietary of the Labouring Classes of Birmingham with Special Reference to its Bearing upon Tuberculosis* (Birmingham, 1914), p. 13.

2. In both the American and British censuses of 1910 and 1911, statistics of women at work explicitly included women regularly employed in assisting relatives in trade or business: Great Britain, *Census*, 1911, Vol. 10, Pt. 1, p. cxxviii; U.S. *Census*, 1910, Vol. 4, p. 87. In 1900 and 1901 such women—primarily shopkeepers and boardinghouse or lodging-house keepers within the urban environment—had been underestimated. Adjustments to the earlier data suggest that the number of female workers in Birmingham in 1901 should be increased to 84,101 (33.4 percent of the labor force), and that the number of female workers in Pittsburgh in 1900 should be increased to 36,259 (19.3 percent of the labor force).

3. Women's Industrial Council, *The Case For and Against a Legal Minimum Wage for Sweated Workers* (London, 1909), p. 13.

4. Great Britain, *Census*, 1911, Vol. 10, Pt. 1, p. xxxi.

5. Mrs. M. T. Muirhead, "Home Industries in Birmingham," *Women Workers*, 9 (1899), 10–15; Edward Cadbury, Cecile M. Matheson, and George Shann, *Women's Work and Wages. A Phase of Life in an Industrial City* (London, 1906), p. 150.

6. Comparison of Pittsburgh with Sheffield would not have been fairer. Both Birmingham and Pittsburgh employed a greater percentage of females than their respective national averages: Sheffield, however, employed substantially less. Indeed, it seems probable that there existed more job openings for women in Pittsburgh than in Sheffield. In Sheffield in 1911, the manufacture of metal products, machines, and implements—which employed relatively little female labor—provided jobs for 38.4 percent of the total work force. In Pittsburgh in 1910, such activities occupied only 20.3 percent of the city's laboring population. On the other hand, industries which engaged substantial proportions of women were of greater significance in Pittsburgh: the clothing trades, manufacture of tobacco goods, and food industries together employed 5.3 percent of Pittsburgh's work force, compared to 3.7 percent of Sheffield's. Commercial occupations, excluding retail trade employees, engaged only 5.4 percent of Sheffield workers, whereas in Pittsburgh 10.8 percent were thus employed.

7. Mrs. John van Vorst and Marie van Vorst, *The Woman Who Toils: Being the Experiences of Two Gentlewomen as Factory Girls* (London, 1903), p. 9. See esp. Ch. 2, "In a Pittsburgh Factory," pp. 9–58.

8. Cadbury et al., *Women's Work and Wages*, pp. 53, 62–63; Mrs. M. T. Muirhead, "Report on the Pen Trade in Birmingham," *Women Workers*, 11 (1901), 34–37; Mrs. F. T. Ring, "The Dinner Hour in Our Factories," *Women Workers*, 18 (1908), 3.

9. Tom M. Girdler, *Boot Straps. The Autobiography of Tom M. Girdler*, written in

collaboration with Boyden Sparks (New York, 1944), pp. 98–99; *Pittsburgh Leader*, 27 Dec. 1912, p. 1.

10. Elizabeth Beardsley Butler, *Women and the Trades, Pittsburgh, 1907–1908* (New York, 1911), p. 25. See also p. 227, where the violent job of an opener is detailed: "The sheet of steel comes from the furnaces with five to eight plates welded together . . . . [the women] beat it on the ground . . . [then] forcibly tear apart the plates, holding part of the sheet down with the knee, while tearing the metal with the other."

11. Ibid., p. 337; Eva Smill, "The Stogy Industry on the Hill in Pittsburgh," M. A. thesis, Carnegie Institute of Technology, 1920, p. 7; *Pittsburgh Index*, 24 June 1905, p. 6.

12. Van Vorst and van Vorst, *Woman Who Toils*, pp. 27, 34–35. Discrimination seems to have been common in the factory: for instance, men had exclusive right to use the cheap canteen facilities available.

13. *Mosely Industrial Commission to the United States of America, October to December, 1902. Report of the Delegates* (Manchester, 1903), p. 104; Cadbury et al., *Women's Work and Wages*, p. 68.

14. Cadbury et al., *Women's Work and Wages*, p. 194; Budgett Meakin, *Model Factories and Villages: Ideal Conditions of Labor and Housing* (Philadelphia, 1905), p. 58.

15. S. P. Breckinridge, "Legislative Control of Women's Work," *Journal of Political Economy*, 14 (1906) 107; U.S. *Reports of the Industrial Commission*, Vol. 7 (1901), p. 100; Pittsburgh Christian Social Service Union, *The "Strip": A Socio-Religious Survey of a Typical Problem Section of Pittsburgh, Pennsylvania* (Pittsburgh, 1915), p. 31; William H. Matthews, *Kingsley House Record*, 8 (March 1905), 1.

16. Typewritten draft speech dated 22 Sept. 1906, pp. 5–7, in the University of Pittsburgh Archives of Industrial Society, National Council of Jewish Women, Pittsburgh Chapter, Box 3.

17. Morals Efficiency Commission, George Seibel, sec., *Report and Recommendations of the Morals Efficiency Commission* (Pittsburgh, 1913), pp. 29–30.

18. E. D. McCafferty, *Henry J. Heinz: A Biography* (New York, 1923), p. 130; Meakin, *Model Factories and Villages*, pp. 103–04, 120, 153, 170–72, 236, 265, 281; William H. Tolman, *Social Engineering. A Record of Things Done by American Industrialists Employing Upwards of One and One-Half Million of People* (New York, 1909), pp. 33–37, 54; Cadbury et al., *Women's Work and Wages*, p. 115; Girdler, *Boot Straps*, p. 102.

19. Unfortunately, estimates of the conjugal condition of Pittsburgh's women workers in 1910 had to be based upon 1900 weightings, which probably underestimate married women workers: many would have been shopkeepers and boardinghouse keepers who, it has been noted, were often ignored by census enumerators in 1900. However, even if all these "uncounted" workers had been married, the figures still suggest that only 0.058 married women worked per family unit in Pittsburgh compared to 0.185 in Birmingham: that is, 5.8 percent of Pittsburgh's married women worked, compared to 18.5 percent in Birmingham. Table 18 identifies the minimum estimate (3.5 percent), the maximum (5.8 percent), and calculates the mean probability (4.6 percent).

20. Clementina Black, *Married Women's Work: Being the Report of an Enquiry Undertaken by the Women's Industrial Council* (London, 1915), p. 1.

21. John Robertson, *Report on Industrial Employment of Married Women and Infantile Mortality* (Birmingham, 1910), pp. 4, 7–9, 20.

22. Daniel L. Marsh, *The Challenge of Pittsburgh* (New York, 1917), p. 83; *Iron City Trades Journal*, 3 Dec. 1909, p. 4.

23. Estimates relate to the contribution made to family income by regularly employed

wives and children while engaged in full-time employment. Contributions to annual family income would have been lowered to the extent that female workers were susceptible to higher levels of unemployment and underemployment than their male colleagues, but raised to the extent that women were more likely to seek paid work on an irregular (and unrecorded) basis.

24. It is also true that not all married women would have been living with their husbands. However, the number of separated wives was probably small, and there seems little reason to suppose that the proportion of such women would have been markedly different in Birmingham and Pittsburgh.

25. U.S. *Census,* 1900, Vol. 2, Table 32, and Special Report, "Occupations at the Twelfth Census," 1900, Table 43; U.S. *Census,* 1910, Vol. 1, Table 38; Great Britain, *Census,* 1911, Vol. 3, Table 9.

26. See Table 18 and n. 19.

27. The estimated mean probability receives support from a study of 700 Pittsburgh district families undertaken by the U.S., *Reports of the Immigration Commission,* 1911, Vol. 1, "Iron and Steel Manufacturing," which found that 6.3 percent of native-born wives were employed, and 1.4 percent of foreign-born (p. 269). If these percentages are weighted to take account of Pittsburgh's ethnic structure in 1910, it appears that 5.0 percent of wives worked—very close to the estimate of 4.6 percent.

28. *Women Workers: The Quarterly Magazine of the Birmingham Ladies' Union of Workers Among Women and Children,* 21 (1911); Madame Blanc, *The Condition of Women in the United States: A Traveller's Notes* (Boston, 1895), pp. 250–51.

29. Pennsylvania Department of Factory Inspection, *Fifteenth Annual Report,* 1904, p. 7; "One of the most alarming and pathetic features in . . . child labor is the total ignoring of sex conditions and differences in the employment of children."

30. Pennsylvania Department of the Interior, Bureau of Industrial Statistics, *Annual Report,* 1912, pp. 484–85; U.S. Bureau of the Census, *Census of Manufactures,* 1905, Pt. 2, Table 28, pp. 970–71, 984–85.

31. Butler, *Women and the Trades,* p. 340. Study of core-makers, laundry workers, milliners, and telegraphers convinced Butler that the 2:1 wage ratio was "also the ratio between [male and female] wages when skill was gained by preliminary study or by trade apprenticeship."

32. Margaret Byington, *Homestead: The Households of a Mill Town* (New York: 1910), Appendix 1, Tables 2 and 3, p. 201. Forty men averaged $14.92, while nine women averaged $7.28.

33. Van Vorst and van Vorst, *Woman Who Toils,* pp. 22, 46. Adult women started at 76¢ a day and could earn a maximum of $1.35; the rates paid to men ranged from $1.35 to $3.00.

34. Robertson, *Industrial Employment of Married Women,* pp. 9, 14. Regarding weekly income, 1073 husbands earned a mean weekly wage of 21.02s. ($5.34), while 453 wives earned 10.04s. ($2.44).

35. R. S. Smirke, *Report on Birmingham Trades, Prepared for Use in Connexion with the Juvenile Employment Exchange* (London, 1913–1914): "The Brass Trade," pp. 25, 32, 34, 38; "The Manufacture of Flint Glass," p. 10; "Printing and the Allied Trades," pp. 5, 12; "The General Brush Trade," p. 4; "Electro-Plate Trade," pp. 5–6; "Jewellery," pp. 8–9, 11.

36. Pennsylvania Bureau of Industrial Statistics, *Annual Report,* 1912, pp. 484–85; U.S. *Census of Manufacturers,* 1905, Pt. 2, Table 28, pp. 970–71, 984–85; Cadbury et al., *Women's Work and Wages,* pp. 309–30.

37. Smirke, "The Brass Trade," pp. 6–7; "Vanboy Labour," pp. 5–7.

38. U.S. Department of Commerce and Labor, *Eighteenth Annual Report of the Commissioner of Labor*, 1903, Pt. 1, Table 1I and Table 3I, pp. 242–49, 366–67. If similar calculations are used for the United States as a whole, it can be estimated that children earned 56.9 percent of adult male wages, whereas 51.6 percent was the stated amount; similarly, an estimate for the North Atlantic states suggests 58.2 percent, whereas 53.9 percent was the stated amount. The wage progression suggested in this chapter therefore appears to be an acceptable approximation.

39. Elizabeth Beardsley Butler, "Sharpsburg: A Typical Waste of Childhood," pp. 293–94, 298; Peter Roberts, "Immigrant Wage-Earners," p. 42; and R. R. Wright, Jr., "One Hundred Negro Steel Workers," p. 100, all found in Paul U. Kellogg, ed., *Wage-Earning Pittsburgh* (New York, 1918). See also Butler, *Women and the Trades*, p. 338.

40. U. S. Department of Commerce and Labor, *Report on the Conditions of Women and Child Wage-Earners*, 61st Cong., 2nd sess., 1913, Senate Document No. 645, Vol. 18, "Employment of Women and Children in Selected Industries," Table 8. It will be noted that the average adult female wage was 61.7 percent of the average adult male wage, a figure much higher than the estimate of 50 percent derived from other sources. There are two possible reasons for this discrepancy. First, the report's data were collected in "an actual week in the period December 1908 to April 1909, taken as generally representative of normal conditions," whereas the estimate of Table 20 was derived from annual earnings: it is possible that such earnings were relatively lower because women were more susceptible to unemployment/underemployment than men. Second, the report's sample frame was clearly biased toward industries in which women comprised a substantial share of the work force: it is possible that such industries paid lower male wages than industries in which the work force was overwhelmingly male.

41. Smirke, "The Brass Trade," pp. 8, 25; "The Manufacture of Flint Glass," p. 5; "The General Brush Trade," p. 4; "Jewellery," pp. 6–7; "Printing and the Allied Trades," p. 5.

42. These estimates are rather lower than those presented in Table 19 in order to make allowance for the surprisingly high female wage:male wage ratio indicated in those data.

43. *Weekly People*, 14 Jan. 1905, p. 1.

44. Leon Stern, "Housing Report. (First State of Investigation)," typewritten manuscript, p. 16, in the University of Pittsburgh Archives of Industrial Society, Civic Club of Allegheny County records, Box 6; Samuel Ely Eliot, "Report of the Headworker, April, 1912," typewritten manuscript, p. 4, in the University of Pittsburgh Archives of Industrial Society, Woods Run Industrial House records, Box 3.

45. Byington, in *Homestead*, p. 201, studied 90 families in 1907; Catherine M. Hoyt analyzed the family backgrounds of 96 juvenile delinquents in 1910–1911 (Hoyt Papers, four tabulated sheets in the University of Pittsburgh Archives of Industrial Society); Abraham Oseroff, in "Survey of Working Men's Homes in the Soho District of Pittsburgh" (M.A. thesis, University of Pittsburgh, 1914), investigated 126 families.

46. U.S., *Eighteenth Annual Report of the Commissioner of Labor*, 1903, Pt. 1, Table 3A, p. 306.

47. Stern, "Housing Report," p. 14; Oseroff, "Soho," Chart G; Hoyt, Papers; Byington, *Homestead*, pp. 206–13; U. S., *Eighteenth Annual Report of the Commissioner of Labor*, 1903, Pt. 1, Table 1D, p. 232.

48. Great Britain, Board of Trade, *Report of an Enquiry . . . into Working Class Rents, Housing and Retail Prices, Together with the Rates of Wages of Certain Occupa-*

tions in the Principal Industrial Towns of the United States of America, British Parliamentary Papers, Cd. 5609, 1911, Vol. 88, p. 349; Peter Roberts, "Immigrant Wage Earners," in Kellogg, *Wage-Earning Pittsburgh,* pp. 46–47.

49. These estimates are similar to those for Pennsylvania in 1901. U. S., *Eighteenth Annual Report of the Commission of Labor,* 1903, Pt. 1, Table 3C, pp. 336–67, reveals that 832 Pennsylvania families gained an average annual income of $277.69 from 1,403 boarders or lodgers: that is, that the 1,164 boarders and 239 lodgers paid a yearly mean sum of $135.02, or $2.60 per week.

50. Samuel Ely Eliot, "Report of the Headworker, April 1912," p. 4.

51. Great Britain, *Enquiry into Working Class Rents, Housing and Retail Prices in the U.S.A.,* p. 351.

Chapter 5: Food Prices

1. Andrew Carnegie, *The Empire of Business* (New York, 1902), pp. 248, 254, and 258; Samuel Gompers, *Labor in Europe and America* (New York, 1910), p. 231.

2. *Pittsburgh Post,* 16 Apr. 1902, p. 6. *Mosely Industrial Commission to the United States of America, October to December, 1902. Report of the Delegates* (Manchester, 1903), pp. 34, 215.

3. Mosely Industrial Commission, *Report,* p. 62. In his foreword to the commission's report, Mosely expressed a similar view: "Food is as cheap (if not cheaper) in the United States as in England, whilst general necessaries may . . . be put on the same level. Rent, clothes made to order, and . . . all luxuries, are considerably dearer" (p. 8); Price Collier, *England and the English from an American Point of View* (London, 1912), p. 273.

4. The description of bureau efforts to present reliable price information is from Charles P. Neill, Commissioner of Labor, before U.S Senate, 61st Cong., 2nd sess., 1910, *Report of the Select Committee on Wages and Prices of Commodities,* "Hearings Held," Vol. 1, pp. 28–29. After 1911, eighteen Pittsburgh retailers were sampled.

5. The price series are derived from U.S. Department of Commerce and Labor, *Eighteenth Annual Report of the Commissioner of Labor, 1903; and U.S. Bureau of Labor, Bulletin,* Nos. 59 (1905), 65 (1906), 71 (1907), 77 (1908), and 105 (1902); Bureau of Labor Statistics, *Bulletin,* Nos. 115 (1913), 125 (1913), 132 (1913), 136 (1913), 138 (1913), and 140 (1914).

6. Western Pennsylvania Hospital, *Annual Report,* 1900–1901, p. 6.

7. Pennsylvania Bureau of Industrial Statistics, *Annual Report of the Secretary of Internal Affairs,* No. 35 (1907), Pt. 3, "Report of the Commission to Enquire into the Price of Food Stuffs in Pennsylvania," pp. 14, 16–20; Pennsylvania, *Senate Journal,* 1907, Pt. 2, pp. 1250–53; Pennsylvania, *Legislative Record,* 1907, Vol. 2, p. 2444; [Pittsburgh] *Searchlight,* 1 Oct. 1907, p. 15.

8. *National Labor Tribune,* Jan. 1907, p. 1; [Pittsburgh] *Searchlight,* 1 Oct. 1907, p. 15.

9. *Literary Digest,* 19 Oct. 1907, p. 559; *National Labor Tribune,* 10 Oct. 1907, p. 1; 25 Oct. 1907, p. 1; 2 Apr. 1908, p. 1; *Pittsburgh Dispatch,* 24 Nov. 1907, p. 1; 16 Nov. 1908, p. 6.

10. *National Labor Tribune,* 25 July 1907, p. 3.

11. *Pittsburgh Dispatch,* 1 Nov. 1907, p. 6; 20 May, 1909, Sec. 2, p. 2; *National Labor Tribune,* 16 June 1908, p. 1; 2 Apr. 1908, p. 1; 11 June 1908, p. 1. Horace Fletcher had lived on half the rations of the "normal" adult male since 1898: at age fifty-eight, in

1907, he sauntered through fitness tests arranged at the Yale gymnasium by Dr. William G. Anderson. See *New York Times*, 29 Nov. 1907, p. 6.

12. The report was published in full as Appendix 9 by Margaret Byington, *Homestead: The Making of a Mill Town* (New York, 1910). John O'Connor, Jr., *The Cost of Living Studies in Pittsburgh* (Pittsburgh, 1914), noted that if it was assumed that food comprised 40 percent of the family budget, the chamber of commerce estimates meant that a Pittsburgh family would have required an annual income of $1,500! Not only Pittsburghers viewed the price rises with shock. Walter E. Clark, *The Cost of Living* (Chicago, 1915), p. 120, claimed that "prices had generally rebounded by the end of 1909 to as high a point as before the [economic] crisis"—contrary to behavior in the depressions of 1873 and 1893.

13. Great Britain, Foreign Office, *Diplomatic and Consular Reports* (Annual Series), "Reports on the Trade and Commerce of the Consular District of Philadelphia," No. 4499 (1909), p. 32; Pennsylvania Department of Factory Inspection, *Annual Report*, No. 20 (1909), p. 7.

14. *Pittsburgh Dispatch*, 16 Nov. 1910, p. 6.

15. Pittsburgh Executive Department, *Annual Report*, 1912, Bureau of Food Inspection, "Some Notes on Pittsburgh Food Supply and Costs of Living," p. 1164; Pittsburgh Chamber of Commerce, *The Year Book and Directory, 1913* (Pittsburgh, 1913), p. 30; *Pittsburgh Index*, 27 Apr. 1912, p. 10; 1 May 1912, p. 5; 8 June 1912, p. 6; F. C. Wilkes, "Annual Review of 1912," *Pittsburgh Post*, 1 Jan. 1913, p. 9.

16. John T. Holdsworth, *Economic Survey of Pittsburgh* (Pittsburgh, 1914), p. 3; U.S. Bureau of Labor Statistics, *Bulletin*, No. 156 (1916), p. 16.

17. Great Britain, Board of Trade, *Report of an Enquiry . . . into Working Class Rents, Housing, Retail Prices and Standard Rates of Wages in the United Kingdom*, British Parliamentary Papers, Cd. 3864, 1908, Vol. 53, and Cd. 6955, 1913, Vol. 63.

18. Great Britain, Board of Trade, *Report on Wholesale and Retail Prices in the United Kingdom in 1902, With Comparative Statistical Tables for a Number of Years*, British Parliamentary Papers, Cd. 321, 1903, Vol. 68, Pt. 3, "Prices Paid by Certain Families in the United Kingdom, 1900–01," pp. 403–05; U. S. Senate, *Wages and Prices Abroad*, 61st Cong., 2nd sess., 1910, Pt. 1, pp. 28–46 (hereafter referred to as Halstead, "Report on Prices"); A. E. Carver, *Investigation into the Dietary of the Labouring Classes of Birmingham, with Special Reference to its Bearing upon Tuberculosis* (Birmingham, 1914), pp. 46–47. The statistical data presented in these reports, and the comparative estimates made, are collated in Appendix 7.

19. Evidence from the *Enquiry by the Board of Trade into Working Class Rents, Housing, Prices, and Wages in the U.K.* suggests that the price movement of the meat and nonmeat food samples was similar between 1905 and 1912, and that the comparison of Halstead's 1901–1910 and 1903–1910 commodity frames was justified.

20. Pittsburgh wage movements are based upon Table 5, estimates i and ii; Birmingham wage movements are derived from Table 5, estimates i and iii. The increase in Pittsburgh real food prices is based upon the assumption that wages rose by 38.3 percent while prices advanced by 46.4 percent and the decrease is based upon the assumption that wages rose by 45.6 percent while prices advanced by 38.3 percent.

21. Board of Trade, *Report on Prices in the United Kingdom in 1902*, p. 227; Philip Snowden, *The Living Wage* (London, 1914), p. 65; Halstead, "Report on Prices," p. 28.

22. *Birmingham Daily Post*, 7 June 1910; U. S. Department of Commerce and Labor, Bureau of Manufacturers, *Daily Consular and Trade Reports*, July–Sept. 1910, Vol. 1, p.

206; July–Sept. 1911, Vol. 3, pp. 104, 1120, 1159; Oct.–Dec. 1911, Vol. 4, pp. 775–76. Hereafter referred to as Halstead, *Consular Reports.*

23. Halstead, *Consular Reports*, Jan.–Mar. 1912, Vol. 1, pp. 394, 510; Birmingham Co-operative Society Ltd., *The Wheatsheaf. A Monthly Co-operative Record and Magazine*, Jan. 1912, p. x; Birmingham Chamber of Commerce, *Journal*, 29 Feb. 1912, p. 50; 30 Sept. 1912, p. 158; 31 Dec. 1912, p. 211.

24. *Birmingham Daily Post*, 10 May 1912, p. 3; 31 May, 1912, p. 3.

25. *Birmingham Daily Post*, 22 Nov. 1912, p. 3.

26. Weighted estimates are presented in Table 60.

27. 1905 estimate based upon $(P.1905/P.1900) \times (110/1)$ and 1912 estimate based upon $(P.1912/P.1900) \times (110/1)$, where P is the Pittsburgh mean retail food price expressed as a percentage of the mean Birmingham price; 1905 $(137.7/126.7) \times (110/1)$ and 1912 = $(154.2/126.7) \times (110/1)$: see Table 27.

28. U.S. Bureau of Labor Statistics, *Bulletin*, No. 105, Pt. 1, pp. 6, 37.

29. *National Labor Tribune*, 19 Sept. 1907, p. 1; 3 Oct. 1907, p. 1; Board of Arbitration in the Controversy between the Pittsburgh Railways Company and the Motormen and Conductors, *The Award of the Board of Arbitrators* (Pittsburgh? 1914), pp. 53–54, 59.

30. Carver, *Investigation into the Dietary of the Labouring Classes of Birmingham*, p. 38; F. J. Cross, *How I Lived on Three-Pence a Day and What I Learnt from It* (London, 1912), pp. 24–42.

Chapter 6: Shopping

1. Pittsburgh, Executive Department, *Annual Report*, 1912, p. 1165; Great Britain, Board of Trade, *Report of an Enquiry . . . into Working Class Rents, Housing and Retail Prices, Together with the Rates of Wages in Certain Occupations in the Principal Industrial Towns of the United States of America*, British Parliamentary Papers, Cd. 5609, 1911, Vol. 33, p. 355; *Pittsburgh Post*, 29 Dec. 1900 (advertisement); *Pittsburgh Dispatch*, 5 Nov. 1899, p. 5 (advertisement); *Iron City Trades Journal*, 4 Sept. 1908 (advertisement). It seems likely that the data presented in this chapter underestimate the numerical importance of chain stores: a study made in Philadelphia in 1913, for instance, disclosed that there were six companies in that city operating a total of 490 stores. See Clyde Lyndon King, *Lower Living Costs in Cities* (New York and London, 1915), p. 70.

2. John T. Holdsworth, *Economic Survey of Pittsburgh* (Pittsburgh, 1914), p. 74.

3. Holdsworth's data, suggesting that cut-rate stores were about 9 to 10 percent cheaper than neighborhood stores, received support from Pittsburgh congressman S. C. Porter who, in 1914, claimed that the city's chain stores—notably Charter's—had prices 7 to 10 percent below those of "ordinary" stores. Board of Arbitration in the controversy between the Pittsburgh Railways Company and the Motormen and Conductors, *The Award of the Board of Arbitrators* (Pittsburgh? 1914), p. 54.

4. For a detailed explanation of the construction of this series and an examination of its strengths and deficiencies, see Peter R. Shergold, "Newspaper Advertisements as a Source of Retail Price Data: A Tentative Methodology," *Historical Methods Newsletter*, 10 (1976), 29–38.

5. U. S. Senate, 61st Cong., 2nd sess., 1910, *Select Committee on Wages and Prices*, "Hearings Held," Vol. 1, p. 30; *Pittsburgh Railways Company Arbitration*, pp. 54, 59; John O'Connor, Jr. *The Cost of Living Studies in Pittsburgh* (Pittsburgh, 1914), p. 12.

6. Holdsworth, *Economic Survey of Pittsburgh*, pp. 74–75. A useful analysis of retailing economics, which summarizes much of the contemporary debate, may be found

in Paul H. Nystrom, *The Economics of Retailing* (New York, 1915). Nystrom, professor of economics at the University of Minnesota, agreed with Holdsworth that the chain stores' large purchasing power comprised their main cost-saving advantage, but he also noted their economies of scale with regard to accounting, advertising, and the delivery of goods; their ability to transfer stock to more effective sales points; and their price-cutting wars against retail opposition in chosen locales. See esp. pp. 219–26.

7. *Select Committee on Wage and Prices,* "Hearings Held," Vol. 1, p. 31.

8. See, for instance, *Pittsburgh Dispatch,* 7 May 1905 (advertisement).

9. *Industry. A Magazine of Commerce and Finance,* 1, No. 1 (1906), 3; 1, No. 3 (1906), 4; 3, No. 2 (1908), 4.

10. *Select Committee on Wages and Prices,* "Hearings Held," Vol. 1, pp. 384, 406, testimony of John A. Green: "There were a good many men [in 1907–1908] that were out of work and didn't have a dollar, and the retailers today have hundreds of thousands of dollars on their books for credit that was given at that time."

11. Joseph Hallsworth and Rhys J. Davies, *The Working Life of Shop Assistants: A Study of Conditions of Labour in the Distributive Trades* (Manchester, 1910), p. 3. See also James B. Jeffreys, *Retail Trading in Britain 1850–1950* (Cambridge, 1954), esp. pp. 26–29.

12. *Kelly's Directories of Birmingham (Including the Suburbs and the Boroughs of Smethwick and Aston Manor),* 1901, 1911; *The Birmingham Magazine of Art and Industries,* 1 (1898), 210; *The Birmingham Pictorial and Dart,* 1 Jan. 1909, p. 15 (advertisement).

13. *Kelly's Directories of Birmingham,* 1901, 1911.

14. A. E. Carver, *An Investigation into the Dietary of the Labouring Classes of Birmingham, with Special Reference to its Bearing upon Tuberculosis* (Birmingham, 1914), p. 39; Birmingham and Midland Counties Grocers' Protection and Benevolent Association, *Annual Report and Balance Sheet,* No. 33 (1906), p. 25.

15. Edward Cadbury, Cecile M. Matheson and George Shann, *Women's Work and Wages. A Phase of Life in the Industrial City* (London, 1906), pp. 176–78. The store-keepers displayed prominently among their wares homemade pickles, ginger beer and cakes, and frequently supplemented income by cooking workmen's dinners and early breakfasts. Yet so small was the normal transaction that Cadbury's survey of eighty-six such retailers found that the average weekly profit totaled only 11s. ($2.68).

16. *Birmingham Sunday Echo,* 27 May 1900, p. 1 (advertisement). Lilley's customers were retailers.

17. R. H. Best, W. J. Davis, and C. J. Perks, *The Brassworkers of Berlin and of Birmingham* (London, 1905), p. 23; Birmingham Chamber of Commerce, *Journal,* 31 July 1908, p. 100.

18. Cadbury, *Women's Work and Wages,* pp. 177, 179.

19. Birmingham Chamber of Commerce, Council Minute Books, 1905–1907 (Birmingham Chamber of Commerce Library), pp. 260–61. Birmingham Chamber of Commerce, *Journal,* 30 Sept. 1908, p. 140. The Birmingham Grocers' Association considered establishing a Debt Collecting Department but had to shelve the idea "owing to the already heavy demands made upon the Committee." See Birmingham Grocers' Association, *Annual Report,* No. 35 (1908), p. 41.

20. G. Henry Wright, *Chronicle of the Birmingham Chamber of Commerce A.D. 1813–1913, and of the Birmingham Commercial Society A.D. 1783–1812* (Birmingham, 1913), pp. 510, 559–60.

21. Pittsburgh Department of Public Works, Bureau of City Property, "Annual Report," in Executive Department, *Annual Report,* 1912–1913, pp. 763–64; *Annual Re-*

port, 1909–1910, Pt. 1, p. 47; W. T. Pike, ed., *Birmingham at the Opening of the Twentieth Century* (Brighton, 1905), pp. 13, 33; Birmingham Markets and Fairs Committee, *The Birmingham Market Hall, 1835–1935* (Birmingham, 1935), p. 5.

22. Holdsworth, *Economic Survey of Pittsburgh,* p. 75.

23. [City of] Allegheny, "Annual Report" of Superintendent of Markets, Department of Public Works, in *Municipal Reports,* 1906–1907, p. 529; *The Banker,* 23 (1912), 371; Pittsburgh, *Statement of Hon. J. O. Brown, City Recorder, to Municipal Committee Appointed under Resolution of Councils of December* 12, 1901 (Pittsburgh, 1902), p. 7; Pittsburgh Chamber of Commerce, *Yearbook and Directory,* 1910, p. 24; Pittsburgh, "Annual Report" of the Mayor [W. A. Magee]," in Executive Department, *Annual Report,* 1911–1912, p. 29; Pittsburgh, "Annual Report" of Ordinance Officers, in Executive Department, *Annual Report,* 1910–1911, Pt. 1, p. 321; *Pittsburgh Dispatch,* 25 Nov. 1911 (advertisement).

24. Pike, *Birmingham,* p. 33. See also T. Renshaw, "The History of the Market Hall," in *Birmingham Market Hall* (Birmingham, 1934); Birmingham and District Butchers' and Pork Butchers' Trade and Benevolent Association, *Annual Report,* No. 32 (1909), p. 5.

25. Carver, *An Investigation into the Dietary of the Labouring Classes of Birmingham,* pp. 38–40.

26. Pittsburgh, "Annual Report of the Department of Public Works," in Executive Department, *Annual Report,* 1911–1912, Vol. 2, p. 23.

27. There were 2,500 groceries in Pittsburgh (1912) compared to 1,098 in Birmingham (1911). In contrast, the number of multiple-store branches was much greater in the British city. Two large chain stores in Pittsburgh had forty-one branches locally (1909) compared to five with seventy-two branches in Birmingham (1911): this excludes the Birmingham Co-operative, which possessed twenty-eight grocery branches (1913). There were two large chain butchers in Birmingham with ninety-two local branches (1911). In Pittsburgh, the retail butcher of most numerical significance locally had only six branches (1909). Data thus support the claim of Douglas Knoop, *American Business Enterprise: A Study in Industrial Organization* (Manchester, 1907), p. 101, that while "the department store is essentially American . . . the 'multiple' firm . . . has reached its highest development in the United Kingdom."

28. New York Bureau of Municipal Research, *The City of Pittsburgh: Report on a Survey of the Department of Public Health, Department of City Controller . . . June-July, 1913* (Pittsburgh, 1913?), pp. 13, 21; Mary E. Bakewell, "Pittsburgh Fifty Years Ago As I Recall It," *Western Pennsylvania Historical Magazine,* 30, Nos. 1–2 (1947), 2; Dr. J. F. Edwards, "The Municipal Milk Supply," *Pittsburgh Index,* 23 May, 1908, p. 7. A similar situation prevailed in Birmingham which, as late as the 1920s, still had no less than 3,800 registered milk sellers, "mostly small hucksters' shops, where a gallon or two of milk was sold daily in small quantities." See Birmingham Public Health Department, *The Milk Supply. Report on a Visit to American Cities in regard to Milk Supplies* (Birmingham, 1922), p. 23.

29. Pittsburgh, "Annual Report of the Bureau of Food Inspection," in Executive Department, *Annual Report,* 1912–1913, p. 1166; *National Labor Tribune,* 17 Jan. 1907, p. 1.

30. *Industry,* 2, No. 2 (1907), 104–05.

31. *Birmingham Daily Post,* 15 Nov. 1912, p. 3; Birmingham Butchers' Association, *Annual Report,* No. 32 (1909), p. 5; No. 35 (1908), p. 47.

32. *Birmingham Daily Post,* 15 Nov. 1912, p. 3.

33. Birmingham Grocers' Association, *Annual Report*, No. 37 (1910), p. 27; Birmingham Co-operative Society Ltd., *The Wheatsheaf. A Monthly Co-operative Record and Magazine.* Apr. 1911, p. i.

34. T. Smith, ed., *History of the Birmingham Co-operative Society Ltd., 1881–1931* (Birmingham, 1931), esp. pp. 25, 31, 37, 42, 55, 56, 61, 159; *Wheatsheaf*, Mar. 1913, p. vi.

35. *The Searchlight of Greater Birmingham*, 9 Oct. 1913, p. 7; Birmingham Grocers' Association, *Annual Report*, No. 35 (1908), p. 43; No. 36 (1909), p. 47; No. 50 (1913), p. 41.

36. Birmingham Chamber of Commerce, *Journal*, 31 Jan. 1913, p. 8; 30 Apr. 1913, p. 67; Birmingham Industrial Co-operative Society, *Report and Balance Sheets*, half-year ending Jan. 1913, p. 3, and half-year ending July 1913, p. 3; *Searchlight of Greater Birmingham*, 9 Oct. 1913, p. 7.

37. Birmingham Grocers' Association, *Annual Report*, No. 39 (1912), p. 25; *Wheatsheaf*, Apr. 1911, p. i; Mar. 1913, p. ii.

38. *Wheatsheaf*, May 1911, p. iv; Apr. 1913, p. v; Birmingham Industrial Co-operative Society, *Report and Balance Sheets*, quarter ending June 1911, p. 10.

39. *Wheatsheaf*, Feb. 1912, p. ix.

40. *Wheatsheaf*, Feb. 1912, p. ix; July 1913, p. vi.

41. Great Britain, *Enquiry into Working Class Rents, Housing and Retail Prices in the U.S.A.*, p. 355; *National Labor Tribune*, 27 Apr. 1905 (advertisement); Andrew Carnegie, *Autobiography* (London, 1920), p. 250.

42. *Pittsburgh Dispatch*, 5 May 1912 (advertisement).

43. Great Britain, *Enquiry into Working Class Rents, Housing and Retail Prices in the U.S.A.*, p. 355.

44. Clementina Black, *Married Women's Work: Being the Report of an Enquiry Undertaken by the Women's Industrial Council* (London, 1915), p. 9; Hallsworth and Davies, *Working Life of Shop Assistants*, pp. 77–78; Mrs. Pember Reeves, *Round About a Pound a Week* (London, 1913), pp. 78–79; 105–06; [London] Economic Club, *Family Budgets: Being the Income and Expenses of Twenty-Eight British Households, 1891–1894* (London, 1896), p. 8.

45. Great Britain, Board of Trade, *Report on Wholesale and Retail Prices in the United Kingdom in 1902, With Comparative Statistical Tables for a Number of Years*, British Parliamentary Papers, Cd. 321, 1903, Vol. 68, Pt. 3, "Prices Paid by Certain Families in the United Kingdom, 1900–01," pp. 403–05; Carver, *Dietary of the Labouring Classes of Birmingham*, pp. 24–25. Family incomes cited by Carver were 36s. to 42s. per week.

46. See *National Labor Tribune*, 19 May 1906; 18 Nov. 1906; *Iron City Trades Journal*, 14 May, 1909; 26 Nov. 1909; *Pittsburgh Dispatch*, 5 May 1900; 7 and 21 May 1909 (advertisements).

47. Carnegie, *Autobiography*, p. 250; *Pittsburgh Dispatch*, 5 and 12 May 1900 (advertisements).

48. F. J. Cross, *How I Lived on Three-Pence a Day and What I Learnt from It* (London, 1912), p. 42; U. S. Department of Commerce and Labor, Bureau of Manufactures, *Daily Consular and Trade Reports*, Oct.–Dec. 1910, Vol. 2, pp. 228–29.

49. Seasonality was estimated as $S = A - T - R$, where S represents the seasonality component of price, A represents the actual price, T represents the secular price trend, and R represents the residual price component. See K. A. Yeomans, *Statistics for the Social Scientist* (Harmondsworth, Eng., 1968), 1: 208–32.

50. Calculated as *APM/SPM*. This probably understates the significance of seasonality, for it should be remembered that the annual secular price movement from 1907 to 1913 was greater than it was earlier in the century.

Chapter 7: Rent

1. Great Britain, Board of Trade, *Report of an Enquiry . . . into Working Class Rents, Housing and Retail Prices, Together with the Rates of Wages in Certain Occupations in the Principal Industrial Towns of the United States of America, British Parliamentary Papers.* Cd. 5609, 1911, Vol. 88, p. 351.

2. Joseph M. Gillman, *Rent Levels in Pittsburgh, Pennsylvania and Their Causes* (New York, 1926), pp. 19–20.

3. Great Britain, *Enquiry into Working Class Rents, Housing and Retail Prices in the U.S.A.,* p. 350; Great Britain, Board of Trade, *Report of an Enquiry . . . into Working Class Rents, Housing, Retail Prices and Standard Rates of Wages in the United Kingdom, British Parliamentary Papers,* Cd. 6955, 1913, Vol. 63, pp. 130, 234.

4. Based on wage data for 1906–1907, presented in Table 8, and on the rent statistics tabulated in Table 35.

5. Birmingham Special Housing Inquiry, 1913–1914, *Appendix to the Report of the Special Committee Containing Evidence of Witnesses* (Birmingham, 1914), evidence of Miss A. R. Wills, a lady health visitor, p. 69. Hereafter referred to as Birmingham, Special Housing Inquiry, 1913–1914, *Appendix.*

6. Board of Arbitration in the Controversy between the Pittsburgh Railways Company and the Motormen and Conductors, *The Award of the Board of Arbitrators* (Pittsburgh? 1914), pp. 15, 56.

7. Albert Rees, *Real Wages in Manufacturing, 1890–1914* (Princeton, 1961), Table 22, p. 74.

8. The *Pittsburgh Bulletin,* 7 Feb. 1903, p. 18, claimed that "rents [were] going up everywhere" in the city.

9. Rees, *Real Wages in Manufacturing,* p. 74, estimated that rents, indexed at 100 in 1913, rose from 85 in 1900 to 102/99 in 1907–1908.

10. U.S. Senate, *Wages and Prices Abroad,* 61st Cong., 2nd sess., 1910, Pt. 1, p. 36 (hereafter referred to as Halstead, "Report on Prices"); Samuel Gompers, *Labor in Europe and America* (New York, 1910), p. 199. British commentators sometimes agreed.

11. Birmingham, *Report of the Special Housing Committee* (Birmingham, 1914), p. 2; Birmingham Housing and Town Planning Committee, *Memorandum on the Housing Problem in Birmingham and Acquisition of Land* (Birmingham, 1918), p. 7; *Speech Made by the Chairman of the Housing Committee [J. Nettlefold] to the Birmingham City Council on Presentation of the Housing Committee's Report, 3rd July, 1906* (Birmingham, 1906), p. 3. For a vivid account of the city's worst housing conditions, see J. C. Walters, *Scenes in Slumland* (Birmingham, 1902).

12. Birmingham, *Report of the Special Housing Committee,* p. 3; Birmingham, Special Housing Inquiry, 1913–1914, *Appendix,* p. 10; Birmingham Medical Officer of Health, *Annual Report,* 1913, p. 18.

13. Paul S. Cadbury, *Birmingham—Fifty Years On* (Bournville, Birmingham, 1952), p. 13.

14. Birmingham, Special Housing Inquiry, 1913–1914, *Appendix,* p. 10. Cadbury Bros., *Our Birmingham* (Bournville, Birmingham, 1943), p. 37, contains excellent archi-

tectural plans of nineteenth-century back-to-back houses. These suggest that rooms were 14.5′ by 11′ in three-story buildings and 12.5′ by 11′ in two-story dwellings.

15. Halstead, "Report on Prices," p. 36: "In many of the cheaper houses there is no running water; it is obtained from a hydrant outside, while bathrooms would be the exception, and sanitary conveniences would be found common to a number of houses." Dr. John Robertson agreed: "It is generally thought that back-to-back houses are bad mainly because of the lack of through ventilation, but in my opinion this is by no means the most important reason. Back-to-back houses are objectionable because they are not self-contained, with a result that decent women object to using the common conveniences." Birmingham, Special Housing Inquiry, 1913–1914, *Appendix*, p. 5.

16. Birmingham, Medical Officer of Health, *Annual Report*, 1913, p. 18.

17. Birmingham, Special Housing Inquiry, 1913–1914, *Appendix*, pp. 5, 379.

18. Cadbury Bros., *Our Birmingham*, p. 37. Rooms, however, were often smaller than in the back-to-back. The parlor and bedroom above were generally 13′ by 11′; the living room and bedroom above, 13′ by 12′.

19. A. E. Carver, *Investigation into the Dietary of the Labouring Classes of Birmingham, with Special Reference to its Bearing upon Tuberculosis* (Birmingham, 1914), p. 21. Birmingham, *Report of the Special Housing Committee*, p. 17, noted that until 1913–1914, "a constant migration of the working classes from the centre to the suburbs was taking place" in order to secure more modern housing accommodation.

20. Robert H. Sherard, *The Cry of the Poor* (London, 1901), p. 213; Birmingham Housing Committee, *Report of Representatives Attending the Ninth International Housing Congress Held at Vienna, June, 1910* (Birmingham, 1910), p. 26.

21. Birmingham Housing and Town Planning Committee, *Memorandum on the Housing Problem in Birmingham*, pp. 2–7.

22. Birmingham, Medical Officer of Health, *Annual Report*, 1914, p. 95; Birmingham Special Housing Inquiry, 1913–1914, *Appendix*, p. 14; Birmingham, Housing Committee, *Report of the Housing Committee. Presented to the Council on the 3rd July, 1906*, (Birmingham, 1906), p. 10; Birmingham, *Report of the Special Housing Committee*, p. 4.

23. Birmingham City Association, *The City Association (Non-Political) Year Book, 1903–1904* (Birmingham, 1904), pp. 9–10; Halstead, "Report on Prices," p. 36; Lee Galloway, "Impressions of Birmingham Past and Present," *Women Workers*, 24 (1914), 40–44.

24. *Mosely Industrial Commission to the United States of America, October to December 1902. Report of the Delegates* (Manchester, 1903), pp. 60, 187, 225; Arthur Shadwell, *Industrial Efficiency: A Comparative Study of Industrial Life in England, Germany, and America* (London, 1906), 1, 322–27; J. Stephen Jeans, "General Report on American Industrial Conditions," in British Iron Trade Association, *American Industrial Conditions and Competition. Report of the Commissioners* (London, 1902), p. 329.

25. Pittsburgh Civic Commission, *Civic Bulletin*, 1 (Oct. 1911), 2; Pittsburgh Chamber of Commerce, *Year Book and Directory*, 1912, p. 40; William H. Matthews, *A Pamphlet Illustrative of Housing Conditions in Neighborhoods Popularly Known as the Tenement House Districts of Pittsburgh* (Pittsburgh, 1907).

26. Kingsley House Association, *Directory of the Philanthropic Agencies of the City of Pittsburgh* (Pittsburgh, 1910), pp. 54, 56–57; E. D. McCafferty, *Henry J. Heinz: A Biography* (New York, 1923), pp. 212–14.

27. *Kingsley House Record*, 8 (Mar. 1905), 2; Pittsburgh Chamber of Commerce, *Year Book and Directory*, 1908, pp. 4, 19; Pittsburgh Chamber of Commerce, *Report of Committee on Housing Conditions of Workmen's Dwellings* (Pittsburgh? 1911?) p. 6.

Roy Lubove, *Twentieth-Century Pittsburgh: Government, Business and Environmental Change* (New York, 1969), gives a good account of the concern of Pittsburgh business leaders with housing reform. Lubove's well-substantiated thesis is that the business and professional leadership of Pittsburgh, operating through voluntary civic organizations, initiated and dominated the environmental reform tradition.

28. For good accounts of Pittsburgh's boss system, see Lincoln Steffens, "Pittsburgh: A City Ashamed," *McClure's Magazine,* 21 (1903), 24–36; Harold Zink, *City Bosses in the United States: A Study of Twenty Municipal Bosses* (Durham, N.C., 1930), Chs. 12, 13; and Gerald W. Johnson, "The Muckraking Era," in Stephan Lorant, ed., *Pittsburgh: The Story of an American City* (New York, 1964), pp. 261–319.

29. Pittsburgh, Department of Public Safety, Bureau of Health, *Annual Report,* 1907, "Report of the Division of Sanitary Inspection," pp. 111, 138.

30. *Iron City Trades Journal,* 12 Feb. 1909, p. 1; National Housing Association, *Proceedings of the Second National Conference on Housing, Philadelphia, December 1912* (Cambridge, Mass., 1913), pp. 169–70.

31. National Housing Association, *Proceedings,* p. 295.

32. Pittsburgh Department of Public Health, *Annual Report,* 1910, "Report of the Bureau of Sanitation," p. 296; Executive Department, *Annual Report,* 1912–1913, "Report of the Bureau of Sanitation," p. 1132.

33. Julia Shelley Hodges, *George Hodges: A Biography* (New York, 1926), p. 100; Joint Annual Convention of the National Municipal League and American Civic Association, *Manual of the Civic and Charitable Organizations of Greater Pittsburgh* (Pittsburgh, 1908), p. 27.

34. Laurie Billstone, "Soho Community House, 1905–1940," M. S. thesis, University of Pittsburgh, 1942, p. 10; Pittsburgh Christian Social Service Union, *"The Strip": A Socio-Religious Survey of a Typical Problem Section of Pittsburgh, Pennsylvania* (Pittsburgh, 1915), pp. 11, 27. Remarkably little residential building took place in early twentieth-century Pittsburgh. A 1934 survey revealed that 58.2 percent of dwellings had been built before 1905. In working-class areas, houses were even older: in wards 1, 2 and 3, 93.2 percent of dwellings had been constructed before 1905. University of Pittsburgh, Bureau of Business Research, *Real Property Inventory of Allegheny County* (Pittsburgh, 1937), pp. 69–71.

35. Charles H. Steinecke, "The Housing of the Working Classes," in Pittsburgh Department of Public Safety, Bureau of Health, *Annual Report,* 1907, pp. 176, 184; Pittsburgh Council of the Churches of Christ, *"The Up-Town": A Socio-Religious Survey of a Section of Pittsburgh, Pennsylvania* (Pittsburgh, 1917), p. 4.

36. Billstone, "Soho Community House, 1905–1940," pp. 11–12; Great Britain, *Enquiry into Working Class Rents, Housing and Retail Prices in the U.S.A.,* p. 351. The Pittsburgh terrace had four rooms of 12′ × 11.75′, while the Birmingham tunnel-back had two rooms of 13′ × 11′ and two rooms of 13′ × 12′. The three-story back-to-back had three rooms of 14.5′ × 11′.

37. Pittsburgh Council of the Churches of Christ, *"The Up-Town,"* p. 11; William H. Matthews, "A Discussion of Housing Conditions in Pittsburgh," *Kingsley House Record,* 10 (Jan.–Feb. 1907), 2.

38. Pittsburgh Department of Health, Bureau of Sanitation, *Annual Report,* 1909, p. 983; Dr. Frank J. Edwards [Superintendent, Pittsburgh Bureau of Health], "Condition of Our Tenements," *Humanity,* 8 (1906), 4.

39. *Industry. A Magazine of Commerce and Finance,* 10 (1907), 108.

40. Pittsburgh Chamber of Commerce, *Year Book and Directory,* 1902, p. 80; *Manual of the Civic and Charitable Organization of Greater Pittsburgh,* pp. 42, 83, 101, 125–

26; Kingsley House Association, *Directory of the Philanthropic Agencies of the City of Pittsburgh,* 1910, pp. 48–49; Allegheny County Civic Club, *Handbook,* 1907, p. 12.

41. Great Britain, *Enquiry into Working Class Rents, Housing and Retail Prices in the U.S.A.,* p. 349. See also Pittsburgh, Council of the Churches of Christ, *"The Up-Town,"* where conditions in that area in 1916 are described. "There are still the outside, old-fashioned privies in scores of back yards. In other houses the pipes and bowls in the bathrooms are worn out or in disrepair. Hundreds of people have to go outside for their water supply, sometimes a half-a-dozen families depending on one outdoor spigot" (p. 11).

42. Birmingham, *Report of the Special Housing Committee,* p. 10; Birmingham, Housing and Town Planning Committee, *Memorandum on the Housing Problem in Birmingham,* p. 4; Birmingham, Special Housing Inquiry, 1913–1914, *Appendix,* p. 6.

43. Steinecke, "Housing of the Working Classes," p. 166; Theodore Dreiser, *A Book About Myself* (New York, 1922), p. 391. Not only areas were crowded: so, too, were individual dwellings. See, for instance, *Manual of the Civic and Charitable Organizations of Greater Pittsburgh,* where it is noted that "many familes [had] been crowded [into tenements] often without much regard to the sanitary requirements of light, ventilation and toilet accommodation" (p. 27). Also the Rev. E. Earl Boyd attested that "the chief problem of housing is the result of the terrible overcrowding in the one or two family houses and in the court dwellings" ("Housing Conditions," in Pittsburgh Christian Social Service Union, *"The Strip,"* p. 27). Similar evidence abounds.

44. National Conference on Housing, *Housing Problems in America. Proceedings of the Third National Conference* (Cambridge, Mass., 1914?), p. 169.

45. Halstead, "Report on Prices," p. 36; Great Britain, *Enquiry into Working Class Rents, Housing and Retail Prices in the U.S.A.,* p. 340.

46. Shadwell, *Industrial Efficiency,* 1:326; Mosely Industrial Commission, *Report,* p. 118; [Pittsburgh] *Searchlight,* 1 Oct. 1907, pp. 7, 17–18; *Kingsley House Record,* 6 (1902), 3.

47. Pittsburgh Department of Health, *Annual Report,* 1912, pp. 1128, 1132; Mary Roberts Rinehart, *My Story* (New York, 1931), pp. 26, 30–31.

Chapter 8: *Fuel, Clothing, Furniture*

1. A. P. Kirtland, "Pittsburgh, With Its Black Diamonds," *Engineers' Society of Western Pennsylvania Proceedings,* 15 (1899), 203–21; Edgar P. Allen, "The Natural Resources of Pittsburgh," *Engineers' Society of Western Pennsylvania Proceeding,* 3 (1891), 9–26; William Gilbert Irwin, "Pittsburgh, The Metropolis of Iron and Steel," *Gunton's Magazine,* 26 (1904), 226.

2. J. H. Hillman, Jr., "Coal—Basis of Pittsburgh's Industrial Supremacy," in Pittsburgh Chamber of Commerce, *Pittsburgh and the Pittsburgh Spirit* (Pittsburgh, 1928?), p. 35.

3. U. S. Bureau of Labor Statistics, *Bulletin,* No. 115, Table 5, pp. 164–65.

4. Great Britain, Board of Trade, *Report of an Enquiry . . . into Working Class Rents, Housing, Retail Prices and Standard Rates of Wages in the United Kingdom, British Parliamentary Papers,* Cd. 6955, 1913, Vol. 63, pp. 412–13.

5. Based upon price information presented in U. S. Senate, *Wages and Prices Abroad,* 61st Cong., 2nd sess., 1910, Pt. 1, p. 42 (hereafter referred to as Halstead, "Report on Prices"); Great Britain, Board of Trade, *Report on Wholesale and Retail Prices in the United Kingdom in 1902, With Comparative Statistical Tables for a Number of Years, British Parliamentary Papers,* Cd. 321, 1903, Vol. 68, Pt. 3, "Prices Paid by

Certain Families in the United Kingdom, 1900–01," pp. 403–05; and Great Britain, *Enquiry by the Board of Trade into Working Class Rents, Housing, Prices and Wages in the U. K.*, 1913, p. 131.

6. Based upon descriptions in U. S. Bureau of Labor, *Bulletins.*

7. Great Britain, *Enquiry by the Board of Trade into Working Class Rents, Housing, Prices and Wages in the U. K.*, 1913, p. 413.

8. Great Britain, Board of Trade, *Report of an Enquiry . . . into Working Class Rents, Housing and Retail Prices, Together with the Rates of Wages in Certain Occupations in the Principal Industrial Towns of the United States of America, British Parliamentary Papers*, Cd. 5609, 1911, Vol. 88, p. 355; *Pittsburgh Dispatch*, 20 Nov. 1903, p. 3. Coal prices, like food prices, also varied according to the quantity purchased and in response to seasonal factors. The *Pittsburgh Bulletin* noted that the "man who can buy several hundred bushels in the fall may get it for six or so cents a bushel, while his poor washerwoman, having no place to store any quantity, buys by the bushel, at varying prices during the winter" (6 Oct. 1900, p. 12).

9. Halstead, "Report on Prices," p. 42; Great Britain, *Enquiry into Working Class Rents, Housing, Prices and Wages in the U.K.*, 1913, p. 131; Charles Anthony Vince, *History of the Corporation of Birmingham*, Vol. 4, "1900–1915" (Birmingham, 1923), p. 401.

10. U.S. Bureau of Labor, *Bulletin*, No. 105; U. S. Bureau of Labor Statistics, *Bulletin*, Nos. 115, 125, 136, 138.

11. *National Labor Tribune*, 16 June 1904, p. 8.

12. Pittsburgh Chamber of Commerce, *Year Book and Directory, 1900* (Pittsburgh, 1900), pp. 62–63; Harry Huse Campbell, *The Manufacture and Properties of Iron and Steel* (New York, 1903), p. 660.

13. Pittsburgh Select and Common Councils, *Official Municipal Program of the Sesqui-Centennial Celebration of the City of Pittsburgh* (Pittsburgh, 1908?), p. 47; *Public Service*, 23 (1934) [50th Anniversary Issue], 3; Philadelphia Company, *Day and Night for Fifty Years* (Philadelphia, 1925), pp. 47–48. G. H. Neilson, Jr., "Pittsburgh's Story of Natural Gas Full of Romance," *Public Service*, 23 (May, 1934), 16.

14. James D. Van Trump, " 'Solitude' and the Nether Depths: The Pittsburgh Estate of George Westinghouse and Its Gas Well," *Western Pennsylvania Historical Magazine*, 42 (1959), 167; George S. Davidson, "Annual Address," *Engineers' Society of Western Pennsylvania*, 15 (1899), 12–13; Sumner B. Ely, "Important Events in the History of Smoke Control," *Western Pennsylvania Historical Magazine*, 32 (1949), 94–95.

15. Neilson, "Pittsburgh Story of Natural Gas," p. 13; Philadelphia Company, *Annual Reports of the Board of Directors . . . to the Stockholders*, No. 15 (year ending 31 Mar. 1899) through No. 30 (year ending 31 Mar. 1914).

16. Vince, *History of the Corporation of Birmingham*, pp. 395–415; Paul S. Cadbury, *Birmingham—Fifty Years On* (Bournville, Birmingham, 1952), p. 29.

17. Vince, *History of the Corporation of Birmingham*, p. 415; *The Ironmonger*, 7 Nov. 1903, p. 226; 5 Dec. 1903, p. 394.

18. *Pittsburgh Dispatch*, 18 May 1907, p. 4; 26 May 1907, p. 1; [Pittsburgh] *Searchlight*, 1 Oct. 1907, p. 9.

19. Halstead, "Report on Prices," p. 42.

20. Great Britain, *Enquiry into Working Class Rents, Housing and Retail Prices in the U.S.A.*, p. 340.

21. Great Britain, Board of Trade, *Report on Prices in the United Kingdom in 1902*, pp. 403–05.

22. Vince, *History of the Corporation of Birmingham*, pp. 403, 430.

23. "Reminiscences of Sales and Service Growth," and S. S. Pack, "The Electric Light and Power Industry in Pittsburgh," in *Public Service*, 23, No. 5 (1934), 36–37, 19–24; Great Britain, *Enquiry into Working Class Rents, Housing and Retail Prices in the U. S. A.*, p. 340.

24. U. S. Senate, Select Committee on Wages and Prices, *Hearings Held*, 1910, Vol. 1, p. 32. Assessing the quality of shoes was equally problematic. Leather in 1912 ranged from 5¢ to 50¢ per foot, gradations not easily recognized in the final product. See Fred Hammond Nichols, ed., *The Building of a Shoe* (Lynn, Mass., 1912): "After the soles are cut, they go to the sorters, who select five different qualities; and in three of the qualities there are grades made for every half inch; . . . about fifty grades of sole are made from each side of leather. . . . Through this specialization, any manufacturer can buy just the grade he wants, to cover his particular needs, for from 5½ cents to 28 cents in women's, 10 cents to 50 cents in men's—a range that covers every demand" (pp. 20–21).

25. Albert Rees, *Real Wages in Manufacturing, 1890–1914* (Princeton, 1961), Table 22, p. 74, considerably understates the difficulty of compiling a price index for clothing and home furnishings from mail-order catalogues. Whereas Paul H. Douglas, *Real Wages in the United States, 1890–1926* (Boston, 1930), Table 8, p. 38, employing whole-sale statistics, estimated an 11.1 percent increase in clothing prices between 1900 and 1910, Rees calculated a 10 percent decrease. It is likely that Rees' more optimistic picture resulted from his inability to assess the decreased quality of products from advertised descriptions.

26. Nichols, *Building of a Shoe*, pp. 73, 143; *Ladies' Home Journal*, Mar.–Sept. 1911 (advertisements); *Pittsburgh Dispatch*, Nov. 1910 (advertisements).

27. *National Labor Tribune*, 2 May 1907, p. 8; 13 June 1907, p. 8 (advertisements); *Pittsburgh Dispatch*, Nov. 1908 (advertisements).

28. Halstead, "Report on Prices," p. 42.

29. *Ibid.* This conclusion is in line with the national price index for clothing constructed by A. R. Prest and A. A. Adams, *Consumers' Expenditure in the United Kingdom 1900–1949* (Cambridge, 1954), Table 80, p. 123, which estimated a price rise in the decade of 10 percent.

30. As Sidney Pollard has noted, "It is better to include an informed guess than exclude a value altogether, since omission may distort the index even more than an approximation." ("Real Earnings in Sheffield, 1851–1914," *Yorkshire Bulletin of Economic and Social Research*, 9 [1957], 61.)

31. *Birmingham Sunday Echo*, 3 Dec. 1905, pp. 1, 3; *Bargains. A Monthly Journal for Bargain Hunters*, Dec. 1910, 24, 30; *Birmingham Tramways Gazette*, Dec. 1908, front cover (advertisements).

32. Halstead, "Report on Prices," p. 40; *Birmingham Pictorial and Dart*, 6 July 1906, p. 14; 12 and 26 Jan. 1906, back covers (advertisements). Another large footwear chain that attempted to attract Birmingham workers was Freeman, Hardy and Willis: see Birmingham Independent Labour Party, *Federation Year Book*, 1909, p. 1 (advertisements).

33. Great Britain, *Enquiry into Working Class Rents, Housing and Retail Prices in the U.S.A.*, p. 355. Douglas Knoop, *American Business Enterprise: A Study in Industrial Organization* (Manchester, 1907), claimed that American stores did "not appear to follow the English idea of having a general sale once or twice a year. They [preferred] to have a kind of permanent sale, first in one department then in another" (p. 18).

34. Advertisements in the *Pittsburgh Dispatch* throughout 1905 give evidence of the sales at Rosenbaum's and Kaufmann's; *Justice*, 11 Oct. 1913, provides details of the bargain basement at Frank and Seder's.

35. *Searchlight of Greater Birmingham*, 27 Mar. 1913, p. 13; Trades Union Congress, Joint Committee on the Cost of Living, *Final Report* (London, 1920), pp. 27–28.

36. See, for example, Eleanor McGrew, "How I Dressed on $50 a Year," *Ladies' Home Journal*, Sept. 1911, p. 86; Mary Haniman, "How I Dressed on $100 a Year," *Ladies' Home Journal*, Oct. 1911, p. 102.

37. James R. Cox, diary, entry for 1 July 1904, in the James R. Cox Papers, University of Pittsburgh Archives of Industrial Society.

38. *National Labor Tribune*, 17 Oct. 1907, p. 8; *Justice*, 11 Oct. 1913, p. 2 (advertisements).

39. W. Shaw Sparrow, *Hints on Home Furnishings* (London, 1909), pp. 22–23.

40. *Searchlight of Greater Birmingham*, 16 Jan. 1913, p. 12; 27 Mar. 1913, p. 2. Similar price rigidity also prevailed in the United States: see R. R. Williams, ed., *Hardware Store Business Methods* (New York, 1901), p. 160.

41. Trades Union Congress, *Report on the Cost of Living;* Army and Navy Stores, *Catalogue*, 1907; *National Labor Tribune*, 1907; *Pittsburgh Dispatch*, May and Nov. 1907 (advertisements); Martha Cutler, "The Cost of Home Furnishings—A Review," *Harper's Bazaar*, 41 (1907), 768. Cooperative prices refer to 1914 but appear to have been stable since 1907.

42. Cutler, "Cost of House Furnishings," p. 768.

Chapter 9: Expenditure

1. Board of Arbitration in the Controversy between the Pittsburgh Railways Company and the Motormen and Conductors, *The Award of the Board of Arbitrators* (Pittsburgh? 1914), p. 11; U. S. Department of Commerce and Labor, *Annual Report of the Commissioner of Labor*, 1903, Pt. 1, Table 3C, pp. 336–37; Table 3I, pp. 366–67; Margaret Byington, *Homestead. The Households of a Mill Town* (New York, 1910), Appendix 2, pp. 206–14.

2. Great Britain, Board of Trade, *Report of an Enquiry . . . into Working Class Rents, Housing, Retail Prices, and Standard Rates of Wages in the United Kingdom*, British Parliamentary Papers, Cd. 3864, 1908, Vol. 53, "Memorandum—Detailed Returns of Food Consumption," pp. 11, 14; A. E. Carver, *Dietary of the Labouring Classes of Birmingham, with Special Reference to its Bearing upon Tuberculosis* (Birmingham, 1914), pp. 16–30.

3. For a good account of the development, use (and misuse) of the law, see George J. Stigler, "The Early History of Empirical Studies of Consumer Behaviour," *Journal of Political Economy*, 62 (1954), 95–113.

4. U. S., *Eighteenth Annual Report of the Commissioner of Labor*, 1903, Pt. 1, Table 4C, pp. 416–17; Table 4L, pp. 496–97.

5. Great Britain, Board of Trade, *Report of an Enquiry . . . into Working Class Rents, Housing and Retail Prices, Together with the Rates of Wages in Certain Occupations in the Principal Industrial Towns of the United States of America*, British Parliamentary Papers, Cd. 5609, 1911, Vol. 88, p. 355.

6. U. S., *Eighteenth Annual Report of the Commissioner of Labor*, 1903, Pt. 1, Table 4C, pp. 416–17. Cheese was also a far more popular item of diet in Britain, and British migrants retained their taste for it in their new home: whereas American workers spent only $3.75 per annum on cheese, British immigrants disbursed $5.31.

7. Carver, *Dietary of the Labouring Classes of Birmingham*, p. 38. Certainly, as Table 53 reveals, there was a surprising similarity between the food expenditure re-

corded by the Board of Trade in 1904 and that collected by Dr. Carver in 1914—a fact which justifies using Carver's more detailed study as a basis for comparison with the Pennsylvania data.

8. For circumstantial evidence of the American workers' greater expenditure for fruit, see *Mosely Industrial Commission to the United States of America, October to December 1902. Report of the Delegates* (Manchester, 1903), p. 259; G. W. Steevens, *The Land of the Dollar* (Edinburgh and London, 1900), p. 183.

9. According to Mrs. Pember Reeves, *Round About a Pound a Week* (London, 1913), p. 103, British workers viewed vegetables more as condiments than food, and generally bought only small bunches of "potherbs."

10. U.S., *Eighteenth Annual Report of the Commissioner of Labor*, 1903, Pt. 1, p. 19. It was assumed that the children in both Pennsylvania and the British Midlands were equally distributed between 0 and 14 years, inclusive. Consumption units per family were estimated to be 3.237 in Pennsylvania (1901), 3.916 in Midlands towns (1904), and 3.972 in northern towns (1904).

11. Carver, *Dietary of the Labouring Classes of Birmingham*, p. 43; Edward Cadbury, Cecile M. Matheson and George Shann, *Women's Work and Wages. A Phase of Life in an Industrial City* (London, 1906), p. 233. Anna Martin, *The Married Working Woman. A Study* (London, 1911), pp. 21–22; Phyllis D. Winder, *The Public Feeding of Elementary School Children. A Review of the General Situation, and an Inquiry into Birmingham Experience* (London, 1913), p. 39.

12. Great Britain, Board of Trade, *Report of an Enquiry . . . into Working Class Rents, Housing, Retail Prices and Standard Rates of Wages in the United Kingdom, British Parliamentary Papers*, Cd. 3864, 1908, Vol. 53, p. 413; Carver, *Dietary of the Labouring Classes of Birmingham*, p. 43.

13. Stephen Potter, *The Magic Number: The Story of "57"* (London, 1959), p. 67.

14. Cadbury et al., *Women's Work and Wages*, pp. 236–37; Mrs. John van Vorst and Marie van Vorst, *The Woman Who Toils: Being the Experiences of Two Gentlewomen as Factory Girls* (London, 1903), p. 25.

15. Pember Reeves, *Round About a Pound a Week*, p. 131; van Vorst and van Vorst, *Woman Who Toils*, pp. 39–40; Mrs. F. T. Ring, "The Dinner Hour in Our Factories," *Women Workers*, 18 (1908), 3.

16. Carver, *Dietary of the Labouring Classes of Birmingham*, p. 43; Pember Reeves, *Round About a Pound a Week*, p. 58. According to Carver, if a child could "be induced to take porridge for breakfast for a week or two he almost infallibly [acquired] the taste" (pp. 43–44). Perhaps with this in mind, Birmingham children who qualified for a free school breakfast were generally given porridge with treacle or sugar, followed by bread and dripping: Winder, *Public Feeding of Elementary School Children*, p. 34.

17. Pember Reeves, *Round About a Pound a Week*, p. 98.

18. Carver, *Dietary of the Labouring Classes of Birmingham*, pp. 42–43.

19. Moreover, milk and butter were used far more extensively by Britain's northern urban workers, and slightly more butter was eaten in that area than in Pennsylvania. The data, in short, suggest that regional differences in diet *within* Britain were often as significant as those between that country and the United States: certainly this was true of butter, cheese, and bacon consumption, and possibly of bread and flour also. With diet, even more than with wage rates or price levels, the national average is likely to hide a good deal more than it reveals.

20. This assertion, and similar estimates throughout the chapter, are based upon R. A. McCance and E. M. Widdowson, *The Composition of Foods* (London, 1960).

21. Carver, *Dietary of the Labouring Classes of Birmingham*, p. 42. Whereas Birmingham milk generally cost 7.1¢ per quart in 1905, the more hygienic, sterilized variety cost 9.2¢: see *Birmingham Pictorial and Dart*, 5 Jan. 1906, p. 2 (advertisement).

22. Dr. J. F. Edwards, "The Municipal Milk Supply," *Pittsburgh Index*, 23 May 1908, pp. 7, 16; Pennsylvania Department of Health, *Pennsylvania Health Bulletin*, No. 14 (1910), "The Conservation of Child Life in Pennsylvania," p. 9; Pittsburgh Bureau of Health, *Bulletin*, 9 May 1908, p. 3; Pittsburgh Department of Public Health, *Annual Report*, 1914, "Report of Bureau of Registration," pp. 206–11; *Pittsburgh Index*, 10 Oct. 1908, p. 5.

23. Great Britain, *Enquiry by the Board of Trade into Working Class Rents, Housing, Prices and Wages in the U.K.*, 1913, p. 131; Carver, *Dietary of the Labouring Classes of Birmingham*, p. 41.

24. The 1902 (Grout) Act, amending the law of 1896, imposed a tax of 0.25¢ per pound upon uncolored margarine and a tax of 10¢ per pound on margarine colored to look like butter. Moreover, the manufacturer was obliged to pay an annual tax of $600, the wholesale dealer a tax of $200, and the retailer (selling only the uncolored product) a tax of $6.

25. For a detailed description of the laws against oleomargarine, with particular reference to the state of Pennsylvania, see Edward Wiest, *The Butter Industry in the United States* (New York, 1916), pp. 241–64; Pennsylvania Department of Agriculture, *Bulletin*, No. 560 (1938–1939).

26. *Pittsburgh Bulletin*, 20 Oct. 1900, p. 3; *National Labor Tribune*, 12 Nov. 1908, p. 1; 7 Oct. 1909, p. 5.

27. Great Britain, *Enquiry into Working Class Rents, Housing and Retail Prices in the U. S. A.*, p. 355.

28. Catherine C. Osler, "State Interference with Parental Responsibility," *Women Workers*, 16 (1906), 4.

29. Carver, *Dietary of the Labouring Classes of Birmingham*, p. 40.

30. Cadbury et al., *Women's Work and Wages*, p. 233.

31. Carver, *Dietary of the Labouring Classes of Birmingham*, p. 48.

32. For an account of how these estimates of meat consumption were constructed, see Appendix Table 9.

33. Carver, *Dietary of the Labouring Classes of Birmingham*, p. 40.

34. *Ibid.*, pp. 40–1; Birmingham Industrial Co-operative Society, *Report and Balance Sheet*, quarter ending Sept. 1911, p. 20 (advertisement).

35. Great Britain, *Enquiry into Working Class Rents, Housing, Prices and Wages in the U.K.*, 1913, p. 131.

36. F. J. Cross, *How I Lived on 3d. a Day and What I Learnt from It* (London, 1912), p. 81; Cadbury et al., *Women's Work and Wages*, p. 233; Mrs. Isabella Beeton, *The Book of Household Management* (London, 1861), pp. 878–79. Estimates are not quite accurate for, as Mrs. Beeton reminded her readers, although one should allow one teaspoonful of tea leaves per person, one should also add "one for the pot." It is difficult to make the art of tea-making conform to the science of statistics.

37. Carver, *Dietary of the Labouring Classes of Birmingham*, p. 45.

38. Cadbury et al., *Women's Work and Wages*, p. 197. Club organizers generally received a 2.5 to 5 percent discount from retailers and were thereby able to profit from their enterprise.

39. Carver, *Dietary of the Labouring Classes of Birmingham*, p. 18; U.S. Department of Commerce and Labor, Bureau of Manufactures, *Daily Consular and Trade Reports*,

July–Sept. 1910, Vol. 1, p. 303; *Bargains. A Monthly Journal for Bargain Hunters,* July 1910, pp. 29, 32 (advertisements).

40. Robert H. Sherard, *The Cry of the Poor* (London, 1901), p. 221.

41. Cadbury et al., *Women's Work and Wages,* p. 245.

42. Sidney Pollard, "Real Earnings in Sheffield, 1851–1914," *Yorkshire Bulletin of Economic and Social Research,* 9 (1957), 58. In fact, this study estimates that clothing comprised 12 percent of income, not expenditure, but as is noted in chapter 10, the difference would have been fractional.

43. George J. Barnsby, "The Standard of Living in the Black Country in the Nineteenth Century," *Economic History Review,* 24 (1971), 228–29. The Black country is a common epithet for the industrial West Midlands, an area of about 100 square miles comprising the county boroughs of Dudley, Walsall, Warley, West Bromwich and Wolverhampton. It includes Birmingham.

44. [London] Economic Club, *Family Budgets* (London, 1894), Tables A–D, pp. 70–76.

45. U. S., *Eighteenth Annual Report of the Commissioner of Labor,* 1903, Pt. 1, Tables 3B, 3C, 4D, 4F, pp. 317, 336–37, 430–31, 464–65.

46. Byington, *Homestead,* Appendix 11, pp. 206–13.

47. A separate survey of 1,666 "normal" Pennsylvania familes found that annual clothing expenditure for families with no children was $61.37 (native-born) and $55.68 (foreign-born); with one child, $62.63 (n-b) and $56.54 (f-b); with two children, $71.17 (n-b) and $62.95 (f-b); with three children, $75.07 (n-b) and $62.33 (f-b); with four children, $75.70 (n-b) and $74.27 (f-b); and for families with five children, $91.35 (n-b) and $66.05 (f-b). See U.S., *Eighteenth Annual Report of the Commissioner of Labor,* 1903, Pt. 1, Table 5A, p. 528.

48. Whiskey cost $1.00 a quart; *National Labor Tribune,* 3 Oct. 1907 (advertisement). Beer cost 5¢ a pint; *New York Times,* 15 Dec. 1907, p. 6 (advertisement).

49. These are rough estimates only, based upon two key assumptions: (a) that the relative price differential that prevailed in 1907 was true also in 1901, and (b) that the percentage of expenditure in Birmingham in 1901 was equal to that in 1914.

50. Cadbury et al., *Women's Work and Wages,* p. 179; Great Britain, *Enquiry into Working Class Rent, Housing and Retail Prices in the U.S.A.,* p. 348; Carver, *Dietary of the Birmingham Labouring Classes,* p. 26.

51. Carver, *Dietary of the Birmingham Labouring Classes,* pp. 17–18.

52. Byington, *Homestead,* Tables 24, 25, pp. 84–86, 104.

53. Douglas Knoop, *American Business Enterprises: A Study in Industrial Organization* (Manchester, 1907), pp. 96–97.

54. Steevens, *Land of the Dollar,* p. 311.

55. Mosely Industrial Commission, *Report,* p. 153. Sue Ainslie Clark and Edith Wyatt, "Working-Girls' Budgets," *McClure's Magazine,* 35 (1910), 609.

56. Samuel Gompers, *Labor in Europe and America* (New York, 1910), p. 10; Lee Galloway, "Impressions of Birmingham, Past and Present," *Women Workers,* 24 (1914), 40–41; Sherard, *Cry of the Poor,* p. 214.

57. Galloway, "Impressions of Birmingham," pp. 41–42.

58. Van Vorst and van Vorst, *Woman Who Toils,* pp. 11, 35.

59. U. S. *Consular Reports,* Jan.–Mar. 1912, Vol. 1, p. 930; Clark and Wyatt, "Working-Girls' Budgets," 601; *Wheatsheaf,* June 1911, p. iv; U. S. Senate, *Wages and Prices Abroad,* 61st Cong., 2nd sess., 1910, Pt. 1, p. 40.

60. Clark and Wyatt, "Working-Girls' Budgets," 601.

Chapter 10: The Standard of Living

1. E. H. Phelps Brown and Margaret Browne, *A Century of Pay and Production in France, Germany, Sweden, the United Kingdom and the United States of America, 1860–1960* (London, 1968), p. 52.

2. *Ibid.*, p. 53. This is equally true of the Paasch and Laspeyre indices compiled for temporal comparisons. Where changes in prices (or quantities) are measured by the two methods, different results will probably result, in consequence of the different weights (base-year or given-year) employed. But it makes little sense to inquire which formula is more accurate: "Each of them is meaningful in the sense that it has a simple and precise physical interpretation. In a way, we can actually consider the difference as a meaningful range of values." Ya-lun Chou, *Statistical Analysis: With Business and Economic Applications* (New York, 1969), pp. 494–97.

3. It should be noted that the Birmingham weights had to be derived from income, not expenditure. However, the practical effect of this substitution would have been minimal. There can be little doubt that Birmingham families spent almost all received income; only 4.1 percent of income was not accounted for by Carver, and some of this would have gone to purchase liquor, tobacco, newspapers and for recreation. (A. E. Carver, *An Investigation into the Dietary of the Birmingham Labouring Classes, with Special Reference to its Bearing upon Tuberculosis* [Birmingham, 1914], pp. 16–30.) Similarly, in Homestead in 1907 expenditure was exactly equal to income: see Margaret Byington, *Homestead. The Households of a Mill Town* (New York, 1910), pp. 206–13. U. S., *Eighteenth Annual Report of the Commissioner of Labor*, 1903, Table 3C, p. 336, suggested that 3,702 Pennsylvania families spent, on average, 94.3 percent of income in 1901.

4. This estimate is based upon a cost-of-living index weighted in relation to the Pennsylvania pattern of expenditure. If a Sheffield budget had been compiled and used as a basis for weighting, the comparative cost-of-living differential would probably have appeared narrower, and the Pittsburgh real hourly rate concomitantly lower.

5. The index for the United Kingdom was derived from A. L. Bowley, *Wages and Income in the United Kingdom since 1860* (Cambridge, 1937), Table 8, p. 30: those for the U.S. from Albert Rees, *Real Wages in Manufacturing, 1890–1914* (Princeton, 1961), Table 44, p. 120; Paul H. Douglas, *Real Wages in the United States, 1879–1926* (Boston, 1930), Table 24, p. 108. All indices were converted to base year 1906.

6. An additional statistical problem is that Bowley's index refers to weekly rather than hourly earnings. However, M. A. Bienefeld, *Working Hours in British Industry: An Economic History* (London, 1972), indicates that there were no substantial changes in the standard work week in the 1890–1913 period, so that an index of hourly rates is unlikely to be very different from one based upon earnings received in a normal week (pp. 145–61).

7. Phelps Brown and Browne, *Century of Pay*, p. 165.

8. Chapter 9 suggests that the ratios that coal, gas, and paraffin comprised of fuel and lighting expenditure were 60, 25, and 15 respectively. When paraffin was excluded, the coal:gas ratio became 71:29, and it was upon this basis that the fuel index in Table 64 was estimated.

9. Bowley, *Wages and Income in the United Kingdom*, notes that not only was his food price index based exclusively upon London data (and there was "no certainty that the movements in the provinces were the same"); but that the data were derived "mainly from large stores, where the movement may have differed from that in shops in working-class districts" (p. 115).

10. Phelps Brown and Browne, *Century of Pay*, p. 163.

11. Real earnings for a standard week.

12. Werner Sombart, *Why is there no Socialism in the United States?* trans. Patricia M. Hocking and C. T. Husbands (1906; rpt. London, 1976), pp. x, xxiv.

13. Tom Bottomore, "Class Structure and Social Consciousness," in István Mészáros, ed., *Aspects of History and Class Consciousness* (London, 1971), p. 58.

14. Adolph Sturmthal, "Comment 1," in John H. M. Laslett and Seymour Martin Lipset, *Failure of a Dream? Essays in the History of American Socialism* (New York, 1974), p. 609.

15. David M. Potter, *People of Plenty: Economic Abundance and the American Character* (Chicago, 1954), p. 84.

16. Seymour Martin Lipset argues that "the American rate of mass social mobility is not uniquely high, but a number of European countries have had comparable rates" ("Comment," in Laslett and Lipset, eds., *Failure of a Dream?* p. 528). However, Stephan Thernstrom remains convinced that at least in the nineteenth century American upward mobility remained comparatively great. ("Socialism and Social Mobility," in Laslett and Lipset, eds., *Failure of a Dream?*, pp. 509–28, 549–50.)

17. Figures on American unemployment are from Stanley Lebergott, *Manpower in Economic Growth: The American Record Since 1800* (New York, 1964). Figures on British unemployment and on the wider fluctuations in American industrial activity and unemployment compared to European countries are from Phelps Brown and Browne, *Century of Pay*, pp. 82, 220–22.

18. Susan J. Kleinberg, "Technology and Women's Work: The Lives of Working-Class Women in Pittsburgh, 1870–1900," *Labor History*, 17 (1976), 58–72, draws a revealing portrait of the way in which inequalities in wages and incomes were reflected in inequalities in the distribution of social services.

Index

Labor market, dual, 226
Labor scarcity, 3–4, 265*n4*
Labor turnover: in Pittsburgh, 55; in Birmingham, 55–56; comparative, 274*n48*
Lapping, G. J., Moseley Industrial Commission, 12
Leader Department Store (formerly Gusky's), 131
Leisure activities: in Pittsburgh, 60–61; in Birmingham, 60–61; and standard of living, 219; comparative, 230
Levasseur, Emile, 13
Light fitting prices, comparative, 177–78
Lipton's (grocery stores), 123
Lodgers. *See* Boarders
London Woolen Mills, 171
Lyons' (tailors), 171

McCann's (grocery stores), 134
McDowell, J., secretary of Birmingham Industrial Co-operative Society, 131
MacKintosh, Hemphill, and Company (engineers), 55
McKnight, Kate, president of Pittsburgh Civic Club, 154
Macmaster, Donald, member of Parliament, 10
McNeil, J. S., superintendent of Pittsburgh Bureau of Food Inspection, 103
Magee, Chris, mayor of Pittsburgh, 150
Magee, William, mayor of Pittsburgh (nephew of Chris M.), 151
Manfield and Sons (shoe stores), 170
Market facilities, comparative, 125–28
Marshell's (grocery stores), 121, 134
Marx, Eleanor, 8
Mason's (grocery stores), 123
Matthews, William, director of Kingsley House Settlement, 72, 149
Mayoralty elections, Pittsburgh, 150–51
Maypole's (grocery stores), 122–23
Methodist Episcopal Church Union, Pittsburgh, 77
Methodology: level of disaggregation, 14; income measure, choice of, 14–15, 268*n23;* limitations on, 15; locations, choice of, 15–21; time period, choice of, 21–28; wages, ratio correlation of, 47–50, 272–73*n35;* consumer goods, comparative quality of, 91; weights and

measures, comparative, 91. *See also* Estimates
Metropolitan Life Insurance Company, 51
Midland Leather Trades Federation, 24
Migration. *See* Immigration
"Mike Finks," 59
Milk supply, comparative, 191–92, 284*n28*
Mosely, Alfred, 11. *See also* Mosely Industrial Commission
Mosely Industrial Commission (1902), 11–12, 61, 91, 148, 267*n16*, 280*n3*. *See also* Standard of living, views of Mosely Industrial Commission

National Association of Retail Grocers, U.S.A., 122
National Tube Company, 152
National Consumers' League, U.S.A., 206
Neale's (grocery stores), 123
Neill, Charles P., U.S. secretary of labor, 117, 121, 165–66
Nelson and Sons (butchers), 123
New York Building Trades Employers' Association, 39
North Side Market, Pittsburgh, 125

O'Connor, John, Jr., 120
O'Donnell, Hugh, Pennsylvania factory inspector, 68
Oleomargarine sales, legislative opposition to, 192–93, 294*n24*
Oliver, David B., director of the Pittsburgh Board of Education, 67
Oliver, George T., 27
Oliver and Snyder Steel Company, 26
Oliver Iron and Steel Company, 67, 73
Oseroff, Abraham, 86
Outwork. *See* Homework

Paraffin. *See* Kerosene
"Peaky blinders," 41
Peddlers: in Pittsburgh, 127–28, 158; in Birmingham, 128, 202
Pennsylvania Department of Health, 191
Pennsylvania Railroad, 25, 26
Peto, Basil, member of Parliament, 9